Ethics, Information and Technology
Readings

D0170977

Ethics, Information and Technology
READINGS

Richard N. Stichler *and*
Robert Hauptman, *Editors*

McFarland & Company, Inc., Publishers
Jefferson, North Carolina, and London

British Library Cataloguing-in-Publication data are available

Library of Congress Cataloguing-in-Publication Data

Ethics, information and technology : readings / Richard N. Stichler and
   Robert Hauptman, editors.
      p.   cm.
   Includes bibliographical references and index.
   ISBN 0-7864-0392-6 (library binding : 50# alkaline paper) ∞
   1. Communication—Moral and ethical aspects.   2. Communication
and technology.   3. Freedom of information.   4. Internet (Computer
network)—Moral and ethical aspects.   I. Stichler, Richard N.
II. Hauptman, Robert, 1941–
P94.E795   1998
175—dc21   97-24655
                                                                      CIP

Manufactured in the United States of America

McFarland & Company, Inc., Publishers
   Box 611, Jefferson, North Carolina 28640

Acknowledgments

Mark Alfino, "Information Ethics in the Workplace," in *Journal of Information Ethics*, 2.2 (Fall 1993), pp. 15–19, is reprinted by permission of Mark Alfino and the *Journal of Information Ethics*.   Henry T. Blanke, "Librarianship and the Public Culture in the Age of Information Capitalism," in *Journal of Information Ethics*, 5.2 (Fall 1996), pp. 54–69, is reprinted by permission of the *Journal of Information Ethics*.   Partha Dasgupta, "Utilitarianism, Information, and Rights," in *Utilitarianism and Beyond*, edited by Amarta Sen and Bernard Williams (Cambridge University Press, 1982), pp. 199–218, is reprinted by permission of Cambridge University Press and Partha Dasgupta.   Daniel C. Dennett, "Information, Technology, and the Virtues of Ignorance," in *Daedalus* 115.3 (Summer 1986), pp. 135–153, is reprinted by permission of the Journal of the American Academy of Arts and Sciences. Ronald Doctor, "Justice and Social Equity in Cyberspace," in *Wilson Library Bulletin* (January 1994), pp. 35–39, is reprinted by permission of the H. W. Wilson Company.   Susan M. Hallam, "Misconduct on the Information Highway: Abuse and Misuse of the Internet," in *Online Information 94* (1994), pp. 593–602, is reprinted by permission of Susan M. Hallam and Learned Information Ltd.   Robert Hauptman, "Professionalism or Culpability? An Experiment in Ethics," in *Wilson Library Bulletin* (April 1976), pp. 626–27, is reprinted by permission of the H. W. Wilson Company.   Robert Hauptman, "Professional Responsibility Reconsidered," in *RQ* (Spring 1996), pp. 327–329, is reprinted by permission of the American Library Association. Grant Kester, "Access Denied: Information Policy and the Limits of Liberalism," in *Afterimage* 21.6 (January 1994), pp. 5–10, is reprinted by permission of Grant Kester and *Afterimage*.   John Kultgen, "The Ideological Use of Professional Codes," in *Business and Professional Ethics Journal* (Spring 1982), pp. 53–69, is reprinted by permission of John Kultgen.   Senator Patrick Leahy, "The Freedom of Information Act: Public Access in the Computer Age," in *Journal of Information Ethics*, 2.1 (Spring 1993), pp. 22–25, is reprinted by permission of the *Journal of Information Ethics*.   Lisa Newton, "The Origin of Professionalism: Sociological Conclusions and Ethical Implications," in *Business and Professional Ethics Journal* (Summer 1982), pp. 33–43, is reprinted by permission of Lisa Newton. Neil Postman, "Education and Technology: Virtual Students, Digital Classrooms," in *The Nation* (October 9, 1995), pp. 377–382, is reprinted by permission of *The Nation* magazine. © The Nation Company, L.P. Jonathan Rauch, "New Threats to Free Thought," in *Kindly Inquisitors,* by Jonathan Rauch (University of Chicago Press, 1993), pp. 1–29, is reprinted by permission of University of Chicago Press. Virginia Rezmierski, "Computers, Pornography, and Conflicting Rights," in *Educom Review* (March/April 1995), pp. 42–44, is reprinted by permission of Virginia Rezmierski. Marc Rotenberg, "Communications Privacy: Implications for Network Design," in *Communications of the ACM,* 36.8 (August 1993), pp. 61–68, is reprinted by permission of Marc Rotenberg. Kirkpatrick Sale, "Unabomber's Secret Treatise: Is There Method to His Madness?" in *The Nation* (September 25, 1995), pp. 305–311, is reprinted by permission of *The Nation* magazine. © The Nation Company, L.P. Richard N. Stichler, "Ethics in the Information Market," in *Journal of Information Ethics,* 2.1 (Spring 1993), pp. 48–62, is reprinted by permission of the *Journal of Information Ethics.* Nadine Strossen, "Academic Freedom and Artistic Freedom," in *Academe,* 78.6 (1992), pp. 8–15, and 79.1 (1993), pp. 30–37, is reprinted by permission of Nadine Strossen. John C. Swan, "Untruth or Consequences?" in *Library Journal* (July 1986), pp. 44, 46–52 (copyright © 1992 by Reed Elsevier, USA), is reprinted by permission of Cahners Publishing Company. Michael F. Winter, "Umberto Eco on Libraries: A Discussion of De Bibliotheca," in *The Library Quarterly* 64.2 (April 1994), pp. 117–29, is reprinted by permission of Michael F. Winter. "Statement on Professional Ethics," "A Statement of the Association's Council: Freedom and Responsibility," and "Statement on Plagiarism," in *AAUP Policy Documents and Reports* (1995 Edition), pp. 105–110, are reprinted by permission of the American Association of University Professors. The *ALA Code of Ethics* and the *Library Bill of Rights* are reprinted by permission of the American Library Association.

Contents

Introduction

Richard N. Stichler and *Robert Hauptman*

The Information Age has been widely acclaimed as a great benefit for humanity, but the massive global change it is producing brings with it new ethical dilemmas. Proponents of the information revolution often portray the new technology as a panacea that will free us to build a better world, promote democratic equality, improve the quality of education, and create new economic opportunities for underdeveloped nations. But others are concerned about its dangers. They contend that information technology itself is inherently biased toward centralized decision-making. They worry that it will assume an autonomous life of its own and bring with it social consequences that no one intended and no one can control. Rather than serving our needs, they fear that the new technology may become our master.

In response to these concerns it is often said that any technology is merely a tool that can be used for either good or bad ends. How we use it is up to us. But critics such as Jacques Ellul and others have argued that technology is neither neutral nor within our power to regulate.[1] Modern technology is not a simple tool but a complex interdependent network that behaves like an ecosystem that no single individual or group can control. Just when it seems that we have solved one technical problem here, an unintended consequence springs up over there. As each new technical solution leads us inevitably on to new and more complex technical problems, the technology we use shapes and guides our actions in ways that we cannot immediately foresee or control. Thus, Ellul maintains, in the technological society we have unwittingly become the slaves of our own techniques.

Will the new information technology become our master or our servant? Contemporary issues in information ethics arise within the context of conflicting views on the effects of technology on society. This volume brings together essays that deal with issues in information ethics from a variety of divergent standpoints.

Information ethics includes a broad range of topics in the areas of data, information, and knowledge production, dissemination, and application. Rafael Capurro in Germany and Robert Hauptman in the United States came up with both the concept and the phrase at about the same time; it is first mentioned in 1988 in a paper by Capurro[2] and (again in 1988) in a monograph by Hauptman.[3] Although topics in information ethics often overlap other areas of professional ethics, there are certain disciplinary areas that are generally abjured especially in the pages of the *Journal of Information Ethics*. These include legal, medical, and business ethics, since all of these disciplines produce their own specialized periodicals.

Martha Montague Smith has developed a concise taxonomy that helps to delineate the boundaries of information ethics.[4] Information ethics can be divided into three major areas: ownership, access and security. Ownership covers the production, dissemination and financial aspects of data, information and knowledge. It includes the privatization and commodification of information that was formerly held in the public domain. Access is linked to financial matters such as cost and the information rich and poor, but it also concerns control of information, censorship, freedom of expression, and technology transfer. Security concerns issues of privacy, confidentiality and integrity. Each of these is complex and multi-faceted. Privacy includes legal and cultural issues, invasions, fraud and theft, credit abuse, and related matters. Confidentiality is most blatantly manifested in the current medical records controversy but also covers all areas where secrecy is professionally mandated. Integrity is a term used to indicate that data and information are accurate, i.e., that truth is not distorted or perverted either purposely or inadvertently by the document's author or by an interloper, or in cyberspace, by a hacker who has altered what others consider to be a permanent record.

There are two distinct types of question that can be raised about ethical issues; there are those about ends to be pursued and those about means for attaining ends. Questions about means assume a given end to be pursued; hence they are narrower in focus. But questions about ends are directed at the basic principles of action and challenge the foundations of our character and conduct. Many of the essays included in this volume raise questions about the ends and purposes of information technology. We have tried to select essays that challenge some of the traditional assumptions about the value of information and the pursuit of knowledge. It is our hope that this anthology will provide a stimulus for students of the information sciences to reconsider some of our basic assumptions about ethics and information technology.

NOTES

1. Jacques Ellul. *The Technological Society*. Tr. John Wilkinson. New York: Vintage, 1964.
2. Rafael Capurro. "Informationsethos und Informationsethik—Gedanken zum verantwortungsvollen Handeln im Bereich der Fachinformation." *Nachrichten für Dokumentation* 39 February 1988, pp. 1–4.
3. Robert Hauptman. *Ethical Challenges in Librarianship*. Phoenix: Oryx, 1988, p. 3.
4. Martha Montague Smith. "Information Ethics: An Hermeneutical Analysis of an Emerging Area in Applied Ethics." Diss., University of North Carolina, 1996, p. 3.

I
Freedom of Information and the Pursuit of Knowledge

John Stuart Mill *Of the Liberty of Thought and Discussion*
Jonathan Rauch *New Threats to Free Thought*
Nadine Strossen *Academic and Artistic Freedom*
John C. Swan *Untruth or Consequences?*

Of the Liberty of Thought and Discussion*

John Stuart Mill

The time, it is to be hoped, is gone by, when any defence would be necessary of the "liberty of the press" as one of the securities against corrupt or tyrannical government. No argument, we may suppose, can now be needed, against permitting a legislature or an executive, not identified in interest with the people, to prescribe opinions to them, and determine what doctrines or what arguments they shall be allowed to hear. This aspect of the question, besides, has been so often and so triumphantly enforced by preceding writers, that it needs not be specially insisted on in this place. Though the law of England, on the subject of the press, is as servile to this day as it was in the time of the Tudors, there is little danger of its being actually put in force against political discussion, except during some temporary panic, when fear of insurrection drives ministers and judges from their propriety; and, speaking generally, it is not, in constitutional countries, to be apprehended, that the government, whether completely responsible to the people or not, will often attempt to control the expression of opinion, except when in doing so it makes itself the organ of the general intolerance of the public. Let us suppose, therefore, that the government is entirely at one with the people, and never thinks of exerting any power of coercion unless in agreement with what it conceives to be their voice. But I deny the right of the people to exercise such coercion, either by themselves or by their government. The power itself is illegitimate. The best government has no more title to it than the worst. It is as noxious, or more noxious, when exerted in accordance with public opinion, than when in opposition to it. If all mankind minus one, were of one opinion, and only one person were of the contrary opinion, mankind would

*From John Stuart Mill, On Liberty (1859; 4th edition, 1869), Chapter 2.

be no more justified in silencing that one person, than he, if he had the power, would be justified in silencing mankind. Were an opinion a personal possession of no value except to the owner; if to be obstructed in the enjoyment of it were simply a private injury, it would make some difference whether the injury was inflicted only on a few persons or on many. But the peculiar evil of silencing the expression of an opinion is, that it is robbing the human race; posterity as well as the existing generation; those who dissent from the opinion, still more than those who hold it. If the opinion is right, they are deprived of the opportunity of exchanging error for truth: if wrong, they lose, what is almost as great a benefit, the clearer perception and livelier impression of truth, produced by its collision with error.

It is necessary to consider separately these two hypotheses, each of which has a distinct branch of the argument corresponding to it. We can never be sure that the opinion we are endeavouring to stifle is a false opinion; and if we were sure, stifling it would be an evil still.

First: the opinion which it is attempted to suppress by authority may possibly be true. Those who desire to suppress it, of course deny its truth; but they are not infallible. They have no authority to decide the question for all mankind, and exclude every other person from the means of judging. To refuse a hearing to an opinion, because they are sure that it is false, is to assume that their certainty is the same thing as absolute certainty. All silencing of discussion is an assumption of infallibility. Its condemnation may be allowed to rest on this common argument, not the worse for being common.

Unfortunately for the good sense of mankind, the fact of their fallibility is far from carrying the weight in their practical judgment, which is always allowed to it in theory; for while every one well knows himself to be fallible, few think it necessary to take any precautions against their own fallibility, or admit the supposition that any opinion, of which they feel very certain, may be one of the examples of the error to which they acknowledge themselves to be liable. Absolute princes, or others who are accustomed to unlimited deference, usually feel this complete confidence in their own opinions on nearly all subjects. People more happily situated, who sometimes hear their opinions disputed, and are not wholly unused to be set right when they are wrong, place the same unbounded reliance only on such of their opinions as are shared by all who surround them, or to whom they habitually defer: for in proportion to a man's want of confidence in his own solitary judgment, does he usually repose, with implicit trust, on the infallibility of "the world" in general. And the world, to each individual, means the part of it with which he comes in contact; his party, his sect, his church, his class of society: the man may be called, by comparison, almost liberal and large-minded to whom it means anything so comprehensive as his own country or his own age. Nor is his faith in this collective authority at all shaken by his being aware that other ages, countries, sects, churches, classes, and parties have thought, and even now think, the exact reverse. He devolves upon his own world the responsibility of being in the right against the dissentient worlds of other people; and it never troubles him that mere accident has decided which of these numerous worlds is the object of his reliance, and that the same causes which make him a Churchman in London, would have made him a Buddhist or a Confucian in Peking. Yet it is as evident in itself, as any amount of argument can make it, that ages are no more infallible than individuals; every age having held many opinions which subsequent ages have deemed not only false but absurd; and it is as certain that many opinions, now general, will be rejected by future ages, as it is that many, once general, are rejected by the present.

The objection likely to be made to this argument, would probably take some such form as the following. There is no greater assumption of infallibility in forbidding the propagation of error, than in any other thing which is done by public authority on its own judgment and responsibility. Judgment is given to men that they may use it. Because it may be used erroneously, are men to be told that they ought not to use it at all? To prohibit what they think pernicious, is not claiming exemption from error, but fulfilling the duty incumbent on them, although fallible, of acting on their conscientious conviction. If we were never to act on our opinions, because those opinions may be wrong, we should leave all our interests uncared for, and all our duties unperformed. An objection which applies to all conduct, can be no valid objection to any conduct in particular. It is the duty of governments, and of individuals, to form the truest opinions they can; to form them carefully, and never impose them upon others unless they are quite sure of being right. But when they are sure (such reasoners may say), it is not conscientiousness but cowardice to shrink from acting on their opinions, and allow doctrines which they honestly think dangerous to the welfare of mankind, either in this life or in another, to be scattered abroad without restraint, because other people, in less enlightened times, have persecuted opinions now believed to be true. Let us take care, it may be said, not to make the same mistake: but governments and nations have made mistakes in other things, which are not denied to be fit subjects for the exercise of authority: they have laid on bad taxes, made unjust wars. Ought we therefore to lay on no taxes, and, under whatever provocation, make no wars? Men, and governments, must act to the best of their ability. There is no such thing as absolute certainty, but there is assurance sufficient for the purposes of human life. We may, and must, assume our opinion to be true for the guidance of our own conduct: and it is assuming no more when we forbid bad men to pervert society by the propagation of opinions which we regard as false and pernicious.

I answer, that it is assuming very much more. There is the greatest difference between presuming an opinion to be true, because, with every opportunity for contesting it, it has not been refuted, and assuming its truth for the purpose of not permitting its refutation. Complete liberty of contradicting and disproving our opinion, is the very condition which justifies us in assuming its truth for purposes of action; and on no other terms can a being with human faculties have any rational assurance of being right.

When we consider either the history of opinion, or the ordinary conduct of human life, to what is it to be ascribed that the one and the other are no worse than they are? Not certainly to the inherent force of the human understanding; for, on any matter not self-evident, there are ninety-nine persons totally incapable of judging of it, for one who is capable; and the capacity of the hundredth person is only comparative; for the majority of the eminent men of every past generation held many opinions now known to be erroneous, and did or approved numerous things which no one will now justify. Why is it, then, that there is on the whole a preponderance among mankind of rational opinions and rational conduct? If there really is this preponderance—which there must be unless human affairs are, and have always been, in an almost desperate state—it is owing to a quality of the human mind, the source of everything respectable in man either as an intellectual or as a moral being, namely, that his errors are corrigible. He is capable of rectifying his mistakes, by discussion and experience. Not by experience alone. There must be discussion, to show how experience is to be interpreted. Wrong opinions and practices gradually yield to fact and argument: but facts and arguments, to produce any effect on the mind, must be brought before it. Very few facts are able to tell their own story, without comments to bring out their meaning. The whole strength and value, then, of human judgment, depending on the one property, that it can be set right when it is wrong, reliance can be placed on it only when the means of setting it right are kept constantly at hand. In the case of any person whose judgment is really deserving of confidence, how has it become so? Because he has kept his mind open to criticism of his opinions and conduct. Because it has been his practice to listen to all that could be said against him; to profit by as much of it as was just, and expound to himself, and upon occasion to others, the fallacy of what was fallacious. Because he has felt, that the only way in which a human being can make some approach to knowing the whole of a subject, is by hearing what can be said about it by persons of every variety of opinion, and studying all modes in which it can be looked at by every character of mind. No wise man ever acquired his wisdom in any mode but this; nor is it in the nature of human intellect to become wise in any other manner. The steady habit of correcting and completing his own opinion by collating it with those of others, so far from causing doubt and hesitation in carrying it into practice, is the only stable foundation for a just reliance on it: for, being cognizant of all that can, at least obviously, be said against him, and having taken up his position against all gainsayers—knowing that he has sought for objections and difficulties, instead of avoiding them, and has shut out no light which can be thrown upon the subject from any quarter—he has a right to think his judgment better than that of any person, or any multitude, who have not gone through a similar process....

There are, it is alleged, certain beliefs, so useful, not to say indispensable to well-being, that it is as much the duty of governments to uphold those beliefs, as to protect any other of the interests of society. In a case of such necessity, and so directly in the line of their duty, something less than infallibility may, it is maintained, warrant, and even bind, governments, to act on their own opinion, confirmed by the general opinion of mankind. It is also often argued, and still oftener thought, that none but bad men would desire to weaken these salutary beliefs; and there can be nothing wrong, it is thought, in restraining bad men, and prohibiting what only such men would wish to practise. This mode of thinking makes the justification of restraints on discussion not a question of the truth of doctrines, but of their usefulness; and flatters itself by that means to escape the responsibility of claiming to be an infallible judge of opinions. But those who thus satisfy themselves, do not perceive that the assumption of infallibility is merely shifted from one point to another. The usefulness of an opinion is itself matter of opinion: as disputable, as open to discussion, and requiring discussion as much, as the opinion itself. There is the same need of an infallible judge of opinions to decide an opinion to be noxious, as to decide it to be false, unless the opinion condemned has full opportunity of defending itself. And it will not do to say that the heretic may be allowed to maintain the utility or harmlessness of his opinion, though forbidden to maintain its truth. The truth of an opinion is part of its utility. If we would know whether or not it is desirable that a proposition should be believed, is it possible to exclude the consideration of whether or not it is true? In the opinion, not of bad men, but of the best men, no belief which is contrary to truth can be really useful: and can you prevent such men from urging that plea, when they are charged with culpability for denying some doctrine which they are told is useful, but which they believe to be false? Those who are on the side of received opinions, never fail to take all possible advantage of this plea; you do not find them handling the question of utility as if it could be completely abstracted from that of truth: on the contrary, it is, above all, because their doctrine is the 'truth,' that the knowledge or the belief of it is held to be so indispensable. There can be no fair discussion of the question of usefulness, when an argument so vital may be employed on one side, but not on the other. And in point of fact, when law or public feeling do not permit the truth of an opinion to be disputed, they are just as little tolerant of a denial of its usefulness. The utmost they allow is an extenuation of its absolute necessity, or of the positive guilt of rejecting it....

Let us now pass to the second division of the argument, and dismissing the supposition that any of the received opinions may be false, let us assume them to be true, and examine into the worth of the manner in which they are likely to be held, when their truth is not freely and openly canvassed. However unwillingly a person who has a strong opinion may admit the possibility that his opinion may be false, he ought to be moved by the consideration that however true it may be, if it is not fully, frequently, and fearlessly discussed, it will be held as a dead dogma, not a living truth.

There is a class of persons (happily not quite so numerous as formerly) who think it enough if a person assents undoubtingly to what they think true, though he has no knowledge whatever of the grounds of the opinion, and could not make a tenable defence of it against the most superficial objections. Such persons, if they can once get their creed taught from authority, naturally think that no good, and some harm, comes of its being allowed to be questioned. Where their influence prevails, they make it nearly impossible for the received opinion to be rejected wisely and considerately, though it may still be rejected rashly and ignorantly; for to shut out discussion entirely is seldom possible, and when it once gets in, beliefs not grounded on conviction are apt to give way before the slightest semblance of an argument. Waving, however, this possibility—assuming that the true opinion abides in the mind, but abides as a prejudice, a belief independent of, and proof against, argument—this is not the way in which truth ought to be held by a rational being. This is not knowing the truth. Truth, thus held, is but one superstition the more, accidentally clinging to the words which enunciate a truth.

If the intellect and judgment of mankind ought to be cultivated, a thing which Protestants at least do not deny, on what can these faculties be more appropriately exercised by any one, than on the things which concern him so much that it is considered necessary for him to hold opinions on them? If the cultivation of the understanding consists in one thing more than in another, it is surely in learning the grounds of one's own opinions. Whatever people believe, on subjects on which it is of the first importance to believe rightly, they ought to be able to defend against at least the common objections. But, some one may say, "Let them be taught the grounds of their opinions. It does not follow that opinions must be merely parroted because they are never heard controverted. Persons who learn geometry do not simply commit the theorems to memory, but understand and learn likewise the demonstrations; and it would be absurd to say that they remain ignorant of the grounds of geometrical truths, because they never hear any one deny, and attempt to disprove them." Undoubtedly: and such teaching suffices on a subject like mathematics, where there is nothing at all to be said on the wrong side of the question. The peculiarity of the evidence of mathematical truths is, that all the argument is on one side. There are no objections, and no answers to objections. But on every subject on which difference of opinion is possible, the truth depends on a balance to be struck between two sets of conflicting reasons. Even in natural philosophy, there is always some other explanation possible of the same facts; some geocentric theory instead of heliocentric, some phlogiston instead of oxygen; and it has to be shown why that other theory cannot be the true one: and until this is shown, and until we know how it is shown, we do not understand the grounds of our opinion. But when we turn to subjects infinitely more complicated, to morals, religion, politics, social relations, and the business of life, three-fourths of the arguments for every disputed opinion consist in dispelling the appearances which favour some opinion different from it. The greatest orator, save one, of antiquity, has left it on record that he always studied his adversary's case with as great, if not with still greater, intensity than even his own. What Cicero practised as the means of forensic success, requires to be imitated by all who study any subject in order to arrive at the truth. He who knows only his own side of the case, knows little of that. His reasons may be good, and no one may have been able to refute them. But if he is equally unable to refute the reasons on the opposite side; if he does not so much as know what they are, he has no ground for preferring either opinion. The rational position for him would be suspension of judgment, and unless he contents himself with that, he is either led by authority, or adopts, like the generality of the world, the side to which he feels most inclination. Nor is it enough that he should hear the arguments of adversaries from his own teachers, presented as they state them, and accompanied by what they offer as refutations. That is not the way to do justice to the arguments, or bring them into real contact with his own mind. He must be able to hear them from persons who actually believe them; who defend them in earnest, and do their very utmost for them. He must know them in their most plausible and persuasive form; he must feel the whole force of the difficulty which the true view of the subject has to encounter and dispose of; else he will never really possess himself of the portion of truth which meets and removes that difficulty. Ninety-nine in a hundred of what are called educated men are in this condition; even of those who can argue fluently for their opinions. Their conclusion may be true, but it might be false for anything they know: they have never thrown themselves into the mental position of those who think differently from them, and considered what such persons may have to say; and consequently they do not, in any proper sense of the word, know the doctrine which they themselves profess. They do not know those parts of it which explain and justify the remainder; the considerations which show that a fact which seemingly conflicts with another is reconcilable with it, or that, of two apparently strong reasons, one and not the other ought to be preferred. All that part of the truth which turns the scale, and decides the judgment of a completely informed mind, they are strangers to; nor is it ever really known, but to those who have attended equally and impartially to both sides, and endeavoured to see the reasons of both in the strongest light. So essential is this discipline to a real understanding of moral and human subjects, that if opponents of all important truths do not exist, it is indispensable to imagine them, and supply them with the strongest arguments which the most skilful devil's advocate can conjure up.

To abate the force of these considerations, an enemy of free discussion may be supposed to say, that there is no necessity for mankind in general to know and understand all that can be said against or for their opinions by philosophers and theologians. That it is not needful for common men to be able to expose all the misstatements or fallacies of an ingenious opponent. That it is enough if there is always somebody capable of answering them, so that nothing likely to mislead uninstructed persons remains unrefuted. That simple minds, having been taught the obvious grounds of the truths inculcated on them, may trust to authority for the rest, and being aware that they have neither knowledge nor talent to resolve every difficulty which can be raised, may repose in the assurance that all those which have been raised have been or can be answered, by those who are specially trained to the task.

Conceding to this view of the subject the utmost that can be claimed for it by those most easily satisfied with the amount of understanding of truth which ought to accompany the belief of it; even so, the argument for free discussion is no way weakened. For even this doctrine acknowledges that mankind ought to have a rational assurance that all objections have been satisfactorily answered; and how are they to be answered if that which requires to be answered is not spoken? or how can the answer be known to be satisfactory, if the objectors have no opportunity of showing that it is unsatisfactory? If not the public, at least the philosophers and theologians who are to resolve the difficulties, must make themselves familiar with those difficulties in their most puzzling form; and this cannot be accomplished unless they are freely stated, and placed in the most advantageous light which they admit of. The Catholic Church has its own way of dealing with this embarrassing problem. It makes a broad separation between those who can be permitted to receive its doctrines on conviction, and those who must accept them on trust. Neither, indeed, are allowed any choice as to what they will accept; but the clergy, such at least as can be fully confided in, may admissibly and meritoriously make themselves acquainted with the arguments of opponents, in order to answer them, and may, therefore, read heretical books; the laity, not unless by special permission, hard to be obtained. This discipline recognises a knowledge of the enemy's case as beneficial to the teachers, but finds means, consistent with this, of denying it to the rest of the world: thus giving to the elite more mental culture, though not more mental freedom, than it allows to the mass. By this device it succeeds in obtaining the kind of mental superiority which its purposes require; for though culture without freedom never made a large and liberal mind, it can make a clever *nisi prius* advocate of a cause. But in countries professing Protestantism, this resource is denied; since Protestants hold, at least in theory, that the responsibility for the choice of a religion must be borne by each for himself, and cannot be thrown off upon teachers. Besides, in the present state of the world, it is practically impossible that writings which are read by the instructed can be kept from the uninstructed. If the teachers of mankind are to be cognizant of all that they ought to know, everything must be free to be written and published without restraint.

If, however, the mischievous operation of the absence of free discussion, when the received opinions are true, were confined to leaving men ignorant of the grounds of those opinions, it might be thought that this, if an intellectual, is no moral evil, and does not affect the worth of the opinions, regarded in their influence on the character. The fact, however, is, that not only the grounds of the opinion are forgotten in the absence of discussion, but too often the meaning of the opinion itself. The words which convey it, cease to suggest ideas, or suggest only a small portion of those they were originally employed to communicate. Instead of a vivid conception and a living belief, there remain only a few phrases retained by rote; or, if any part, the shell and husk only of the meaning is retained, the finer essence being lost. The great chapter in human history which this fact occupies and fills, cannot be too earnestly studied and meditated on....

But what! (it may be asked) Is the absence of unanimity an indispensable condition of true knowledge? Is it necessary that some part of mankind should persist in error, to enable any to realize the truth? Does a belief cease to be real and vital as soon as it is generally received—and is a proposition never thoroughly understood and felt unless some doubt of it remains? As soon as mankind have unanimously accepted a truth, does the truth perish within them? The highest aim and best result of improved intelligence, it has hitherto been thought, is to unite mankind more and more in the acknowledgment of all important truths: and does the intelligence only last as long as it has not achieved its object? Do the fruits of conquest perish by the very completeness of the victory?

I affirm no such thing. As mankind improve, the number of doctrines which are no longer disputed or doubted will be constantly on the increase: and the well-being of mankind may almost be measured by the number and gravity of the truths which have reached the point of being uncontested. The cessation, on one question after another, of serious controversy, is one of the necessary incidents of the consolidation of opinion; a consolidation as salutary in the case of true opinions, as it is dangerous and noxious when the opinions are erroneous. But though this gradual narrowing of the bounds of diversity of opinion is necessary in both senses of the term, being at once inevitable and indispensable, we are not therefore obliged to conclude that all its consequences must be beneficial. The loss of so important an aid to the intelligent and living apprehension of a truth, as is afforded by the necessity of explaining it to, or defending it against, opponents, though not sufficient to outweigh, is no trifling drawback from, the benefit of its universal recognition. Where this advantage can no longer be had, I confess I should like to see the teachers of mankind endeavouring to provide a substitute for it; some contrivance for making the difficulties of the question as present to the learner's consciousness, as if they were pressed upon him by a dissentient champion, eager for his conversion.

But instead of seeking contrivances for this purpose, they have lost those they formerly had. The Socratic dialectics, so magnificently exemplified in the dialogues of Plato, were a contrivance of this description. They were essentially a negative discussion of the great questions of philosophy and life, directed with consummate skill to the purpose of convincing any one who had merely adopted the commonplaces of received opinion, that he did not understand the subject—that he as yet attached no definite meaning to the doctrines he professed; in order that, becoming aware of his ignorance, he might be put in the way to attain a stable belief, resting on a clear apprehension both of the meaning of doctrines and of their evidence. The school disputations of the middle ages had a somewhat similar object. They were intended to make sure that the pupil understood his own opinion, and (by necessary correlation) the opinion opposed to it, and could enforce the grounds of the one and confute those of the other. These last-mentioned contests had indeed the incurable defect, that the premises appealed to were taken from authority, not from reason; and, as a discipline to the mind, they were in every respect inferior to the powerful dialectics which formed the intellects of the "Socratici viri": but the modern mind owes far more to both than it is generally willing to admit, and the present modes of education contain nothing which in the smallest degree supplies the place either of the one or of the other. A person who derives all his instruction from teachers or books, even if he escape the besetting temptation of contenting himself with cram, is under no compulsion to hear both sides; accordingly it is far from a frequent accomplishment, even among thinkers, to know both sides; and the weakest part of what everybody says in defence of his opinion, is what he intends as a reply to antagonists. It is the fashion of the present time to disparage negative logic—that which points out weaknesses in theory or errors in practice, without establishing positive truths. Such negative criticism would indeed be poor enough as an ultimate result; but as a means to attaining any positive knowledge or conviction worthy the name, it cannot be valued too highly; and until people are again systematically trained to it, there will be few great thinkers, and a low general average of intellect, in any but the mathematical and physical departments of speculation. On any other subject no one's opinions deserve the name of knowledge, except so far as he has either had forced upon him by others, or gone through of himself, the same mental process which would have been required of him in carrying on an active controversy with opponents. That, therefore, which when absent, it is so indispensable, but so difficult, to create, how worse than absurd it is to forego, when spontaneously offering itself! If there are any persons who contest a received opinion, or who will do so if law or opinion will let them, let us thank them for it, open our minds to listen to them, and rejoice that there is someone to do for us what we otherwise ought, if we have any regard for either the certainty or the vitality of our convictions, to do with much greater labour for ourselves.

It still remains to speak of one of the principal causes which make diversity of opinion advantageous, and will continue to do so until mankind shall have entered a stage of intellectual advancement which at present seems at an incalculable distance. We have hitherto considered only two possibilities: that the received opinion may be false, and some other opinion, consequently, true; or that, the received opinion being true, a conflict with the opposite error is essential to a clear apprehension and deep feeling of its truth. But there is a commoner case than either of these; when the conflicting doctrines, instead of being one true and the other false, share the truth between them; and the nonconforming opinion is needed to supply the remainder of the truth, of which the received doctrine embodies only a part. Popular opinions, on subjects not palpable to sense, are often true, but seldom or never the whole truth. They are a part of the truth; sometimes a greater, sometimes a smaller part, but exaggerated, distorted, and disjoined from the truths by which they ought to be accompanied and limited. Heretical opinions, on the other hand, are generally some of these suppressed and neglected truths, bursting the bonds which kept them down, and either seeking reconciliation with the truth contained in the common opinion, or fronting it as enemies, and setting themselves up, with similar exclusiveness, as the whole truth. The latter case is hitherto the most frequent, as, in the human mind, one-sidedness has always been the rule, and many-sidedness the exception. Hence, even in revolutions of opinion, one part of the truth usually sets while another rises. Even progress, which ought to superadd, for the most part only substitutes, one partial and incomplete truth for another; improvement consisting chiefly in this, that the new fragment of truth is more wanted, more adapted to the needs of the time, than that which it displaces. Such being the partial character of prevailing opinions, even when resting on a true foundation, every opinion which embodies somewhat of the portion of truth which the common opinion omits, ought to be considered precious, with whatever amount of error and confusion that truth may be blended. No sober judge of human affairs will feel bound to be indignant because those who force on our notice truths which we should otherwise have overlooked, overlook some of those which we see. Rather, he will think that so long as popular truth is one-sided, it is more desirable than otherwise that unpopular truth should have one-sided asserters too; such being usually the most energetic, and the most likely to compel reluctant attention to the fragment of wisdom which they proclaim as if it were the whole....

We have now recognised the necessity to the mental well-being of mankind (on which all their other well-being depends) of freedom of opinion, and freedom of the expression of opinion, on four distinct grounds; which we will now briefly recapitulate.

First, if any opinion is compelled to silence, that opinion may, for aught we can certainly know, be true. To deny this is to assume our own infallibility.

Secondly, though the silenced opinion be an error, it may, and very commonly does, contain a portion of truth; and since the general or prevailing opinion on any subject is rarely or never the whole truth, it is only by the collision of adverse opinions that the remainder of the truth has any chance of being supplied.

Thirdly, even if the received opinion be not only true, but the whole truth; unless it is suffered to be, and actually is, vigorously and earnestly contested, it will, by most of those who receive it, be held in the manner of a prejudice, with little comprehension or feeling of its rational grounds. And not only this, but, fourthly, the meaning of the doctrine itself will be in danger of being lost, or enfeebled, and deprived of its vital effect on the character and conduct: the dogma becoming a mere formal profession, inefficacious for good, but cumbering the ground, and preventing the growth of any real and heartfelt conviction, from reason or personal experience.

Before quitting the subject of freedom of opinion, it is fit to take some notice of those who say, that the free expression of all opinions should be permitted, on condition that the manner be temperate, and do not pass the bounds of fair discussion. Much might be said on the impossibility of fixing where these supposed bounds are to be placed; for if the test be offence to those whose opinion is attacked, I think experience testifies that this offence is given whenever the attack is telling and powerful, and that every opponent who pushes them hard, and whom they find it difficult to answer, appears to them, if he shows any strong feeling on the subject, an intemperate opponent. But this, though an important consideration in a practical point of view, merges in a more fundamental objection. Undoubtedly the manner of asserting an opinion, even though it be a true one, may be very objectionable, and may justly incur severe censure. But the principal offences of the kind are such as it is mostly impossible, unless by accidental self-betrayal, to bring home to conviction. The gravest of them is, to argue sophistically, to suppress facts or arguments, to misstate the elements of the case, or misrepresent the opposite opinion. But all this, even to the most aggravated degree, is so continually done in perfect good faith, by persons who are not considered, and in many other respects may not deserve to be considered, ignorant or incompetent, that it is rarely possible on adequate grounds conscientiously to stamp the misrepresentation as morally culpable; and still less could law presume to interfere with this kind of controversial misconduct. With regard to what is commonly meant by intemperate discussion, namely invective, sarcasm, personality, and the like, the denunciation of these weapons would deserve more sympathy if it were ever proposed to interdict them equally to both sides; but it is only desired to restrain the employment of them against the prevailing opinion: against the unprevailing they may not only be used without general disapproval, but will be likely to obtain for him who uses them the praise of honest zeal and righteous indignation. Yet whatever mischief arises from their use, is greatest when they are employed against the comparatively defenceless; and whatever unfair advantage can be derived by any opinion from this mode of asserting it, accrues almost exclusively to received opinions. The worst offence of this kind which can be committed by a polemic, is to stigmatize those who hold the contrary opinion as bad and immoral men. To calumny of this sort, those who hold any unpopular opinion are peculiarly exposed, because they are in general few and uninfluential, and nobody but themselves feels much interested in seeing justice done them; but this weapon is, from the nature of the case, denied to those who attack a prevailing opinion: they can neither use it with safety to themselves, nor, if they could, would it do anything but recoil on their own cause. In general, opinions contrary to those commonly received can only obtain a hearing by studied moderation of language, and the most cautious avoidance of unnecessary offence, from which they hardly ever deviate even in a slight degree without losing ground: while unmeasured vituperation employed on the side of the prevailing opinion, really does deter people from professing contrary opinions, and from listening to those who profess them. For the interest, therefore, of truth and justice, it is far more important to restrain this employment of vituperative language than the other; and, for example, if it were necessary to choose, there would be much more need to discourage offensive attacks on infidelity, than on religion. It is, however, obvious that law and authority have no business with restraining either, while opinion ought, in every instance, to determine its verdict by the circumstances of the individual case; condemning every one, on whichever side of the argument he places himself, in whose mode of advocacy either want of candour, or malignity, bigotry, or intolerance of feeling manifest themselves; but not inferring these vices from the side which a person takes, though it be the contrary side of the question to our own: and giving merited honour to every one, whatever opinion he may hold, who has calmness to see and honesty to state what his opponents and their opinions really are, exaggerating nothing to their discredit, keeping nothing back which tells, or can be supposed to tell, in their favour. This is the real morality of public discussion: and if often violated, I am happy to think that there are many controversialists who to a great extent observe it, and a still greater number who conscientiously strive towards it.

New Threats
to Free Thought

Jonathan Rauch

In 1900 the French national assembly passed new laws to toughen the existing measures against racism. At the time people were in an uproar over the desecration of Jewish graves in France, and the newspapers were full of concern about France's extremist right wing and the revival of anti–Semitism in Europe and the Soviet Union. So the new legislation surprised no one. But there was something disturbing in it, passed over incidentally, as though hardly worth mention, in newspaper accounts like this one: "The measures also outlaw 'revisionism'—a historical tendency rife among extreme right-wing activists which consists of questioning the truth of the Jewish Holocaust in World War II."

Some of those words stir memories: "measures" that "outlaw ... questioning." We have seen that before.

Taken by itself, the French action was a curious and vaguely troubling incident, but little more. The intentions were good, and it is a fact that many and probably most of the so-called Holocaust "revisionists" were Jew-haters and Jew-baiters who were acting in bad faith, and it is a fact also that the Holocaust *did* happen; so let the matter pass. Fair enough.

No. The French action could not be taken by itself. It was part of a pattern.

In Australia the New South Wales parliament amended the Anti-Discrimination Act in 1989 to ban public racial vilification. Since most people are against racial vilification, most could sympathize with the legislature's intentions. But it was hard to be enthusiastic about the mechanism: "The law invests in the Anti-Discrimination Board the power to determine whether a report is 'fair,' and whether a discussion is 'reasonable,' 'in good faith,' and 'in the public interest.' The board will pronounce upon the acceptability of artistic expression, research papers, academic controversy, and scientific questions. An unfair (i.e., inaccurate) report of a public act may expose the reporter and the publisher to damages of up to $40,000."[1]

In Austria you can get a prison sentence for denying the existence of the Nazi gas chambers. In 1992 the government, seeking to make the offense clearer, proposed language which would make it a crime "to deny, grossly minimize, praise or justify through printed works, over the airwaves or in any other medium the National Socialist genocide or any other National Socialist crime."[2] In Denmark the national civil-rights law forbids "threatening, humiliating, or degrading" someone in public on the basis of race, religion, ethnic background, or sexual orientation. When a woman wrote letters to a newspaper calling the national domestic-partnership law "ungodly" and homosexuality "the ugliest kind of adultery," she and the editor who published her letters were targeted for prosecution.[3] In Great Britain the Race Relations Act forbids speech that expresses racial hatred, "not only when it is likely to lead to violence, but generally, on the grounds that members of minority races should be protected from racial insults."[4]

In Canada a reputable research psychologist named Jean Philippe Rushton presented a paper in 1989 in which he looked at three very broad racial groups and hypothesized that, on average, blacks' reproductive strategy tends to emphasize high birthrates, Asians' tends toward intensive parental nurturing, and whites' tends to fall in between. The man was vilified in the press, he was denounced on national television (to his face) as a neo–Nazi, and his graduate students were advised to find a new mentor. That was not all. The Ontario provincial police promptly launched a six-month investigation of Rushton under Canada's hate-speech prohibition. They questioned his colleagues, demanded tapes of his debates and media appearances, and so on. "The provincial police officially assessed the question of whether Rushton might be subject to two years in prison for such actions as 'using questionable source data.'"[5]

So it goes in France, Australia, Austria, Canada—and the United States. In the United States, however, there is an important difference. The U.S. Constitution makes government regulation of upsetting talk difficult. There is not much the government can do to silence offensive speech or obnoxious criticism. In America, therefore, the movement against hurtful speech has been primarily moral rather than legal, and nongovernmental institutions, especially colleges and universities, have taken the lead. All around the country, universities have set up anti-harassment rules prohibiting, and establishing punishments for, "speech or other expression" (this is from Stanford's policy, adopted in 1990 and more or less representative) which "is intended to insult or stigmatize an individual or a small number of individuals on the basis of their sex, race, color, handicap, religion, sexual orientation or national and ethnic origin."[6]

Those rules are being enforced. One case became particularly well known, because it generated a lawsuit in the federal courts, which eventually struck down the rule in question. At the University of Michigan, a student said in a classroom discussion that he considered homosexuality a disease treatable with therapy. Now, as of this writing the evidence is abundant that the student's hypothesis is wrong, and any gay man or woman in America can attest to the harm that this particular hypothesis has inflicted over the years. But the people at Michigan went further than to refute the student or ignore him. They summoned him to a formal disciplinary hearing for violating the school's policy prohibiting speech that "victimizes" people on the basis of "sexual orientation."[7]

What is disturbing is not just that this sort of thing happened, but that it happens all the time now and intellectual opinion often supports it. The Michigan incident was just one among many. In 1990 at Southern Methodist University, "five white students and one black student reported to university officials that a freshman had denounced Dr. [Martin Luther] King as a Communist and had sung 'We Shall Overcome' in a sarcastic manner during a late-night discussion in a residence hall."[8] A university judicial board sentenced the offending freshman to thirty hours of community service at minority organizations.

Cases of that kind are controversial—off campus, at least—and are drawing their share of outrage from civil libertarians. However, to understand the French and Australian and Michigan incidents as raising only civil-liberties issues is to miss the bigger point. A very dangerous principle is now being established as a social right: Thou shalt not hurt others with words. This principle is a menace—and not just to civil liberties. At bottom it threatens liberal inquiry—that is, science itself.

If that statement sounds too alarmist, I won't contest the point here but will ask you to read on. I will ask you, also, to remember this: In English we have a word for the empanelment of tribunals—public or private, but in any case prestigious and powerful—to identify and penalize false and socially dangerous opinions. The word applies reasonably well to a system in which a university student is informed against, and then summoned to a hearing and punished, for making incorrect and hurtful remarks during a conversation late at night. The word has been out of general circulation for many years. It is "inquisition."

This book is about the liberal social system for sorting truth from falsehood: arguably our greatest and most successful political system. It is also about that system's political enemies: not only the ancient enemies, the old-fashioned authoritarians, but also the newer ones, the egalitarians and humanitarians. It is partly a book about free speech, to the extent that the principles it discusses affect the laws and governments' policies. But enough has been written elsewhere in defense of the First Amendment. This book tries to defend the morality, rather than the legality, of a knowledge-producing social system which often causes real suffering to real people. It tries to defend the liberal intellectual system against a rising anti-critical ideology.

We have standard labels for the liberal political and economic systems—democracy and capitalism. Oddly, however, we have no name for the liberal intellectual system, whose activities range from physics to history to journalism. So in this book I use the term "liberal science," for reasons to be explained later. The very need to invent a label for our public idea-sorting system speaks volumes about the system's success. Establishing the principles on which liberal science is based required a social revolution; yet so effective have those principles been, and so beneficent, that most of us take then for granted. We rarely take the time to stop and cherish them, any more than we stop to cherish the right to own property or to vote—less so, indeed. The liberal regime for making knowledge is not something most of us have ever though about. That fact is a tribute to its success. Sadly, it is also a reason so many Americans are dozing through the current attack.

And just what kind of "attack" is going on? Let me try to make it clearer in the following way.

The question which forms the central issue of this book is, What should be society's principle for raising and settling differences of opinion? In other words, what is the right way, or at least the best way, to make decisions as to who is right (thus having knowledge) and who is wrong (thus having mere opinion)?

There are a million ways to ask that question, and they come up every day. On May 10, 1989, the Nashville *Tennessean* reported that George Darden, a city councilman, had filed a resolution asking the city to build a landing pad for unidentified flying objects. "What it was," he said, "people were reporting all these strange creatures coming to town, and they have nowhere to land." He said that he had never seen the creatures himself but that he was "very serious." He wanted to know, "When people see them, do you want to just cast them off as a lunatic?"

George Darden was no clown. He was raising nothing less than what philosophers refer to as the problem of knowledge: What is the right standard for distinguishing the few true beliefs from the many false ones? And who should set that standard? Everybody laughed at George Darden—but he deserves an answer. After all, what is a politician supposed to do when his constituents start reporting UFOs?

To the central question of how to sort true beliefs from the "lunatic" ones, here are five answers, five decision-making principles—not the only principles by any means, but the most important contenders right now:

- *The Fundamentalist Principle*: Those who know the truth should decide who is right.
- *The Simple Egalitarian Principle*: All sincere person's beliefs have equal claims to respect.
- *The Radical Egalitarian Principle*: Like the simple egalitarian principle, but the beliefs of persons in historically oppressed classes or groups get special consideration.
- *The Humanitarian Principle*: Any of the above, but with the condition that the first priority be to cause no hurt.
- *The Liberal Principle*: Checking of each by each through public criticism is the only legitimate way to decide who is right.

The argument of this book is that the last principle is the *only* one which is acceptable, but that it is now losing ground to the others, and that this development is extremely dangerous. Impelled by the notions that science is oppression and criticism is violence, the central regulation of debate and inquiry is returning to respectability—this time in a humanitarian disguise. In America, in France, in Austria and Australia and elsewhere, the old principle of the Inquisition is being revived: people who hold wrong and hurtful opinions should be punished for the good of society. If they cannot be put in jail, then they should lose their jobs, be subjected to organized campaigns of vilification, be made to apologize, be pressed to recant. If government cannot do the punishing, then private institutions and pressure groups—thought vigilantes, in effect—should do it.

Strange, fully three and a half centuries after the Roman Catholic Inquisition arrested and tried Galileo, to be writing about a new anti-critical ideology, and about public and private movements to enforce it. Strange to use words like "Inquisition" and "thought vigilantes." What has happened? And why now?

Consider, then, the stories of two new challenges to liberal science. One story is about fairness, the other about compassion.

The story about fairness begins in the last century, when the strong claims of conservative religious forces finally collapsed under the onslaught of Lyell and Darwin and T. H. Huxley and the whole implacable advance of establishment science. God and the Bible had long since been mostly banished from physics and astronomy. The last redoubts were geology and biology, the histories of the earth and of life; the Bible, after all, said little about the laws of motion but a great deal about the creation of the world and its occupants. Yet even in the life sciences and earth sciences, time was running out for those who believed in religious authority. By the 1830s even pious geologists like the Reverend Adam Sedgwick were declaring that there was no evidence of a worldwide Noachian flood. The Bible, he and others said, simply could not be taken literally. If one read between the lines, they were saying that the Bible was only for moral guidance, not for knowledge of the world around us.

Twenty years after the publication of Darwin's *Origin of Species* in 1859, there was hardly a naturalist in the world who did not support some version of evolutionary theory.[9] Yet the public was much slower to come around to evolution than the scholars. The new scientific consensus left millions of ordinary people behind. To fundamentalist Christians in particular, the issue was a moral one. In the 1920s they led a crusade to evict ungodly evolutionism from the public schools, and by the end of the decade four states had banned the teaching of Darwinism and more than twenty had considered doing so. Among the states that had adopted the ban was Tennessee, where the law was challenged in the famous Scopes trial of 1925. The ban was upheld, but the fundamentalists' leader, William Jennings Bryan, was humiliated on the witness stand, the press mocked the anti-evolutionists, and by the end of the decade anti-evolutionists had run out of steam. The movement turned inward and sank almost—though not quite—into oblivion.

When liberal Americans like me and, probably, you look at the creationists of that day, we see a gang of ignorant troglodytes out to abolish progress. But surely we commit an injustice if we fail to think how terrible it must be to see one's holy book dragged through the mud and an ungodly secular idol erected in its place. The creationists were trying to defend their world, their decency.

They failed, utterly. But their complaint did not go away; it gnawed like a stomachache. The creationists, indeed, began to see that they had done worse than to lose the battle for supremacy; they had lost even the battle to have their beliefs considered an equally legitimate alternative. In the 1960s came a revival of creationism, but this time with a twist. It was "creation *science*" now, they said: an alternative theory. As had been the case in the decades before, scientists and liberal intellectuals dismissed creation science with a laugh; hardly any reputable scholars would go anywhere near it. It was the old biblical story purged of all references to God or the Bible and dressed up with such scraps of evidence, real or imagined, as could be gathered. But the public was more receptive than the professionals. And in the 1970s the creationists discovered an appealing new cause: Equal time for creationism!

They argued that evolution was religion just as much as creation, and they argued that "creation science" was just as scientific as "evolution science." They even argued that creationism was more scientific than evolution. They argued every which way, but the point was always the same: There is more than one way to view the world, and all we want (they said) is a little fairness, a chance to make our case.

Although it was often dismissed casually, their position in fact had deep philosophical strength. Science and skeptical inquiry are one path to belief about the world; looking in the Bible or consulting your guru is another. If both paths are subject to uncertainty—as skeptical science must admit!—then why not present them both in the classroom, as alternatives? Why grant privileges? "Your belief in, say, Darwin's theory rests, finally, no less on faith—faith in science—than does my belief in special creation; and so on what grounds can you claim a monopoly on truth, since my beliefs are held just as strongly and as sincerely as yours?"

Thus the creationists began to portray themselves as an oppressed minority. "Under the present system ... the student is being indoctrinated in a philosophy of secular humanism," one typical creationists complained. "The authoritarianism of the medieval church has been replaced by the authoritarianism of rational materialism. Constitutional guarantees are violated and free scientific inquiry is stifled under this blanket of dogmatism."[10] That is what a fundamentalist Christian state education official in Arizona was getting at when he said that if parents tell their children that the earth is flat, teachers have no right to contradict them. No one has a right to impose his opinion on others—and the idea that humans evolved from earlier species is, the Christians said, ultimately just some people's opinion. A common opinion, true; the experts' opinion, true. But minorities have rights, and experts can be wrong.

In response to their complaint, they got little but scorn from the establishment. When a creationist protests that what is being tossed in the ditch happens to be the truth about human genesis, he is told, "Well, you're wrong." Then when he asks what gives *you* the right to set the standard for truth, he is told, "Because we're right." And when he begs to know why his view of the world should not at least be presented as a fair alternative, someone will tell him, "Because you're a nut." Those are bad answers, arrogant and self-dealing. It is quite useless to pretend that it is "fair," in the sense of evenhanded, to kick someone's beliefs out of the canon if they do not happen to be deemed science by the intellectual establishment. If we on the Darwinian side of the question are going to insist on preferential treatment for our way of looking at the world (and we should), and if in the process we are going to cause pain and outrage to people who do not happen to look at the world our way, then we had better have an awfully good reason—a much better reason than "Because we're right and you're wrong and that's that." If we do not, then shame on us.

But dismissed the creationists' complaint was. They lost a court case in 1982 when Arkansas' Balanced Treatment for Creation-Science and Evolution-Science Act was struck down by a federal judge as unconstitutionally injecting religious instruction into public schools. They lost again over a similar law in Louisiana—this time before the U.S. Supreme Court.[11] Yet the Supreme

Court decision brought a dissent from two justices who argued passionately that a majority was indeed oppressing a minority. And elsewhere there were signs of softening in the face of the creationists' demands for fairness. In November 1989 the California state board of education, under pressure from evangelical Christians, adopted textbook guidelines that deleted a reference to evolution as "scientific fact." (The nature of the process by which evolution works remains a matter of some controversy, but the occurrence of evolution, the *fact* of evolution, is as settled as any proposition in science.) Banished from the guidelines was the true statement "There is no scientific dispute that evolution has occurred and continues to occur; this is why evolution is regarded as scientific fact" and also "These sequences show that life has continually diversified through time, as older species have been replaced by newer ones."[12]

There was a reason for the softening. Fair-minded observers had to admit that the creationists were on to something. It was one thing to demand supremacy, but quite another to demand equal time. Why should the evolutionary, "officially" scientific story be the *only* legitimate story? No less a personage than Ronald Reagan himself said that if evolution was going to be taught, then the biblical story of creation should also be taught; one poll found that three-fourths of the public agreed with him.

If the story ended there it would not be so very interesting. But in the 1970s and especially the 1980s it acquired a new dimension. The battle for intellectual "fairness"—for the Egalitarian Principle—was joined by a new and more powerful faction.

By the 1980s the creationists were not alone. Exactly the same line of attack was now being pursued by their enemies on the political left. What about minority viewpoints? Why were they not being taught, at least as valid alternatives to the all-male, all-European tradition of "mainstream" history and social science? "Native people say they were created here, that they sprang from Earth, not from Europe or Asia," said one activist. "Why not give those theories equal time? To present theory as truth and disregard people's religious beliefs is racist."[13] In 1989 a task force on minorities reported to the New York state education commissioner that "African-Americans, Asian-Americans, Puerto Ricans/Latinos, and native Americans have all been the victims of an intellectual and educational oppression that has characterized the culture and institutions of the United States and the European-American world for centuries."[14] The task force said that even when dealing with topics like the writing of the Constitution, curriculum developers must find a contribution from every major ethnic group.[15] The creationists had argued that the question of human creation was too important to be monopolized by professional biologists, who are biased by dint of being secular humanists. Now came others arguing that the question of America's constitutional heritage was too important to be left to the conventional historians, who are biased by dint of being privileged white males.

Here again were charges of indoctrination, of alternative points of view being oppressed and locked out. Because of their Eurocentric worldview, "the education systems in New York State and throughout the United States of America have produced processes of 'miseducation' that must be challenged and changed."[16] A growing number of minority activists were rejecting outright the legitimacy of the mainstream scientific and intellectual establishment ("white European" science). One television producer said, "African-Americans are now smart enough to know that historically we have been written out of history, and so we are not waiting for the approval of white scholars to believe the research that these African and African-American scholars have done."[17] There was evolution science, creation science, male science, female science, white science, black science. It was about this time when people took to wearing T-shirts with the slogan "It's a black thing. You wouldn't understand."

Thus the rise of minority activists' version of the creationist argument. They said that classical scholarship had lied about blacks' role in history—for example, about the African ethnicity of the ancient Egyptians. An outline for "multicultural" curriculum reform, adopted in various school districts, said that Africa—specifically Egypt—was "the world center of culture and learning in antiquity" and that ancient Egypt was a black nation. Leave aside why it should matter what color people were; the agenda here was to use political pressure to obtain at least equal time for an "outsiders'" viewpoint—the creationists' agenda precisely. As it was with creationism, the science of the matter was dubious. As to the claim that ancient Egypt was a black nation, the essayist John Leo reported that he "phoned seven Egyptologists at random around the country, and all seven said it is completely untrue, then asked that their names not be used. 'It's politically too hot to say this [in public],' said one."[18] (Not so long ago, there were parts of the United States where a biologist had to have some courage to say outright that creationism was bunk.) Undoubtedly, there will be more such claims as other interest groups demand respect and attention for their own versions of the facts.

Adding strength to the challenge was that fair-minded academics were also coming around. They produced an egalitarian argument far more sophisticated than anything the creationists had been able to develop. It goes more or less as follows:

Not to be biased is not to be human. We are all biased and interested, we all have preferences, an intellectual temperament, and a point of view; it is only that our biases go in different directions. The secular Western notion of objectivity, of how to sort reality from myth, has prevailed largely by a kind of imperialism—by trampling on other traditions and stepping on the aspirations of women and Africans and Asians and others who were excluded from European male culture. The Zande who believes he is a witch or the Bororo who asserts he is a red macaw or the Christian who believes the Bible is literally true—none of those is a "lunatic" at all, but merely a minority, a victim of the scientific order's hegemony, shut out by dint of weakness. Science embodies a white European worldview, and to impose it or insist on it, or to deny the equal merit of other ways of thinking, is a form of domination. The biologist and feminist theorist Ruth Hubbard says, in a phrase that could come from any of a variety of contemporary writers on knowledge, "The pretense that science is objective, apolitical and value-neutral is profoundly political."[19] Which is to say, she adds, that the scientific method "rests on a particular definition of objectivity that we feminists must call into question"—a definition very much a culprit in the social exclusion of women, nonwhites, and other minorities. (She might have added fundamentalist Christians, but did not.)

In all honesty, one must confess that there is justice in this challenge. Any system for deciding who is objectively right is a social system and so has political consequences. Liberal science does not throw its opponents in jail, but it does deny their beliefs' respectability, and to deny respectability is to cause anguish and outrage. In the modern West, the liberal, scientific view of knowledge *has* asserted a unique claim to legitimacy, and that *is* a form of intellectual imperialism, as is *any* person's or system's claim to special legitimacy in sorting true beliefs from false ones. Anyone who doubts that this is so might ponder the fate of Christian Scientists in today's America.

On December 4, 1984, a four-year-old girl named Natalie died very painfully of an infection. The cause was a common bacterium that is almost always killed by antibiotics. Her parents, however, did not use antibiotics; they used prayer. To many of us, that sounds preposterous. But imagine what it is to believe fervently in the healing power of your Lord. Imagine that your child is sick, and you want the best treatment, the one that is right and most likely to work. That treatment is prayer, or so you believe with all your heart. And that treatment you use. "We say those parents chose the method of care they felt was the most likely to make their child well," a church official said; and unquestionably he was right.

Then the child dies, and the parents are charged with manslaughter and child endangerment. Over the last ten years there have been dozens of such cases. In 1990 a two-year-old boy named Robyn died of a bowel obstruction after a five-day illness; his parents, David and Ginger Twitchell, were convicted of manslaughter and sentenced to ten years' probation. Pictures in the paper showed the mother, after the trial, cowering in her husband's arms as he faced news photographers. David Twitchell said, "If I try a method of care I think is working, I will stick with that. If I think it's not working, I will try something else."[20] By his own lights, he had done his best for his child. Anyone who did not happen to share the worldview of medical science could only view the prosecution and conviction of the Twitchells as the most blatant kind of scientific imperialism. True, in Robyn's case and Natalie's the prayer treatment had failed. But sometimes antibiotics and surgery fail, too. When surgery fails, should parents be put on trial for not having first tried prayer?

People like the Twitchells feel the full force of the liberal intellectual system's power to declare who is right and who is wrong. They know what it means to be declared losers in the game of science. Tell them about liberalism's being "tolerant" and they will snicker. The truth is that liberal science insists absolutely on freedom of belief and speech, but *freedom of knowledge it rejects absolutely*. When we are deciding whether or not a medical treatment is effective, we turn to liberal science and reject all other claimants. That is why Christian Scientists who unsuccessfully treat their children with prayer are charged with manslaughter, while parents who unsuccessfully try surgery are not. Is that "fair"?

If we do not have an answer to the demands for fairness, if we cannot justify the imperialism of liberal science and the refusal to recognize the validity of other systems, then we are forced to admit that the scientific order is indeed nothing more than the rule of the strong. In that case we must concede that David and Ginger Twitchell were in fact political prisoners, condemned because they and their fellow churchmen lacked the strength or numbers to impose on society *their* idea of truth. That is the egalitarian challenge.

Another challenge was also emerging. Though it advanced on a separate track, ultimately it would lead to much the same place as the challenge from fairness. This was the challenge from compassion.

America, like every country, has always had its share of bluenoses. H. L. Mencken taunted them as Puritans—people driven by the "haunting fear that someone, somewhere, may be happy." Their favorite target was pornography, which they attacked in the name of godliness and later decency and family values. Like the creationists, they came to be deplored and ridiculed by the intellectual establishment; but as did the creationists, they made an argument whose deep strength was unanswered and ignored for too long.

The claim of the bluenoses was that pornography was hurtful because it eroded morality and so was a menace to society. Opponents of bans on obscenity often pointed out that the line between smut and art, between the obscene and the beautiful, was impossible to draw, even in principle. And they pointed out that because there was no line, bans on the gross would also reach serious art—a point which was timelessly proved by the banning of Joyce's *Ulysses* in Great Britain and America, where shipments of the book were seized by the authorities and burned.

Yet battles like the one to save *Ulysses* from the bluenoses were soon won, with the help of liberal courts. Today, every so often the bluenoses resurface, as they always will. In 1989 came the high-visibility trial of the director of Cincinnati's Contemporary Art Center for showing homoerotic photographs by Robert Mapplethorpe, and the 1990 members of the rap group 2 Live Crew were tried for their explicit and rank lyrics.[21] But by the 1980s the anti-pornography activists no longer controlled the terms of debate; the presumption was against them, except perhaps where public money was involved.

Once again, however, the story was not over. Alongside and underlying the puritanical moral fear was the objection that people and communities were being *hurt* by foul words or gross images. And that argument did not go away as society grew more permissive of pornography. Instead, the argument slept in a pupal cocoon and then reemerged stronger than before.

The context was again pornography. But this time the attack was more sophisticated and it came from feminists, not from bluenoses. The feminists' argument bears a moment of examination, because it soon became part of a broader pattern.

The core argument was that pornography hurt women by degrading them, aiding in their repression, denying them their rights. Pornography, said the influential feminist critic and scholar Catharine A. MacKinnon in 1983, "causes attitudes and behaviors of violence and discrimination that define the treatment and status of half of the population."[22] Real people were being hurt. Mary S. or Beth W. was raped or killed by a filth-inspired criminal. And against the actuality of those real-horrors, the traditionalist male power structure was upholding the rights of pornographers to traffic in scenes of sexual violence and domination. The feminists were incredulous. Here, they said, was one more sign of the patriarchy's contempt for the human rights of women.

They made some inroads. Spurred by MacKinnon and others, the city of Indianapolis enacted an anti-pornography statute making pornography actionable as sex discrimination. (The law was later ruled unconstitutional.) By 1989 legislation to similar effect had been introduced in Congress. If you were the victim of a sex crime, and if you could show a link between the crime against you and some "specific pornographic material," then the legislation would give you the right to sue the material's maker or distributor for damages.[23] Setting aside the constitutional problems with such a law, the logic seemed compelling: if you are hurt, you can sue.

The trouble was that particular individuals were raped and bruised by criminals, not by dirty movies. "No respectable study or evidence has shown any causal link between pornography and actual violence."[24] "In countries where pornography is legalized, the crime rates for rape and sex offenses have actually decreased, according to a Danish report."[25] Showing a connection between any particular crime and any particular piece of pornography was difficult or impossible. Anyway, traditional doctrine said that you punish the criminal, not the ideas which might have been in his head or the person who might have put them there. Should selling *Mein Kampf* be illegal because some cretin read it and then killed a Jew? Traditional doctrine said, Certainly not. Nor should selling the Bible be illegal because someone reading the story of Cain and Abel might kill his brother, or someone reading "Thou shalt not suffer a witch to live" might kill a woman, or someone reading the story of Elisha (2 Kings 2:24) might kill rude children. To ban books or words which cretins find exciting is to let the very lowest among us determine what we may read or hear.

Faced with problems like those, feminists broadened their argument; and here, is where, for our purposes, the argument gets especially interesting. The issue was not only that particular people might be hurt by particular crimes inspired by particular dirty books or movies. The issue was also that pornography hurt women *as a class*. "It does hurt individuals, not *as* individuals in a one-at-a-time sense, but as members of the group 'women,'" MacKinnon said.[26]

> Pornography, in the feminist view, is a form of forced sex, a practice of sexual politics, an institution of gender inequality. In this perspective, pornography is not harmless fantasy or a corrupt and confused misrepresentation of an otherwise natural and healthy sexuality. Along with the rape and prostitution in which it participates, pornography institutionalizes the sexuality of male supremacy, which fuses the erotization of dominance and submission with the social construction of male and female. Gender is sexual. Pornography constitutes the meaning of that sexuality. Men treat women as who they see women being. Pornography constructs who that is.[27]

In other words, by portraying male domination of women, pornography transmits the ethic of male supremacy and makes it real. Thus pornography *in itself*—never mind any crimes which it might (or might not) inspire— oppresses women.

You might ask for evidence of such harm; but you should not expect to find it, because one of pornography's harms is to hide the damage it does. "If pornography is an act of male supremacy, its harm is the harm of male supremacy made difficult to see because of its pervasiveness, potency, and success in making the world a pornographic place .... To the extent pornography succeeds in constructing social reality, it becomes *invisible as harm*."[28] In the world constructed by pornography, people who are not radical feminists can no more see the harm of pornography than a fish can see water. How, then, do we know if pornography is really doing the harm that feminists allege? Because it must be. By its very nature—by the images it expresses and the psychological climate it creates—pornography is oppressive.

I linger here because something interesting is going on. An old complaint against standard free-speech theory is that it lets people say harmful things (e.g., "You can get AIDS from a dirty toilet seat"). And the old reply is that "harmful" is in the eye of the beholder, and that while harmful actions should be punished, words and expressive images are the coin of opinion and thought and so are special. I can say "Republicans should be rounded up and shot," but I cannot have Republicans rounded up and shot. But now the complexion of the argument was changing. MacKinnon, in the passages quoted above and others, was within a metaphysician's eyelash of saying, not that pornography *causes* hurt, but that it *is* hurt. It *is* violence; specifically, it is *group* violence against women. And, sure enough, MacKinnon again and again wrote of pornography as an act. It is "an act of male supremacy," it is the sexist social order's "quintessential social act," it "is a political practice," it "is a form of forced sex," it "is more actlike than thoughtlike," it is "a practice of sex discrimination," and so on.[29]

The old, and admittedly sometimes tricky, distinction between talk and action was being methodically blurred—and not just in theory. In 1980, influenced by feminist legal theorists, the U.S. Equal Employment Opportunity Commission adopted three tests for deciding whether speech in the workplace constitutes sexual harassment punishable under civil-rights laws. Among those tests was whether the words at issue create an "intimidating, hostile, or offensive working environment." If words make the social situation uncomfortable for somebody, the commission seemed to be saying, then they are not mere words at all; rather, they are acts of harassment (just as pornography is an act of oppression).

So here was a theory which said that images and expressions and words could be, for all practical purposes, a form of hurt or violence. Keep your eye on this theory. Remember its face: you will see it again.

In the 1980s it began to be commonplace for activists and intellectuals to conspicuously take offense. Here, there, everywhere, they were offended. People began demanding public apologies when they were offended. Often jokes were the target. Organized groups—gay activists, for instance—began patrolling the presses and airwaves for offensive statements and promptly demanding apologies and retractions when they found cause for complaint. "From gays to American Indians to Asians to the disabled to environmentalists," reported the *Washington Post*, "Hollywood at the end of 1991 seems besieged by interest groups." In hopes of staying out of trouble, producers in Hollywood began vetting their screenplays with activists before shooting, to make sure, as one producer said, that the film "has nothing they would find offensive."[30] Activists began compiling and distributing lists of "offensive" expressions. (From the University of Missouri journalism school's *Dictionary of Cautionary Words and Phrases*: "*Burly*: An adjective too often associated with large black men, implying ignorance, and considered offensive in this context. *Buxom*: Offensive reference to a woman's chest. Do not use. See 'Woman.'

Codger: Offensive reference to a senior citizen.")[31] Professors began to tape their classes in case they were charged with saying something offensive. As more and more people realized that they could win concessions and moral victories by being offended, more and more offended people became activists.

All of those activists were perfectly well within their legal rights, and no legal attempt was made to stop them. Nor did there seem to be any moral reason to want to stop them. Indeed, they seemed to have occupied the moral high ground. One could dismiss them as the new Puritans, the new bluenoses, which in part they were. But they were also acting on morally unimpeachable motives: to protect the weak, to salve hurt feelings, and to weed out hateful and hurtful ideas—racist ideas, sexist ideas, homophobic or unpatriotic ideas. There was to be no place in civil society for people who said "nigger" or "queer" (or "burly" or "buxom"), no place for those who were disrespectful or demeaning. "People do not understand the pain and hurt that these words can inflict on their victims," said one university dean.[32] And, as they had with the creationists, fair-minded people had to admit that the humanitarians were on to something. The humanitarians had discovered what liberals rarely realize and almost never admit: the liberal intellectual system, whatever else it may be, is not "nice."

Somehow the idea has grown up that "liberal" means "nice," that the liberal intellectual system fosters sensitivity, toleration, self-esteem, the rejection of prejudice and bias. That impression is misguided. The truth is that liberal science demands discipline as well as license, and to those who reject or flout its rules, it can be cruel. It excludes and restricts as well as tolerates. It thrives on prejudice no less than on cool detachment. It does not give a damn about your feelings and happily tramples them in the name of finding truth. It allows and—here we should be honest—sometimes encourages offense. Self-esteem, sensitivity, respect for others' beliefs, renunciation of prejudice are all good as far as they go. But as primary social goals they are incompatible with the peaceful and productive advancement of human knowledge. To advance knowledge, we must all sometimes suffer. Worse than that, we must inflict suffering on others.

Just as the losers in the game of science—creationists, Afrocentrists, and so on—had risen up and demanded inclusion, so did the offended demand redress and an end to the hurting. The time had come, they said, to reconsider the liberal-science system, to retreat from it or revise it or put sensible and humane controls on it—perhaps even to junk it.

Then came a defining moment, though to this day it has not, I believe, been properly recognized as such. All at once lightning illuminated a garish landscape which until then had been seen only in patches here and there. In February 1989, fundamentalist Muslims rose up against the British writer Salman Rushdie, who had written a novel which they regarded as deeply, shockingly, offensive to Islam's holy truths and to the Muslim community. As they understood it, the novel implied that Muhammad had made up the Koran, an outrageous (to them) slander against their holy book's divine origin. The novel fantasized about a whorehouse where each whore takes on the name, even the personality, of one of Muhammad's wives. It suggested that Muhammad might have bent his divine inspirations to suit his political needs or even his convenience. It referred to him as "Mahound." That was what they saw.

The Ayatollah Ruhollah Khomeini proclaimed that it was the duty of all good Muslims to kill Salman Rushdie: "It is incumbent on every Muslim to employ everything he has got, his life and his wealth, to send him to hell." Rushdie went underground. "I feel as if I have been plunged, like Alice, into the world beyond the looking glass," he wrote a year later, "where nonsense is the only available sense. And I wonder if I'll ever be able to climb back through."[33]

Happening as it did in the year when communism crumbled, the Rushdie affair flashed into headlines but then sank into history. It soon became a historical footnote, partly because Khomeini himself died soon afterwards. And the attack itself was not so very surprising; fundamentalists have made a hobby of harassing the unorthodox for centuries. The surprise was that the reply from the liberal democracies was muttered and utterly incoherent. A long week of silence passed before President George Bush got around to saying, unimpressively, that the death decree was "deeply offensive." The Japanese government said, "Mentioning and encouraging murder is not something to be praised."

In the end the Rushdie affair showed us graphically two things, one which we knew already and one which we did not know at all. What we knew already was that fundamentalism—not just religious fundamentalism, but any fundamentalist system for settling differences of opinion—is the enemy of free thought. More frightening was what we had not known: Western intellectuals did not have a clear answer, many had no answer at all, to the challenge that Khomeini set before them.

That challenge was at least twofold. First, it was a restatement of the creationists' challenge, the angry outsiders' cry from the heart: Who gave you, the arrogant West, the right to make the rules? You are imperialists with your view of truth, with your insistence on the intellectual ways of secularism and of science. How dare you flout and mock our view of truth?

The point was noted at the time. What was not so widely noted was the second dimension of Khomeini's challenge: the humanitarian dimension. This is not to say that Khomeini was a humanitarian, only that the argument which his supporters commonly made was humanitarian in principle: "You have *hurt* us with your evil words, your impious words, disrespectfully and needlessly written in utter disregard of Muslim sensibilities. You have caused pain and offense to many people. And this you have no right to do."

We liberals will never be able to answer those complaints honestly or consistently until we grit our teeth and admit the truth. Yes, Rushdie's words caused many people anger and pain. *And that is all right.* But no such honest admission, and therefore no clear defense, was forthcoming. People often did not seem even to know what it was—free speech? religious liberty? nonviolence? respect for other cultures?—that they were defending. They certainly seemed not to understand the principles upon which the liberal intellectual system is based. A lot of people seemed to have the impression that the Western intellectual system is a kind of anything-goes pluralism in which all ways of believing are created equal and the only rule is "Be nice." "Well," quite a few people said apologetically at the time of the Rushdie incident, "for Khomeini to have ordered Rushdie's death was of course bad, and he shouldn't have done that, but Rushdie certainly did write a book which was offensive to Islamic truths, and he shouldn't have done that, either." The chief rabbi of Great Britain said that the book should not have been published. "Both Mr. Rushdie and the Ayatollah have abused freedom of speech."[34]

That was the sense in which the Rushdie affair was a defining moment. It showed how readily Westerners could be backed away from a fundamental principle of intellectual liberalism, namely that there is nothing whatever wrong with offending—hurting people's feelings—in pursuit of truth. That principle seemed to have been displaced by a belief in the right not to be offended, which was quickly gaining currency in America. At Harvard in 1989, about the same time as the Rushdie affair, a professor of ichthyology reportedly said at a panel discussion on race relations that in a lecture one should never "introduce any sort of thing that might hurt a group." He said, "The pain that racial insensitivity can create is more important than a professor's academic freedom."[35]

You can hear that sort of thing on campuses across America nowadays, and echoes of it in the newspapers and practically everywhere else. America is full of people who deplored Khomeini's attack on Rushdie but launched similar, if less deadly, attacks on "offensive" persons here at home. On the first anniversary of the death sentence, Rushdie, from his hiding place, published an article in which he said that, without the freedom to offend, freedom of expression ceases to exist.[36] That very same week, the columnist and television commentator Andy Rooney, to save his job, found himself apologizing for a statement which he denied ever having made. (He had been quoted as saying that "most people are born with equal intelligence, but blacks have watered down their genes because the less intelligent ones are the ones that have the most children. They drop out of school early, do drugs, and get pregnant.") Rooney got off with a suspension from his job at CBS News after offering "his deepest apologies to any in our society who were given offense."

CBS was legally entitled to suspend its commentators for allegedly making statements which offended people, for having white hair, or even for being embarrassingly banal. What was disturbing was not the legality of CBS's action but the mentality which seemed to impel it: the activists' belief that they had a right not to be offended, and the network's readiness to concede that right. Meanwhile, where were other commentators who may someday also be accused of offending? "Call [it] censorship if you like," wrote Walter Goodman of the *New York Times*, assessing CBS's action. "American television lives by that sort of censorship and so makes a considerable contribution to the country.... And whatever the justice of his punishment, [Rooney] can take comfort in having served as a sacrifice to the cause of public tranquillity."[37] As for Rooney, he seemed to have learned his lesson. He decided to kill a critical commentary on black colleges. "I just decided it was so touchy I'd better not do it," he said. "In view of my problems, I decided not to push it."[38]

Every day brings new reports of thought vigilantism—citizen posses organized to punish people with wrong and dangerous ideas. In December 1990 the *Philadelphia Inquirer* ran an editorial suggesting as a possibility (though not advocating) that welfare mothers be offered incentives to use a contraceptive implant. ("No one should be compelled.") People immediately rose up to denounce the editorial as racist; to have even raised the idea was insensitive. The paper, feeling obliged to redress the "pain and suffering" caused by the editorial, soon followed with another editorial, headlined "An Apology: The Editorial on 'Norplant and Poverty' Was Misguided and Wrong-Headed." At about the same time, Puerto Rican activists took up the cause of getting Carlos Alberto Montaner fired. He was a Cuban-American TV commentator who was asked on the air why Puerto Ricans in the United States suffer worse economic conditions than other Hispanic groups. He replied, "There's probably more than one explanation, but the one that seems the most important to me is this: because there is a grave family problem in the Puerto Rican ghettos of the United States, where there are thousands of single mothers, very young, who try to escape poverty through welfare or through new partners who then leave, and leave behind other children to worsen the problem." When the uproar—"sexism," "stereotypes," and the like—began, he apologized, but (reported the *New York Times*) "a coalition of 25 Puerto Rican organizations in New York City that has led efforts to have Mr. Montaner dismissed said yesterday that it was not appeased." The spokesman for a company that joined a boycott designed to get Montaner fired said: "His comments were an insult to the Puerto Rican community. Freedom of speech is not the right to insult a community."[39]

Those words—"Freedom of speech is not the right to insult a community"—could have come straight from the mouths of the Muslims who demanded that the hurtful, insulting Rushdie be punished. It is important to see that Khomeini, the angry Puerto Ricans, the college anti-bigotry activists, and all the others were acting, not just desultorily and emotionally, but consistently and in the cause of a principle: that you are not entitled to hurt me or others with words or ideas. You should not inflict pain and suffering on others with ideas and talk any more than with clubs and knives.

That principle has caught on fast. It has, indeed, begun to shape the law. Recent years have seen the rapid rise of what have become known as hate-crime statutes, which typically create special criminal offenses or require special sentences for crimes committed "with specific intent to intimidate or harass another person because of that person's race, color, religion, gender, or national origin." (The language is from Michigan's ethnic intimidation law and is more or less typical.) Well over half the states in the union, and many localities, have such laws. The hate-crimes approach (as distinct from the hate-*speech* approach) says that the expression of prejudice or bigotry by itself should not be punished, but the expression of prejudice accompanied by violence or vandalism should be.

The constitutionality of such laws is a subject of hot debate; in June 1992 the U.S. Supreme Court cast a pall over hate-crime laws by overturning a particularly broad St. Paul, Minnesota, ordinance that criminalized bigoted insults and symbols. But the *idea* behind the laws also needs debating: that a prosecutor or politician can put his finger on particularly hurtful words and ideas and, when they are accompanied by other crimes, punish people for expressing or even thinking them.

In the U.S. Congress in 1992, a bill was introduced "to provide sentencing enhancements" (in English, harsher penalties) for crimes "in which the defendant's conduct was motivated by hatred, bias, or prejudice." Such a law could not be enforced without putting the defendant's opinions on trial. (What was he thinking about the blacks at the time of the crime? What does he think about them generally? Is that a "prejudice"?) Ohio passed an ethnic intimidation law that deemed crimes more serious if committed "by reason of the race, color, religion, or national origin of another person or group of persons." That verged on making what a defendant said or believed about race a part of the criminal charge (and, as a state appellate court pointed out in overturning the law, it "vests virtual[ly] complete discretion in the hands of the state to determine whether a suspect committed the alleged acts based on ... race, color, religion, or national origin"). St. Paul's ordinance—the one that the Supreme Court struck down—went a step further by making it a misdemeanor to place "on public *or private* property a symbol, object, appellation, characterization, or graffiti, including but not limited to a burning cross or a Nazi swastika, which one knows or has reasonable grounds to know arouses anger, alarm, or resentment in others on the basis of race, color, creed, or religion" (italics added). The ordinance seemed to say that it was a hate crime to upset someone. In Florida a black man was charged under the state's hate-crime law for calling a white policeman a "cracker." In Massachusetts state legislators tried to make it a "crime against humanity" to satirize or modernize religious figures and texts.[40] (Those legislators might have been interested to know that in Pakistan thirty-year-old Tahir Iqbal was languishing in Lahore's Kot Lakhpat jail, "accused of having made 'insulting remarks against the religion of Islam' and defiling the Koran—'as a result of which the religious feelings of Muslims were wounded.'")[41] In all of those cases, the underlying ethical principle was the same: that people who cause grave offense have committed a kind of crime. True, many people, not least of them the justices on the Supreme Court, questioned whether the American government could constitutionally punish such crimes. Yet few seemed to question whether, as a moral matter, the crime existed.

Today a new ethical concept has been established, one with extraordinary implications. It is the notion of "verbal harassment," "words that wound," "assaultive speech." Hurtful words are a kind of violence, that notion holds. It is, of course, a form of the Humanitarian Principle mentioned above. And it is immediately appealing in a way that liberal science is not. Its strong moral traction tugs at anyone who cares about others, and it has a wonderful moral clarity: Thou shalt not hurt others with words. That precept looks harmless, even admirable. Yet as the concern not to offend ascended the ethical scale from good manners to social imperative, a long-familiar side effect was ascending with it, like a childhood nightmare returning to haunt the adult: if hurting people with words is wrong, then the people who commit the offense must be called to account. And called to account they were—by offended activists and sympathetic authorities in France, in Canada, in American universities. "Only when insults, harassment, disrespect and obscenity are banned [in universities] can people engage in truly substantive argument," wrote a syndicated columnist and a prominent scientist in the *New York Times*.[42] Intellectual authoritarianism, so long disgraced, was returning to favor—this time not among religious reactionaries or fringe radicals or cultural primitives or McCarthyite paranoiacs, but among Western educated elites. Opposition to unfettered criticism was now arising from within criticism's core constituency. Intellectuals' ranks were deeply divided, and the humanitarians who called for bans on "insults, harassment, disrespect and obscenity" had seized the moral offensive.

And this is where our two stories converge. From modest beginnings with creationists and bluenoses have grown two full-fledged and linked challenges to the legitimacy of liberal science. Taken together, they are the most conceptually cogent and far-reaching challenges since the days of the great battles between science and religion. One challenge says that the liberal intellectual system is unfair, the other that it is hurtful, both that it must therefore be regulated. Exclusion is unfair—exclusion of creationism from biology classes, of Afrocentrism from history classes, of Christian Science from medical respectability. Therefore exclusion should be stopped. And offensive words and ideas hurt. Therefore they also should be stopped.

Of the two, the humanitarian challenge is the more dangerous. We will pay a heavy price if the principle takes root in our ethical code that the offended, having been hurt, have the right to an apology and to redress. It is crucial to understand that the Humanitarian Principle is deadly—inherently deadly, not incidentally so—to intellectual freedom and to the productive and peaceful pursuit of knowledge. The principle takes aim not just at freedom of speech but at *liberal science itself*. It is equally deadly whether espoused by Islamic fundamentalists ("Rushdie owes Muslims an apology"), by Christians, or by minority activists ("Andy Rooney owes an apology to 'any in our society who were given offense'"). It leads to the doctrine that people should be punished for holding false or dangerous beliefs. It leads, in other words, toward an inquisition.

I hope to show that the humanitarians' and egalitarians' claim to the moral high ground is false and that intellectual liberalism, with its commitment to allow and even sometimes encourage offense, is the only genuinely humane system. I hope to show that people who are "hurt by words" are morally entitled to nothing whatsoever by way of compensation. What is the right answer to the person who demands something because he is offended? Just this: "Too bad, but you'll live." As for people who call for punishment of "racists," "homophobes," "sexists," "blasphemers," "Communists," or whoever the bogeyman happens to be—those people are enemies of inquiry and their clamor deserves only to be ignored, never humored.

More specifically, this book will try to establish the following points. First, there are not two great liberal social and political systems but three. One is democracy—political liberalism—by which we decide who is entitled to use force; another is capitalism—economic liberalism—by which we decide how to allocate resources. The third is liberal science, by which we decide who is right.

Second, the third system has been astoundingly successful, not merely as a producer of technology but also, far more important, as a peacemaker and builder of social bridges. Its great advantages as a social system for raising and settling differences of opinion are inherent, not incidental. However, its disadvantages—it causes pain and suffering, it creates legions of losers and outsiders, it is disorienting and unsettling, it allows and even thrives on prejudice and bias—are also inherent. And today it is once again under attack.

Third, the attackers seek to undermine the two social rules which make liberal science possible. For the system to function, people must try to follow those rules even if they would prefer not to. Unfortunately, many people are forgetting them, ignoring them, or carving out exemptions.

That trend must be fought, because, fourth, the alternatives to liberal science lead straight to authoritarianism. And intellectual authoritarianism, although once the province of the religious and the political right in America, is now flourishing among the secular and the political left.

Fifth, behind the new authoritarian push are three idealistic impulses: Fundamentalists want to protect the truth. Egalitarians want to help the oppressed and let in the excluded. Humanitarians want to stop verbal violence and the pain it causes. The three impulses are now working in concert.

Sixth, fundamentalism, properly understood, is not about religion. It is about the inability to seriously entertain the possibility that one might be wrong. In individuals such fundamentalism is natural and, within reason, desirable. But when it becomes the foundation for an intellectual system, it is inherently a threat to freedom of thought.

Seventh, there is no way to advance knowledge peacefully and productively by adhering to the principles advocated by egalitarians and humanitarians. Their principles are poisonous to liberal science and ultimately to peace and freedom.

Eighth, no social principle in the world is more foolish and dangerous than the rapidly rising notion that hurtful words and ideas are a form of violence or torture (e.g., "harassment") and that their perpetrators should be treated accordingly. That notion leads to the criminalization of criticism and the empowerment of authorities to regulate it. The new sensitivity is the old authoritarianism in disguise, and it is just as noxious.

NOTES

1. Tony Katsigiannis, "How the NSW Anti-Discrimination Laws Threaten Free Speech," *Policy*, Summer 1989, p. 29.

2. *New York Times*, January 24, 1992.

3. Lindsy Van Gelder and Pamela Robin Brandt, *Are You Two ... Together? A Gay and Lesbian Travel Guide to Europe* (Random House, 1991), p. 116.

4. Ronald Dworkin, "Liberty and Pornography," *New York Review of Books*, August 15, 1991, p. 13.

5. Barry R. Gross, "The Case of Philippe Rushton," *Academic Questions*, Fall 1990, pp. 35–46. In the end, the attorney general decided not to prosecute and settled for denouncing Rushton's ideas as "loony."

6. Quoted by Nat Hentoff in the *Washington Post*, op-ed page, July 21, 1990, and confirmed by the university's public-affairs office.

7. See, for example, Jon Wiener in the *Nation*, February 26, 1990, p. 272.

8. *New York Times*, May 6, 1990.

9. For historical information here and elsewhere I am indebted to Ronald L. Numbers's superb little essay, "The Creationists," in *But Is It Science? The Philosophical Question in the Creation/Evolution Controversy*, ed. Michael Ruse (Prometheus, 1988).

10. Duane T. Gish, "Creation, Evolution, and the Historical Evidence," reprinted from *American Biology Teacher*, March 1973, in *But Is It Science?* pp. 270, 281.

11. In *Edwards v. Aguillard* (1987). Chapter 5 has more on the case.

12. *New York Times*, November 10, 1989.

13. Beverly Slapin of Communities United against Racism in Education. Quoted in David L. Kirp, "Textbooks and Tribalism in California." *Public Interest*, Summer 1991, p. 27.

14. *A Curriculum of Inclusion*, Report of the [Education] Commissioner's Task Force on Minorities: Equity and Excellence, July 1989, opening words.

15. *New York Times*, February 7, 1990.

16. *A Curriculum of Inclusion*, p. 36.

17. Quoted in the *New York Times*, February 4, 1990.

18. "A Fringe History of the World," *U.S. News & World Report*, November 12, 1990, p. 25. Bracketed insertion is in the original.

19. "Science, Facts, and Feminism," in *Feminism & Science*, ed. Nancy Tuana (Indiana University Press, 1989), pp. 125, 126, 128.

20. *New York Times*, July 5, 1990.

21. Both trials ended in acquittals.

22. "Not a Moral Issue," in *Feminism Unmodified: Discourses on Life and Law* (Harvard University Press, 1987), p. 147.

23. As of this writing in 1992, the legislation has been approved by the Senate Judiciary Committee but stands well short of final passage.

24. Ronald Dworkin, "The Coming Battles Over Free Speech," *New York Review of Books*, June 11, 1992, p. 61.

25. Wendy Melillo, "Can Pornography Lead to Violence?" *Washington Post*, Health section, July 21, 1992, p. 12.

26. *Feminism Unmodified*, p. 156.

27. Ibid., p. 148.

28. Ibid., pp. 154–55. Italics in original.

29. The quotations are from various essays in MacKinnon's *Feminism Unmodified*, pp. 130, 154, 147, 148, 154, 176.

30. "Hollywood's Sensitivity Training," *Washington Post*, December 28, 1991.

31. Quoted in the *New Republic*, February 18, 1991, p. 39. See also Walter Goodman, "Decreasing Our Word Power: The New Newspeak," *New York Times Book Review*, January 27, 1991, p. 14.

32. Quoted in the *Chronicle of Higher Education*, March 20, 1991, p. A-36.

33. *Newsweek*, February 12, 1990, p. 57.

34. His statement was quoted by Paul Berman in the *New Republic*, October 8, 1990. The rabbi, Immanuel Jakobovits, was writing in the *Times* (London), March 4, 1989.

35. Quoted by Robert R. Detlefsen in the *New Republic*, April 10, 1989, p. 19.

36. *Newsweek*, February 12, 1990, p. 53.

37. February 13, 1990. p. C-18.

38. *Washington Post*, January 20, 1991.

39. December 31, 1990, and January 20, 1991.

40. *Chicago Sun-Times*, March 23, 1991.

41. *The Economist*, October 5, 1991, p. 367. Iqbal's lawyer said that his client had done nothing except underline passages in the Koran.

42. Judith Martin and Gunther Stent, op-ed page, March 20, 1991.

43. Khomeini interview with Oriana Fallaci, *New York Times Magazine*, October 7, 1979, p. 21.

Academic and
Artistic Freedom

Nadine Strossen

Artistic and academic freedom are closely intertwined. This interconnection is indicated by the fact that so many recent arts censorship controversies have occurred on university campuses. For example, shortly after she became acting chair of the National Endowment for the Arts (NEA), Anne-Imelda Radice stirred strong protests throughout the artistic and academic communities by vetoing two grants that the NEA's advisory panel, the National Council on the Arts, had strongly recommended for approval. She apparently rejected these grants because the artistic works in question involved sexually explicit imagery. Both grants would have gone to university art galleries, one at the Massachusetts Institute of Technology and the other at Virginia Commonwealth University.

The *Joint Statement on Academic Freedom and Artistic Expression*, adopted by the AAUP and other organizations in 1990, powerfully explains the connection between artistic and academic freedom. A key opening phrase summarizes the argument: "Essential as freedom is for the relation and judgment of facts, it is even more indispensable to the imagination." In fact, AAUP members should be proud to know that this Association-endorsed statement was quoted and relied upon in an important judicial decision upholding artistic freedom that was issued in June 1992. In that ruling, U.S. District Court Judge A. Wallace Tashima held that a congressionally imposed requirement that NEA grantees abide by "general standards of decency" was too broad and vague, in violation of the First Amendment. I will comment further about this decision later. For now, I simply want to note that, in rejecting the government's argument that there is no First Amendment-protected interest in government-funded artistic expression, Judge Tashima's opinion quoted extensively from the Statement on Academic Freedom and Artistic Expression. In concluding that there is such an interest, Judge Tashima endorsed that statement's formulation of its nature and importance.

Arts Censorship as Part of the "Family Values" Agenda

The issues of artistic and academic freedom are important in their own right. Their significance is magnified because of their interrelationship with other issues as part of the right-wing, fundamentalist assault on culture and freedom. Vice-President Dan Quayle has spearheaded this charge, attacking academic and artistic freedom as well as other liberties that he views as undermining "family values." He started sounding this alarm in June 1992. George Bush then took up the theme, and the Republican Party tried to make it a major issue in the presidential campaign.

Typical of Dan Quayle's message on the "traditional values" theme was a speech he delivered to the Southern Baptist Convention in Indianapolis in June. The vice president attacked what he called "a cultural elite," charging it with mocking the nation's values.

According to Quayle, the "cultural elite" consists of "the Hollywood establishment, the academic world, and the press." Thus, members of the AAUP are among this targeted group—congratulations or condolences, as the case may be! Quayle accused the "cultural elite" of undermining "conventional American values" by supporting reproductive freedom, parental rights for gay men and lesbians, and sex education in public schools. "The changes in our culture in recent decades have created a cultural divide in our country," Quayle said. "We have two cultures, the cultural elite and the rest of us."

Two First Amendment Martyrs

Art is on the cutting edge of both cultural change and freedom. It is therefore not surprising that the right-wing, fundamentalist assault on culture and freedom has targeted the arts. News stories about it appear regularly. I have saved two especially dramatic stories that happened to appear in the *New York Times* on the same day. The first was headed, "Rushdie, in U.S., Speaks on Freedom"; the second, an editorial, was entitled "John Frohnmayer's Noisy Exit." The first article reported on Salman Rushdie's rare emergence from hiding to make a plea for artistic freedom before a free speech conference in the U.S.:

> Mr. Rushdie emphasized ... that his persecution is but the most extreme and obvious case of mounting threats to freedom of expression around the world. "What we are witnessing is a war against independence of mind ... The case

of *The Satanic Verses* is ... the most public battle in that war. It is a [war] that can only be won, because the consequences of losing it are horrendous."

And yet, we are losing many battles in that war, as shown by the *New York Times* editorial that appeared on the same day. The editorial commented on the farewell speech of John Frohnmayer, the NEA chair who was fired by the Bush administration in response to right-wing attacks on some NEA-funded projects:

> In a speech at the National Press Club, [Mr. Frohnmayer] lambasted Patrick Buchanan, the Bush administration, and certain members of Congress for undermining the [NEA], and chastised complacent politicians and religious leaders for letting it happen unchallenged. They all deserved the tongue-lashing.
> Take Mr. Buchanan, who ... shamelessly used a few controversial grants by the [NEA] as an inflammatory campaign issue against President Bush. Mr. Buchanan ... branded the NEA as "the upholstered playpen of the arts and crafts auxiliary of the Eastern liberal arts establishment."

I had the honor of meeting Salman Rushdie in England in October 1991. Since then, as he requested, I have been using every possible opportunity to remind people of his plight. Unfortunately, too many have forgotten that he still suffers under a recently renewed death threat and associated bounty offer (Rushdie's murderer has been promised not only the equivalent of sainthood, but also payments of about $2 million). The *fatwa*, or edict, first issued by the Ayatollah Khomeini in February 1989, applied not only to Rushdie but to anyone who had any connection with the book's distribution. Unfortunately, too few people realize that, following the *fatwa*, the Japanese translator of *The Satanic Verses* was murdered, and its Italian translator was brutally attacked and critically injured. In response, a planned Polish translation was canceled.

Occasionally, when I recount these events to American audiences, even people who are concerned about free speech here ask what all of this has to do with them. After all, they note correctly, we have enough free speech problems right here in the United States. Why, then, should we spread ourselves thin by trying to do something about the Rushdie situation? Indeed, the Bush administration showed an even more insouciant attitude toward his plight. Rushdie came to this country in March 1992 for the express purpose of trying to persuade U.S. officials to use their diplomatic influence to secure the lifting of the *fatwa*. He was cavalierly rebuffed by the Bush administration as not raising any kind of free speech issue. In explaining the administration's refusal to meet with Rushdie, White House spokesperson Marlin Fitzwater dismissed Rushdie's visit to Washington as nothing more than an author on a publicity swing, "doing book tours and things that authors do." No doubt showing more candor about the refusal, State Department spokesperson Margaret Tutwiler said that such a meeting "could, and possibly might, be misinterpreted."

Far away as we are from Iran, where the *fatwa* was issued, and even from Great Britain, where Salman Rushdie continues to live the life of a prisoner, the late ayatollah's attacks nonetheless have had a seriously damaging impact on the free flow of artistic expression right here at home. First, we must not forget that when the death threat was first issued, two of the three major U.S. bookstore chains stopped selling *The Satanic Verses*, out of fear for the safety of their employees. Moreover, the publisher with the rights to issue a paperback version of the novel refused to do so, for similar reasons. Therefore, no paperback edition was available until 1992, when a consortium of anonymous human rights organizations issued it. Even more than three years after the *fatwa* was pronounced, no commercial publisher dared to take this step.

The *fatwa*'s damage to artistic freedom in this country has gone beyond simply making it difficult for American readers to get a copy of *The Satanic Verses*. Many writers and other artists have said that the Rushdie situation has deterred them from creating works that might be perceived as sacrilegious or blasphemous, arousing public hostility. The recent brouhaha over the NEA shows that this concern is hardly far-fetched. President Bush's dismissal of John Frohnmayer seems to have been motivated by a Pat Buchanan televised commercial. It berated the administration for "investing our tax dollars in pornographic and blasphemous art too shocking to show." Blasphemy, of course, was precisely the sin of which *The Satanic Verses* was accused.

To be sure, an artist's loss of federal funding is hardly as severe a sanction as his loss of life or freedom, but for many artists, the cut-off of NEA funds means a loss of private funds, too. For example, many corporations used to buy visual art as a safe, non-controversial form of investment or charitable contribution. Thanks to recent controversies such as those swirling around the NEA, this is no longer the case.

The ayatollah's *fatwa* against Salman Rushdie and the religious right's attacks against artistic expression and other freedoms in the U.S. are different in degree only. This was most dramatically revealed in Pat Buchanan's opening night address at the Republican Party's convention in August. He declared a "religious war" against those who do not share his views on religion, art, culture, family life, human right, and other important issues.

The increasing assaults on artistic expression in the U.S. led the ACLU in 1991 to form a special national project, the Arts Censorship Project, to counter these threats. Although the ACLU has defended free expression since its formation in 1920, it did not establish a special unit devoted to defending free artistic expression until this decade, one indication of the unprecedented nature of the current challenges in that area.

As I indicated at the outset, to be fully understood, the current assaults on artistic freedom should be seen in a larger context, as part of the broader right-wing, fundamentalist attack on various cultural and legal changes. The threats to artistic freedom are part of the call for "family values" and "decency" that are epitomized—or caricatured—by Dan Quayle's criticisms of the television character Murphy Brown and other members of what he calls "the cultural elite." This outlook is typified by Quayle's statement that the Los Angeles riots were caused more by a "poverty of values" than by economic poverty. It also underlies the unprecedented threats we now face on many civil liberties fronts, including academic freedom, women's equality, civil rights for lesbians and gay men, reproductive freedom, and religious freedom.

A recent statement by Gary Bauer, former advisor to President Reagan and now president of the Family Research Council, shows the scope of what is at stake. He said that we are in "an ongoing cultural civil war revolving around morality," which pits Americans "with a fairly traditional religious faith, who feel that the culture is out of control, against secular people who believe in a pluralistic society." From Bauer's perspective, the real enemy in our society is not racial discrimination or the lack of diversity in our cultural and political institutions. It is the opposite—too much diversity, pluralism, and multiculturalism!

These kinds of statements contain ugly overtones of the nativism that so often marks backlashes against artistic and cultural freedom. During his brief presidential campaign, Pat Buchanan made some of the most explicit statements of this sort: "Conservatives need to exploit this mood of national rage against filthy and blasphemous art, against general coarseness and crudity, to rally a movement to recapture America's culture." Thus, the current movement against artistic and cultural freedom is also connected to an opposition to immigration and to refugees, of which Haitian refugees have been the most recent victims.

Censorship of artistic expression is part of a larger pattern. This is an important point, especially concerning sexually oriented artistic expression, because too many otherwise enlightened people are still too defensive about upholding such expression. The integral connection between sexually oriented expression and human rights was powerfully explained by Gary Mongiovi, an economist who teaches at St. John's University:

> Sexual expression is perhaps the most fundamental manifestation of human individuality. Erotic publications, art, films, etc. are subversive in the sense that they celebrate, and appeal to, the most uniquely personal aspects of an individual's emotional life. Thus, to allow freedom of expression and freedom of thought in this realm, is to ... promote diversity and non-conformist behavior in general. Is this not what the Falwells, the Meeses, the Helmses of the world really wish to suppress?
>
> It is no coincidence that one of the first consequences of democratization and political liberalization in the former Soviet Union, Eastern Europe, and China was a small explosion of erotic publications.
>
> Suppression of [sexually oriented expression] is not just a free speech

issue: attempts to stifle sexual expression are part of a larger agenda directed at the suppression of human freedom and individuality more generally.

Specific Threats to Artistic Expression: The Supreme Court

So far I have tried to give a "macro" view of the broader context in which it occurs. The remainder of this article will give a "micro" view, examining some specific elements in the current wave of arts censorship. I see four major sources of threats to artistic freedom: the United States Supreme Court; other governmental bodies; private pressure groups; and—last but not least—public opinion. In the remainder of this article, I will outline the dangers posed by the Supreme Court. In the sequel to this article, to be published in the next issue of *Academe*, I will discuss the other factors that endanger artistic freedom.

The Supreme Court is an appropriate place to begin an analysis of recent threats to artistic expression. Unfortunately, the current court is cutting back on constitutionally protected rights in general, and free expression is no exception. To be sure, the court recently upheld several important free speech claims, but it also rejected other, equivalently important, free speech claims.

Of particular concern are a pair of decisions, issued in 1991, which severely undermined two core free speech principles that until then had been securely established. The first of these principles is known to lawyers as that of "content-neutrality" or "viewpoint-neutrality." This principle, which the court described as "a bedrock of our free speech jurisprudence," holds that government may never limit speech merely because the majority of the community disagrees with or is offended by the ideas or viewpoint it expresses. The court reaffirmed that principle in several recent Supreme Court decisions, including one issued in June 1992, in a case entitled *R.A.V. v. St. Paul*. The *R.A.V.* ruling unanimously invalidated a St. Paul, Minnesota, ordinance that criminalized symbolic expression that "arouses anger, alarm, or resentment in others on the basis of race, color, creed, religion, or gender." The majority opinion, authored by Justice Scalia, struck down the law precisely because it singled out for punishment certain disfavored viewpoints.

The Rehnquist court strictly enforced the viewpoint neutrality principle in cases such as *R.A.V.* In contrast, in a decision issued in 1991, the court greatly eroded that principle in a very important context. *Rust v. Sullivan* upheld the "gag rule" that had been promulgated by the Department of Health and Human Services (HHS) during the Reagan administration. Under that rule, doctors, nurses, and other health professionals working at family planning clinics that receive federal funds are prohibited from giving any information about abortion, even in situations where abortion is medically indicated—i.e., where the woman's health would be adversely affected by carrying the pregnancy to term. Worse yet, the rule provides a script that these health professionals must recite, in case the woman herself asks about abortion. They must say, "This clinic believes that abortion is not an appropriate method of family planning."

Rust, of course, was a disaster in terms of the reproductive rights and health of the five million women whose only access to any sort of medical care—even beyond the context of family planning and pregnancy—is through federally funded clinics. As severe a blow as it dealt to constitutional privacy rights, though, *Rust* had a more pervasive adverse impact on free speech rights by making a significant exception to the previously sacrosanct principle of viewpoint neutrality. The court's reasoning has implications far beyond the particular "gag rule" at issue, which could undermine free speech for those who oppose abortion, as well as those who support the right to choose—not to mention for countless others. The court reasoned that whenever an individual or institution receives government funds, the government may tie strings to those funds. The strings may include a waiver of constitutional rights, including the right to be free from governmental prohibition of speech based upon its viewpoint.

The *Rust* rationale is as threatening to those who oppose reproductive freedom as to those who support it. This can be illustrated by imagining a future—some would describe it as a utopian future!—in which a pro-choice president is elected. Her secretary of health and human services could issue exactly the opposite type of gag rule from the one that the court upheld, yet the court's broad rationale would make it equally constitutional. Under the hypothetical new rule, health care professionals at clinics that receive federal funding would be required to urge, advocate, and encourage abortion, and would be prohibited from giving any information about carrying a pregnancy to term. No wonder that so many "pro-life," as well as pro-choice, members of Congress voted in favor of legislation that would have undone the *Rust* ruling.

Even beyond the context of abortion altogether, the *Rust* rationale has devastating consequences for free speech. To say that the central right to be free from governmental viewpoint discrimination against speech disappears whenever there is any government funding is to create an exception large enough to swallow the rule. How many institutions in our society do not receive some government funding? Surely the vast majority of academic and arts institutions fit within this category, and therefore are especially endangered by *Rust's* implications. Although lawyers for academic and artistic institutions have framed arguments that seek to limit *Rust's* applicability to these other contexts, the government is aggressively asserting counterarguments. For example, in cases involving, respectively, an HHS research grant to Stanford

University Medical School and NEA funding for artists, the government has argued that *Rust* forecloses any First Amendment rights on the part of the grantees, including when the grantees are academics and artists.

Indeed, in a letter to the Senate, the Justice Department expressed a sweeping view of *Rust*'s implications. It asserted that *Rust* "states certain general constitutional principles relevant to the government's power to impose conditions on government subsidies," and that *Rust* "is likely to be pertinent whenever the Justice Department defends funding legislation from judicial challenges similar to those raised in *Rust*."

As I mentioned above, in June 1992, there was a big victory in the effort to check *Rust*'s adverse implications for the viewpoint neutrality principle (not to mention other free speech guarantees) in the government funding context. This was a ruling in a lawsuit brought by the ACLU Arts Censorship Project and other organizations on behalf of performance artists who were denied NEA funding because of the controversial content of their artistic expression. The government had argued that, in light of *Rust*, the NEA could deny funds for any reason, including the politically controversial nature of the artist's themes, ideas, and perspectives. In rejecting that argument, U.S. District Court Judge Tashima limited *Rust*'s application to the arts funding context. Specifically, he ruled that the "decency" standard, which Congress had imposed on NEA grant applications in 1990, violated artists' free speech rights.

Important a victory as Judge Tashima's ruling was, it is no guarantee that *Rust* can in the long run be cabined specifically within its own factual context. First, the government will probably appeal that ruling, and it is unclear whether the Supreme Court shares Judge Tashima's narrow reading of its reasoning in *Rust*. Second, the NEA may evade the import of Judge Tashima's ruling even before any appeal. This possibility was suggested by Congressman Ralph Regula, an Ohio Republican, who was an architect of the decency requirement. Shortly after Judge Tashima's decision, the *New York Times* reported, "Mr. Regula [said] that he thought the ruling would make little difference, [expressing his belief that NEA's new acting chair, Anne-Imelda] Radice, favored the decency standard and would continue to use it. 'I think that she will continue to apply [the standard] under the rubric of artistic excellence.'"

If Regula is correct, his comment sheds interesting light on the Bush administration's avowed commitment to law and order. Whether or not he is correct, *Rust v. Sullivan* will continue to cast a shadow over all government-funded expression unless or until the Supreme Court itself explicitly reins in its apparently broad rationale.

The Erosion of the Actual or Imminent Harm Requirement

The second core free speech principle that the Supreme Court severely undermined through a decision in 1991 complements the viewpoint neutrality principle. The viewpoint neutrality principle specifies what is not a sufficient justification for censoring expression—namely, disagreement with its viewpoint. This second principle specifies what is the only acceptable justification for limiting expression—namely, that the speech causes actual or imminent harm. This is often summarized as the "clear and present danger" requirement. In other words, speech may be suppressed only if it would inevitably cause danger. The most familiar example of this principle comes from an opinion by Supreme Court Justice Oliver Wendell Holmes in which he said that the free speech guarantee would not extend to someone falsely shouting "Fire!" in a crowded theater and causing a panic.

Barnes v. Glen Theatres gutted the imminent harm requirement. The 1991 decision is often referred to as the "nude dancing decision," since it upheld a South Bend, Indiana, ordinance that prohibited nude barroom dancing. I prefer not to describe Supreme Court decisions in terms of the particular facts they happened to involve, since these decisions are based upon principles that will have precedential impact in many other factual contexts as well. Just as *Rust*'s ruling should trouble even those who oppose a constitutional right to choose an abortion, so, too, the *Barnes* ruling should disturb even those who do not believe that nude dancing is an important form of constitutionally protected expression.

In *Barnes*, the court initially ruled that nude dancing is expressive conduct that comes within the scope of the First Amendment. The court did not create another category of sexually oriented speech and declare such speech to be wholly outside the First Amendment, as it has done with respect to obscenity and child pornography. Rather, the court recognized that nude dancing expresses important themes of eroticism, sexuality, and sensuality, and has been practiced throughout history and in many different cultures.

Supporters of free expression should not take comfort in the court's ruling that nude dancing is *prima facie* protected expression, because it then went on to hold that such expression could nonetheless be prohibited without evidence that it caused actual or imminent harm. Having assimilated nude dancing within the scope of constitutionally protected expression, the court offered a broad rationale for permitting prohibitions upon nude dancing that will apparently extend to other constitutionally protected expression too. Therefore, in the long run, the court did more damage to free expression by holding nude dancing to be within the free speech clause than if it had reached the opposite conclusion.

In *Barnes* there was no evidence that the prohibited nude dancing had caused any harm. To the contrary, the record revealed that there were no adverse "secondary effects" in terms of crime, prostitution, and the like. Therefore, in asserting a purported justification for prohibiting nude dancing, the court was forced to rely on a generalized community interest in "morality." In short, free speech became the casualty of the sense of moral affront felt by some members of the community in realizing that some consenting adults were choosing to pay to watch other consenting adults dance without clothes.

If all *prima facie* protected speech can be outlawed because the community's sense of morality is offended, then speech is hardly free in any durable sense. Rather, the expressions of minorities or individuals within the community can be held hostage to prevailing majoritarian notions of morality.

The Court's Class-Based Approach to Free Speech

Both *Rust* and *Barnes* illustrate another distressing aspect of the Rehnquist court's cutback on significant free speech rights: an economic or class bias. In the past, when the court was more protective of rights generally, it also was especially careful to safeguard the rights of relatively powerless groups, including the poor. It did so in recognition both that such individuals were more likely to be victims of rights abuses and that the exercise of their rights could facilitate their interests more broadly. In stark contrast, the Rehnquist court has been particularly aggressive in undermining the rights of those who lack financial resources. *Rust*, for example, in effect creates a caste system of constitutional rights. As long as you are wealthy enough not to need governmental financial aid, or aid from an institution that itself receives government assistance, only then do you still have full constitutional rights.

The *Barnes* decision revealed another form of class bias. The justices who voted to uphold the ban on nude dancing took pains to emphasize that they were not antagonistic to art. Therefore, they stressed that if the nude dancing had occurred in another setting, such as an opera at Lincoln Center, it would have been protected. This distinction prompted New York University law professor (and former ACLU legal director) Burt Neuborne to observe that whether you have a constitutional right to watch nude dancing depends on what you are drinking while you are watching the dancing. If you are drinking white wine, your viewing is constitutionally protected, but if you are drinking beer, it's not! He calls this the "Chablis theory" of free speech. In the same vein, Duke University law professor Walter Dellinger has summarized the Barnes court's class bias by quipping that nude dancing is protected, but naked dancing is not.

Important a role as the Supreme Court plays in connection with our free speech rights—and their erosion—such rights are also subject to pressures from other governmental bodies, from the organizations, and from public opinion. Part II of this article, to be published in the next issue of *Academe*, will outline these other sources of threats to artistic freedom.

Part I of this article gave a "macro" perspective on the current threats to artistic freedom in the United States. It showed that those threats are part of a worldwide pattern of attacks on free speech and other individual freedoms, many of which are initiated by religious fundamentalists. The death threat against Salman Rushdie for having written a "blasphemous" book is the most extreme example of this pattern, but it is no different in kind from the attacks in the U.S. against allegedly "blasphemous" artistic works funded by the NEA. The most telling acknowledgment of the connection between the Ayatollah's *fatwa* against Rushdie and the religious right's attack on artistic and other freedoms was Patrick Buchanan's declaration of "religious war" in his opening night speech at the Republican Party Convention in August 1992. Dan Quayle and other prominent public figures have used similarly bellicose rhetoric, declaring that we are engaged in a "cultural war." These campaigns are being waged not only against free speech, but also against other civil liberties and civil rights. These include academic freedom, artistic freedom, the civil rights of lesbians and gay men, gender equality, religious freedom, reproductive freedom, and the rights of refugees and immigrants.

After placing the recent attacks on artistic expression in this larger context of worldwide attacks on human rights, Part I of the article turned to a "micro" perspective. It began to examine some examples of the recent attacks on artistic expression in the U.S. These attacks can be divided into four broad groups, according to their sources. Part I discussed the U.S. Supreme Court, outlining the Court's constricted interpretation of the free speech guarantee in the First Amendment. Part II will discuss three remaining sources of such threats: other governmental agencies, private organizations, and public opinion.

Threats to Artistic Freedom: Other Governmental Bodies

The second force of threats to artistic expression is other governmental units, besides the Supreme Court. Too often, discussions of free speech (and other rights) focus exclusively on the Supreme Court. The court plays an important role as the final interpreter of the Constitution. We must remember, however, that other branches of government also have great power either to promote or to curtail our rights. The Supreme Court simply sets a floor under our rights; it cannot impose a ceiling over them. In other words, the Court specifies the level below which other governmental bodies may not sink in terms of protecting our rights, but these other bodies may still choose to afford broader protection for those rights.

For example, the Supreme Court ruled in *Rust* that the "gag rule" does not violate the First Amendment's free speech guarantee. Nevertheless, the Department of Health and Human Services could have chosen not to enforce the gag rule, and Congress could have chosen to pass legislation barring the Department from imposing it. (Congress did in fact pass such legislation, but it was vetoed by President Bush, and Congress did not override the veto.) Likewise, even though the Supreme Court ruled in *Barnes* that local governments may prohibit nude barroom dancing consistent with the First Amendment, local governments may still choose to allow adults the option of enjoying this form of expression.

Unfortunately, though, too many other governmental entities are joining the Supreme Court in making significant incursions into artistic expression. For the sake of brevity, I will give only one or two examples involving each unit or level of government. Alas, there is a wealth of such examples from which to choose!

The Executive Branch of the Federal Government: The Department of Justice's Obscenity Unit

Turning first to the executive branch of the federal government, the Obscenity Unit within the Department of Justice poses a major threat to artistic expression. This unit, a legacy of the widely discredited Meese Pornography Commission, has expended major resources in a broad-gauged attack on all sexually oriented expression. As the publisher of the trade magazine *Adult Video News*, Paul Fishbein, commented, "The Justice Department has apparently won the war on drugs, beaten inner-city crime, solved the savings and loan crisis, and decided to focus on something really important. Now it's going after videos that portray adults engaging in consensual sexual behavior that people enjoy in the privacy of their own homes."

Beyond their direct victims, the activities of this unit were not widely known prior to the publication of a major exposé issued by the ACLU Arts Censorship Project in 1991, entitled "Above the Law: The Justice Department's War Against the First Amendment." That report documented the questionable tactics used by the Obscenity Unit in an attempt to drive much constitutionally protected sexually oriented material from the market. Under the unit's direction, government agents have raided artists' homes and studios, seized (and sometimes destroyed) their works and equipment, entrapped previously law-abiding individuals into violating the law, and instituted multiple prosecutions against distributors of targeted work in carefully selected forums where the juries are less tolerant and the defense is more burdensome. The harassing strategies have coerced distributors of sexually oriented works into settlements in which they agree not to distribute even works that are constitutionally protected, including popular magazines like *Playboy* and popular books like *The Joy of Sex*.

Even some law enforcement agents with experience in combating obscenity have denounced the extremist goals and tactics of the Justice Department's Obscenity Unit. For example, Robert Marinaro, who ran the FBI's anti-obscenity operations, decried the leaders of this unit as "religious zealots," and denounced their operations in harsh terms: "Much of the material they targeted is protected by the First Amendment. They became zealots about pornography, and their religious beliefs overstepped good judgment."

In a challenge to the Obscenity Unit's operations that the ACLU Arts Censorship Project supported, the U.S. Court of Appeals for the Tenth Circuit issued a ruling in May 1992 that strongly criticized the unit's harassing tactics. The court condemned what it termed "a coordinated campaign of questionable prosecutorial activity." Welcome as this ruling is, it must be recognized that most producers and distributors of the material that has been targeted do not have the resources to fight even those legal battles that they should ultimately win. Therefore, their rights—and those of the individuals who are deprived of access to the material they create or disseminate—are effectively eliminated by the Obscenity Unit, with no meaningful recourse to judicial review.

Congress: The Pornography Victims Compensation Act

The final branch of the federal government, of course, is the Congress. Like the Supreme Court and the executive branch, Congress also has been particularly unsupportive of sexually oriented expression. One measure that Congress is currently considering focuses directly on such expression, but if passed, it would have an enormous adverse impact on many other types of expression as well. The measure in question is officially named the Pornography Victims Compensation Act (PVCA), but has popularly been dubbed the "Bundy Bill." This nickname refers to convicted rapist-murderer Ted Bundy's claim, on the eve of his execution, that exposure to pornography caused him to commit sex crimes. The PVCA endorses the "porn-made-me-do-it" theory of sexual assaults by enabling victims of such assaults to recover damages from creators or distributors of certain sexually oriented work that the jury finds to be a causal factor in the underlying crime. In June 1992, the Senate Judiciary Committee approved a version of the PVCA that should soon come before the full Senate.

Senator Mitch McConnell (R-Ky.), the PVCA's chief sponsor, has said that its purpose is to bankrupt purveyors of sexually oriented work through large damages. Even if such lawsuits do not result in large damage awards, the financial and other costs of defending against them would likely be so onerous as to persuade many businesses to forgo the distribution of any sexually oriented works. The enormous chilling impact that this bill would have on constitutionally protected speech motivated organizations such as the American Booksellers Association and the American Library Association to testify against it.

Moreover, in reaction to the apparent perception by some members of the Judiciary Committee that women and feminists generally supported the bill, many prominent individual women and feminists, as well as organizations representing them, mobilized to express their opposition to it. This opposition has been based both on the bill's adverse impact on free expression, which has been especially important in the movement for women's equality, and on its failure to provide any meaningful response to the serious problem of sexual assault. On these grounds the PVCA has been opposed, for example, by Feminists for Free Expression, the Feminist Anti-Censorship Task Force, and the two largest chapters of the National Organization for Women (those located in California and New York).

It should also be recognized that the PVCA subscribes to a third-party liability theory regarding expressive works that could lead to sweepingly devastating encroachments on much free expression beyond the sexual realm. Once we allow one type of expression to be scapegoated as the cause of anti-social conduct, why not others? Why not license victims of any violent crime to sue the creators and distributors of violent words and imagery? And why not license victims of serious non-violent crimes—for example, various forms of white-collar crimes—to sue the creators and distributors of words and imagery about those anti-social acts? Once we begin to limit the depictions of criminal or immoral conduct, or other depictions that might spur some anti-social act, our bookshelves empty rapidly.

State and Local Government Censorship Efforts

Turning from the national level of government to the state and local levels, we find that artistic expression recently has been under siege here too. In the past few years, we have witnessed many sad "firsts" in grassroots governmental censorship. For example, in 1990, we saw the first criminal prosecution of an art museum and an art museum director for obscenity. I am referring to the prosecution of the Cincinnati Art Museum and its director, Dennis Barrie, for exhibiting Robert Mapplethorpe's photographs.

In that same year, we also saw another first in visual arts censorship: a painting was actually arrested! The painting, depicting former Chicago Mayor Harold Washington wearing women's lingerie, had been included in a display of student art work at the School of the Art Institute of Chicago. Outraged at the perceived insult to the memory of Harold Washington, several members of the Chicago City Council removed the painting from the wall and brought it to the office of the school's director, demanding that he destroy it. He refused, and a lengthy stalemate ensued, which the Chicago Police Department decided to terminate by arresting the painting. It was charged with posing a "threat to public order."

The year 1990 also brought us another first in arts censorship by local governments: the first criminal prosecutions of musical works for obscenity. In Broward County, Florida, the rap group 2 Live Crew was prosecuted for performing songs from *As Nasty as They Wanna Be*. A record store owner was also prosecuted for having sold the album.

These two prosecutions showed one of the major flaws inherent in all obscenity prosecutions—namely, the inevitably subjective nature of the determination whether any particular work fits the vague "definition" of obscenity that the Supreme Court articulated in 1973. The two 1990 2 Live Crew prosecutions were brought against the very same album in the very same county. Nonetheless, the two juries came out with opposite results: one concluded that the piece was obscene and convicted, while the other concluded that it was not, and acquitted. This episode brings to mind the best-known pronouncement about obscenity ever made by a Supreme Court justice, former Justice Potter Stewart's assertion that, although he could not define obscenity, "I know it when I see it." The problem is that no two people, and no two juries—even those drawn from the same geographical pool—see obscenity in the same way. Therefore, artists who produce sexually explicit work always have to fear that some prosecutor or jury, sometime, somewhere, might well find it to be obscene.

The foregoing incidents of local obscenity prosecutions engendered a great chill in the artistic community, even though they all resulted in legal victories for the artists or distributors. For example, with the ACLU's support, the Cincinnati and Chicago cases resulted in acquittals; one 2 Live Crew case resulted in an acquittal, and the other one ended in a appellate court's reversal of the initial conviction. Nonetheless, despite the ultimate legal victories, these proceedings imposed substantial unrecoupable costs on the defendants: the expenditure of money for lawyers' fees and court costs, the investment of time and energy by the defendants themselves and their associates, and much adverse publicity. The final lesson that these and similar prosecutions have taught to those in the arts communities is to steer clear of sexually explicit and other controversial works.

Threat Number Three: Private Pressure Groups

Free speech recently has been subject to incursions from across the political spectrum. For example, many left-of-center individuals, including some feminists, have spearheaded assaults on sexually explicit speech. However, the major source of well-organized private pressure against artistic expression has come from the opposite end of the political spectrum—in particular, from the religious right.

Because of the demise of the Moral Majority as an organization, too many people have assumed—incorrectly—that the religious right's political influence has likewise disappeared. To the contrary, other religious right groups are flourishing, with an impact on the political process. For example, Pat Robertson's Christian Coalition has helped to lead the charge against the NEA by mobilizing its members to lobby for restrictions on grants. Other organizations that have played leading roles in the arts censorship movement are the Eagle Forum and Concerned Women of America, in both of which Phyllis Schlafly is prominent, and the American Family Association, headed by the Rev. Donald Wildmon. These groups have organized boycotts of companies advertising in media that carry stories or messages to which they object. In consequence, many advertisers have pressured the media, which in turn have decided not to carry the targeted material. This strategy has led to the withdrawal of articles or programs that are offensive to well-organized pressure groups from the print media, broadcast television, and cable television.

Another example of how private pressure has led to the curtailment of artistic expression is through "voluntary" record labeling. In response to efforts to pass laws that would require musical recordings to bear warning labels about the sexually explicit or otherwise controversial nature of their lyrics, the record industry "volunteered" to impose such labels upon its own members. To underscore the fact that threats to artistic free expression come from across the political spectrum, it should be noted that one of the original leaders of the record-labeling movement was Tipper Gore, wife of Vice President Al Gore. Advocates of these labels contend that they are consistent with free speech values, since they simply provide information. True as that is, the actual impact of such labels may well be to lessen the free flow of expression and information, since too many record stores refuse to sell any material that bears a label, and too many mall owners refuse to lease space to record stores that sell labeled materials.

All the private organizing efforts to restrict artistic expression are themselves exercises of free speech and other First Amendment rights. Certainly, the ACLU defends the rights to speak, write letters, organize boycotts, and lobby government officials to advocate any position, including a position that is itself anti-civil liberties. Therefore, we would not seek to stop the activities of the Christian Coalition and like organizations.

However, we would urge other individuals and groups who espouse different philosophies about how free artistic expression should be, and what materials should be carried in the media, to engage more actively in their own speaking, organizing, and boycotting efforts. As always in a free society, the appropriate way to counter speech with which one disagrees is not by suppressing it, but rather, with more speech. Those who raise their voices to restrict the free flow of ideas and expression have a negative impact on First Amendment values. Those of us who champion such values accordingly have a special responsibility not only to defend their expressive rights, but also to raise our own voices in support of a more robust, open, and varied societal discourse.

Threat Number Four: Public Opinion

This leads to the last source of challenge to free artistic expression that I have identified—namely, public opinion. Earlier in this century, the great free speech scholar Zechariah Chafee said, "In the long run, the public will have just as much freedom of speech as it really wants." That, alas, is the root of the problem! Public opinion surveys consistently show that public understanding of and support for free expression is a thin reed upon which to lean.

For example, to commemorate the bicentennial of the First Amendment in 1991, a comprehensive survey of public attitudes toward free speech was conducted by the American Society of Newspaper Editors and Middle Tennessee State University. That survey asked whether the respondents believed that certain types of expression should be protected. In every case, the expression at issue was clearly protected as a matter of constitutional law. Nevertheless, large percentages of the respondents answered that the speech should never be protected, and only small percentages gave the constitutionally correct answer that it would always be protected.

I will illustrate these attitudes, and the challenge they present for protecting artistic expression, by sharing with you the survey results concerning types of expression that are particularly relevant to the arts context. Before giving you a sampling of these survey results, I want to reemphasize that even the current Supreme Court, with its relatively unsympathetic attitude toward free speech, would no doubt reaffirm that every type of expression asked about is constitutionally protected.

When asked whether there should be a right to dance in a sexually suggestive manner, only 27 percent of the survey respondents said that right should always be protected. When asked whether there should be a right to use slang words that refer to sexual acts, only 21 percent said that right should always be protected. When asked whether there should be a right to say sacrilegious things, only 32 percent said yes, and when asked whether there should be a right to use words or phrases that may offend people from a certain religious group, a mere 12 percent said yes. In light of these last two responses, Salman Rushdie might well be almost as embattled in the U.S. as in other parts of the world. When asked whether television should have a right to show music videos that deal with sexual themes, only 14 percent said yes. As one final example, when asked whether there should be a right to sell magazines or books with nude pictures, only 20 percent said yes, thus raising real problems for anthropological and medical texts.

As the results show, a pervasive theme that characterizes much of the public (as well as official) unwillingness to protect artistic expression is hostility or suspicion toward sexuality or nudity. Another manifestation of this attitude was a recent Gallup Poll, which revealed that an overwhelming 76 percent of the public wants to ban "dial-a-porn," and almost half would ban all striptease performances. The lyrics to one of Madonna's songs contain the following paean: "Martin Luther King, Malcolm X/ Freedom of speech is as good as sex." For many members of the U.S. public and government, a more apt phrasing would apparently be, "Freedom of speech is as *bad* as sex"!

Scapegoating Speech

A consistent rationale seems to underlie many of the incidents of arts censorship that this article has described. In situation after situation, the expression is targeted because it conveys messages related to some troubling societal problem—for example, sexual assault, other forms of violence, and intergroup hatred. But to limit speech on this theory amounts to an unjustified blaming of the messenger. No causal connection has been demonstrated between expression that depicts various types of anti-social conduct and the actual conduct itself. For example, no credible scientific evidence supports claims that exposure to sexually explicit, degrading images of women incite actual violence or discrimination against women. Likewise, despite Dan Quayle's assertions, no causal link can be established between the positive message about single motherhood conveyed by the television show *Murphy Brown* and the Los Angeles riots.

Censoring expression that portrays pressing societal problems is always a politically effective "quick fix" which creates the illusion that government leaders are addressing the problems. In fact, though, scapegoating speech is at best ineffective and at worst counterproductive in addressing the actual underlying problems. For example, the "Bundy Bill" does nothing to bolster prosecutions of actual criminals who sexually assault women. Nor does it address the underlying causes of sexual assault and gender discrimination.

Ironically, many of the politicians who claim to demonstrate their commitments to women's equality by supporting this bill do not support constructive measures that are directly focused on that goal. These include the elimination of the caps on damages for gender-based employment discrimination in the 1991 Civil Rights Act, legislation mandating that employers provide family leave, and government-supported child care.

In conclusion, this survey of current challenges to artistic expression shows that such challenges are enormous. Nevertheless, I remain optimistic about the ability of free speech advocates to meet those challenges. I am buoyed in my optimism by the many courageous and talented individuals who are actually exercising their artistic expression, or fighting to do so. The one I find most inspiring is Salman Rushdie, who personifies both the exercise and the suppression of artistic free speech. Therefore, I will end where I began, by quoting Mr. Rushdie. I would like to share with you a passage from Rushdie's first public speech since the death threat and bounty were put on his head in February 1989. Fittingly, he chose to risk this public appearance to address a conference at Columbia University in New York in December 1991, to celebrate the two hundredth anniversary of the First Amendment.

From Mr. Rushdie's eloquent, powerful plea for artistic freedom—hearing it in person was one of the most memorable experiences in my life—I will share with you a passage in which he describes how he overcomes his occasional bouts of despair that the world will remember him and champion his cause:

> What is a novelist under terrorist attack worth? Despair whispers in my ear, "Not a lot." But I refuse to give in to despair.
> Our lives teach us who we are. I have learned the hard way that when you permit anyone else's description of reality to supplant your own—and such descriptions have been raining down on me—then you might as well be dead.
> Obviously, a rigid, blinkered, absolutist world view is the easiest to keep hold of, whereas the fluid, uncertain, metamorphic picture I've always carried about is rather more vulnerable. Yet I must cling with all my might to ... my own soul; must hold on to its mischievous, iconoclastic, out-of-step clown instincts, no matter how great the storm. And if that plunges me into contradiction and paradox, so be it; I've lived in that messy ocean all my life. I've fished in it for my art. This turbulent sea was the sea outside my bedroom window in Bombay. It is the sea by which I was born, and which I carry within me wherever I go.
> "Free speech is a non-starter," says one of my Islamic extremist opponents. No, sir, I reply, it is not. Free speech is the whole thing, the whole ball game. Free speech is life itself.
> What is my single life worth?
> Ladies and gentlemen, you must decide what you think a writer is worth, what value you place on a maker of stories, and an arguer with the world.

Untruth
or Consequences?

John C. Swan

A few years ago an Illinois man named Paul Heinrich became so angry with a certain young woman of his acquaintance that he took the unusual step of producing and distributing a leaflet about her. In that document he called her a promiscuous, drug-using social deviate and an unfit mother who ought to have her daughter taken away from her. He also wrote a letter to the woman's mother, calling her "mother of a whore," "grandmother of a bastard," and "white trash." Just to make things perfectly clear, he added, "I hope to God you take me to court for distributing the enclosed newsletter."[1]

Heinrich's prayer was answered. He was charged in McLean County for criminal defamation under the Illinois Criminal Code. At this point the case began to get interesting to lawyers and, incidentally, librarians. According to the statute in question (Ill. Rev. Stat. 1981, Ch. 38, par. 27-1), a criminal libel defendant must not only show that his offending utterance is true, but also that he did the deed with "good motivation" and for "justifiable ends." This "qualified truth defense," as lawyers call it, is mandated not only by the law but also by the Illinois Constitution.

Heinrich moved that the charges against him be dismissed on the grounds that this chink in the armor of a defense based upon the truth was a violation of the First and Fourteenth Amendments to the U.S. Constitution. The circuit court agreed and dismissed the charges. On appeal, the Illinois Supreme Court reversed this decision and upheld the statue.

The U.S. Supreme Court refused to take *The People of the State of Illinois v. Paul Heinrich* under review. This probably means that Paul Heinrich will be taken to trial back in McLean County and whatever the outcome there, this landmark libel case will make its way back to the Supreme Court via another appeal.

An Absolute Defense

A lot of people are interested in the outcome, particularly those who have a healthy dislike of a law that imposes "criminal liability on a declarant, regardless of the truthfulness of the statements made or the declarant's knowledge of the truth or falsity of those statements."[2] The Freedom to Read Foundation has agreed with the assertion of the defense that this is bad business. Truth *must* be an absolute defense in such cases for a number of vital First Amendment reasons. Otherwise libel action could stop the flow of necessary information merely on the grounds that those releasing it have difficulty proving they are properly motivated to tell the truth.

The Freedom to Read Foundation has put money into this case, money that is largely from, and for the sake of, us librarians. We should applaud this investment. Truth is the most precious commodity in the information market for practical as well as idealistic reasons—the "truth" here being that of Mill, Milton, and Socrates, not the far more common version, which Ambrose Bierce defined as "an ingenious compound of desirability and appearance."[3]

Truth, Untruth, & Libraries

The commitment of librarians to the truth as an absolute legal defense should never be confused with our basic professional commitment to the flow of all kinds of information without regard to its truth or falsehood. One of the Freedom to Read Foundation lawyers made that important observation when the Foundation affirmed its support for the defense in *Heinrich*.

Truth may be, must be, an absolute criterion under the law, but it has no such place in the selection, classification, storage, and weeding decisions made by librarians.

One hopes it is self-evident that we are not arbiters of the truth. The first tenet of the Library Bill of Rights, our primary professional interpretation of the Constitution as it applies to us (and our patrons), states that:

> Books and other library resources should be provided for the interest, information, and enlightenment of all people of the community the library serves. Materials should not be excluded because of the origin, background, or views of those contributing to their creation.

The document's second point commits us to a broad diversity and tolerance:

> Libraries should provide materials and information presenting all points of view on current and historical issues. Materials should not be proscribed or removed because of partisan or doctrinal disapproval.[4]

These statements make no reference to the truth or untruth of library materials, and that is as it must be. Another ALA document, "Diversity in Collection Development," a particularly vital and hard-won interpretation of the Library Bill of Rights, addresses this point most directly:

> Intellectual freedom, the essence of equitable library services, promotes no causes, furthers no movements, and favors no viewpoints. It only provides for free access to all expressions of ideas through which any and all sides of a question, cause or movements may be explored. Toleration is meaningless without tolerance for what some may consider detestable.[5]

This openness is necessary simply because Ambrose Bierce was right: the real world offers us a multiplicity of "truths" compounded of desirability and appearance, often contradictory, sometimes in violent conflict with one another. As human beings we inevitably hold cause with one or many of these truths, but as librarians our cause is, in a very practical sense, not truth but freedom. Indeed, our truth *is* freedom, freedom of access, freedom for our patrons to draw upon our resource, to sort their own truths out of our carefully collected and managed mélange of truths, half-truths, untruths, and non-truths.

Slow Evolution & Hard Politics

It takes very little knowledge of the development of the library profession to realize that this position is the result of slow evolution and hard politics.

The renowned and influential librarian of the San Francisco Free Public Library, F.B. Perkins, was expressing the dominant sentiment of the profession when he wrote, "I say that a Free Public Library has no business to furnish licentious, immoral, or vulgar books .... A Free Public Library is an educational institution .... Its first requisite is, therefore, that it should be useful—should do good; its office as to amusement is of very minor importance. The business of teaching immorality it ought not to practice at all."[6] Perkins asserted this belief in a particular set of library truths almost exactly one hundred years ago.

If the library profession's current official policy statements are to be believed, we have evolved as a profession from the position of guardians of one set of truths to guardians of access to all information.[7]

Duty to "Untruth"

It is paradoxical, then, if also somewhat platitudinous, that the librarian's duty is as much to preserve the untruth on the shelves as the truth. But it cannot be denied that Perkin's delineation of the moral chasm between "Free Libraries and Unclean Books" has a contemporary ring to it, despite its century of age.

Perkins is certainly echoed by many today who devote themselves to translating their religious and social convictions into pressure for the censorship of other people's religious and social convictions. This external pressure, however, is only part of the problem. The process of accommodating mutually exclusive versions of the truth can be a most challenging exercise in political communication.

The sharper issue here, however, is not the external push and pull, but the complications that arise from our personal allegiances. We do indeed bring our own versions of the truth to the job. We don't put them behind us when we make professional judgments. Selection and weeding and organizing and providing access and guidance are all carried out with at least one eye cocked on the truth, or at least a consensus thereof established by the review media, public opinion, and other measures.

We prefer to buy books that tell the truth about life or dog grooming or history or solar panels, rather than those which distort, mislead, lie, or just make mistakes.

Demand is obviously important also, but demand is itself usually conditioned by some ingredient of truth, whether it is that perceived by a few scholars or that mirrored in the desires and dreams of a multimillion Harlequin readers.

This truth is older than Plato: People do not deliberately seek falsehood, however twisted a thing they make of the truth they do seek. In itself, this is not the problem, but it leads to the problem, which is a deep, even structural ambiguity in our commitment to untruth as it is presumably protected by those first two tenets of the Library Bill of Rights.

There is much more to this issue than the old and unresolvable clash between ideal standards and real practices. It is a problem with concrete professional and political implications. They can be demonstrated by way of a recent and usefully notorious case in California—especially useful because it involves a group with a mission that is just about as free of the truth as any defender of untruth could wish for.

Truth & Truth Missions

In June 1984, David McCalden, the guiding spirit of an organization called Truth Missions, contracted with the California Library Association to rent exhibit space and to reserve a meeting room at the December CLA convention.

In September, after considerable discussion and pressure from Jewish and other sympathetic, outraged groups, the CLA canceled McCalden's contract. In October he responded with a threat to sue them for breach of contract and again, on advice from counsel, the CLA Conference Planning Committee voted to rescind the cancellation. This in turn resulted in widespread protest, threats from extremist groups, and a banner headline in the *Los Angeles Times*. A resolution passed by the Los Angeles City Council stated that:

> While we must protect the right of all Americans to express their views, there is no obligation to provide the forces of hatred such respected platforms. We therefore call on the California Library Association to recognize their grave error of judgment and urge them to remove these individuals from their program.[8]

The City Council backed this suggestion with a threat to withdraw all support, "formal or informal," from CLA.

As you could guess, the CLA decided again, finally to cancel the Truth Missions contract. In the letter of cancellation CLA Executive Director Stefan Moses used an escape clause in the contract allowing CLA "to restrict exhibits that may be objectionable or to order the removal of any portion of an exhibit which in the judgment of the association is detrimental to or detracts from the general order of exhibits."[9] The hollow ring of this statement is the sound of librarians caving in.

The CLA had itself sent McCalden the regular exhibitor's packet at the suggestion of one of its members because he had been denied space to exhibit his banned books during the 1983 observation of Banned Books Week by the Torrance Public Library. The CLA knew what he had to offer, and it was not McCalden who was detracting from the "order of exhibits" but the host of protesters aroused by what he had to offer.

McCalden's Message

Just what did McCalden have to offer? Truth Missions is dedicated to the proposition that the Holocaust is an entirely overrated event, and that evidence for it is largely a fabrication of a vast Zionist conspiracy. (McCalden refers to the American Jewish Committee as the "Kosher nostra.")

Formerly a leader of the notorious Institute for Historical Review, which through such books as *The Hoax of the Twentieth Century* has reviewed the Holocaust right out of history, McCalden does admit that some Jews died in concentration camps, mostly of starvation and disease when times were tough for everybody near the end of the war. He claims, however, that no Jews were gassed to death in the concentration camps, that the gas was used only to delouse clothing.

It was McCalden who, in 1979, issued the challenge of a $50,000 prize to anyone providing proof that any Jews were put to death in the gas chambers at Auschwitz. McCalden used the name Lewis Brandon at that time. A Los Angeles businessman and Auschwitz survivor, Mel Mermelstein, took up the challenge and provided the proof—rejected, of course, by McCalden but accepted by a Los Angeles Superior Court in an important suit.[10] (The case is still in the courts on appeal.)

The banning of the Truth Missions banned-books display and meeting has a disproportionate place in my argument precisely because of the utter lack of truth to the message peddled by McCalden and his ilk. The point here is not to chastise the California Library Association. Their waffling had the virtue of self-examination, and it is doubtful whether any similar organization would have behaved differently under the circumstances.

The ACLU Response

True, one thinks immediately of the ACLU and its brave and almost ruinous tenacity in attacking what was essentially an unconstitutional parade ordinance used against the Nazis in Skokie. But part of the point here is that the ACLU and a library association are not similar organizations.

In a letter to the *Los Angeles Times*, Ramona Ripston, executive director of the Southern California ACLU, asserted that the CLA, as "a private group, does not have to permit David McCalden to speak at its conference." She went on to add: "However, the ACLU remains committed to the principle that freedom of thought also includes freedom for those ideas we hate."

This sounds like our very own *Intellectual Freedom Manual*. Ripston cites Woodrow Wilson in words that reflect the healthy reasoning behind her position: "I have always been among those who believe that the greatest freedom of speech was the greatest safety, because if a man is a fool, the best thing to do is to encourage him to advertise the fact by speaking."[11] Jeff Selth, librarian at UC-Riverside and chair of the Southern California Coalition for Intellectual Freedom, in a long, arduous letter to the *Los Angeles Times* defending McCalden's right to a place at the convention maintained that: " ... my beliefs about the Holocaust were totally irrelevant, since all I was doing was defending free speech, as I will do for everybody, regardless of their views, since that is supposed to be the American way."[12]

Those are brave words—especially considering that the chancellor of Selth's place of employment had a letter in the same *Times* issue. Like most everyone else, he managed to divorce the Nazis from free speech, noting that he was "gratified" that the CLA recognized the "distinction between freedom of speech, which no one disputes, and the obligation to provide a forum for a person whose views have been repudiated as neo-Nazi propaganda by recognized academic authorities."[13]

The ACLU is devoted to the preservation of civil liberties; that is an extremely difficult legal, political, and social commitment. Librarians are devoted to putting those civil liberties into practice, and that is a different sort of commitment. Once the ACLU had seen where its path lay in the Skokie case, it took only relentless legal warfare and appalling courage to stick to it.

Librarians, on the other hand, must confront political and social reality in a very different way. Remember the marvelous dictum of Mark Twain: "It is by the goodness of God that in our country we have those three unspeakably precious things: freedom of speech, freedom of conscience, and the prudence never to practice either of them."[14] It will not do to underrate prudence, even this embarrassing kind, because we all rely on it heavily. They certainly did in California.

Freedom for Untruth

So what is the California problem doing in the middle of an argument about the importance of untruth to librarians? After all, external pressure had more to do with CLA's welshing on McCalden than any internal distaste for his mission. While the real issue is related both to the external protest and to internal intolerance, it is distinct from both.

We are caught in a dilemma that we have generally failed to appreciate: We are committed both to the search for the truth and to the freedom of expression of untruth. It is a truism that these commitments are not mutually contradictory, that they are, in fact, necessary to one another. However, when they are translated into real political terms, they often, in fact, collide. Like the L.A. City Council and that Riverside chancellor, many people are ready to grant the untruth some theoretical place in the network of free debate, but no place that will somehow grant that untruth legitimacy.

In the political arena, belief in the corrective powers of the marketplace of ideas is rapidly supplanted by a fear that bad ideas, especially bad ideas that excite base instincts, will drive out good ideas. This is not merely an irrational fear. A quick glance at the world of politics could lead to the conclusion that the bad ideas have taken the field.

Bad ideas certainly had a field day in Nazi Germany. But Hitler did not rise to power as the result of a contest of ideas. Is it not obvious that grim forces well beyond the reach of ideas were at work to select out and promote the worst elements in that society? Is it not also obvious that the worst ideas prevailed, not because they were aired, but because they had the forces of coercion and fear behind them. As the brutal stifling of debate progressed, the hold of untruth became stronger.

70   Freedom of Information and the Pursuit of Knowledge

This connection was made more eloquently by another interested party in the McCalden debate. Elli Wohlgelernter, editor of the *B'nai B'rith Messenger*, in splendid, lonely sentiments, put it this way:

> Was something really accomplished by denying him his lunatic pronouncements? And is our community really better off because we shut him up? ... Having already invited him, a library should never "cave in" based on the unpopularity of an idea. Or do we agree with those who would ban Mark Twain from libraries? Where do we draw the line? Let the marketplace of ideas determine the validity of an argument, not the prior censorship of its presentation. What next? Do we burn the books? Or have we forgotten the lessons of 50 years ago, that where they would burn books, they would burn people.[15]

Our task is to convince ourselves and our public that this must be the basis of our practical library politics as well as good theory. It is essential to this process of conviction that we truly grant a place in the intellectual freedom scheme of things for that which we *know* to be untrue.

Indivisible Freedom

The simple theoretical point is, as the *Intellectual Freedom Manual* tells us, that freedom is indivisible. Yet even as we assert this, we know in our collections, our meetings, and our hearts, that we must live with a more or less distinct hierarchy of truths and untruths. We give more space to the truth. We also tend to evaluate each item, each idea, each datum according to that hierarchy.

I *know* that there is no truth to Truth Missions, but if that alone is the determining factor for my treatment of their ideas, my treatment is not likely to conform to that necessary indivisibility of freedom. There are a lot of influential people who *know* that abortion is murder, and some of them liken abortion-on-demand to the Holocaust. They are about as interested in maintaining an open forum on the subject as most of us are interested in seriously debating the Nazis.

There is another influential group that *knows* that the theory of evolution is the false doctrine of a powerful cabal of atheist humanists. They have managed to have it demoted and even removed from a number of widely used biology textbooks, which is an indication of their approach to debate—but then, like Phyllis Schlafly's Stop Textbook Censorship Committee, they believe they have been shut out of the marketplace of ideas.

It Might Turn Out to Be True

We all have our firm beliefs and commitments. We all *know* some things are true and some are false. This line of reasoning is usually used to support the practical relativism that we all adopt to some degree in a world where we generally have no choice but to see through a glass darkly. That which looks false today may tomorrow be found to be true. History is full of that sort of thing. Ask any member of the Flat Earth Society. This argument is not good enough. We are not defending the presence of untruth in our libraries just because it might turn out to be true.

McCalden's arguments will never turn out to be true, and "Creation science" will always be apologetics masquerading as empiricism, but both have a place in our libraries.

The crisis in the California Library Association reminded many of the storm that surrounded the ALA film, *The Speaker*. One of the problems with that troubled ALA intellectual freedom film is that it puts a great deal of emphasis on the argument that today's falsehoods may be tomorrow's truths. Mildred Dunnock wisely intones to her beleaguered student lecture committee that some of our greatest truths were first rejected as foolishness, and that is why it is so important that this man be allowed to speak.

The man is a racist modeled upon a real-life, much-censored proponent of racial hierarchies. The brave little teacher is right, of course, to defend his right to speak, but her argument is one dimensional, as oversimplified as the political situation the film portrays. The speaker has a right to speak, not because his brand of racism just may be one of those truths waiting for vindication, but he also has the right to utter untruths that will never be vindicated. The suppression of any idea can be dangerous to the flow of all ideas.

This is not merely purist pontification; it is the necessary consequence of the fact that we do see through a glass darkly. Someone has said that the truth may be simple, but *we* are complex, and therefore our paths to the truth must be complex. Our road map is a bewildering maze of smudged and partial truths thoroughly enmeshed in falsehoods. To stumble upon a whole truth is a rare and lucky event, and we're usually not equipped to appreciate it. In this state of affairs bad ideas and untruths are a necessary part of the search. Like mosquitoes—nasty, sometimes fatal malaria mosquitoes, if you will—they may be utterly detestable, but they are a vital ingredient in the overall ecology. To suppress them is to affect the ecology of the whole system of discourse.

This is not to say that many restrictions and compromises are not necessary, just as it has proven necessary to extinguish, or try to extinguish, some of the most malevolent forms of life. But there are always tradeoffs.

The effort to kill off an untruth by suppressing its expression is always risky. For example, child pornography is a very serious problem which anyone with any claim to healthy humanity considers to be an expression of purest untruth. The Supreme Court chose to attack this untruth with a sweeping declaration that it is unprotected speech. The *Ferber* decision was nine to zero in favor of broadly defined suppression, but it is doubtful whether this noble unanimity has had any serious effect upon the flow of this particular untruth. It has certainly made its mark on the world of legitimate publishing, as witness the suppression of *Show Me* and other sex education materials.

Note also the growing acceptance in schools of the expurgated *Romeo and Juliet*, the original of which is literally actionable in the terms of the *Ferber* decision. The political potency of this decision is demonstrated in a small but telling way by the fact that we Indiana librarians have been unable to find a legislative sponsor for our affirmative defense amendment to the state's child pornography law, a similarly all-encompassing spawn of *Ferber*.

No one wants to be associated with this evil in any way, even to secure a straightforward, even traditional defense for libraries, museums, and other educational institutions. We are assured that the law is not aimed at "real literature." Apparently those 400 words in *Romeo and Juliet* are a small price to pay for a political kiester.

Lessons from Bad Ideas

It is our job to provide access not to the truth, but to the fruit of human thought and communication; not to reality, but to multiple representations thereof. Truth and reality must fend for themselves within each of the complicated creatures who uses the materials we have to offer. We can and do learn a great deal from bad ideas and untruths.

It is obvious enough that we learn about the motivations and the twisted psyches of those who cherish them. Late in his life Ezra Pound admitted something to Allen Ginsberg that is to the point: "The worst mistake I made was that stupid, suburban prejudice of anti–Semitism." Ginsberg replied, "It's lovely to hear you say that … because anyone with any sense can see it as a humour, in that sense part of the drama, a model of your consciousness. Anti–Semitism is your fuck-up … but it's part of the model and the great accomplishment was to make a working model of your mind. Nobody cares if it's Ezra Pound's mind but it's a mind like everybody's mind."[16] It takes a clarity, an enormous tolerance to learn so much from the struggle with untruth, but we would do well to try it ourselves, even as we know that Ezra Pound's mind is not like everybody's mind, and anti–Semitism is a disease not like everyone else's diseases.

We shall inevitably and properly give our personal and professional preference to the truth, but it is vital that we recognize the place of untruth in helping us get at the truth. In most of the controversies before us the difficulty of the issue, the heat of the debate, and the pressure from one or all sides to rig the debate by silencing the opposition are all directly proportional.

According to the introductory lines of the Library Bill of Rights, "all libraries are forums for information and ideas." This phrase is the bland fruit of compromise, but it does make the point: We provide an arena for debate; very often we are both the battlefield and the arsenal in the war of ideas; we very naturally and humanly get caught up in the cause of one side or another. We are prochoice or prolife, proevolution or pro-creation, even pro- and anti-censorship. Although this is another platitude, it must be said: We are all pro-truth. That is why we support the truth as an absolute defense in a defamation case involving a very emotional man who took the distasteful step of writing some nasty things about a young woman.

Access Is the Mission

It is this simple fact that we are committed to the truth that makes it utterly necessary that we formulate our mission as librarians not in terms of truth but in terms of access. It is why we must make it clear to ourselves and our public that access means a professional responsibility to, among other things, as much untruth as we can politically and practically manage.

We live within a freedom necessarily circumscribed by many legal and political realities, as the California librarians have helpfully reminded us. It is a real and precious freedom. McCalden is wrong when he says, "there is no free speech in America."[17] But to the extent that there is no free speech for *him*, for all the other hatemongers, the racists, or those who would coerce us with their version of god, McCalden has a point, and we have a problem.

The knowledge of truth and the knowledge of untruth, like the knowledge of good and evil, are indissolubly joined. Our cause, professionally and politically, is with both of them.

NOTES

1. *The People of the State of Illinois v. Paul Heinrich*, Docket No. 59239, Agenda 11, May 1984, p. 2. Quoted in opinion of the court delivered by Justice Moran. Materials provided here by the ALA Office for Intellectual Freedom and the Freedom To Read Foundation.

2. Brief and Argument for Defendant–Appellee, No. 59239 in the Supreme Court of Illinois, p. 2.

3. Bierce, Ambrose, *The Devil's Dictionary*. 1911; reprint, Dover, 1958, p. 136.

4. *Intellectual Freedom Manual*, ALA, 1983, p. 14.

5. *Ibid.*, p. 43.

6. Perkins, F.B., *Free Libraries and Unclean Books*. San Francisco Free PL, November 22, 1885, p. 3–4. This copy of the pamphlet located in the *Tuttle Miscellany*, Vol. 100, Wabash College.

7. For an excellent account of the evolution of the profession in this regard, see Evelyn Geller, *Forbidden Books in American Public Libraries, 1876–1939*. Greenwood, 1984.

8. Kamm, Susan, "'Holocaust hoax' publisher barred from annual convention of California LA after controversy spreads through state," *American Libraries*, January 1985, p. 5.

9. *Ibid.*

10. Beck, Melinda, "Footnote to the Holocaust," *Newsweek*, October 18, 1981. p. 73.

11. Ripston, Ramona, Letters to the Times, *Los Angeles Times*, November 26, 1984, Pt. 2, p. 4. This and several of the following citations courtesy of McCalden himself, who devoted an issue of his *Revisionists' Reprints* (No. 8, January 1985) to off–print of a large number of the press responses to his "martyrdom"—including many columns very unfavorable to him: he may be "using" the First Amendment, but at least he does so with some consistency. Naturally, this particular issue of his serial was treated to a special mass mailing for fundraising purposes. McCalden has decided to ride the issue further by fulfilling everyone's worst expectations and taking the CLA to court; the case is still there and already a considerable drain on the resources of the association.

12. Selth, Jeff, *ibid.*

13. Aldrich, Daniel G., Jr., *ibid.*

14. Twain, Mark, *Following the Equator: A Journey Around the World*. Vol. 1. Harper, 1899, p. 198. (Headnote to Chapter XX, ascribed to "Pudd'nhead Wilson's New Calendar.")

15. Wohlgelernter, Elli, "Free Speech," *B'nai B'rith Messenger*, November 23, 1984, p. 14.

16. Quoted in James J. Wilhelm, *Il Miglior Fabbro: the Cult of the Difficult in Daniel, Dante, and Pound*. Univ. of Maine Pr., 1982, p. 96. Originally in *Evergreen Review*, Vol. 55, 1968, Michael Reck, "A Conversation Between Ezra Pound and Allen Ginsberg."

17. Quoted in "CLA Cancels 'Holocaust Hoax' Publisher," *Newsletter on Intellectual Freedom*, Vol. XXXIV, No. 1, January 1985, p. 31.

II
Information, Technology, and Education

Information, Technology and the Virtues of Ignorance

Daniel C. Dennett

When I was about ten years old, I read *Robinson Crusoe* for the first time and could scarcely contain my delight with the ingenious and resourceful ways Crusoe transformed his island world, bending its inventory to his own purposes, surrounding himself with contrivances of his own design and manufacture for enhancing his powers, and providing for his safety, nourishment, and pleasure. I discovered right then that I was in love with technology, as no doubt many of you are. We should recognize—we technophiles—that our love affair with technology, like all good love affairs, is not entirely rational, try as we may to rationalize our devotions. Crusoe the technocrat—it is one of the great fantasy themes, right up there with sexual adventure, athletic triumph, being able to fly, being invisible. It rivals them all in its captivation, in the luxuriousness of its details in our minds' eyes. It is far more satisfying than magic, precisely because it is *not* magic; it is something *we create*, and hence are presumably responsible for; it is something we *understand*, presumably, and hence, presumably, control.

We live today in a wonderful world in which the fantasy of unlimited technological enhancement seems to be coming true. This is convenient for us technophiles, for we can point to the many blessings our loved one has provided for us all—even the ingrates. Which technophobe would choose to live the harrowing and desperate life of the medieval peasant or the Stone Age hunter? Yet, like Crusoe, we pay some price for whatever we gain, requiring some minor revision in our habits, some curtailing of our options, some petty irritations that crop up as side effects with the adoption of each new marvel. Some find it easy to push these slightly nagging debits into the background;

they say "Yes, there are costs of course, but it's not worth our while trying to sum them—whatever they come to, they are a small price to pay for the obvious gains." Others find their uneasiness harder to quell; they wonder if, when the total costs of some of the more indirect effects of new technology are rendered, we may not find that we have moved imperceptibly into a world we do not know how to inhabit and cannot leave.

I propose to focus attention on certain troubling aspects of this relationship between technology and morality.[1] I wish to consider the possibility that information technology, which has been a great boon in the past, is today poised to *ruin our lives*—unless we are able to think up some fairly radical departures from the traditions that have so far sustained us.

We all want to lead good lives—in at least two senses. We want to lead lives that are interesting, exciting, fulfilling, and happy, and we want to lead lives that are morally good as well: we would like to be useful, and to make a difference—a difference in the right direction, whatever direction that is. There is no doubt that technology in the past has facilitated both these aspirations, freeing us from drudgery and misery, making it possible for many of us to improve the lives of others. But unless we can find solutions to certain problems, the curve will turn. We have reached a point where the advance of technology makes the *joint realization* of these two goals less likely—we may have to make an unpalatable choice between lives that are morally good, and lives that are interesting.

Since my message is one that many may find unpalatable, it may be useful for me to start with a very specific instance of the trend that concerns me, before drawing on it for wider implications. As technology imposes new sources of knowledge, it renders obsolete the standards that guided our individual actions in the past. Consider, for example, the base of the rural doctor. Today, there are doctors who have chosen, commendably, to forsake lucrative urban or suburban practices for more valuable and meaningful lives as doctors in small rural communities. Their virtues have often been sung;[2] there is little need for me to dwell on them. These doctors know their patients well; their personal, intricate, involved knowledge stands them in good stead when they come to diagnose, treat, and advise the members of their communities.

Such doctors, for better or worse, are an endangered species. Technology is on the verge of rendering their style of medical treatment obsolete,

---

[1]*These reflections have grown out of discussion in the Norbert Wiener Forum, a policy workshop at Tufts, funded by the CSK corporation of Japan, and under the co-directorship, currently, of Professors Tadatoshi Akiba and David Isles. Earlier versions of parts of this paper were presented at the joint meeting of the Norbert Wiener Forum with its counterpart forum at Tokai University in Japan, July, 1985, and in lectures at the MIT Laboratory for Computer Science, and the Yale Humanities Center this spring.*
[2]*Most recently and convincingly by John McPhee, in "Heirs of General Practice," which first appeared in* The New Yorker, *and has since been reprinted in McPhee's collection,* Table of Contents *(New York: Farrar, Straus, Giroux, 1985).*

and—because of its obsolescence—morally indefensible. As expert systems for medical diagnosis become available, these doctors will have to decide whether to avail themselves of the new technology. Let us suppose, for the sake of argument, that the systems will work as well as their supporters claim; they really will provide swift, reliable, and accurate diagnoses of ailments across the wide spectrum of medical cases the average physician is likely to encounter.

If so, the doctors, in good conscience, will have no choice: they will have to avail themselves of the new expert systems. To choose not to equip themselves with the best available means of securing accurate diagnosis would be a gross dereliction of duty, just as if—for some romantic whim—they chose to deny themselves use of a telephone, or insisted on making their rounds on horseback, or refused to consult x-rays before operating. Quaintness is acceptable when matters of life and death are not at stake; but few would be enthusiastic about a doctor who insisted on relying on old-fashioned methods, particularly if it entailed a serious and avoidable risk of misdiagnosis or mistreatment.

Doctors have always been obliged to keep up-to-date with their medicine, and typically have responded to this obligation with fairly serious efforts to stay abreast of medical journals, to take refresher courses. The generation of information has recently been getting out of hand; until now, rural doctors have been excused from knowing everything that their urban colleagues were held responsible for—there are limits to what people can be expected to carry around in their heads.

Now, however, a technology is promised that will render such limits obsolete. All you will have to do is install a modem and a cellular telephone in your four-wheel-drive van and there, at your fingertips, will be a credible approximation of the finest corps of specialist consultants, available twenty-four hours a day. You would have to take a curious moral stand indeed to resist becoming reliant on such a system. How dare you turn your back on such a fine new source of information, when lives—lives entrusted to you—depend on you making the best informed diagnoses of which you are capable?

The standards of excusable ignorance for even the most isolated of rural doctors will shift, and the doctors will be required to alter their practices to meet wholly new standards. All doctors will be expected to avail themselves of the new technology, just as all doctors now are required to maintain standards of antiseptic practice. We may suppose that expert systems will enable doctors to practice much better medicine, but in order to use these systems they will have to relinquish some practices they may well have prized in their earlier *modus operandi*.

At present, rural doctors can take a varied, even informal, approach to gathering facts about their patients. If old Sam looks OK, sounds just about the way he always sounds at this time of year, and does not complain about anything new, the doctor can leave well enough alone. Besides, if there really is anything new wrong with old Sam, it is too esoteric, or too obscure at this stage, for the rural doctor to be expected to diagnose it. After all, rural medicine is not the Massachusetts General Hospital. But expert systems will change all this. Doctors will be obliged to ask all their patients a battery of questions they never felt the need to ask before—for what use could they have made of the answers?

They will also be obliged to perform a variety of largely simple tests they never felt bound to perform before. They will do so because the feeding of expert systems with such data will supposedly have proven to bear valuable results—permitting a higher rate of early diagnosis of treatable cancer, for instance. Gathering information by these two methods—asking questions and performing simple tests—will be made as easy, straightforward, unequivocal as possible. Indeed, the procedure will be *as routine as possible*, for the more routine it is, the more uniform the feeding of the expert systems will be, and hence the less likelihood there will be of misinforming them.

In this way, the "art" of diagnosis, and the "art" of "taking a patient's history" will be reduced, as far as possible, to an exercise in which the art is displaced by the mere capacity to follow directions. I am not claiming that such systems would place a positive value on the deliberate suppression of imaginative, artful investigation and diagnosis, but just that such activities would be relegated to whatever room remained *after* the doctors had done their duty by asking all the *obligatory* questions and performing all the *obligatory* tests.

Since "progress" in medicine (and technology generally) proceeds by replacing art with obligatory practices whenever the principles governing the art can be well enough understood and justified to be codified, we can expect that, insofar as the technology of medical diagnosis succeeds, insofar as it becomes so demonstrably reliable that doctors will be obliged to use it, it will do so by diminishing the regular, daily contribution of the medical practitioners who use it. Once in a while, the artful doctor may find a moment in which to exercise his or her art, and even save a life by filling a gap in the technology, but such opportunities will become rarer as the technology improves.

A subspecies of doctor will thus become extinct, succeeded by a new species that will delegate more and more diagnostic responsibility to expert systems, not because of their indolence or stupidity, but simply because they will not be able to defend the claim that they can do as well or better without the systems.

Should we mourn the passing of this species of practitioner? If we adopt the doctors' own point of view, we can see why they might well regret this development: it will make their own lives less exciting, less indispensable; they will begin to sink into the role of mere go-betweens, living interfaces between patient and system, who consolidate their direct observations into machine-readable symptomatology, and execute the therapeutic directives of the system.

It may help us to conceive of their predicament if we imagine their secret yearnings: they will occasionally be tempted to "live dangerously," to "fly by the seat of their pants," to take risks with their patients' lives just to prove to themselves that they still have the "right stuff"—that they can make bare-handed diagnoses as well as the best of the old-time doctors, the swashbuckling specialists of the 1970s and '80s. The more adventurous (or self-indulgent) of them may seek out the few exotic environments where they can practice medicine free from the obligation to use the boring technology—much the way some like to "rough it" by going camping, or by sailing small boats across the ocean. Yet, thanks to communication satellites, even Robinson Crusoe's island will provide no asylum for the physician who seeks refuge from expert systems. Being a doctor simply won't be anywhere near as much fun in the future.

This extinction of social roles is a familiar process in history. Artists, calligraphers, potters, and tailors used to be more indispensable to their communities than they are now. Although there still is a role for such artists, it is a luxury role; some people are willing to pay extra for that special, personal, artistic touch—but the realm in which the hand-made is superior to the machine-made has shrunk to an almost purely ceremonial, even mystical remnant of its former status.

Fortunately for potters, there are still enough people who prize hand-made pottery so that it is possible to sustain a career as a potter, but the social position of the potter has been ineluctably damaged; potters are simply no longer indispensable as they once were. While being a potter is still a good life compared with most others—it has more than its share of satisfactions and delights—it is not as fulfilling a life as it used to be, since any reflective potter must recognize that he or she survives by gratifying the desires of a rarified subset of the population. Doctors will not even be that lucky, for who in his right mind would acquire a taste for funky, hand-made medical care—just like Grandma used to get?

No doubt the rich and foolish would recognize a certain *cachet* in keeping a personal—and personable—physician in their entourage. Compare the doctor of the future with the apartment doorman. This descendant of the *concierge*, who had a relatively challenging and varied life work, has an almost purely ceremonial function today. You can telephone for a taxi with greater ease than your obliging doorman can lure one to the door, and the security he provides is typically almost redundant, given the twenty-four-hour surveillance and alarm system. But it looks nice to have a doorman. He adds a personal touch—of sorts. It is posh to live somewhere that is so well-heeled that it can afford to pay a grown human being to stand around in a uniform smiling all day. The doorman's life is not pleasant to contemplate; it is a travesty of human service, however well reimbursed.

Every doctor must begin to worry that he or she is heading towards becoming a health-care doorman. Can it be that, in a future generation, all that will be left of today's doctor will be minimal "computer literacy" and a bedside manner?

The advocates of expert systems in medicine may wish to intervene here, pointing out that, far from diminishing the life of the physician, expert systems will enhance it. The physician will have *more* time to deal personally with patients, and can care effectively for greater numbers, because the drudgery and galling uncertainty of poring through textbooks and journals for snatches of half-remembered wisdom will be eliminated. Indeed, and today's apartment doorman can "deal personally" with ten times as many inhabitants as the old-fashioned concierge, since all the drudgery has been removed from his life as well. The doorman has certainly been relieved of such menial labor, but also of responsibility, variety of challenge, and autonomy. Like the Cheshire cat, all that is left is the smile. As the responsibility for diagnosis and treatment shifts imperceptibly away from the physician—the "field operative"—and lodges in the expert system (or system of expert systems), doctors will suffer a similar, if less drastic, diminution of role.

I am not for one minute maintaining that today's rural doctors are heroes, and that their sad fate is the result of evil, rapacious technocrats seducing them from their noble lives. Greed and evil intentions do not enter this equation—though they are not in short supply. It is precisely because doctors want to practice the best medicine they can that they will find it incumbent on them to make these choices; for they will see that they will actually be able to save lives more reliably and efficiently by availing themselves of the technology. The interesting and risky life they had been leading will no longer be morally defensible. Wanting to be responsible and to do good, they will have to settle for a less exciting service role. We may suppose equally pure and altruistic motives on the part of those who design, develop, and promote the technology. They do not *intend* to spoil career opportunities; it is simply one of the foreseeable side effects of their effort to do a better job of saving lives through technology. What I am referring to is not a cheap melodrama with a convenient villain at which I can shake my finger, but more in the nature of a tragedy.

In a tragedy, the hero's ultimate fate must be seen to be inevitable; that is one reason why I hesitate to call this a tragedy. If I thought that this unhappy *dénouement* were strictly inevitable, I would perhaps have decided to keep the grim news to myself. How, then, might some alternative future await the physicians?

First, the technology of expert systems may turn out not to work all that well. We may discover the expert systems are so limited and unreliable, taken by themselves, that doctors will still have to be very self-reliant, very knowledgeable individually, very artful in the use they make of technology. Perhaps they will not even be obliged to use it, so untrustworthy will it prove to be. (In several conversations with advocates of such technology I have been amused to be assured, most solemnly, that I have vastly overestimated the actual powers of expert systems. These spokespeople for expert systems have failed to see the irony in their protestations: "Don't worry!" they say. "These expert systems aren't going to be *reliable!*—they won't be *foolproof!* Why, in the hands of an unskilled practitioner they would be positively dangerous!" I am strongly inclined to agree, but to suggest that to them would be to risk being dismissed as a technology-hating humanist.)

We have found one escape route: this particular technology will not work after all, and hence will not be obligatory, and hence will not spread to destroy this enviable and admirable variety of human life. There are several other ways out. If one thought that the technology *might* work, and thought that preserving the way of life of today's physician was of prime importance, one could take steps to avert this future: either by the Luddite tactic of destroying expert systems as they appeared; or by attempting to prohibit or prevent the development and improvement of the technology in the first place. But Luddism has never worked well in the past. It tends to postpone crises and aggravate situations, and is in any event not likely to inspire those who would have to support the policy today.

Alternatively, it may turn out that I have overestimated the physicians' commitment to practicing the best medicine they can. According to several observers, many doctors have given the new expert systems a lukewarm reception largely because they are more interested in "talking shop" with consultants, and in spreading liability, then in obtaining diagnostic assistance. If such resistance is widespread, it may prevent the public from perceiving the value of expert systems, and thereby keep the obligation to use them at bay.

Finally, of course, one could decide that saving the role of the *mid-twentieth-century physician* was, in the end, no more defensible than saving the role of the linotype operator in the production of newspapers. These roles must pass, perhaps, and as long as we ease the plight of the current holders of the positions, and prevent the recruitment of a new generation, little harm will be done to specific individuals. People in the future will just have other, no doubt better, occupations.

While that sentiment has a certain plausibility when the displaced workers are miners, linotype operators, or secretaries, it is far from clear what exalted work will remain for displaced physicians. If a social role as obviously valuable and impressive as that of the physician is in jeopardy, what future awaits the rest of us?[3]

Let us review the situation: if expert systems in medicine live up to their promise, then the tradition and the current trajectory of development suggest that they will probably ruin one of the most exciting and fulfilling careers in modern life. Without destroying it, they will diminish it enormously; people who want to live a good life—not just do good in life—will think twice before entering this part of the service sector. Perhaps the role of physician is not worth preserving. Alternatively, perhaps expert systems will not prove all that powerful, so that physicians will not be obliged to cede their responsibility to them. Or, in the hope that expert systems will fail to establish themselves, we might even take steps, violent or legislative, to forestall their deployment.

I see two further possibilities. The first and most probable outcome is that we shall be faced with the worst of both worlds: expert systems will not work anywhere near well enough for physicians to be *obliged* to rely on them, but the physicians will come to depend on them anyway, succumbing to the pressure of over-optimistic public opinion, their lack of self-confidence, and even laziness, greed, and fear of malpractice suits. A second somewhat utopian possibility is certainly worth striving for: perhaps we can design computer systems to support only the wily and self-reliant physician. We should look for design principles that would lead to the creation of systems that preserve or (better yet) enhance the contribution of the individual physician, while not sacrificing diagnostic power. I do not think that creating such systems is impossible, but it will not be easy; it will require rethinking the basic design task.

Compare expert systems to musical instruments: today's expert systems are similar to autoharps, designed so that anyone can learn to play them, and with an easily reached plateau of skill. We should aim instead to develop systems more like violins and pianos—instruments that indefinitely extend and challenge the power of the individual.

I have some inklings about how this might be accomplished. They stem from ideas I have been developing at Tufts' Curricular Software Studio with my colleague, George Smith.[4] We are creating several different kinds of "concept pianos" for the exploration of complex phenomena—such as population genetics and the computer's own internal architecture. If our ideas survive their current testing, we shall subsequently present them as steps towards a new design philosophy for expert systems, but in the meanwhile there is still

---

[3] *"Even physicians, formerly a culture's very symbol of power, are powerless as they increasingly become mere conduits between their patients and the major drug manufacturers."* Joseph Weizenbaum, Computer Power and Human Reason, *San Francisco: Freeman, 1976), p. 259.*

[4] Daniel C. Dennett, *"Notes on Prosthetic Imagination,"* Boston Review 7 (3) (June, 1982), pp. 3–7; George E. Smith, *"The Dangers of CAD,"* Mechanical Engineering 108 (2) (Feb. 1986), pp. 58–64.

plenty of philosophical work to be done on these issues, to which I shall devote my remaining observations.

Why should doctors find themselves riding this obligation-train to tedium? To understand this particular phenomenon, we must step back and take a more general view of the relations between information technology and our ethical lives as decision-making agents.

Our ancestors were, relative to us, epistemically impoverished: there were few means of finding out much about non-local, non-immediate effects and problems, so they could plan and act with a clear conscience on the basis of a more limited, manageable stock of local knowledge. They were thus *capable* of living lives of virtue—of a virtue that *depended on* unavoidable ignorance. Modern technology has robbed us of the sorts of virtue that depend on such ignorance, for ignorance is all too avoidable today. Information technology has multiplied our *opportunities to know*, and our traditional ethical doctrines overwhelm us by turning these opportunities into newfound *obligations to know*.

We have always had "principles of excusable ignorance." According to tradition, we are responsible for knowing whatever is "common knowledge," plus whatever is the received wisdom of those who occupy our specialized social role—such as the role of physician—plus whatever is obviously and directly relevant to our particular circumstances of the moment. We are all responsible for knowing the standardly understood relationships between smoke and fire, rainstorms and slippery roads, voting and democracy. Plumbers—but only plumbers—have been responsible for knowing the particular effects, opportunities, and hazards of the plumbing trade, and everyone is responsible for knowing whether anyone is standing behind one's car before backing out of a parking place.

The rough-hewn boundaries of these classes of knowledge were fixed by default by the limitations of human capacity. One could not be expected to carry around vast quantities of information in one's head, nor to calculate, in the time available, any of the longer-range effects of action. The example of the physician showed in some detail how technology interacts with the obligation to know in a specialized field, but its effects on "common knowledge" are even more severe and imponderable.

"Common knowledge" is no longer the relatively stable, inertial mass it once was. We *can* acquire knowledge with little effort on almost any topic; when knowledge is "at your fingertips," how can you not be responsible for acquiring it? The obligation to know—a burden of guilt that weighs heavily on every academic, but that in milder forms is ubiquitous today—creates the situation where, if we read everything we "ought" to read, we would have time to do nothing else. Thanks to science and mass communication, we *all* now know that, in addition to worrying about whether someone is standing behind our car when we back up, we also have to wonder about the effects of our personal auto-driving (and auto-buying) activities on air pollution, acid rain, the local and global economy, and so forth.[5]

The well-known glut of information has inspired a host of responses from those who must cope with it, or wish to exploit it. Since everyone knows that no one can possibly keep abreast of all this information, meta-techniques, meta-strategies, meta-meta-structures, meta-meta-meta-tactics have arisen. The "common knowledge" we are now held responsible for is not the whole of what is almost instantaneously *available* to almost everyone, but rather a small, shifting core of what might be called "temporarily famous" common knowledge. (Recall Andy Warhol's prediction of the future time when each person will be famous for ten minutes.) Getting items of information into the spotlight of temporary fame has become a major enterprise. Whether your problem is the eradication of Third World hunger, the deposition of an evil dictator, stopping the Star Wars lunacy, or selling cornflakes, your solution must begin with "advertising"—attracting the fleeting attention of the well-intentioned, and *imposing* that item of information on them.

So much information is available that mere accessibility is no better than invisibility. Most books that are published are not read, and even being read does not guarantee their influence. This depends on higher-order effects: a book must not only be reviewed, but (thanks to the reviews) be included on an influential list of books to be read, for example. If it achieves sufficient visibility in the higher-order structures, it need not even be read to have vast influence. This profusion of information filters, duplicators, and amplifiers is the product of helter-skelter competition, and there is little reason to suppose such a process is even approximately optimizing. On the contrary, there is probably scant direct relationship between the value of items of information and their capacity to exploit the publicity environment and reproduce themselves across the society.

Richard Dawkins' excellent book, *The Selfish Gene*, introduces the idea of what he calls *memes*—a "new kind of replicator" living in "the soup of human culture." Memes are, to a first approximation, ideas in particular forms—the sort of thing one might be able to patent or copyright:

> Examples of memes are tunes, ideas, catch-phrases, clothes fashions, ways of making pots or of building arches. Just as genes propagate themselves in the gene pool by leaping from body to body via sperm or eggs, so memes propagate themselves in the meme pool by leaping from brain to brain via a process which, in the board sense, can be called imitation.[6]

The analogy between memes and genes runs deep, as Dawkins shows. Recasting my argument in his terms, my claim is that, thanks to *some* technological

---

[5]One is reminded of the James Taylor song "Damn This Traffic Jam."
[6]Richard Dawkins, The Selfish Gene (Oxford: Oxford University Press, 1976), p. 206.

memes, we have entered a population explosion of memes—parasites that are overwhelming their hosts. Unless we can find some new ideas, some antibodies for these new antigens, hard times are in store for us. The new memes we need are *conceptual* innovations, not just new technology.

It is technology that has created this embarrassment of riches. Consider, in this respect, our obligations to those in misery on other planets. It is quite possible that there is life elsewhere in the universe, and if there is life there is almost certainly misery as well. Fortunately for us, however, the most shocking and gruesome calamities on other planets—plagues, dictatorships, nuclear holocausts—are nothing to us, because even if we knew about them (which, fortunately for our peace of mind, we do not) there would be absolutely nothing we could do about them. Perhaps we should be wary about proceeding with the project Carl Sagan champions of trying to communicate with the civilizations on other planets; after all, we might succeed and find that their first message to us was a heart-rending plea for help—together with detailed information on just how we could be of assistance![7]

Not long ago, measured by the astronomical or even the biological time scale, the Western Hemisphere was as remote from the Eastern as any planet is from us now. Even well into the nineteenth century, few people had the knowledge and power to have any clear obligations to anyone or anything beyond their local communities. The average person could not reasonably expect to have much effect on the lives of those in distant lands, and hence was absolved from worrying about them. Such questions just did not arise—any more than the question of what to do about starvation in other solar systems arises for us.

A few people of enhanced power and knowledge found, however, that they could not hide behind their powerlessness. Their attitude was captured in the slogan *noblesse oblige*—those of noble birth had special obligations.[8] While the slogan applied originally only to the titled few, the idea was subsequently extended to all those who had power, inherited or otherwise acquired. The price they paid for their "*noblesse*," in the extended sense of not having to devote their waking hours to providing daily bread and shelter, was an enlarged social purpose. In the nineteenth century, every well-read person could ask whether he or she should become fully committed to ending slavery, for instance, and many decided they should. Their efforts succeeded in practically eradicating slavery.

Others took on different causes, with varying degrees of success. It is often noted how curious and sometimes eccentric the focus of such people's

---

[7]*There are suggestive observations on the role of technology in expanding our moral universe in Peter Singer,* The Expanding Circle *(Oxford: Oxford University Press, 1981), and Derek Parfit,* Reasons and Persons *(Oxford: Oxford University Press, 1984), part I.*

[8]*Duc de Lévis, (1764–1830* Maxims, Préceptes et Reflexions) *is the first use I have uncovered so far in my casual inquiries.*

moral sensitivities can be, both then and now. Some anti-slavery crusaders were strikingly oblivious of the suffering of their own poor, the degradation of their own servants, the exploitation of the workers in their factories. Today single-minded zealots may uphold the cause of environmentalism or animal rights, apparently unmoved by the outrages committed against their own species by various dictators—at least they devote none of their energies to action on these fronts. Similarly, there are ardent nuclear disarmers who do not care to reform the sexism out of their own language and practices, or who routinely discard unopened all mail beseeching them to enlist in the cause of Amnesty International or Oxfam.

There can be little doubt how these exotic specimens of do-gooder come into existence. We are *all* of the *noblesse* these days. We all have the daunting luxury of the time, energy, knowledge, and power to undertake a broader purpose than merely staying alive and keeping our immediate kin in the same condition. Technology has created innumerable opportunities for us to know, and to act. We want to deal responsibly with this bounty, but *we do not know how*. When we turn to the question of which priority should engage our best efforts, we drown in the available information, unable to make truly principled decisions. Our responses exhibit a sort of Rorschach magnification of whatever minor personal proclivities emerge from the noise of competing and imponderable alternatives. The results, as we have seen, may often be eccentric, but they are arguably better than the course chosen by those who sit on their hands and ignore all appeals, on the grounds that they cannot calculate—have no time to calculate—which appeal is the worthiest.

One would think that any solution there might be to this practical dilemma would stem from philosophy, and more narrowly from ethics, but much as I would like to relate that the humanists either have the answer or at least have undertaken the research program that ought to yield the answer, I must report that almost no direct attention has yet been paid to this troubling moral problem by professional philosophers.

The reason for this is not hard to find. Ethics, like any theoretical enterprise in science, has always been conducted with the aid of idealizations. Reality, in all its messy particularity, is simply too complicated to theorize about taken straight. A favorite idealization in ethics has been the useful myth of the moral agent with unlimited knowledge and time for ethical decision-making. For instance, consequentialist theories, such as the various brands of utilitarianism, declare that what ought to be done is always whatever course of action will have the best expected consequences *all things considered*. Although consequentialists know perfectly well that no one can ever truly consider all things—even all relevant things—they still choose to couch their theories in terms of what the ideally reflective and conscientious decision-maker would have made of all the available facts. This presumably gives one a standard of conduct at which to aim, if never in fact to reach. *In practice*, we tend to overlook important considerations and bias our thinking in numerous idiosyncratic ways, but *in principle* what we should do is what this ideal calculator of consequences decides will most probably maximize utility (or whatever we call the good consequences).

The plain fact that we are all finite, forgetful, and have to rush to judgment is standardly recognized, not implausibly, as a real but irrelevant element of friction in the machinery whose blueprint we are describing. It is as if there might be two disciplines—ethics proper, which undertakes the task of calculating the principles of what one ought to do under all circumstances—and then the less interesting, "merely practical" discipline of *Moral First Aid*, or *What to Do Until the Doctor of Philosophy Arrives*, which tells, in rough and ready terms, how to make decisions under time pressure.

My suspicion is that traditional theories of ethics all either *depend on* or *founder on* the very elements of friction that are ignored by the standard idealization. Information technology, by removing the friction, helps expose the weakness of much that has passed for sound in ethics. For instance, a bench test that most ethical theories pass with ease is the problem: what should you do if you are walking along, minding your own business, and you hear a cry for help from a drowning man? But almost no one faces predicaments with that logical form anymore; instead we hear, every day, while desperately trying to mind our own business, a thousand cries for help, complete with volumes of information on how we might oblige.[9] On this ubiquitous problem, traditional ethical systems are essentially reduced to silence or transparent handwaving.

This is too large a claim to support here, but I can at least sketch the problem as I currently envision it. How could we write the *Moral First Aid Manual?* Or, might we replace the manual with something fancier—an Expert System for Moral Advice-Giving in Real Time?

The fantasy of just such an expert system often lurks in the shadows of ethical theory. "If what I ought to do is whatever has the highest expected utility, how on earth shall I calculate it in the time available?" This question has been familiar for over a hundred years, and the standard response from the moral philosophers is well expressed by John Stuart Mill, who borrowed a metaphor from the technology of his own day:

> Nobody argues that the art of navigation is not founded on astronomy because sailors cannot wait to calculate the Nautical Almanac. Being rational creatures, they go to sea with it ready calculated; and all rational creatures go out

[9]*John Stuart Mill, in* Utilitarianism, 1863, *thought he could defend his utilitarianism thus: "... the occasions on which any person (except one in a thousand) has it in his power to ... be a public benefactor ... are but exceptional; and on these occasions alone is he called on to consider public utility; in every other case, private utility, the interest or happiness of some few persons, is all he has to attend to." I doubt that this was an entirely convincing claim in 1863; it is transparently unrealistic today.*

upon the sea of life with their minds made up on the common questions of right and wrong ....[10]

This is as fine an idea today as it was in Mill's time, but the metaphor mis-leadingly invites us to ignore the fact that the future position of the heavenly bodies could *actually* be calculated in advance, using the technology of the day. Where is the Moral Almanac that would guide the moral chooser through the stormy seas of life? We are still debugging it.[11] Jeremy Bentham, Mill's contemporary, set out to create a "hedonic calculus," and while no one takes it seriously today, the descendants of this quaint museum piece are still being produced, elaborated, and, above all, advertised, not just by philosophers, but by "cost-benefit analysts," computer modelers, and other futurologists.

What should be evident to computer scientists, if still easily overlooked by philosophers, is that the idea of actually producing a reliable or authoritative consequentialist almanac of any generality is sheer fantasy, now and at any future time. Compare the demanding specifications for such a system with the now well-known limitations on far simpler forecasting and problem-solving tools. *Short*-range real-time weather forecasting, for instance, has reached useful levels of reliability by restricting itself severely to a handful of measures, coarse-grained data-grids, and relatively simple equations, and then exhausting the powers of the world's fastest super-computers. Detailed forecasting of the weather months into the future is probably computationally intractable under any circumstances.[12] If it proves not to be intractable, it will be only because micro-climate effects will be shown not to propagate chaotically after all. Yet, we already know, from countless every-day experiences, that "micro-social" effects—some unknown individual's dislike for Tylenol, for example—can create major perturbations in the best-laid human plans and social trends.

Even supposing the prediction problem could somehow be tamed, the evaluation problem would remain. In chess-playing programs, the problem of when to terminate look-ahead and evaluate the resulting position has led to the framing of the *principle of quiescence*: Always look several moves beyond any flurry of exchanges and postpone final evaluation until a relatively quiescent board position obtains. This satisfactory, though not foolproof, strategy of chess design, is systematically inapplicable to the design of our moral advice-giver, because of what we might call the Three Mile Island effect. It

---

[10]*Ibid., p. 31.*

[11]*Mill's idea was that the everyday maxims of morality that people had "made up their minds" about could be shown to be reliable rules of thumb that followed, somehow, from the more laborious and authoritative calculations of utilitarianism.*

[12]*Very short range forecasting of local disturbances such as thunderstorms and tornadoes is proving extremely difficult, but is currently receiving considerable attention from NASA and the expert systems community, among others.*

has now been several relatively quiescent years since the melt-down at Three Mile Island, but can we yet say, with confidence better than a coin flip, whether that was one of the good things that have happened or one of the bad? If our imagined system were to generate a future path of probability p with Three Mile Island as its terminus, should it assign a high or low utility to the event? The trouble is, of course, that in life there is no checkmate, no fixed point finitely in the future at which we get one definitive result or another, from which we might calculate, by retrograde analysis, the actual values of the alternatives that lie along the paths followed and not followed. So there is no way, and *could be* no way, to tune the parameters of any prototype expert system we designed—except the invocation, as usual, of ideology and handwaving.

The suspicion that consequentialist theories are systematically infeasible is nothing new. It has fueled support for the so-called Kantian or duty-based ethical alternative for over a century.[13] As the Pirate King says to Frederick, the self-styled "slave of duty" in *The Pirates of Penzance*, "Always follow the dictates of your conscience, me boy—and chance the consequences!" The trouble is that such duty-based theories, while not always leading to results as comical or pathetic as Frederick's myopic posings and blunderings in *The Pirates of Penzance*, have hardly coalesced into a stable and compelling system of recipes for action. Kant's own *categorical imperative*, which he quite consciously conceived as the one and only rule that needed to be printed in the *Moral First Aid Manual*, appears today about as naive and impractical a guide as Bentham's hedonic calculus.

It is a step in the right direction however, and what *is* new is the opportunity to reconceive of these alternatives to consequentialism through the lens of artificial intelligence as responses to the inescapable demands of real-time heuristic decision-making. When viewed from this perspective, for instance, what would count as justification or defense of an ethical principle shifts significantly. This opens up a promising research program in philosophy, in my opinion, and I think it will gain more than just jargon from its engineering perspective.

The first, general result is appealing: we can already see that, since *any* "system" for ethical decision-making must be bounded arbitrarily by limitations that are far from content-neutral, no technological black-box oracle can give you a principled, objective, reliable answer to your ethical problems, no

[13] *The Kantian philosopher, Onora O'Neill, in "The Perplexities of Famine Relief," in* Matters of Life and Death, *ed. Tom Regan (New York: Random House, 1980) offers a convincing analysis of the fundamental embarrassment of utilitarianism; two competent and well-informed utilitarians, Garrett Hardin and Peter Singer, addressing the same issue (what if anything to do about famine relief), holding the same ethical theory, and having access to the same empirical information, arrive at opposing counsels: one thinks the case is compelling for dramatic forms of aid; to the other it is equally "obvious" that all such aid should be withheld. See also O'Neill's* Faces of Hunger *(Boston, MA: Allen and Unwin, 1986).*

matter what anyone advertises. When the choice is between "flying by the seat of your own pants" on the one hand and paying to fly by the seat of somebody else's pants on the other, you are entitled to keep both the responsibility and the excitement to yourself.

Do Expert Systems
Have a Moral Cost?

Mark Alfino

When professionals are asked about the value of information technology to their work, they typically give two kinds of answers. Some see the advent or arrival of sophisticated information technology as a great boon to their professional lives. For them, the only question is how soon can the technology be deployed to open up new horizons for professional activity and end dull tedious work. Others sense more acutely the serious *dislocation* of familiar work patterns and interactions that the arrival of personal computers, networked information systems, and global information access has caused. Both responses are justified. The thick instruction manuals that come with the hardware and software of information technology are mixed blessings; we ignore them at our peril, but if we read them and adopt new information practices, the character of our work may change. The question I will consider in this column is whether and under what circumstances that change poses a threat to our pursuit of the good life. I will focus this question on a particular kind of information technology, expert systems. One of the most prominent philosophers of our day, Daniel Dennett, has argued that this technology can indeed pose a significant moral threat to us. My view is that the danger is overstated, but the problem of integrating information technology into our lives (especially our work lives) does pose moral challenges.

Previously, I argued that there is, in addition to a moral right to information, an "information virtue," and that managers and other workers with special access to information have a moral responsibility to realize this virtue in their work. The information virtuous do not just use information to promote excellence and opportunities for growth among their coworkers, but they also think critically about how information handling is tied to patterns of institutional power and whether such power relationships are encouraging moral virtues such as worker responsibility, autonomy, and leadership. This entire line of thinking assumes that information technology does not, in general, pose a moral threat to our personal and professional lives. Daniel Dennett thinks that it does, so it is especially important that we look at his argument carefully.

Since Dennett's argument is that expert systems in particular threaten our ability to pursue the good life, we should first describe some of the features of expert systems before presenting his argument. Most expert systems are in fact large databases that use rules of various kinds to answer questions people are likely to have about the information they contain. For instance, I might assemble data about a particular economic market and rules that I think govern that market to create an expert system that models the market in a way that allows the system to predict future events. In a more sophisticated expert system, one that takes advantage of recent advances in "machine learning," the distinction between data and rules is somewhat looser. For instance, suppose I want to predict the likelihood that an entering freshman law student will complete law school. Instead of giving the machine the rules that I think determine success in law school, I might just give it a lot of information relevant to predicting success and have it derive rules by weighing competing variables on the basis of actual data on actual law students. In this more sophisticated model it appears that the machine has "learned" the very rules that it will then use to answer my question about a particular incoming student. Some people believe that these more sophisticated systems, since they appear to develop the rules for answering questions on their own, usurp a more significant domain of human judgment than less sophisticated systems.[1]

Dennett wants readers "to consider the possibility that information technology, which has been a great boon in the past, is today poised to *ruin our lives*—unless we are able to think up some fairly radical departures from the traditions that so far sustained us."[2] He is particularly worried that two features of the good life, a moral life and an interesting life, may not be jointly realized because of information technology such as expert systems. The general reason for this is that expert systems remove elements of human judgment, which are the subject of specific human virtues and make life interesting.

To make these general claims concrete, Dennett considers the case of the "country doctor" who must decide whether to use an expert system to make diagnoses. Suppose this system had the most up-to-date information on medical science as well as rules for weighing particular information about

---

[1] *This brief description oversimplifies some features of these artificially intelligent expert systems. We did give the computer rules for handling the data.*

[2] *Daniel C. Dennett, "Information, Technology, and the Virtues of Ignorance," Daedalus 115 (Summer 1986); 135–153.*

particular patients. If such a system could produce more reliable diagnoses, the country doctor would have no choice but to use it. But Dennett believes that the doctor's reliance on the system represents a loss. Not only is life now less interesting for the doctor, but the art of medical judgment will be "displaced by the mere capacity to follow directions." Dennett is claiming that the moral loss is not so much the result of something immoral being done *to* the doctor, but inheres in a loss of some morally significant features of his or her work.

To make his argument general, Dennett draws from the example of the country doctor a general claim that modern technology is robbing us of some virtues that depend upon ignorance: "The obligation to know—a burden of guilt that weighs heavily on every academic, but that in milder forms is ubiquitous today, creates the situation where, if we read everything we 'ought' to read, we would have time to do nothing else." By a "virtue that depends upon ignorance," Dennett probably has in mind those situations in which we give moral praise to someone for a judgment that required him or her to bridge some gap between knowledge and action. People rarely get our admiration for giving answers about which there is easily attained absolute certainty. But we do often praise and admire people for their ability to use intuition and judgment to reach good decisions in the face of great uncertainty. Sometimes we say, in retrospect, that they were lucky, but other times, especially when we see a pattern of such judgments, we credit the person with a kind of wisdom or judgment. The expert system, since it may have better "judgment" than its rival human doctors, would appear to rob them of the admiration they might formerly have received. Dennett is quite candid about identifying the basis of that admiration in terms of the ability to operate successfully in relative ignorance.

Although I am very unsympathetic to Dennett's argument, I must admit that it is ingenious and correctly shows the ethical implications of a given economy of information. Since many people think of information ethics in terms of isolated ethical problems (like confidentiality, copyright, proprietary information, etc.) rather than general and pervasive features of experience, Dennett's approach is refreshing. But I think his analysis has two serious weaknesses: he misunderstands the way expert systems operate and he uses a narrow analysis of the impact of information technology on the workplace.

Given Dennett's expertise in following developments in artificial intelligence and philosophy of mind, it is surprising that he would actually believe that an expert system would eliminate the role of professional judgment in very significant ways. Sometimes information technology involves trade-offs between skills, but we should not assume that when one area of judgment is eliminated it is not replaced by another. Library automation, for example, places a premium on good judgment in the pursuit of information, but de-emphasizes some other virtues more appropriate to older technologies. Similarly, the expert system in medicine, since it will open up the possibility of searching more literature, will require more practicing doctors to be good researchers. But this is a trade-off between moral goods—the virtue of good judgment in the face of ignorance and the virtue of good judgment in the face of an information rich environment.

Like many science fiction writers, Dennett conceives of expert systems as "closed" systems in which the doctor interacts with front end software that exhaustively describes the search possibilities for the particular case or illness. But there is good reason to believe that this situation will only emerge when (and if) we achieve certainty about a large percentage of the causal relations at work in the human body and environment. Until then, any expert system will be limited to providing doctors with a variety of possible diagnoses. The doctor's virtue will still consist in judging well in light of what is known and not known about the patient's illness at any given time.[3]

The second problem with Dennett's argument is more interesting for the light it sheds on information ethics in the workplace and how the analysis of such problems should proceed. There is little dispute that information technology is radically reorganizing many professional work patterns and workplaces. Someone might argue that such technology is liberating because it frees professional time for satisfying other unmet responsibilities and for taking on new responsibilities. These new efficiencies could allow professionals (especially doctors) to meet more client and patient needs. When Dennett considers this objection, he likens his poor country doctor to a doorman working in a world with automatic doors. He agrees that the doorman might have more time now to deal more personally with more customers. Yet he thinks the net result is a loss: "The doorman has certainly been relieved of such menial labor, but also of responsibility, variety of challenge, and autonomy."

In tallying the moral costs and benefits from new technology, Dennett presumes that professionals are morally entitled to insist on the relative stability of their professional job description. But why should we assume that? One of the most exciting (and threatening) aspects of information technology is that it has the power to force reappraisals and changes in the way we live and work. This is a background condition of technological change in general, but it is especially true of information technology. Perhaps the moral "virtues of ignorance" of the country doctor will be transformed into moral "virtues of access, education, and deliberation," which can be enjoyed by far more people living in an information rich world in which expert systems do

[3]In light of this criticism, we could recast Dennett's argument as a concern about the moral implications of achieving relatively complete knowledge about the subject, not about the advent of better information technology. Indeed, deep philosophical issues are raised by advances in our knowledge of human physiology and behavior.

make medical knowledge more understandable to more people. Dennett is right to warn us that there are moral trade-offs to information technology. But we cannot assess those trade-offs if we assume arbitrarily that some things, like country doctors and doormen, ought to be permanent fixtures of the landscape. When the analysis is broadened we can better judge which future scenarios we should work toward.

The ethical analysis of information issues in the workplace cannot be divorced from an organizational analysis of work and a social analysis of the position of the organization in the larger values of the society. When we fail to broaden the analysis in this way, we risk placing an unjustified value on just those aspects of a *status quo* that we are trying to assess. As I indicated in my last column, the development of the virtuous information manager may indeed include changes in the way work patterns and power relationships are configured. For example, with networked information technology the question of information sharing in an organization is no longer resolved by asking about the practical limits of sharing documents. The new technology usually makes room for electronic copies of a large amount of information such as budgets, blueprints, plans, and schedules, as well as forums that allow workers to contribute to deliberative processes. The *basis* for decisions about what to share has changed, and there is a clear need, in my opinion, not to shrink from the ethical challenge of creating information policies that realize both organizational goals and the morally significant goals of the organization's stakeholders.

Umberto Eco on Libraries: A Discussion of "De Bibliotheca"

*Michael F. Winter**

Librarians have a perennial interest in scholars' reactions to libraries, librarians, and library services. Yet with few exceptions scholars rarely take the opportunity to comment directly on libraries. This article discusses some exploratory observations made by Umberto Eco in "De Bibliotheca," a lecture later published as an essay. Eco's point of view is scholarly and yet somewhat whimsical, mixing fantasy, satire, and reflective analysis for a broadly intellectual effect, and makes a plea for embracing technological change in libraries through increased reliance on the instruction of the user. He also develops the idea of the library as a locus of creative work—rooted in the most fundamental meanings of the act of collection—which is at partial odds with the reality of the library as a hierarchically structured organization. On the way to these conclusions he makes some points that deserve wider attention.

Scholars not only regularly use but highly value libraries.† But they do not often take them as a theme for analysis, reflection, or public discussion. Perhaps, as more than one philosopher has suggested, there is a certain inevitability to this: we tend to take for granted the settings in which we all routinely operate. The busy scholar—often also a busy teacher—may not only rely heavily on the library but indeed also hold it in high esteem as a place where many of the essential tools and materials of scholarly work are found,

288 Shields Library, University of California, Davis, Davis, California 95616. I would like to extend thanks to Ellen R. Robert of the University of California, Berkeley, and to Axel Borg of the University of California, Davis. I also thank the editor and the anonymous reviewers of the Library Quarterly for a number of useful critical observations.
†*This finding is by now so common that a recent study suggests that it is no longer necessary to confirm it [1, p. 11].*

and yet at the same time ignore is as a topic worthy of reflection in its own right.*

This is certainly understandable, but unfortunate; it would be useful for all librarians, especially those working in research settings and thus frequently serving researchers, to look at the library from the standpoint of the scholar. What appears from that point of view might well surprise and interest them. This is not to say that librarians and other information professionals should ignore the wider range of user groups. In fact we now have a rather substantial body of library user studies, some of them relying on advanced forms of survey research and covering this basic range quite well. But we do not seem to know nearly as much about the firsthand experiences of scholars [1, p. 12]. Thus it is informative to focus, as time and resources permit, on the firsthand observations of this very advanced and articulate group of users. Surely their observations will tell us much about what kinds of places libraries are in which to work and would form a useful complement to our existing body of professional knowledge.

This brief article cannot, of course, hope to accomplish anything like this in a systematic way, but it can make a small start by examining Umberto Eco's essay "De Bibliotheca," an intriguing example of a scholar's reflections on libraries as places where scholarly work is done, as centers of applied technological innovation, and as key sites in the creation and transmission of knowledge.† More broadly, the scholar's analysis sheds some light on the library as one aspect of a cluster of social institutions and processes that create, maintain, and transmit the ideas, values, worldviews, and traditions of human cultures.§

Umberto Eco's fascination with libraries, particularly medieval ones, is well known. Indeed an article recently published in these pages [7] provides an example of how Eco's famous mystery novel set in a medieval monastery, *The Name of the Rose*, can be read as an example of "library criticism." In addition to shedding a good deal of interesting light on the novel—no one who reads it will think of the novel quite in the same way again—Jeffrey Garrett also reviews a large body of literary criticism dealing with the same subject.

*I would like to thank an anonymous reviewer for the Library Quarterly for (however inadvertently) pointing this out to me. For a useful elaboration, see [2, p. 3].
†Originally a lecture delivered March 10, 1981, at the Bibliotheca Comunale di Milano and first printed in [3], "De Bibliotheca" was later published in one of Eco's many essay collections [4]. A French translation appeared in 1986 [5]. In the discussion that follows, the passages quoted are my translations from [4], in some cases along with the original material and the French version for purposes of comparison.
§One is tempted, in the traditional fashion, to simply say "human culture" in the singular, but by now the cumulative ethnocentrism of that seemingly innocent phrase has been well-exposed by more recent work in cultural anthropology and culture theory. Much the same could be said of the term "tradition," whose ideal singularity conceals an actuality of competing and conflicting pluralities of traditions, some indigenous, some imposed, some invented, etc. [6, pp. 5–7].

In Garrett's article, "De Bibliotheca" appears only briefly, since his main interest is in the longer and more complex fictional treatment of libraries found in *The Name of the Rose* [7, pp. 376–77]. Understandably, the shorter piece gets only tangential treatment. Unfortunately, however, the rather narrow focus on Eco's ironic catalog of criticisms may give the reader a somewhat skewed view of the material. Perhaps this is because Garrett's reading of *The Name of the Rose*, which stresses Eco's treatment of the traditional negative images of librarians as powerful gatekeepers, causes him to miss the much broader sweep that "De Bibliotheca" actually has. Yet while there are certainly some critical observations, "De Bibliotheca" is hardly, as Garrett claims, "one long philippic against libraries he has known" [7, p. 376]. By the same token it is not accurate—nor is it fair—to report Eco's major goal in writing the essay as "venting his spleen" [7, p. 337]. But let us look at the essay in more detail.

The occasion is the twenty-fifth anniversary of the Milan Public Library. The speaker begins with a famous quotation from the Argentine writer Jorge Luis Borges, the celebrated "Library of Babel" text, which vividly and dramatically depicts the cultural, linguistic, and epistemological fragmentation of contemporary world cultures.* He does this, he tells us, because "in such an august location it is appropriate to begin, as in a religious ceremony, with a reading from the Book" [4, p. 237], not because of its content, which we all already know anyway—indeed, this is always the case with scriptural readings— but because it induces in us a proper spiritual attitude. From this it appears that Eco sees the library first in ceremonial and second in functional terms. More specifically, his descriptions, despite (or perhaps because of) this ironic allusion to liturgical sobriety, are quasi-religious.

But unlike the Borges of this particular passage, Eco is interested in actual, not metaphorical, libraries. (If we missed the ironic cue of the "invocation," we might have suspected this anyway from *The Name of the Rose*, where the descriptions recall a highly imaginative library historian steeped in the medieval, not a contemporary critic committed to the priority of symbol over referent.) As if to emphasize this point, Eco lists some typical functions of libraries from ancient times to the present: (1) collecting (*reccogliere*), (2) hoarding (*tesaurizzare*), (3) transcribing (*trascrivere*), (4) the encouragement of reading (*far leggere*), (5) providing public access to materials ("permettere al publico di leggere"), (6) concealing or not providing access to materials (*non far leggere*),† and finally (7) providing the opportunity for discovery or retrieval of materials (*ritrovare*) [4, p. 239]).

---

*The Library of Babel text is from [8].

†The original reads as follows: "Ma in seguito credo che siano nate delle bibliotheche la cui funzione era quella di non far leggere, de nascondere, di celare il libro" [4, p. 239]. Celare and nascondere are roughly synonymous, but nascondere, in addition to suggesting concealment, also bears the meanings

In ancient society, libraries performed the primitive or foundational function of gathering materials together in one place "so that scrolls and books would not remain dispersed" ("per non lasciare in giro rotoli o volumi") [4, p. 239]. This has the effect of transforming a practical act of accumulation, with obvious implications for the accessibility of texts, into a de facto intellectual synthesis by bringing disparate works into proximity. The collecting practices of libraries, in other words, reverse the presumably natural tendency for materials to remain dispersed and thus uncontrolled. Though this is not Eco's language, he is here suggesting the idea that a library is a larger and more ambitious version of the anthology and is, thus, like a giant text with an indefinite range of subtexts; and what it brings together, often with little or no conscious sense of creation, presents an indefinite range of possibilities for the discovery of new knowledge. We can explain this briefly as follows. Texts that never take up residence near each other, whether the neighborhood is defined by the covers of a single volume or by the wider precincts of shelf locations, to say nothing of the purely symbolic locations that texts occupy in indexes and catalogs, are texts that live in isolation. We forget this perhaps because it is so obvious and so basic—it is the foundation of any library, private or public, and also of the bookstore. (No doubt we also forget it because as librarians we focus on the library in technical terms.) This comparison between the library and the anthology as collections recalls French social historian Roger Chartier's exploitation of two contrasting though related uses of the word "library": it refers on the one hand to a place or sited organization, on the other to a collection or series of works—for example, the Muirhead Library of Philosophy, the Oxford Home Library, or the Collection Que Sais-Je? [9].

Collecting is a function that, however venerable, we can all recognize as quintessentially contemporary. Hoarding, on the other hand, has an obsolete ring. While it is obvious that libraries contain intellectual materials, at the same time the great expense of producing scrolls and early codices must have made libraries places where certain kinds of material treasures were accumulated and preserved. Thus the library at a certain point acquired the status of an accumulated hoard, recalling the way museums function even today. "After all," Eco observes, "scrolls cost a great deal to produce" [4, p. 239]. Nowadays we are more inclined to give intellectualist readings to the importance of collections, but in ancient times the material dimension may have been more significant, if only because the cost of producing the individual item was so

of "masking," "screening," and "disguising." Thus there are multiple meanings of "hiding," including putting materials where users would not be able to find them, labeling or otherwise marking materials in such a way as to disguise them, and perhaps by these and other devices screening the user population to ensure that only certain groups are able to access them. All of these options are of course very familiar to librarians who have struggled with problems of access, intellectual freedom, and censorship.

high. Having lowered costs through much larger scales of production and distribution, we are freer to emphasize intellectual content over physical form, though this emphasis carries some inevitable risk.*

Librarians are of course well aware of the importance of cost, but what is interesting here is the notion of a more general theoretical, historical, and even ideological dimension to the subject. Cost, that is to say, is much more than a practical problem; it is a historical and socioeconomic phenomenon that reflects broader social processes and values. And while we tend to view material and intellectual value as incommensurable, they are in this respect closely intertwined. The discussion of ancient libraries as literal treasure troves suggests that this historical fact is part of the general background of the collections of later periods, even though the socioeconomic scale changes dramatically in the process.

It is interesting in this context to reflect on the common etymological roots of the modern words "treasure" and "thesaurus," which are part of the background of Eco's observation that "eventually, the library acquired the function of accumulating treasure."† Both are derived from the Greek *thesaurós*. The modern use of the term "thesaurus," in other words, to refer to a list of terms, is historically and philologically based on the idea of written language as a kind of material resource, which indeed it is, although that is generally suppressed in contemporary discourse. We tend to think of written language, as we do also of texts and other library materials, in intellectual terms, although here etymology reminds us of the earlier connection between material wealth and intellectual activity. Linguistically, this is interesting evidence for a notion of symbolic capital that, though based on the more fundamental capital of goods production, defines a kind of intellectual economy of its own: it is accumulated and carefully redistributed by schools, universities, churches, and, of course, museums and libraries.§

In more modern times, as societies democratize and education expands, the idea of making library materials accessible is added to these older and more venerable functions. The private intellectual and spiritual capital of the

---

*For a discussion of the dangers of an overly simple and unreflective distinction between form and content, see [10].

†The original reads, "In seguito credo abbia avuto la funzione di tesaurizzare" [4, p. 239]. The French version reads, "Par la suite, je crois qu'elle entendait thesauriser" [5, p. 14]. One realizes here how fortunate it is to have a French translation, since this shifting of meanings disappears in English. In English, one loses the shift between "treasure" and "thesaurus," since they do not look enough alike to suggest a common etymology. But in the translation it is obvious that the verbs tesaurizzare and théauriser, which are variously translated as "accumulating treasure," "saving," "hoarding," etc., are closely related to the contemporary term "thesaurus" (Italian tesoro [4, p. 239]; French thésaurus [4, p. 15].

§This use of economic terms to describe erstwhile intellectual activities may wrongly suggest a reductionist attempt to explain scholarship in terms of material production. Actually, however, the comparison leads, if anything, in the opposite direction: what we refer to as "economic" activity is in fact only a specialized form of the much more broadly based exchanges of social life generally [11].

ancient and medieval worlds becomes gradually socially appropriated and treated as a public good. Accordingly, the purpose of the contemporary library, at least in the industrial democracies, is often described in official statements as that of making material accessible and available. Eco agrees that libraries do indeed enable people to find materials, but he also makes the observation that libraries exist not only to make records of knowledge available but, at the same time, to hide them: "I believe that eventually there arose in libraries the function of making materials unavailable, and thus of not encouraging reading" [4, p. 239; 5, p. 15]. At the same time, he goes on to observe, the idea of making such materials available arises as a natural complement to the tendency to conceal: "Naturally, these libraries were also based on the idea of retrieval. We are always astonished by the ability of the great Renaissance humanists to discover lost texts. And where do they find them? They find them in libraries. In libraries which hide, on the one hand, and at the same time provide the opportunity for retrieval" [4, p. 239]. Unlike the head librarian in *The Name of the Rose*, contemporary librarians do not—at least not usually—intentionally hide materials. What Eco is suggesting, I suspect, is a cultural process that has little to do with librarians' intentions. The large, sprawling research collection conceals by labyrinthine default if not by design; but in either case, for the scholar the effect can be much the same, as the advanced user discovers the need to go far beyond the catalog, the index, and the obvious finding aids that map the surfaces. This is really only another way of saying that finding a place for something is also finding a place where it can become hidden.

But it is not only because libraries and their collections are often large and complex, not to say Byzantine, that materials become as easily hidden as they are revealed, though this is a part of the story. It is also because the professional expertise that controls them is, like all professional knowledge, a barrier as well as a gateway. One typical way of looking at systems of cataloging and classification, for example, is as systems of rules for locating materials. But though they have a clear and inescapable logic to the initiated, it could hardly be said that such systems reveal materials in any straightforward or obvious way. The same could be said of systems of legal and medical classification, which require professional interpretation to reveal anything at all. Of course the dedicated and intelligent user can figure out the organizational scheme unaided, and the more adept library users do this all the time, just as the jailhouse lawyer and the chronic patient figure out the systems used simultaneously to conceal and to reveal the complexities of legal precedent and medical procedure, respectively.* These kinds of claims are worth considering, since

*The connection between the classification and control systems found in large and complex organizations and the activities of the occupational groups employed in them was suggested to me by Axel Borg, personal communication, March 8, 1993.

organizations seldom acknowledge all of their ends and may not even realize the underlying social and cultural functions they are fulfilling.

In any case, what this dialectic of revealing and concealing rests on is a characteristic and perhaps unresolvable tension at the heart of librarianship, which is experienced rather differently by librarians and library users, but which is really the same thing looked at in two different ways. On the one hand, material is collected in order to be used, and thus regularly taken away for private consultation; on the other, material is there to occupy a certain place in the collection, like a piece of a puzzle. This is one of the great taken-for-granted oppositions in libraries, usually obscured by technical and professional routine. To frame it for purposes of illustration, we might say that at one extreme of the polarity is pure accessibility, while at the other end lies inviolate integrity. Left in place, the collection is aesthetically and even ontologically whole, but obviously not terribly useful to anyone in particular; when a piece is removed, its utility to a particular user dramatically increases. Yet this utility is purchased at the rather high price of temporary monopolization—a price that all of us recoil at paying when we go to look for something that is not there and discover that the violation of the collection's unity has highly practical consequences. When we can find what we want, we are all for access and utility; when we cannot and may be working against some deadline or other routing pressure, we curse "accessibility" under our breath and suddenly realize why books were once chained to the shelves. In this respect, at least, librarians and library users are united: both live with the constraint that making the material available always makes it simultaneously unavailable. (Whether automation can resolve this contradiction is of course a central unanswered question.)*

There is an appreciation of dialectic here not to mention delight in paradox; and these are driving forces in all of Eco's work. If the idea that libraries hide materials seems ironic, Eco's vision of the "bad" library ("la bibliotheca cattiva") seems almost Rabelaisian in its fantastic exaggeration; it is, in short, "an immense nightmare" ("un immenso cauchemar") [4, p. 240]. In this fictitious model (*modello fittizio* [4, p. 239]) of an antilibrary, catalogs would be divided and subdivided to the point of lunatic confusion, call numbers would be so esoteric and convoluted as to defy transcription, the user would never be able to use more than one book at a time, photocopiers would be either nonexistent or prohibitively expensive, there would be few if any bathrooms, and the librarians would view the user as a kind of shiftless no-good who really should be at the office instead of loitering in the library, etc. [4, pp. 240-42;

All of this suggests something that Eco only hints at and that may be worth further study: the logic of parts and wholes, and perhaps also the relevance of a gestalt psychology to the understanding of collections and their users. More remotely, it also suggests the idea of a dialectical approach to information retrieval, a notion implausible enough to be genuinely interesting.

5, pp. 15—19]. Fantasy, of course, even with a twist of caricature, is not to be confused with literal observation, but nonetheless there is just enough truth in the absurdities of the "bad" library to cause mild discomfort: it is ridiculous enough to seem humorously remote and yet accurate enough to enable us to recognize the outlines of our own libraries in the caricature. "But as in all fictitious models ... I think each of us can discover in this negative model some distant memories of our adventures" in the libraries we have visited [4, p. 240]. He is discreet enough not to be more specific, but Eco may be drawing most deeply, at least in the case of this exercise in the description of the fictitious bad library, on his experiences in European libraries more than on his experiences in North American libraries.*

Eco freely admits that he has no correspondingly systematic notion of the "good" library, but supplies instead an idiosyncratic reading of two of his favorite libraries, at the universities of Toronto and Yale. (That his choices are both North American no doubt explains his care in the preceding passages to reassure his Italian audience that the only reason he chooses foreign examples is because when he is traveling he has much more time at his disposal to visit libraries!) Both of these show an interesting mix of the closed and the open and, for a European writer, are no doubt instructive to think about on that score alone. To a European, even the partial freedom of access to library materials that is commonly found in the great private research collections of North America must seem exhilarating.

The principal value of these passages is that they provide examples of firsthand accounts of scholars' reactions to libraries as places where creative work is done. What librarians know about users is normally confined to the standard survey, where respondents are kept to a strict schedule of response; and the focus, to borrow the language of a recent commentator, is on the user's opinions and not on the user's experiences [12, p. 116]. The reason why librarians generally focus on the standard survey is, Eco suggests, because they are measuring a standard and more or less repetitive kind of use; scholars and researchers, on the other hand, may be doing something else, something that is not entirely predictable. For example, librarians and those who administer libraries do not always appreciate that some of the more significant advances that the scholar makes in libraries have to do with items that one is not looking for. In Eco's words: "What then is the importance of having access to the stacks? One of the misunderstandings dominating the library is the idea that one goes in to look for some item whose title is determined in advance ... but the principal function of the library, at least of my own library and those

---

How anyone could read this as "one long philippic" or an exercise in spleen-venting is mysterious enough, but it may well be that it provides some anecdotal evidence for Garrett's contention that Eco seems to doubt librarians' ability to laugh at themselves [7, p. 375].

of other people I visit, is to discover items whose existence we hadn't even suspected and yet which turn out to be of extraordinary importance to us" [4, p. 244].

It is not Eco's purpose to disparage the traditional formal apparatus of information retrieval. Indeed, it is clear from his discussion that this kind of "discovery can be made by using the catalog," but at the same time he suggests that the physical exploration of the stack areas is distinctly revelatory and suggestive in a way that searching the catalog is not [4, p. 244]. Thus, he continues, "the ideal function of the library is a little like the stall of the *bouquiniste,* where one finds such surprising and unexpected things, and this function can only be fulfilled when there is free access to the stacks" [4, p. 244].

Eco's point about the working assumption that one knows what one wants in advance is an important one. The formal user survey, for example, usually makes the assumption that what the patron is looking for is clearly and unambiguously known, and it thus focuses by definition on the more routine forms of library use. By its formulation of the issue, it rules out the more creative and unusual uses of library collections and, thus, in effect unintentionally neutralizes that remarkable notion of the library as the "humanist's laboratory," to which so many claim to adhere. For Eco, the most striking thing about the large North American research library is the freedom that the user has to browse, which permits the discovery of items whose existence one had not even suspected and allows the user to glimpse directly connections among works that would be either missed entirely or barely recognized by even the best catalogs and bibliographies. In the European library, by contrast, these connections remain largely latent and unrealized, since in many cases only the staff circulates with any freedom. What Eco is alluding to here is the difference between the library as a context of discovery and the library as a setting for verification of what is already known. And while it is clear that much routine library use would scarcely be possible without standard tools and schemes of organization for retrieval, it is useful to have the scholar working at the edges of the unknown to remind us that the context of discovery calls for a certain style of work that cannot be easily reduced to routine formulas.*

*It should not but may be necessary, in this methodologically polarized age, to recall that there is no inherent contradiction but, rather, a fruitful contrast between the more nomothetic approach of the survey and the more idiographic style inherent in the report of concrete experience; much of the best research, in fact, combines both points of view. And surely the more creative library users combine the two as well. This basic insight seems missing from much of the literature on library use, but we should nevertheless note that the contrast between the creative and the routine is reflected in the distinction between subjective (or psychological) relevance and objective (or topical) relevance. Further, the notion of subjective relevance has a range of nuances that we must pass over here. For an exploratory discussion clarifying the distinction and spelling out the nuances, see [13, pp. 613 ff.; 14].

There are nonetheless, Eco argues, drawbacks to these typical examples of North American research library organizations. Obviously, there are the problems of missing items, of core reference works that migrate around the building with a disconcerting ease, finding their way into study carrels, incorrect shelf locations, and even bathrooms. These problems are usually temporary and not particularly serious, but theft and mutilation of unique and perhaps even priceless materials is something else again, a kind of cultural hooliganism that is much more damaging [4, p. 245]. Even so, the North American example holds public access to be a greater good than protection of materials though, as Eco points out, one needs to be very wealthy indeed to enjoy this system of values. In addition to this, however, he hits on a central difference between the cultures he is implicitly comparing. In the American setting, our tendency to argue that it is essential to assure public access is based partly on the assumption that almost every item, however rare or expensive, is replaceable, and this is reflection, perhaps, of American mass culture.*

In his conclusion Eco makes an observation that speaks clearly to the question of the library's role in contemporary culture when he addresses questions of the authority of writers and texts and the responsibilities of readers in relation to the technology of photocopying. In its friendliness to public access, Eco argues, the "open" library encourages the spread of what he calls *xerociviltà* [4, p. 246]. The French word *xérocivilisation* [5, p. 25] is only a little more transparent to the English reader. But even though the alert reader can decode this, the general idea is at best awkward to render in English as "xerocivilization." We might call it, instead, the culture of photocopying. (If we view the culture of the copier in visionary terms, we might even call it "copytopia," and although this is a little grand, there is something of this in the idea of *xerociviltà*.) The ubiquitous photocopier, humming day and night and serenely permitting the shifting of much of the cost of production and distribution of scholarly materials to the user, is a unique tool of contemporary pluralistic fragmentation. This is reminiscent of those avant-garde writers who take a finished work, clip it into paragraphs, toss them around in a basket, and create "works" that bypass any significant relation to their "author." The photocopier, of course, *can* be used in a way that respects the integrity of the authored text, but it is just as likely to fragment texts, recombining them in unanticipated unity. The point that Eco is making here is that the technology of photocopying allows a certain reallocation or redistribution of power in the traditional relationships that have existed for centuries between writers and readers. In the earlier world, where print held its almost exclusive sway,

*One thinks here of G. Thomas Tanselle's argument [10] that libraries should treat all materials as items are treated in "special collections." According to this view, every physical format—every material package—carries with it a freight of bibliographic, social, economic, cultural, and intellectual value. This is, perhaps, a more nearly European than American viewpoint.

the reader appears as a more passive receiver of information and intention; with the photocopier, the reader enjoys more freedom to define the text as received.

And indeed one sees precisely this kind of "deconstruction" occurring daily in libraries, as users accumulate stacks of fragments from longer works, disengaging them from their original contexts of authority and giving them a kind of monographic independence of their own, however brief, inconclusive, and inconsequential they may appear in relation to the longer texts from which they are taken. Somehow these longer texts disappear as originals and become only extended fragments detached from authorial intention. From a tool with great utility, photocopying becomes, in Eco's words, "an intellectual alibi" [4, p. 247].

Interestingly, this leads Eco not to an ill-defined critical malaise but, quite sensibly, to a plea for better education of library users [4, p. 248]. The root issue here is not the influence of copy machines, however important that may be, but rather the gradual automation—in the older and more fundamental sense, that is, of using machines to replace labor—of the acts of reading and research. Between the shadow of reading and the act of the word now fall these many machines. As we suggest above, there is liberatory potential here, as readers move out of the traditional shadows of passivity and into the active light of influence. But there is also a threat here, and that is the specter of the surrender of intellectual sovereignty to the "alibi" of the machine. If we are going to embrace the whole range of industrial and postindustrial technology—not just the photocopier and the computer but also the microfilm reader—and yet not allow ourselves to become mechanized, this takes us to a much more fully humanized library, in the sense that using all these machines makes heavy demands on librarians to instruct their users. Obviously, they cannot do this if they themselves fall under the enchanting spell of technology, for they must remain in control of the machines and avoid the traps of an uncritical technocracy. Only thus can the scholar participate in the circulation of this immense accumulated cultural and intellectual capital [11].

NOTES

1. Morton, Herbert C., and Price, Anne J., with Mitchell, Robert Cameron, *The ACLS Survey of Scholars: Final Report of Views on Publications, Computer, and Libraries.* Washington, D.C.; American Council of Learned Societies and the University Press of America, 1989.

2. Dain, Phyllis, "Scholarship, Higher Education, and Libraries in the United States: Historical Questions and Quests." In *Libraries and Scholarly Communication in the United States: The Historical Dimension*, edited by Phyllis Dain and John Y. Cole, New York: Greenwood, 1990, pp. 1–44.

3. Umberto Eco, "De Bibliotheca." *Quaderni di Palazzo Sormani*, vol. 6 (1981).

4. Umberto Eco, "De Bibliotheca." In his *Sette Anni di Desiderio*. Milano: Bompiani, 1983, pp. 27–50.

5. Umberto Eco, *De Bibliotheca*. French translation by Eliane Deschamps-Pria. Caen: L'Echoppe, 1986.

6. Yengoyan, Aram A., "Culture, Ideology, and World's Fairs: Colonizer and Colonized in Comparative Perspectives." In *Fair Representation*, edited by Robert Rydell. Amsterdam: University of Amsterdam Press, in press.

7. Garrett, Jeffrey, "Missing Eco: On Reading *The Name of the Rose* as Library Criticism.: *Library Quarterly* 61 (October 1991): 373–88.

8. Borges, Jorge Luis, *Ficciones*. Edited and with an introduction by Anthony Kerrigan. New York: Grove, 1962.

9. Chartier, Roger, "La Bibliothèque sans Murs: du 15è au 21è Siècle." Paper presented at the conference "La Très Grande Bibliothèque and the Future of the Library," University of California, Berkeley, April 12, 1992. Translated by Lydia Cochrane, under the title "Libraries Without Walls." *Representations* 42 (Spring 1993): 38–52.

10. Tanselle, G. Thomas, "Libraries, Museums, and Reading." *Raritan* 12 (Summer 1992): 63–82.

11. Bourdieu, Pierre, *Language and Symbolic Power*. Translated by Gino Raymond and Matthew Adamson. Edited and with an introduction by John B. Thompson. Oxford: Polity, 1991.

12. Kantor, Paul B., "Marketing User Surveys, and the Library in Transition." In Herbert C. Morton and Anne J. Price, with Robert Cameron Mitchell, *The ACLS Survey of Scholars: Final Report of Views on Publications, Computers, and Libraries*. Washington, D.C.: American Council of Learned Societies and the University Press of America, 1989, pp. 105–23.

13. Harter, Stephen P., "Psychological Relevance and Information Science." *Journal of the American Society for Information Science* 43 (October 1992): 602–15.

14. Park, Taemin K., "The Nature of Relevance in Information Retrieval." *Library Quarterly* 63 (July 1993): 318–51.

Education and Technology: Virtual Students, Digital Classroom

Neil Postman

If one has a trusting relationship with one's students (let us say, graduate students), it is not altogether gauche to ask them if they believe in God (with a capital G). I have done this three or four times and most students say they do. Their answer is preliminary to the next question: If someone you love were desperately ill, and you had to choose between praying to God for his or her recovery or administering an antibiotic (as prescribed by a competent physician), which would you choose?

Most say the question is silly since the alternatives are not mutually exclusive. Of course. But suppose they were—which would you choose? God helps those who help themselves, some say in choosing the antibiotic, therefore getting the best of two possible belief systems. But if pushed to the wall (e.g., God does not always help those who help themselves; God helps those who pray and who believe), most choose the antibiotic, after noting that the question is asinine and proves nothing. Of course, the question was not asked, in the first place, to prove anything but to begin a discussion of the nature of belief. And I do not fail to inform the students, by the way, that there has recently emerged evidence of a "scientific" nature that when sick people are prayed for they do better than those who aren't.

As the discussion proceeds, important distinctions are made among the different meanings of "belief," but at some point it becomes far from asinine to speak of the god of Technology—in the sense that people believe technology works, that they rely on it, that it makes promises, that they are bereft when denied access to it, that they are delighted when they are in its presence, that for most people it works in mysterious ways, that they condemn people who speak against it, that they stand in awe of it and that, in the "born again" mode, they will alter their lifestyles, their schedules, their habits and their relationships to accommodate it. If this be not a form of religious belief, what is?

In all strands of American cultural life, you can find so many examples of technological adoration that it is possible to write a book about it. And I would if it had not already been done so well. But nowhere do you find more enthusiasm for the god of Technology than among educators. In fact, there are those, like Lewis Perelman, who argue (for example, in his book, *School's Out*) that modern information technologies have rendered schools entirely irrelevant since there is now much more information available outside the classroom then inside it. This is by no means considered an outlandish idea. Dr. Diane Ravitch, former assistant secretary of education, envisions, with considerable relish, the challenge that technology presents to the tradition that "children (and adults) should be educated in a specific place, for a certain number of hours, and a certain number of days during the week and year." In other words, that children should be educated in school. Imagining the possibilities of an information super-highway offering perhaps a thousand channels, Dr. Ravitch assures us that:

> in this new world of pedagogical plenty, children and adults will be able to dial up a program on their home television to learn whatever they want to know, at their own convenience. If Little Eva cannot sleep, she can learn algebra instead. At her home-learning station, she will tune in to a series of interesting problems that are presented in an interactive medium, much like video games....
>
> Young John may decide that he wants to learn the history of modern Japan, which he can do by dialing up the greatest authorities and teachers on the subject, who will not only use dazzling graphs and illustrations, but will narrate a historical video that excites his curiosity and imagination.

In this vision there is, it seems to me, a confident and typical sense of unreality. Little Eva can't sleep, so she decides to learn a little algebra? Where does Little Eva come from? Mars? If not, it is more likely she will tune in to a good movie. Young John decides that he wants to learn the history of modern Japan? How did young John come to this point? How is it that he never visited a library up to now? Or is it that he, too, couldn't sleep and decided that a little modern Japanese history was just what he needed?

What Ravitch is talking about here is not a new technology but a new species of child, one who, in any case, no one has seen up to now. Of course, new technologies do make new kinds of people, which leads to a second objection to Ravitch's conception of the future. There is a kind of forthright determinism about the imagined world described in it. The technology is here or will be; we must use it because it is there; we will become the kind of people the technology requires us to be, and whether we like it or not, we will remake our institutions to accommodate technology. All of this must happen because it is good for us, but in any case, we have no choice. This point of view is present in very nearly every statement about the future relationship of learning to technology. And, as in Ravitch's scenario, there is always a cheery, gee-whiz tone to the prophecies. Here is one produced by the National Academy of Sciences, written by Hugh McIntosh.

> School for children of the Information Age will be vastly different than it was for Mom and Dad.
> Interested in biology? Design your own life forms with computer simulation.
> Having trouble with a science project? Teleconference about it with a research scientist.
> Bored with the real world? Go into a virtual physics lab and rewrite the laws of gravity.
> These are the kinds of hands-on learning experiences schools could be providing right now. The technologies that make them possible are already here, and today's youngsters, regardless of economic status, know how to use them. They spend hours with them every week—not in the classroom, but in their own homes and in video game centers at every shopping mall.

It is always interesting to attend to the examples of learning, and the motivations that ignite them, in the songs of love that technophiles perform for us. It is, for example, not easy to imagine research scientists all over the world teleconferencing with thousands of students who are having difficulty with their science projects. I can't help thinking that most research scientists would put a stop to this rather quickly. But I find it especially revealing that in the scenario above we have an example of a technological solution to a psychological problem that would seem to be exceedingly serious. We are presented with a student who is "bored with the real world." What does it mean to say someone is bored with the real world, especially one so young? Can a journey into virtual reality cure such a problem? And if it can, will our troubled youngster want to return to the real world? Confronted with a student who is bored with the real world, I don't think we can solve the problem so easily by making available a virtual reality physics lab.

The role that new technology should play in schools or anywhere else is something that needs to be discussed without the hyperactive fantasies of cheerleaders. In particular, the computer and its associated technologies are awesome additions to a culture, and are quite capable of altering the psychic, not to mention the sleeping, habits of our young. But like all important technologies of the past, they are Faustian bargains, giving and taking away, sometimes in equal measure, sometimes more in one way than the other. It is strange—indeed, shocking—that with the twenty-first century so close, we can still talk of new technologies as if they were unmixed blessings—gifts, as it were, from the gods. Don't we all know what the combustion engine has done for us and against us? At the very least, what we need to discuss about Little Eva, Young John and McIntosh's trio is what they will lose, and what we will lose, if they enter a world in which computer technology is their chief source of motivation, authority and, apparently, psychological sustenance. Will they become, as Joseph Weizenbaum warns, more impressed by calculation than human judgment? Will speed of response become, more than ever, a defining quality of intelligence? If, indeed, the idea of a school will be dramatically altered, what kinds of learning will be neglected, perhaps made impossible? Is virtual reality a new form of therapy? If it is, what are its dangers?

These are serious matters, and they need to be discussed by those who know something about children from the planet Earth, and whose vision of children's needs, and the needs of society, go beyond thinking of school mainly as a place for the convenient distribution of information. Schools are not now and have never been largely about getting information to children. That has been on the schools' agenda, of course, but has always been way down on the list. For technological utopians, the computer vaults information-access to the top. This reshuffling of priorities comes at a most inopportune time. The goal of giving people greater access to more information faster, more conveniently and in more diverse forms was the main technological thrust of the nineteenth century. Some folks haven't noticed it but that problem was largely solved, so that for almost a hundred years there has been more information available to the young outside the school than inside. That fact did not make the schools obsolete, nor does it now make them obsolete. Yes, it is true that Little Eva, the insomniac from Mars, could turn on an algebra lesson, thanks to the computer, in the wee hours of the morning. She could also, if she wished, read a book or magazine, watch television, turn on the radio or listen to music. All of this she could have done before the computer. The computer does not solve any problem she has but does exacerbate one. For Little Eva's problem is not how to get access to a well-structured algebra lesson but what to do with all the information available to her during the day, as well as during sleepless nights. Perhaps this is why she couldn't sleep in the first place. Little Eva, like the rest of us, is overwhelmed by information. She lives in a culture that has 260,000 billboards, 17,000 newspapers, 12,000 periodicals, 27,000 video outlets for renting tapes, 400 million television sets and well over 500 million radios, not including those in automobiles. There are 40,000 new book titles published every year, and each day 41 million photographs are taken. And thanks to the computer, more than 60 billion pieces of advertising junk come into our mailboxes every year. Everything from telegraphy and photography in the nineteenth century to the silicon chip in the twentieth has amplified the din of information intruding on Little Eva's consciousness. From millions of sources all over the globe, through every possible channel and medium—light waves, air waves, ticker tape, computer banks, telephone wires, television cables, satellites and printing presses—information pours in. Behind it in every imaginable form of storage—on paper, on video, on audiotape, on disks, film and silicon chips—is an even greater volume of information waiting to be retrieved. In the face of this we might ask, What can schools do for Little Eva besides making still more information available? If there is nothing, then new technologies will indeed make schools obsolete. But in fact, there is plenty.

One thing that comes to mind is that schools can provide her with a serious form of technology-education. Something quite different from instruction in using computers to process information, which, it strikes me, is a trivial thing to do, for two reasons. In the first place, approximately 35 million people have already learned how to use computers without the benefit of school instruction. If the schools do nothing, most of the population will know how to use computers in the next ten years, just as most of the population learns how to drive a car without school instruction. In the second place, what we needed to know about cars—as we need to know about computers, television and other important technologies—is not how to use them but how they use *us*. In the case of cars, what we needed to think about in the early twentieth century was not how to drive them but what they would do to our air, our landscape, our social relations, our family life and our cities. Suppose in 1946 we had started to address similar questions about television: What will be its effects on our political institutions, our psychic habits, our children, our religious conceptions, our economy? Would we be better positioned today to control TV's massive assault on American culture? I am talking here about making technology itself an object of inquiry so that Little Eva and Young John are more interested in asking questions about the computer than getting answers from it.

I am not arguing against using computers in school. I am arguing against our sleepwalking attitudes toward it, against allowing it to distract us from important things, against making a god of it. This is what Theodore Roszak warned against in *The Cult of Information*: "Like all cults," he wrote, "this one also has the intention of enlisting mindless allegiance and acquiescence. People who have no clear idea of what they mean by information or why they should want so much of it are nonetheless prepared to believe that we live in an Information Age, which makes every computer around us what the relics of the True Cross were in the Age of Faith: emblems of salvation." To this, I would add the sage observation of Alan Kay of Apple Computer. Kay is widely associated with the invention of the personal computer, and certainly has an interest in schools using them. Nonetheless, he has repeatedly said that any problems the schools cannot solve without computers, they cannot solve with them. What are some of those problems? There is, for example, the traditional task of teaching children how to behave in groups. One might even say that schools have never been essentially about individualized learning. It is true, of course, that groups do not learn, individuals do. But the idea of a school is that individuals must learn in a setting in which individual needs are subordinated to group interests. Unlike other media of mass communication, which celebrate individual response and are experienced in private, the classroom is intended to tame the ego, to connect the individual with others, to demonstrate the value and necessity of group cohesion. At present, most scenarios describing the uses of computers have children solving problems alone; Little Eva, Young John and the others are doing just that. The presence of other children may, indeed, be an annoyance.

Like the printing press before it, the computer has a powerful bias toward amplifying personal autonomy and individual problem-solving. That is why educators must guard against computer technology's undermining some of the important reasons for having the young assemble (to quote Ravitch) "in a specific place, for a certain number of hours, and a certain number of days during the week and year."

Although Ravitch is not exactly against what she calls "state schools," she imagines them as something of a relic of a pre-technological age. She believes that the new technologies will offer all children equal access to information. Conjuring up a hypothetical Little Mary who is presumably from a poorer home than Little Eva, Ravitch imagines that Mary will have the same opportunities as Eva "to learn any subject, and to learn it from the same master teachers as children in the richest neighbourhood." For all of its liberalizing spirit, this scenario makes some important omissions. One is that though new technologies may be a solution to the learning of "subjects," they work against the learning of what are called "social values," including an understanding of democratic processes. If one reads the first chapter of Robert Fulghum's *All I Really Need to Know I Learned in Kindergarten*, one will find an elegant summary of a few things Ravitch's scenario has left out. They include learning the following lessons: Share everything, play fair, don't hit people, put things back where you found them, clean up your own mess, wash your hands before you eat and, of course, flush. The only thing wrong with Fulghum's book is that no one has learned all these things at kindergarten's end. We have ample evidence that it takes many years of teaching these values in school before they have been accepted and internalized. That is why it won't do for children to learn in "settings of their own choosing." That is also why schools require children to be in a certain place at a certain time and to follow certain rules, like raising their hands when they wish to speak, not talking when others are talking, not chewing gum, not leaving until the bell rings, exhibiting patience toward slower learners, etc. This process is called making civilized people. The god of Technology does not appear interested in this function of schools. At least, it does not come up much when technology's virtues are enumerated.

The god of Technology may also have a trick or two up its sleeve about something else. It is often asserted that new technologies will equalize learning opportunities for the rich and poor. It is devoutly to be wished for, but I doubt it will happen. In the first place, it is generally understood by those who have studied the history of technology that technological change always produces winners and losers. There are many reasons for this, among them economic differences. Even in the case of the automobile, which is a commodity most people can buy (although not all), there are wide differences between the rich and poor in the quality of what is available to them. It would be quite astonishing if computer technology equalized all learning opportunities, irrespective of economic differences. One may be delighted that Little Eva's parents could afford the technology and software to make it possible for her to learn algebra at midnight. But Little Mary's parents may not be able to, may not even know such things are available. And if we say that the school could make the technology available to Little Mary (at least during the day), there may be something else Little Mary is lacking.

It turns out, for example, that Little Mary may be having sleepless nights as frequently as Little Eva but not because she wants to get a leg up on her algebra. Maybe because she doesn't know who her father is, or, if she does, where he is. Maybe we can understand why McIntosh's kid is bored with the real world. Or is the child confused about it? Or terrified? Are there educators who seriously believe that these problems can be addressed by new technologies?

I do not say, of course, that schools can solve the problems of poverty, alienation and family disintegration, but schools can *respond* to them. And they can do this because there are people in them, because these people are concerned with more than algebra lessons or modern Japanese history, and because these people can identify not only one's level of competence in math but one's level of rage and confusion and depression. I am talking here about children as they really come to us, not children who are invented to show us how computers may enrich their lives. Of course, I suppose it is possible that there are children who, waking at night, want to study algebra or who are so interested in their world that they yearn to know about Japan. If there be such children, and one hopes there are, they do not require expensive computers to satisfy their hunger for learning. They are on their way, with or without computers. Unless, of course, they do not care about others or have no friends, or little respect for democracy or are filled with suspicion about those who are not like them. When we have machines that know how to do something about these problems, that is the time to rid ourselves of the expensive burden of schools or to reduce the function of teachers to "coaches" in the uses of machines (as Ravitch envisions). Until then, we must be more modest about this god of Technology and certainly not pin our hopes on it.

We must also, I suppose, be empathetic toward those who search with good intentions for technological panaceas. I am a teacher myself and know how hard it is to contribute to the making of a civilized person. Can we blame those who want to find an easy way, through the agency of technology? Perhaps not. After all, it is an old quest. As early as 1918, H.L. Mencken (although completely devoid of empathy) wrote, "There is no sure-cure so idiotic that some superintendent of schools will not swallow it. The aim seems to be to reduce the whole teaching process to a sort of automatic reaction, to discover some master formula that will not only take the place of competence and resourcefulness in the teacher but that will also create an artificial receptivity in the child."

Mencken was not necessarily speaking of technological panaceas but he may well have been. In the early 1920s a teacher wrote the following poem:

> Mr. Edison says
> That the radio will supplant the teacher.
> Already one may learn languages by means of Victrola records.
> The moving picture will visualize
> What the radio fails to get across.
> Teachers will be relegated to the backwoods,
> With fire-horses,
> And long-haired women;
> Or, perhaps shown in museums.
> Education will become a matter
> Of pressing the button.
> Perhaps I can get a position at the switchboard.

I do not go as far back as the radio and Victrola, but I am old enough to remember when 16-millimeter film was to be the sure-cure. Then closed-circuit television. Then 8-millimeter film. Then teacher-proof textbooks. Now computers.

I know a false god when I see one.

Unabomber's Secret Treatise: Is There Method In His Madness?

Kirkpatrick Sale

Any day now the powers at the *New York Times* and the *Washington Post* will have to decide whether they will print the full 35,000-word text of the document sent to them in late June by the man the Federal Bureau of Investigation is calling the Unabomber. In the letter that accompanied the text, he gave each paper three months to publish his screed, upon which he promises to "desist from terrorism," but he warned that if they refused he would "start building [his] next bomb." That deadline is September 29.

Naturally the decision has been somewhat complicated for the two papers, since they don't want to seem to "give in to terrorist demands" and don't particularly like giving such publicity to the Unabomber's decidedly anti-establishmentarian opinions. They are especially perturbed by his demand to be allowed to publish additional 3,000-word pieces for the next three years to rebut any critics of the original, thus prolonging the Damoclean threat. And yet they obviously don't want to give the man an excuse to send out more of his mail bombs, two of which have killed and two wounded their recipients in the past three years.

I have read the full text of the Unabomber treatise—the F.B.I. sent along two young female agents with copies of it for me to peruse—and I would recommend that either one of the papers publish it and trust the man will keep his word about ending the mad, unconscionable bombings. They should forget about the "giving in to terrorism" excuse, which is mostly meaningless in this case since there are no grand causes to be satisfied, no hostages to be freed and no reason to think that the threat would be repeated because it then becomes laughable. They needn't worry about the propaganda effect of printing it, since it is a woodenly written term paper, full of academic jargon and pop psychology, repetitive and ill-argued, that will keep only the most dedicated readers awake beyond its opening paragraphs.

Which, I would say, is a shame. Because the central point the Unabomber is trying to make—that "the industrial-technological system" in which we live is a social, psychological and environmental "disaster for the human race"—is absolutely crucial for the American public to understand and ought to be on the forefront of the nation's political agenda.

I say this, of course, as a partisan. The Unabomber stands in a long line of anti-technology critics where I myself have stood, and his general arguments against industrial society and its consequences are quite similar to those I have recently put forth in a book on the people who might be said to have begun this tradition, the Luddites. Along with a number of people today who might be called neo–Luddites—Jerry Mander, Chellis Glendinning, Jeremy Rifkin, Bill McKibben, Wendell Berry, Dave Foreman, Langdon Winner, Stephanie Mills and John Zerzan among them—the Unabomber and I share a great many views about the pernicious effect of the Industrial Revolution, the evils of modern technologies, the stifling effect of mass society, the vast extent of suffering in a machine-dominated world and the inevitability of social and environmental catastrophe if the industrial system goes on unchecked.

We disagree, to be sure, about what is to be done about all this and the means by which to achieve it. In the course of his career, at least as the F.B.I. has reconstructed it, the Unabomber has carried out sixteen bombings, killing three people and injuring twenty-three others, apparently choosing targets in some way connected to modern technology—a technological institute at Northwestern University, the University of Utah business school, a Salt Lake City computer store, a University of California geneticist, and a Yale computer scientist, among others—to try to "propagate anti-industrial ideas and give encouragement to those who hate the industrial system." That strikes me as simple madness. Maiming and killing people does not normally propagate ideas, and in this case no one knew what ideas were in the Unabomber's mind until he started writing letters this past year and then delivered his treatise in June. As for getting the message across, the only message that anyone got for sixteen years was that some nut was attacking people associated with universities and computers (hence the F.B.I.'s tag, *Una*bomber).*

But the bombings are going to get his document published, right or wrong, one way or another, and sooner rather than later. If the two newspapers don't publish it, *Penthouse* has offered to, and failing that, someone is sure to try to get it out as a pamphlet or send it over the Internet. That is what

*The "a" stands for "airline" because one early target was an airline executive, but I remain unconvinced that this was a genuine Unabomber victim. I'd render him "Unibomber," considering nine of the sixteen bombs were aimed at university targets or professors.

moves me to try to assess the treatise now, because I believe it would be a good idea to sort out its sound ideas from its errant ones, and to find the areas that ought not be discredited simply because of the agency that puts them forth—and as a service to all those who would fall asleep over the document itself.

"Industrial Society and Its Future" is the modest-enough title, and it is labeled as "by FC," which the author describes as a "terrorist group" though there is no sign from the writing style here that more than one person is behind it, and the F.B.I. believes that the Unabomber is acting alone. (The fact that he has escaped detection for seventeen years—especially during this past year, when he has become the target of the largest manhunt in the agency's history—would tend to support that.) "FC" is variously cited as the initials for "Freedom Club" or "Freedom Collective," although it is popularly thought to stand for a vulgar comment about computers; it is not explained in his text.

The sixty-six pages that follow begin with two pages of trivial typo corrections, showing the kind of fastidiousness ("sovle" should be "solve," "poit" should be "point") one might expect from a craftsman whose bombs the F.B.I. has described as "meticulously" constructed; then come fifty-six pages of argument divided into twenty-four subtitled sections and 232 numbered paragraphs; and it all ends with thirty-six footnotes, mostly qualifying statements in the text. That form, plus the leaden language and stilted diction, the fondness for sociological jargon and psychobabble, and the repeated use of "we argue that" and "we now discuss" and the like, make it certain that this was written by someone whose writing style, and probably whole intellectual development, was arrested in college.

The F.B.I. has said that it believes he was a student of the history of science, but on the evidence here he was a social psychology major with a minor in sociology, and he shows all the distressing hallmarks of the worst of that academic breed. He spends twelve pages, for example, on a strange and somewhat simplistic explanation of "something that we will call the power process," consisting of four elements "we call goal, effort and attainment of goal," plus "autonomy," all in an effort to explain why people today are unhappy and frustrated. Only someone trapped in the social sciences would talk that way.

Various professor types have been quoted in the papers saying how "bright" this fellow must be, but the arguments here are never very original and the line of reasoning is often quite convoluted. He has read a lot in certain areas—no poetry, though, I'll bet—and has thought a lot about the particular things that concern him, but aside from a few flashes there is no suggestion of anything more than a routine mind and a dutiful allegiance to some out-of-the-ordinary critics of modern society. I'm sure he makes good bombs, but grading him on his intellect I wouldn't give him more than a C+. I venture to say he didn't make it to his senior year.

The opus isn't helped by the fact that at least a third of it is essentially irrelevant, social-psych padding and scholarly back-and-forthing, one-hand-and-the-othering. Two long sections attacking "modern leftism" and "leftish" academics have nothing to do with his thesis, and I suspect they are offered because he had a bad time with certain sectarian groups in the early 1970s—no surprise—and with certain progress-minded, pro-technology Marxists he met in the academy."* Any good editor would have cut it.

But as near as I can fathom it after three careful readings, the Unabomber's argument would seem to be this:

- "Industrial-technological society" has succeeded to the point where, because of its size and complexity, it has constricted human freedom, meaning one's power to "control the circumstances of one's own life." Such freedoms as we do have are those permitted by the system consistent with it own ends—economic freedom to consume, press freedom to expose inefficiency and corruption—and do not in fact give individuals or groups true power, in the same sense that they have control over satisfying "life-and-death issues of one's existence: food, clothing, shelter and defense." Today people live more by virtue of what the system does FOR them or TO them than by virtue of what they do for themselves.... Modern man is strapped down by a network of rules and regulations, and his fate depends on the actions of persons remote from him whose decisions he cannot influence."

- Industrial society *must* perform this way in order to succeed—"The system has to regulate human behavior closely in order to function"—and cannot be reformed to work differently. "Changes large enough to make a lasting difference in favor of freedom would not be initiated because it would be realized that they would gravely disrupt the system."

- Industrial society must increasingly work to constrict freedom and control behavior since "technology advances with great rapidity" and on many fronts: "crowding, rules and regulations, increasing dependence of individuals on large organizations, propaganda and other psychological techniques, genetic engineering, invasion of privacy through surveillance devices and computers, etc."†

- But the problem of "control over human behavior" continues to bedevil this society, and right now "the system is currently engaged in a desperate

*The F.B.I. has leaked the idea the Unabomber is really Leo Frederick Burt, one of the "New Year's Gang" that bombed the Army Math Research Center at the University of Wisconsin in August 1970 and who has been a fugitive ever since. If so, he probably was steeped beyond human endurance in the kind of fractious sectarian stews aboiling in those days and comes by his dislike of what he thinks is leftism legitimately.

†Oddly, the Unabomber's antipathy toward technology is more in the abstract than the particular. He actually likes certain technologies— "electricity, indoor plumbing, rapid long-distance communications ... how could one argue against any of these things?"—and argues that revolutionaries should use "some modern technology."

struggle to overcome certain problems that threaten its survival," primarily social (the "growing numbers" of "rebels," "dropouts and resisters") but also economic and environmental. "If the system succeeds in acquiring sufficient control over human behavior quickly enough, it will probably survive. Otherwise it will break down. We think the issue will most likely be resolved within the next several decades, say 40 to 100 years."

• Therefore, the task of those who oppose the industrial system is to advance that breakdown by promoting "social stress and instability in industrial society," which presumably includes bombing, and by developing and propagating "an ideology that opposes technology," one that puts forth the "counter-ideal" of nature "in order to gain enthusiastic support." Thus, when the system becomes sufficiently stressed and unstable, a "revolution against technology may be possible."

Now, this is a reasonable enough argument—the Unabomber is not irrational, whatever else you can say about him—and I think it is even to some extent persuasive. There is nothing wild-eyed or rabble-rousing about it (it could actually use a lot more Paine-ist fomentation and furor) and the points are most often buttressed with careful arguments and examples—though nowhere, interestingly, a single statistic. It is too slow, too plodding, too repetitive; but you have to say its case is made in a competent, if labored, fashion.

His critique of industrial society today is most telling, I think, and reads as if he's spent a lot of time defending it in the back rooms of bars. (Excerpts presented in the *Times* and the *Post* for some reason concentrate on the treatise's weaker and tangential early parts and give only limited attention to this central message.) Just picking at random, I find these examples;

> The system does not and cannot exist to satisfy human needs. Instead, it is human behavior that has to be modified to fit the needs of the system. This has nothing to do with the political or social ideology that may pretend to guide the technological system. It is not the fault of capitalism and it is not the fault of socialism. It is the fault of technology, because the system is guided not by ideology but by technical necessity.

> • • •

> If the use of a new item of technology is INITIALLY optional, it does not necessarily REMAIN optional, because new technology tends to change society in such a way that it becomes difficult or impossible for an individual to function without using that technology.... Something like this seems to have happened already with one of our society's most important psychological tools for enabling people to reduce (or at least temporarily escape from) stress, namely mass entertainment. Our use of mass entertainment is "optional" ... yet mass entertainment is a means of escape and stress-reduction on which most of us have become dependent.

> • • •

> The technophiles are hopelessly naive (or self-deceiving) in their understanding of social problems. They are unaware of (or choose to ignore) the fact that when large changes, even seemingly beneficial ones, are introduced into a society, they lead to a long sequence of other changes, most of which are difficult to predict .... In fact, ever since the industrial revolution technology has been creating new problems for society far more rapidly than it has been solving old ones.

Not inspired, but thoughtful, perceptive enough, when abstracted from its labored context.

What's surprising about all this, though, is that it reads as if the Unabomber thinks he's the first person who ever worked out such ideas. It is hard to believe, but he seems woefully ignorant of the long Luddistic strain in Western thought going back at least to William Blake and Mary Shelley, and he does not once cite any of the great modern critics of technology such as Lewis Mumford, Jacques Ellul, Paul Goodman, Max Weber, E.F. Schumacher or Rachel Carson, nor any of the contemporary laborers in this vineyard. In one of his letters to the *Times* he does say that "anyone who will read the anarchist and radical environmentalist journals will see that opposition to the industrial-technological system is widespread and growing," so he must know something about the current critics, although he does not mention specific articles or authors or particular periodicals. (If I had to guess which has been most influential on him, I'd say the *Fifth Estate*, a feisty anti-technology paper published out of Detroit for the past thirty years, but he does not name it anywhere.)

That failure to ground himself in the Luddistic tradition, where both utopian and dystopian models proliferate, may be the reason that the Unabomber is so weak on envisioning the future, particularly the kind of revolution he seems to want.

I would agree with the Unabomber's general position that "to make a lasting change in the direction of development of any important aspect of a society, reform is insufficient," and I might even agree that in certain circumstances therefore "revolution is necessary." But I can't figure out at all what kind of revolution this is to be. He says that "a revolution does not necessarily involve an armed uprising or the overthrow of a government," a conviction he is so certain of he repeats it twice more, adding that "it may or may not involve physical violence," and in two footnotes he suggests that it might be "somewhat gradual or piecemeal" and might "consist only of a massive change of attitudes toward technology resulting in a relatively gradual and painless disintegration of the industrial system."

This is a somewhat peculiar position for a man who has been killing and injuring people in service to his dream of a new society, and I'm not sure what he thinks revolutions are or how they are achieved. If he has in mind something more like the Industrial Revolution or the Copernican revolution, he doesn't suggest how that might come about, and the sorts of strategies he ends up advocating—promoting social instability, destroying and wrecking "the system," seeing "its remnants ... smashed beyond repair"—sound an awful lot like a revolution with a good deal of violence. He even suggests at one point that the models are the French and Russian revolutions, both pretty bloody affairs.

The whole question of violence indeed is confused in the Unabomber's mind, oddly enough after seventeen years during which he must have been thinking about it a little. He never once addresses the reasons for his own string of bombings or explains what he thinks he has been accomplishing, other than to say that this was the way to have "some chance of making a lasting impression." He is critical of "leftists" who commit violence, because it is only "a form of 'liberation'" they justify "in terms of mainstream values ... fighting against racism or the like," and later is critical of leftists because they are "against competition and against violence." His revolution is not necessarily to be violent, yet he never confronts the idea of a nonviolent revolution or how it would be strategically carried out.

The one task of revolutionaries the Unabomber is clear about is the business of producing an anti-technology "ideology," although he doesn't anywhere concern himself with the hard business of saying what that would consist of. But it doesn't much matter to him, since the primary purpose of this ideology is "to create a core of people who will be opposed to the industrial system on a rational, thought-out basis," an intellectual cadre who can then dish it out "in a simplified form" for the "unthinking majority" who "like to have such issues presented in simple, black-and-white terms." "History is made by active, determined minorities," you see, and "as for the majority, it will be enough to make them aware of the existence of the new ideology and remind them of it frequently." Lenin couldn't have put it better.

The Unabomber's idea of a systemic breakdown is, I think, more plausible than his concept of revolution; one could see how, as the system was breaking down of its own weight and incompetence, unable to manage the problems its technology creates, this might be "helped along by revolutionaries." Just how the breakdown would come about is not spelled out. The Unabomber gives only a passing glance to the multiple environmental disasters the system is producing for itself and never mentions the likelihood, as chaos theory predicts, that the complex industrial house of cards will not hold. At least he does posit a "time of troubles" after which the human race would be "given a new chance."

I should note that the Unabomber, on the evidence here, does not have any special vision of an ecologically based future, as the newspapers have suggested. Indeed, he is no environmentalist, and I'd say he has only the faintest grasp of the principles of ecology. It's true that he refers to nature at one point—"That is WILD nature!"—as a "positive ideal," but this is almost entirely cynical, nature as a concept that he figures will be useful in propaganda terms because it is "the opposite of technology," because "most people will agree that nature is beautiful" and because "in many people, nature inspires the kind of reverence that is associated with religion." He shows no real understanding of the role of technology in enabling industrial society not only to exploit nature but to pass that off as legitimate, and not one individual environmental problem is addressed here, except overpopulation. (And on that one the Unabomber, though acknowledging that it produces overcrowding and stress, indicates no awareness of its endangerment and extinctions we are causing by our exploding numbers, or for the natural systems of the world, whose degradation we are causing by our exploding consumption.)

It's clear enough that the Unabomber counts "radical environmentalists" as among those rightly opposing technology, and his use of wood in some of his bombs and his killing of a timber lobbyist in California suggests a further affinity. But he indicates no sympathy for the kind of biocentric "deep ecology" and bioregionalism espoused by most of them, and his concerns are exclusively anthropocentric, his appreciation of other species and natural systems nil. He also mocks those who believe in the "Gaia theory" of a living earth, common in many environmental groups: "Do its adherents REALLY believe in it or are they just play-acting?"

In short, it feels to me that his appeal to nature is entirely utilitarian (like adding another little mechanism to your bomb to make sure it works) rather than a heartfelt passion, of which he seems to have very few in any case.

But if nature does not inspire his vision of the future, it is hard to tell what does. Presumably he would want, as a self-described anarchist, some kind of world where "people live and work as INDIVIDUALS and SMALL GROUPS," using "small-scale technology ... that can be used by small-scale communities without outside assistance." But he nowhere bothers to hint at how this future society would operate (other than to say it would burn all technical books), nor does he refer to any in the long line of anarcho-communal writers from Kropotkin to Bookchin who have given a great deal of thought to the configurations of just such a society.

It's true that the Unabomber offers the defense at one point that "a new kind of society cannot be designed on paper" and "when revolutionaries or utopians set up a new kind of society, it never works out as planned." That gives him leeway to avoid discussing what kind of world he wants (even in a three page section called "THE FUTURE"); unfortunately, it also leaves a gaping hole in his treatise. Even those who agree that the industrial system should be torn down will want to get some idea of what is supposed to replace it before they are moved to endorse the cause, much less become the revolutionaries the Unabomber wants.

So, in sum, what are we to make of this strange document? So important to its author that he is prepared to kill people (even though he has written that he is "getting tired of making bombs") to get it published in a major newspaper. So embarrassing to those newspapers that they don't know what to do with it.

It is the statement of a rational and serious man, deeply committed to his cause, who has given a great deal of thought to his work and a great deal of time to this expression of it. He is prescient and clear about the nature of the society we live in, what its purposes and methods are, and how it uses its array of technologies to serve them; he understands the misery and anxiety and constriction this creates for the individual and the wider dangers it poses for society and the earth. He truly believes that a campaign of social disorder led by misfits, rebels, dropouts and saboteurs (and presumably terrorists), coupled with the concerted propaganda work of a dedicated intellectual elite, has a chance to cause or hasten the breakdown of industrial society, and this motivates him in his grisly work.

The document is also the product of a limited and tunnel-visioned man, with a careful and dogged but somewhat incoherent mind, filled with a catalogue of longstanding prejudices and hatreds, academically trained, occasionally inventive, purposeful and humorless. He is amoral, not to say cold-bloodied, about acts of terrorism, which are regarded as an effective tactic in service to the larger cause. He is convinced enough in his cause to have produced this long justification for it, complete with numerous bold assertions and his own "principles of history," but he repeatedly finds qualifications and reservations and indeed ends up calling the article no more "than a crude approximation to the truth," as if to suggest that somewhere within he is not quite confident.

All in all, I think despite its flaws it is a document worth publishing, and not only because that could presumably help stop the killing. There is a crucial message at the core of it for those with fortitude enough to get through it, and unless that message is somehow heeded and acted on we are truly a doomed society hurtling toward a catastrophic breakdown. I can't expect the *Times* and the *Post* to give much credence to that idea—and they can lard it with their own dissents and denials if they choose—but they might just realize that there is a growing body of people these days beginning at last to understand the increasing perils of the technosphere we have created. For, as *The New Yorker* recently put it, there's a little of the Unabomber in all of us.

III
Information, Rights, and Social Justice

Utilitarianism, Information and Rights

Partha Dasgupta*

1 Distributive Justice and Individual Rights

"Social justice," writes Hayek, "can be given a meaning only in a directed or 'command' economy (such as an army) in which individuals are ordered to do.... Indeed ... no free action of the individuals could produce results satisfying any principle of distributive justice" (Hayek 1976, p. 69.). Such an unequivocal position is no doubt rare. But the claim that the demands of distributive justice conflict with individual rights—in particular, the right to decision-making—is one that has often been made.

An individual right (such as the right to be treated with the same respect and concern as anyone else) may be defended on the ground that it is an end in itself. Alternatively, it may be defended on the ground that it is *instrumental* in realising certain desirable ends (e.g. in arguing for the right to private property, because, under certain circumstances, it sustains an efficient allocation of resources). Admittedly, the distinction between these two types of defences is not always sharp. For example, even if a right is regarded as an end, the end may still require justification. Presumably, the justification will be based on the human interests it serves and promotes—for example, by an appeal to the Kantian notion of the autonomy of the individual, or from straightforward utilitarian considerations. In this paper I shall be concerned with *economic decentralisation*, and, therefore, with the right that individuals may be thought to possess to certain private regions of decision-making—an aspect of "protected spheres," as Professor Hayek would call them. I shall ask

*While writing this essay I have gained much from discussions with Ronald Dworkin and Julian LeGrand. This version was completed during a stay at Princeton University which was supported by a grant from the U.S. National Science Foundation.

whether the claims of distributive justice require a systematic violation of rights to individual decision–making, and I shall argue that they do not, that the exercise of rights to *certain* regions of decision-making is *instrumental* in promoting the attainment of distributive justice. The argument is founded on the observation that much information in any society is only privately known; indeed, that no single individual or decision-making unit can feasibly know the sum-total of all information. From this observation it is possible to argue that the goal of distributive justice is best served in an environment where individuals are encouraged to exploit some of their private information; or, in other words, that except for certain very extreme circumstances some form of decentralisation in decision-making is desirable. In particular, this implies that a pure command system is almost never an optimal mode of organisation even from the point of view of distributive justice, let alone from the vantage point of the innate rights that individuals may possess to private decision-making.

For my purposes here I shall be thinking of society as a cooperative venture among individuals for mutual advantage, and shall take it that some form of centralised authority is required for coordinating the activities of the members of society. To be sure, classical criteria of social welfare, such as utilitarianism, require for their furtherance a central authority whose activities far exceed the provision of the limited number of public services, such as the enforcement of contracts, and the protection of persons or groups against force, theft and fraud that delineate the activities of the minimal state. The claims of distributive justice would, as a minimum, require that this central authority be engaged in addition with the task of redistributing purchasing power among individuals via taxes and subsidies.

It has been argued by Nozick (1974) that the imposition of such taxes and subsidies violates the inalienable rights that individuals have to the *actual* goods and services they are historically entitled to. In this paper I shall not concern myself with the question of whether the arguments leading to such a view are compelling.* In any case, it has long been noted by political philosophers that the claims of distributive justice—such as those emanating from utilitarianism—can readily conflict with certain rights that individuals are entitled to. Indeed, Sen (1970a, 1976) has recently noted that certain minimal demands of "liberty" may conflict with even so weak a welfare criterion as the one embodied in the Pareto ranking. Such conflicts do not pose any analytical difficulties. For example, if it is granted that individuals possess innate rights—such as a well-defined region of private decision-making—which considerations of distributive justice, let along "progress" or efficiency, must not override, then an observance of these rights must be viewed as constraints

For extended discussions of this, see e.g. Arrow 1977 and Dasgupta 1980.

that must not be violated in the execution of policies that result in the maximisation of the chosen criterion of social welfare.* Now, it is an observation of the utmost banality that if these constraints are "biting" constraints in the maximisation exercise, then the maximum social welfare that can be achieved in the presence of these constraints is less than the level which could have been achieved had these constraints not been imposed. Indeed, one can even calculate the cost—in terms of forgone social welfare—that the imposition of such constraints leads to. These are familiar matters: that not all rights are typically viewed with equal urgency, that individual rights often clash with one another and that they in turn conflict with other social goals.†Ultimately what one seeks is an ordering of social states. I take it that when one talks of a social state one includes in its characterisation not only the production and distribution of goods and services—"end states" in the sense of Nozick—but also the actions that people choose, those they are entitled to choose, what treatment they are entitled to expect from others, and so on. I recognise that a committed utilitarian will make the claim that if such an extended notion of social states matters to people then it will have found expression in their utility functions. But I take it also that it will be agreed by many that this device misses much of the point raised by non-utilitarian political philosophers in recent years. If political philosophy is much concerned with the characterisation of social states and the arguments that are relevant in seeking an ordering among them, welfare economic theory is much concerned with the design of economic environments that are conducive to the realisation of those social states that are judged desirable in the light of this ordering. Admittedly, in some extreme cases—as in the philosophy of Nozick—this role of welfare economic theory is vanishingly small. Granted that a decision has to be reached on the *degree* of protection which the minimal state is expected to provide, a matter which is hardly touched on in Nozick's work; it must nevertheless be granted that the end of personal rights, as Nozick sees them, dictates that the only economic organisation which is justified is one that is born under the benign indifference of the minimal state. But this is an extreme position, and most political philosophies allow for a certain scope in the design of economic organisations that best serve the purpose at hand. Thus, for example, in his celebrated work Rawls (1971) expresses the opinion that whether the requirements of social justice are best met in a private property system or under a socialist regime cannot be judged in advance, so long

*In what follows I shall suppose that the central authority is concerned with the maximisation of a criterion of social welfare which includes, among other things, a conception of distributive justice. For illustrative purposes I shall often suppose this criterion to be classical utilitarianism.
†When goals conflict one is forced to entertain the idea of tradeoffs among them. The "social weights" attached to these goals typically will depend on the extent to which the goals are realized. At an extreme are lexicographically ordered goals, such as the two principles of justice in Rawls' system.

as market institutions are relied upon in each. And he says "A ... significant advantage of a market system is that, given the required background institutions, it is consistent with equal liberties and fair equality of opportunity ... a system of markets decentralises the exercise of economic power.... It is necessary, then, to recognise that market institutions are common to both private-property and socialist regimes ... which of these systems and the many intermediate forms most fully answers to the requirements of justice cannot ... be determined in advance" (Rawls 1971, pp. 272–4).

In this paper I shall approach matters from a different end and suppose that social welfare depends only on individual welfares and that individual welfares depend solely on the allocation of goods and services. Furthermore, for expositional ease, I shall take it that individual welfares are based on preferences that are entirely *personal*, in the sense that an individual's welfare depends only on the goods and services assigned to him.* I shall suppose that the state is concerned with the maximisation of a criterion of social welfare subject to whatever technological and informational constraints there may be.† Often, for illustrative purposes, I shall take it that the criterion of social welfare is utilitarianism, or the sum of individual utilities (or welfare). It will be noted that in this formulation no account is taken of individual rights, except the right to have one's welfare included in the social ranking of economic states. The question I want to ask is whether economic decentralisation, or the assignment of rights to certain regions of individual decision-making, is instrumental in implementing the optimal allocation of goods and services in the light of the chosen criterion of social welfare. This is discussed in the next two sections.

2 The Fundamental Theorem of Welfare Economics

If welfare economic theory has not usually emphasised the right on the part of individuals to certain areas of personal decision-making, it is because

*As the reader will note, I am borrowing Dworkin's terminology in distinguishing personal from external preferences (see Dworkin 1977, pp. 234 and 275). Actually, unless strong assumptions are made on individual preferences, it is not possible to isolate an individual's personal preferences from his external ones, in that in general a person's preference over his own consumption of wine and beer will depend on the goods consumed by others. For my purpose this does not matter, because much of what I have to say can accommodate the inclusion of external preferences, provided that they are allowed to be counted in the social calculus.

†I shall also abstract from uncertainties in the state of the world—e.g. about tomorrow's weather condition—as well as an individual's uncertainties about his own future preferences. Furthermore, I am abstracting from time here and, therefore, the idea that for any state of nature a person may know that his preferences will change in a predictable way as time passes. Each of these issues can be accommodated in the discussion that follows. But not without further thought and care. Rawls (1971, Chapter 9) presents a deep analysis of the concept of "self" and, in Chapter 8, pp. 416–24, discusses the idea of deliberative rationality. This latter discussion includes an account of what economists call intertemporally consistent preferences on the part of an individual (see Strotz 1956). Both this last and the distinction between ex-ante and ex-post social welfare functions in the face of uncertainty are discussed by Hammond (Chapter 4, above).

in many of the circumstances that have been explored there is, in fact, no necessary conflict between this and the claims of distributive justice. For consider the example of an economy in which individuals possess an initial endowment of goods and services.* Suppose that the state knows the utility (or welfare) function and the initial endowment of each and every individual in society. Then it is a theorem in welfare economics that, provided that the utility functions satisfy certain technical conditions, the *full* optimum allocation of goods and service (i.e. the optimum in the light of the chosen criterion of social welfare constrained only by the total initial endowment of goods and services in the economy) can be realised by way of the following scheme. The scheme consists in the state simultaneously announcing a set of prices, one for each and every commodity and service; rearranging the initial endowments of individuals by imposing lump-sum taxes and subsidies; and allowing individuals to trade at these prices. The rule for trading is precisely what one would expect: the market value of the final consumption bundle each person chooses must not exceed the income allotted to him by the state via the lump-sum taxes (or subsidies). A formal way of stating this is to say that, provided that the utility functions satisfy certain conditions, the full optimum is a competitive equilibrium allocation of goods and services associated with an appropriate distribution of initial endowments among the members of society.†

I want to make three observations about this theorem. First, the structure of the economic organisation described by the theorem has the formal characteristics of a *game*; which is to say that each and every individual, as well as the state, is empowered to *choose* from a personalised set of actions, and in addition there is a publicly known rule which translates the chosen actions of all players (including the state) into a final allocation of goods and services. To be precise, the state wishes to maximise the criterion of social welfare and is empowered to impose lump-sum taxes and subsidies on individuals and to choose prices at which individuals then trade. And each individual is empowered to choose his most preferred bundle of goods and services subject to the constraint that the market value of his final consumption bundle does not exceed the income he has been allotted via the tax system. The theorem says that the (equilibrium) outcome of this game is the optimal

*For simplicity of exposition I shall suppose that it is a pure exchange economy; that is, there is no production. This is not at all crucial in what follows. One can also allow for the passage of time in the model I am describing. For a good account of what follows with the inclusion of features I am abstracting from here, see Malinvaud 1972.
†This result, often called the Fundamental Theorem of Welfare Economics, has been much discussed both in the economics and political philosophy literature, and formed the basis of the socialist pricing debate (see Lerner 1944 and Hayek 1948). For a technical presentation of the theorem, see e.g. Malinvaud 1972. Meade 1964 and Rawls 1971, section 42, provide excellent discussions of it.

allocation of goods and service.* Second, contrary to what is on occasion thought, it is simply not true that in order to sustain the full welfare optimum the state, in the economy we are discussing, must prohibit persons from engaging in mutually beneficial trade among themselves.† The point is that the commodity prices are so chosen and the lump-sum redistribution of assets is so arranged by the state that the outcome of the subsequent market transactions postulated by the Fundamental Theorem leaves no scope for further mutually beneficial trade among persons.§

Third, it will have been noted that in the economy under study a person is characterised by his preferences (or utility function) and his initial endowment of goods and services, and it has been supposed that the state knows each person's characteristics. Thus, in fact, the lump-sum taxes and subsidies required to attain the welfare optimum are person-specific. Thus, while the competitive process is an anonymous one, in the sense that all individuals trade at the same set of prices, the redistributive taxes and subsidies are not. This last should come as no surprise. Since the state knows individual characteristics, it behooves the state to make use of its knowledge for the sake of social welfare. Persons who are needy will have subsidies given to them, obtained via taxes from those who are not.

Now it may be remarked that if the state in fact knows as much as the Fundamental Theorem of Welfare Economics invites it to know, it can rather readily enforce the full optimum directly, by expropriating the initial endowments of individuals and then distributing the (welfare) optimum allocation. This would be a *command* system and the question arises whether there is much to choose between these two allocative mechanisms for attaining the welfare optimum. It may be pointed out that the set of "messages" the state must transmit under the command mode of planning will far exceed the set of messages it must transmit under the price mechanism.** But let us suppose

---

*This leads to the question of whether there are other games, and therefore other economic systems, with this same outcome. The answer is "yes." For a discussion of this in a different context, see Mas-Colell 1978. It should be noted that the Fundamental Theorem envisages the game to be played in two moves. The state makes the first move by announcing prices and imposing transfers. Individuals then make the second move by engaging in transactions. The planning models to be discussed in the next section will also have this "two-moves" structure.

†See Nozick 1974, pp. 161–3, in which the dilemma confronting Wilt Chamberlain and his admirers is based on the contrary supposition.

§Formally, what I am referring to here is the fact that in the economy under study a competitive equilibrium outcome is not merely efficient in the sense of Pareto, but is also in the core, that is, subsequent to the imposition of the appropriate lump–sum taxes and subsidies, no sub–group can, by restricting trade to its members, do better than what it attains at the welfare optimum. For a formal definition of the core and the result I am stating here, see Malinvaud 1972. Nozick 1974, Chapter 10, has a good discussion of the concept.

**If there are m persons and l goods and services then, roughly speaking, the state needs to transmit (m + l) messages (m income transfers and l prices) under the decentralised scheme, and ml messages (l quantities of goods to each individual) under the command system. If m and l are large then obviously ml is greatly in excess of m + l.

that messages can be costlessly transmitted and received. Is there then much to choose between these two special mechanisms as devices for sustaining the full optimum? It may be argued that the freedom enjoyed by individuals under the price mechanism envisaged in the Fundamental Theorem is illusory—that, after all, the state knows precisely what will be chosen by each, and, indeed, that it has so chosen the commodity prices and income transfers that each individual will eventually choose precisely what the state wants it to choose in the light of the social optimum. This argument, plausible at first blush, is not really satisfactory. For the fact that the state knows what an individual will in fact choose does not mean that the individual could not have chosen otherwise. Indeed, the individual will know that the state knows what he will choose. But this in itself is clearly not a good reason for the individuals to think that he is not exercising choice.

3 Differential Information and Economic Decentralisation

The Fundamental Theorem of Welfare Economics states that under certain circumstances a full welfare optimum can be attained through a decentralised mechanism. But it was also noted that under these circumstances the welfare optimum can be attained via a complete command system as well. As an instrument for sustaining the welfare optimum each mode would appear to be equally effective. But, then the operational appeal of the Fundamental Theorem is also minimal. The information that the state is assumed to possess is awesome in amount. For our example it is assumed to know the preferences and endowments of each and every member of society. These observations alone suggest that individual rights to certain private decisions may not only be a moral imperative, but may at once be a necessity prompted by the fact that the state possesses incomplete information.

One supposes that there are certain pieces of information that are known (or which will be known) only by the individuals in question; that is they are costly (or in the extreme, impossible) to monitor publicly. These *private* pieces of information presumably include (i) an individual's personal characteristics (e.g. his preferences and personal endowments); that is, what kind of person he *is* (ii) the actions that he takes (e.g. how hard he works at a given task); that is, what he *does*, and (iii) localised pieces of information about the state of the world—or certain aspects of specialised technological possibilities.* One supposes as well that there are certain pieces of information that are publicly known or which *can* be publicly observed at relatively little cost. These may be precise pieces of information (e.g. the amount of pollution emitted

---

In the insurance literature the terms adverse selection and moral hazard are used to characterise the problems raised by the first and second categories of private information, respectively.

by a firm) or they may be statistical information (e.g. the age distribution in a given society at a given moment of time). Thus we are invited to consider organisations in which the outcome (i.e. an allocation of goods and services) is a function of private decisions that are based on private information and public decisions that are based on publicly known information. And we are invited to choose among them on the basis of their outcomes as measured by the chosen criterion of social welfare.*

This is a difficult task, and it had been neglected until quite recently—the choice among social organisations when the individuals and the state entertain different information structures. But it may first be asked why the state does not require of individuals to make their private information available to it—the point being that if it were to collect all the private information it could implement the full optimum. There are at least two answers to this question and quite clearly both are valid in the world we know. The first is that if an individual knows how the answers will be translated into social action he may have an incentive to lie with a view to tilting the social outcome more towards his favour than the full optimum would allow. The second is that even if all individuals are morally committed to the chosen criterion of social welfare and are truly prepared to act always with a view to maximising this common criterion, the costs of communication—i.e. the costs in transmitting such messages—may be too high.† This second answer, which provided the motivation for the Marschak-Radner theory of teams is of great importance precisely because it alerts us to the fact that even if all individuals act on the basis of a common goal there is still the need for private decision-making—so as to exploit private information. In particular, the construct tells us that a command system—one in which the final allocation is a function solely of *public* information—is almost never optimal (see e.g. Weitzman 1978 and Dasgupta, Hammond and Maskin 1980).

It is, however, the first answer which has prompted an enormous theoretical literature during the past few years.§ For, one is led directly to a consideration of designing *incentive* schemes with a view to maximising the chosen criterion of social welfare. It is clear enough in advance that it may not be possible in general to design social organisations that will yield the full

---

The basic idea, therefore, is the same as the one discussed in the previous section. Myerson 1980 and Laffont and Maskin 1981 have presented a unified formulation of a general planning problem in which each of the three categories of private information mentioned above is present.

†*There is a third answer of course, which has to do with the right that people may be thought to have to "privacy". Since I am concerned here with the instrumental role of decentralised decision-making, I naturally ignore this answer.*

§*The question of incentive compatible resource allocation mechanisms, an issue pioneered by Hurwicz (1972) has been much discussed in recent years. Laffont 1979 contains a rich sample of essays on the subject. See Dasgupta, Hammond and Maskin for a classification of different social organisations designed to implement welfare optima.*

optimum as an (equilibrium) outcome.* Usually the best that can be achieved is what economists clumsily call a "second-best" outcome. I shall illustrate the general problem and the point I wish to make by means of a strikingly simple example due to Mirrlees (1971).

Consider an artisan economy where individuals possess innate abilities for transforming leisure into a single consumption good, which I shall call income. To be precise, I shall suppose that if a person has an innate ability (or productivity) level of n, where n is a positive number, then, if he works l hours at this productivity level, the amount of the consumption good he can produce is nl. A person's utility depends only on his own leisure time and his own disposable income and it increases with both leisure and disposable income. Thus preferences are personal. In fact I shall suppose that individual utility functions are identical. But while individuals have identical utility functions, they are not of identical ability. Thus individuals can be grouped by productivity types. The number of persons of ability n is $N(n)$, by assumption. For the same number of hours worked a more able person obviously *can* produce more income. In what follows I shall take it that even though a person cannot pretend and demonstrate an ability level *greater* than his innate one, he can work at any *lower* ability level, were he to choose to do so.†

I want first to look at the *laissez-faire* outcome in this economy, or, to put it more accurately, the outcome under the minimal state. Notice first that since leisure cannot be transferred from one person to another, there is no scope for trade in this economy. For what can a person offer to another of a higher ability in return for the fruits of his higher productivity? Likewise, there is no scope for exchange between persons of the same productivity. Thus, it is clear that under the minimal state each person will work on his own, at his innate ability level, having chosen his income—leisure mix so as to maximise his utility. Since people, by hypothesis, have identical utility functions, it will come as no surprise that the more able will realise a higher utility level. The distribution of utility levels, as a function of the ability level, n, is depicted in the figure below. I need hardly add that this distribution of realised utilities is efficient in the sense of Pareto.

I want to compare this outcome with the outcome that would be reached if the state were to intervene with a view to maximising a criterion of social welfare. But the point that I wish to emphasise is that the best outcome that can be achieved depends on the information that each of the participants in the economy possesses (or can obtain). By hypothesis each person knows his own utility function and his own innate ability. Thus by varying the amount

---

*The full optimum here is the same as the full optimum of the previous section; i.e. that which is based on the true underlying preferences and endowments of individuals.

†Since by hypothesis a person's utility depends only on his leisure time and disposable income I am assuming that there is no pride in being recognised as an able person.

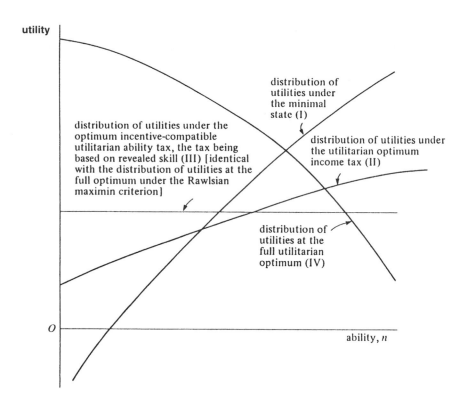

utility

distribution of
utilities under
the minimal
state (I)

distribution of utilities under the
optimum incentive-compatible
utilitarian ability tax, the tax being
based on revealed skill (III) [identical
with the distribution of utilities at the
full optimum under the Rawlsian
maximin criterion]

distribution of utilities under
the utilitarian optimum
income tax (II)

distribution of
utilities at the
full utilitarian
optimum (IV)

O

ability, n

FIGURE 1. If $u_n(x)$ denotes the utility level of person of ability n in scheme x, and if $W(x)$ $(=\sum_n N(n)u_n(x))$ is the *sum* of utilities in scheme x, then $W(\mathrm{IV}) > W(\mathrm{III}) > W(\mathrm{II}) > W(\mathrm{I})$.

of information at the disposal of the state I shall be able to trace the extent to which maximum attainable social welfare can in fact be varied. To bring this out sharply I shall assume that this society is wedded to the philosophy of Sidgwick, so that the criterion of social welfare is the sum of utilities. It is this sum which the state seeks to maximise.

In what follows I shall assume throughout that the state knows the common utility function and that it knows how many persons there are of each ability type. Furthermore, I shall assume that the government can monitor a person's income costlessly. I want first to look at the full utilitarian optimum— the outcome which can be achieved if the state knows each person's innate ability level as well.* Now, it transpires that for a large class of individual utility

*Notice that it is possible for the state to know how many persons there are of each ability type without its being able to distinguish between persons and, therefore, not being able to say who is of what type. It is this distinction which I shall exploit subsequently.

functions (and, therefore, individual preferences), the full utilitarian optimum is characterised by persons of *higher* innate ability attaining *lower* utility levels.* The distribution of utilities at the full utilitarian optimum is also depicted in Figure 1. Quite obviously, this distribution of utilities is also efficient in the sense of Pareto.

The most striking thing about this result is the complete reversal of the *ordering* of utilities from the one under the minimal state. Under the minimal state the more able attain higher utility levels. Under the utilitarian state they attain lower utility levels. Utilitarianism seeks to maximise the *sum* of utilities. The result I am describing says that in order to maximise this sum the really able ought to work much longer hours—so as to help raise the amount of income that is produced in the economy—to such an extent that they emerge with lower utility levels. The point is that the greater income so generated is used to subsidise the less able. The really able will no doubt be worse off under a utilitarian state than under the minimal state—they work a good deal harder. But the less able will be better off, so much so that the sum of utilities will be greater.†

How is this utilitarian optimum to be implemented? Since the state, by assumption, knows the innate ability of each person, and can monitor a person's income, one route is for the state to require of people to produce stipulated amounts of income which the state collects and then proceeds to distribute. Since the state can calculate precisely how long each person ought to work and how much each ought to consume at the full utilitarian optimum, it can enforce these commands. Another option is for the state to impose a tax on each person based solely on his ability, and for individuals to choose their number of working hours. The optimal ability tax schedule will, of course, be a tax on the more able and subsidy on the less able. This is a decentralised mechanism, an application of the Fundamental Theorem of Welfare Economics, where a person is allowed to choose his activity—here the number of hours he works—in the face of the optimal ability tax (or subsidy) imposed on him. The key point is that in the face of the optimal tax (or subsidy) a person, in the light of his own interests, will in fact choose precisely that number of working hours which the utilitarian optimum requires of him. I contrasted these two modes of implementation in the previous section.

Now let us relax our assumptions and suppose that the state does not know who is of what type. In fact, suppose that the state cannot monitor the

---

See Mirrlees 1974 and Allingham 1975 for conditions on individual preferences for which this is true. The conditions are in fact fairly innocuous.

†I am emphasising these stark features precisely because there is a sense in which the more able are "made" to work for the less able under the utilitarian state—a crystalline example of a policy odious to Nozick. A committed utilitarian will, of course, not care. If this is what utilitarianism dictates, he will say, so be it.

number of hours a person chooses to work, but can only monitor a person's income. Thus the state cannot tell merely by observing a person's income whether the person is of "high" ability and has chosen a "high" leisure level or whether he is of "low" ability and has worked long hours.* But now one can see that the full utilitarian optimum cannot be achieved. For example, the state clearly cannot achieve it by asking people to announce their innate abilities. At the full utilitarian optimum the more able are worse off then the less able. Since individuals know that their answers will be used to implement the full optimum, high-ability people will have a strong incentive to announce and act as though they are of low ability, so as to be eligible for state subsidies! What is equally important, the state will know that there are such incentive problems. I want to consider the case where any form of communication between the state and the individuals, other than the enforcement of taxes, is prohibitively costly. Quite clearly the state must impose its tax only on what it can monitor. Since the state can only observe a person's income the only policy it can pursue is to impose an income tax schedule. It is helpful to think of this as a game, in which income tax schedules are the state's strategies, and the choice of leisure (and therefore the number of working hours) is individual choice.† Moreover, the state chooses the income tax schedule with a view to maximising the sum of utilities, knowing the manner in which persons of any given type will respond. It can be shown that if the state imposes the optimum income tax schedule each person will be better off than anyone who is less able then himself, and therefore each will indeed work at his innate ability level. This outcome is depicted in Figure 1. The least able earn very little on their own and, under the tax schedule, receive an income subsidy (a negative income tax). This is financed by income taxes collected from the able who choose to earn a good deal. The sum of utilities achieved under the optimum income tax schedule is the best outcome (from the utilitarian point of view) that can be realised, given the limited information that the government possesses, and given that we have ruled out as prohibitively costly any form of communication between the government and the citizens other than the filing of income tax returns and the imposition of taxes.

Three points bear emphasis. First, we have seen that although a utilitarian government would ideally like to impose an ability tax—i.e. a person-specific tax—it is unable to do so because it does not know who is of what type. By contrast, the optimal income tax is "anonymous": the tax is levied (or subsidy paid) on the income earned. Two people, under such a schedule, are

---

*The example therefore contains both the problem of adverse selection and moral hazard referred to in the footnote, p. 137.
†Since a person can work at an ability level less than his innate one this too is up to a point a choice for the individual. But, as we shall see, persons will in fact wish to choose to work at their innate ability levels when the optimal income tax schedule is imposed.

liable to the same tax (or subsidy) provided they earn the same income.* It does not matter if they are of different types. The state, by hypothesis, cannot distinguish them anyway. People *choose* their income in the face of the tax schedule, by choosing the number of hours they work. In this sense all are treated equally. They are treated unequally if they *reveal* themselves to be different, in the sense of earning different incomes. But the choice is there.

Second, this mode of decentralisation—the one associated with the use of the optimum income tax—is a necessity prompted by the limited information at the disposal of the government. It is not solely a moral requirement. There is no command system which can achieve the outcome resulting from the imposition of the optimal income tax. Given the limited information that the government has been taken to possess all command modes of planning will result in lower social welfare.

Now, the imposition of the optimum income tax introduces what economists call a "distortion" into the economy. The resulting allocation of utilities (scheme II in Figure 1; see also Table 1) is not Pareto efficient: that is, it is possible to imagine technologically feasible alternative allocations of leisure and consumption across persons that result in higher utility to all. This brings me to the third point, namely, that, while indeed there are such *technologically* feasible allocations, because of the limited information at the disposal of the government and because of the incentives problem, such allocations cannot be implemented. That is to say, such allocations are not *informationally* feasible. This implies that the imposition of the optimum tax schedule results in what one might call an "informationally constrained" Pareto efficient allocation. That this is so can be easily confirmed. For, given the limited information of the disposal of the government, if there were an informationally feasible alternative allocation that made all better off, it would lead to a higher sum of utility levels; in which case the income tax schedule being considered would not be the (utilitarian) optimum income tax schedule!

I come now to the final case I wish to consider; one where the government can observe not only a person's income, but also the number of hours he works. But I continue to assume that the government does not know who is of what intrinsic ability (or skill). As the reader will recognise, this case eschews the moral hazard problem but retains the adverse selection feature. This is what makes the problem interesting. It is clear that a utilitarian government will in

---

*It is not difficult to produce models in which the optimum income tax schedule has a random component; that is, the schedule may say, to give an example, that if a person earns £10,000 a year he is liable to an income tax of £2,000 with probability ¼ and £3,000 with probability ¾. In this case, of course, two people earning the same income will not necessarily pay the same tax. That is, ex-post, the principle of horizontal equity is violated here, but not ex-ante. See Stiglitz 1976 and Maskin 1981 for a discussion of optimal random taxation. In the text I am assuming that the optimum income tax does not have a random component.

TABLE 1. Summary of outcomes possible for a utilitarian government. In all cases it is assumed that government knows the (identical) utility function, and the number of persons in each skill (ability) category. Person of ability n can choose labour time l and output y satisfying the relation $y \leq nl$. U_n denotes the utility level of person with intrinsic skill, or ability, level n.

Variables government can observe	Type of optimum	Optimum tax/subsidy based on	Distribution of utilities
y, n	full optimum (Pareto efficient)	true skill (ability), n	for all n and n' with $n > n'$, $U^{n'} > U^n$. (scheme IV in diagram)
y	second-best (informationally constrained Pareto efficient)	income, y	$U^n > U^{n'}$ for all n and n' satisfying $n > n'$ (scheme II in diagram)
y, l	second-best and Pareto efficient (identical to full-optimum for Rawlsian government)	'revealed' ability (or skill) y/l	$U^n = U^{n'}$ for all n, n' (scheme III in diagram)

this case be able to achieve more than it can with the optimal income tax, but typically will still not be able to achieve the *full* utilitarian optimum, since people can pretend and act as though they are of lower ability than they actually are. As we noted earlier, the point is that a person of skill level, say $\bar{n}$, *can*, if he works for l hours, produce output y given by $y = \bar{n}l$. But, should he choose to do so, he can also work below par at any ability level n less than $\bar{n}$ and produce output equal to nl. The government can, by assumption, monitor only y and l. Thus it cannot catch a person working below par if the person finds it in his interest to do so. Dasgupta and Hammond (1980) and Mirrlees (1981) have shown that the best that a utilitarian government can guarantee to be achieved under this information structure is the *maximum uniform* distribution of utilities that is technologically feasible (scheme III in the diagram).* The second of the emphasised adjectives characterising this second-best utilitarian

*The tax-subsidy scheme which enables this second-best optimum to be realised in a decentralised manner is discussed in Dasgupta and Hammond 1980. The tax/subsidy on a person is based on the ability level the person chooses to display; that is, on the value of y/l the government observes in his case. Quite obviously, this allocation cannot be implemented by a command system.

optimum says that all individuals attain the same utility level, and the first implies that the allocation is Pareto efficient in the full sense of the term.* But these two characteristics suggest at once that his second-best utilitarian optimum is in fact the *full* optimum for a government wedded to Professor Rawls' Difference Principle. This is indeed so. That is to say, in the economy we are discussing a Rawlsian government loses nothing if it cannot observe a person's intrinsic ability but can instead observe the number of hours he works. A utilitarian government does lose something: it has to switch from scheme IV to scheme III in the diagram. It is in this sense that unlike the Utilitarian Principle the Difference Principle is "incentive-compatible."†

4 Professor Hayek on Progress and Freedom

Utilitarianism is a consequentialist philosophy, and in the previous two sections I have consciously defined consequences in a very narrow manner—the allocation of goods and services and, by implication, the allocation of utilities. In this essay I have also, consciously, looked at the instrumental role of individual discretion—or the liberty to make certain decisions. I have not taken into account the innate rights that persons may possess to such freedom. I have tried to argue that, contrary to Hayek's view, certain forms of individual discretion are not only not inconsistent with the goals of distributive justice, they must be encouraged if one were to promote distributive justice. I wish now to argue that despite his well-known libertarian views Hayek is very much a consequentialist, and that the value he attaches to individualism in general, and unbridled market forces in particular, is entirely instrumental in origin, and that he is loath to explain why it is instrumental in promoting the goal that he seeks.

Hayek's individualism springs from the fact that a good deal of information in society is not publicly know. For he observes that "practically every individual has some advantage over all others because he possesses unique information of which beneficial use might be made, but of which use can be made only if the decisions depending on it are left to him or are made with his active cooperation" (Hayek 1945, pp. 521–3). If Nozick talks of voluntary transfers and leaves the matter at that, Hayek continually extols the virtues of the spontaneous play of market forces, and in particular the price mechanism. For in his classic essay on the use of knowledge in society he says, "We

---

*Since all attain the same utility level a person gains nothing by working below par. Admittedly he loses nothing either. But we make the innocuous assumption that a person will always choose to work at this intrinsic ability level if he loses nothing by doing so. Thus at this second-best optimum the government can infer the true skill of each person by observing his chosen y and l. But it cannot, obviously, make use of this inference to establish the full-optimum!

†Maskin (1980) has recently demonstrated this last claim in a wider class of economic models than the one I have been analysing in this section.

must look at the price system as ... a mechanism for communicating information if we want to understand its real function ... The most significant fact about this system is the economy of knowledge with which it operates, or how little the individual participants need to know in order to be able to take the right action. In abbreviated form, by a kind of symbol, only the most essential information is passed on and passed on only to those concerned. It is more than a metaphor to describe the price system as a ... system of telecommunications which enables individual producers to watch merely the movement of a few pointers" (Hayek 1945, pp. 526–7).

It can immediately be argued that the fact that much information is private is not on its own sufficient to warrant the unfettered play of market forces to be judged the best possible resource allocation mechanism. If in pointing to the privacy of information all that Hayek intends to assert is that a government ought not to pretend that it knows more than it actually does, or that a social organisation ought to encourage individuals to exploit some of their private information, the point is obviously well taken. But, of course, Hayek intends to assert a great deal more than just that. The problem is that the only alternative to the unfettered play of market forces that Hayek is really willing to consider is an institution in which the government decides everything. For he says at one point, "The concentration of all decisions in the hands of authority itself produces a state of affairs in which what structure society still possesses is imposed upon it by government and in which the individuals have become interchangeable units with no other definite or durable relations to one another than those determined by the all-comprehensive organisation" (Hayek 1948, p. 27). Faced with this as the only alternative it is no wonder that the market mechanism wins hands down. But as the examples I discussed earlier suggested, there are other mechanisms which acknowledge the privacy of a great deal of knowledge and whose outcomes are superior—in the light of the chosen criterion of welfare—to that of the market mechanism. One should note also that the maximisation of a given criterion of social justice does not entail that the state would not wish to rely on prices as an essential ingredient in the mechanism which is chosen.

Hayek would have us believe that the demands of social justice necessitate a fully command system. In this, I have tried to argue, he is wrong. He rejects the claims of distributive justice because he thinks they conflict with individual liberty. But his defence of individual liberty would appear to be based on instrumental considerations. For, in his influential treatise, *The Constitution of Liberty*, Hayek makes clear that the end that he seeks, and what in his mind a spontaneous market process will achieve, is *progress*; and, he says, "progress [is] a process of formation and modification of human intellect, a process of adaptation and learning in which not only the possibilities known to us but also our values and desires continually change" (Hayek 1960,

p. 40); and furthermore that "The changes to which ... people must submit are part of the cost of progress, an illustration of the fact that not only the mass of men but, strictly speaking, every human being is led by the growth of civilisation into a path that is not his own choosing" (Hayek 1960, p. 50).

What is disturbing is not so much the fact that Hayek in his treatise ultimately produces no argument for the supposition that unbridled market forces are the right ones for generating progress, but rather the belief he holds that he has no obligation to provide us with an argument. His escape route is complete; he does not pretend to understand the market mechanism and warns all not to try. For in an earlier article he says that "[true individualism] is a product of an acute consciousness of the limitations of the individual mind which induces an attitude of humility towards the impersonal and anonymous social processes by which individuals help to create things greater than they know" (Hayek 1948, p. 8). Is there any prescription other than that we ought to be humble before this mystical force—the spontaneous process of the market mechanism? There is, for Professor Hayek talks of "the necessity, in any complex society in which the effects of anyone's action reach far beyond his possible range of vision, of the individual *submitting to the anonymous and seemingly irrational forces of society*" (Hayek 1948, p. 24, emphasis mine). If one asks "why," Professor Hayek has a ready answer, one which I alluded to earlier. For he says, "Man in a complex society can have no choice but between adjusting himself to what to him must seem the blind forces of the social process and obeying the orders of a superior" (Hayek 1948, p. 24).

Such an anti-rational view, disagreeable though it may be to many, is still not the most disturbing feature of Hayek's philosophy. Ultimately, it seems to me, what is most disturbing is the degree of authoritarianism that he would appear to be willing to tolerate for the sake of his conception of progress. Indeed, Hayek appears to be willing to renounce individual liberty if that were to be found *useful* to society. For he says, "the case for individual freedom rests chiefly on the recognition of the inevitable ignorance of all of us concerning a great many of the factors on which the achievement of our ends and welfare depends. If there were omniscient men, if we could know not only all that effects the attainment of our present wishes but also our future wants and desires, there would be little case for liberty ... what is important is not what freedom I personally like to exercise but what freedom some person may need in order to do things beneficial for society" (Hayek 1960, pp. 29, 32); and, furthermore, "*if the result of individual liberty did not demonstrate that some manners of living are more successful than others, much of the case for it would vanish*" (Hayek 1960, p. 85, emphasis mine).

Some of Hayek's views are so astonishing that it is hard to believe that he takes them seriously. For example, he seems to think that just as we cannot talk of the "justice" or "injustice" of a drought (a blind act of nature), we cannot use the adjective "just" or "unjust" on the allocation arising from the free-play of market forces. No one, after all, has *consciously* willed such an allocation.* Quite apart from the fact that this last would be the case in any social organisation in which the outcome depends on the actions chosen by everyone, and that "chosen" by Mother Nature, whether to leave society to the mercies of the free-play of market forces is itself a social decision. But while he is convinced that the question as to whether the distribution of incomes resulting from the competitive process is just has no meaning, he certainly approves of whatever distribution results—for the process, in his mind, is fair. If in the unconscious pursuit of progress the economy is littered with the debris of the unsuccessful, it would not seem to matter. The successful few are "the first sign of a new way of living begun by the advance guard" (Hayek 1960, p. 130). Is there a reward scheme he favours? There is, for at one point he says, "The fact is, of course, that we do not wish people to earn a maximum of merit but to achieve a maximum of usefulness at a minimum of pain and sacrifice and therefore a minimum of merit" (Hayek, 1960, p. 96). Comment is superfluous.

5 *Authority and Individual Discretion*

All social organisations operate under a mixed system of commands and individual discretion. Even in a hierarchical structure of authority, such as a firm, each member is allowed a certain amount of discretion. As has been emphasised by Simon (1957) even an employment contract has built within it the agreement that the employer will expect obedience from the employee for certain forms of command, such as the assignment of tasks. But in all cases the employee too can exercise a certain amount of discretion—in the manner in which he undertakes these tasks. In this essay I have tried to emphasise that a central reason why such discretion is desirable from the point of view of the goals of an organisation is the differences in the information that its members possess. When the goals of every member of the organisation coincide there is an advantage in allowing for individual discretion, as the work of Marschak and Radner (1972) implies. This remains true when the goals differ, as the discussion in section 3 makes clear. Furthermore, there is a case for individual discretion simply because an individual's genuine productivity may be weakened if he is under command—a possibility I have ignored in the formal account of sections 2 and 3. It can be argued that an employee, in signing an employment contract—and therefore committing himself to obeying certain commands—does so voluntarily. But his alternative options may be severely limited in an economy with a large dispersion

*See Hayek 1960, p. 99 and 1976, pp. 62–96.

of income and wealth. When the state subsidises one member with the tax collected from another, then, other things remaining the same, the set of options of the first is increased and that of the second is decreased. There is a transference of rights from one to the other. Admittedly, it can be argued, as recently by Nozick (1974), that such redistribution of purchasing power violates individual rights to the actual goods and services that they are historically entitled to. In this essay I have not attempted to evaluate this argument. Instead, I have approached the problem from a different end and have ignored rights, excepting for the right to have one's own welfare given weight in the social calculus. The arguments developed in this essay imply that certain forms of individual discretion—that is, empowering individuals to choose from certain sets of actions—is instrumental in promoting the end of social-welfare. To be sure, there are special circumstances, such as during an emergency, when it will be found *useful* to rely on a command system, such as the rationing of goods during a war or a famine. But even here it will often be better, from the point of view of social welfare, to allow individuals, should they wish, to engage in trade with their rations. And the reason here is the same as the one explored in section 3—the fact that not all private information is publicly known.

All this is not to say that the claims of distributive justice cannot conflict with individual rights. They can, and an enormous literature, both in political philosophy and economics, bears witness to this. But not all rights are equally compelling. In any case, I have not attempted to discuss precisely which rights are instrumental in promoting distributive justice in an economy with dispersed information. They will clearly vary from case to case. My aim has been to argue that a pure command system, narrowly defined, it not the optimum mode of organisation even from the point of view of distributive justice.

BIBLIOGRAPHY

Allingham, M., 1975, "Towards an Ability Tax," *Journal of Public Economics*, 4, pp. 361–76.

Arrow, K.J., 1977, "Extended Sympathy and the Possibility of Social Choice," *American Economic Review*, Supplementary issue of the Proceedings, pp. 219–25.

Dasgupta, P., 1980, "Decentralization and rights," *Economica*, 47, no. 186, pp. 107–24.

Dasgupta, P. and Hammond, P., 1980, "Fully Progressive Taxation," *Journal of Public Economics*, 13, pp. 141–54.

Dasgupta, P., Hammond, P. and Maskin, E., 1979, "The Implementation of Social Choice Rules: Some General Results on Incentive Compatibility," *Review of Economic Studies*, 46, no. 2, pp. 185–216.

Dworkin, Ronald, 1977, *Taking Rights Seriously*, Cambridge, Mass.: also London: Duckworth, 1977. A new impression (corrected) with an appendix came out in 1978, Duckworth.

Hammond, P.J., 1976a, "Changing Tastes and Coherent Dynamic Choice," *Review of Economic Studies*, 43, pp. 159–73.

_____, 1976b, "Equity, Arrow's Conditions and Rawls' Difference Principle," *Econometrica* 44, pp. 793–800. Reprinted in Hahn and Hollis 1979.

_____, 1980, "Some Uncomfortable Options in Welfare Economics Under Uncertainty," Stanford University mimeo.

_____, 1981a, "Liberalism, Independent Rights and the Pareto Principle," in *Logic, Methodology and the Philosophy of Science*, edited by L.J. Cohen, J. T'os, H. Pfeiffer and K.-P. Podewski, Amsterdam: North-Holland, vol. VI, chapter 45. pp. 221–34.

_____, 1981b, "Ex-Post Optimality as a Consistent Objective for Collective Choice Under Uncertainty," Economics Technical Report, Institute for Mathematical Studies in the Social Sciences, Stanford University.

_____, 1981c, "Consistent Dynamic Choice Under Uncertainty and Bayesian Rationality," Economics Technical Report, Institute for Mathematical Studies in the Social Sciences, Stanford University.

_____, 1981d, "On Welfare Economics with Incomplete Information and the Social Value of Public Information," Economics Technical Report, Institute for Mathematical Studies in the Social Sciences, Stanford University.

Hayek, F. von, 1945, "The Use of Knowledge in Society," *American Economic Review*, 35, pp. 519–30.

_____, 1948, *Individualism and Economic Order*, Indiana: Gateway Edition.

_____, 1960, *The Constitution of Liberty*, London: Routledge & Kegan Paul.

_____, 1976, *The Mirage of Social Justice: Law, Legislation Liberty*, vol. 2, London: Routledge & Kegan Paul.

Hurwicz, L., 1972, "On Informationally Decentralized Systems," in *Decision and Organization*, edited by C.B. McGuire and R. Radner, Amsterdam: North-Holland, ch. 14, pp. 297–336. Also in *Studies in Resource Allocation Processes*, pp. 425–59, edited by K.J. Arrow and L. Hurwicz, Cambridge: Cambridge University Press, 1977.

Kant, Immanuel, 1785, *Grundlegung zur Metaphysik der Sitten*, translated by H.J. Paton as *The Moral Law*, London: Hutchinson, 1948.

_____, 1803, *Pädogogik*, translated as *On Education*, Ann Arbor, Michigan, 1960.

Laffont, J.J. (ed.), 1979, *Aggregation and Revelation of Preferences*, Amsterdam: North-Holland Publishing Co.

Laffont, J.J. and Maskin, E., 1981, "The Theory of Incentives: An Overview," mimeo., University of Cambridge.

Lerner, A.P., 1944, *The Economics of Control*, London and New York: Macmillan.

Malinvaud, E., 1972, *Microeconomic Theory*, Amsterdam: North-Holland.

Marschak, J. and Radner, R., 1972, *Economic Theory of Teams*, New Haven: Yale University Press.

Mas-Colell, A., 1978, "An Axiomatic Approach to the Efficiency of Non-cooperative Equilibrium in Economics with a Continuum of Traders," IMSSS Technical Report No. 274, Stanford University.

Maskin, E., 1980, "On First-Best Taxation," in *Limits of Redistribution*, edited by W.R.C. Lecomber.

_____, 1981, "Randomization in the Principal-Agent Problem," mimeo, Cambridge University.

Meade, J.E., 1964, *Efficiency, Equality and the Ownership of Property*, London: George Allen & Unwin.

Mirrlees, J.A., 1971, "An Exploration in the Theory of Optimum Income Taxation," *Review of Economic Studies*, 38, pp. 175–208.

_____, 1974, "Notes on Welfare Economics, Information and Uncertainty," in *Essays on Economic Behaviour Under Uncertainty*, edited by M.S. Balch, D. McFadden and S.Y. Wu, Amsterdam: North-Holland.

_____, 1981, "The Theory of Optimal Taxation," in *Handbook of Mathematical Economics*, edited by K.J. Arrow and M. Intriligator, Amsterdam: North-Holland.

Nozick, R., 1974, *Anarchy, State and Utopia*, New York: Basic Books; Oxford: 1978, *Strategy and Group Choice*, Amsterdam: North-Holland.

Rawls, John, 1971, *A Theory of Justice*, Cambridge, Mass.: Harvard University Press. Also published by Oxford University Press, 1972.

Sen, A.K., 1970a, *Collective Choice and Social Welfare*, San Francisco: Holden Day. Also London: Oliver and Boyd, 1970.

_____, 1976, "Liberty, Unanimity and Rights," *Economica*, 43, pp. 217–46.

Sidgwick, Henry, 1962, *Methods of Ethics*, 7th edition (reissue), London: Macmillan.

Simon, H., 1957, *Models of Man*, New York: John Wiley & Sons.

_____, 1960, *The New Science of Management Decision*, New York: Harper & Brothers.

Stiglitz, J.E., 1976, "Utilitarianism and Horizontal Equity: The Case for Random Taxation," *IMSSS Technical Report No. 214*, Stanford University.

Strotz, R.H., 1956, "Myopia and Inconsistency in Dynamic Utility Maximization," *Review of Economic Studies*, 23, pp. 165–80.

Weitzman, M., 1978, "Optimal Rewards for Economic Regulation," *American Economic Review*, 68, pp. 683–91.

Communications Privacy: Implications for Network Design

Marc Rotenberg

To think that a bit of paper, containing our most secret thoughts, and protected only by a seal, should travel safely from one end of the world to the other, without anyone whose hands it had passed through having meddled with it. —*Ralph Waldo Emerson (1803–1882)*

The American jurist Louis Brandeis described the right of privacy "as the most comprehensive of all rights and the right most cherished by civilized men." The French political theorist Francis Lieber praised "The sacredness of epistolary communion." Privacy has been described by some as the "kernal of freedom" and the right from which other freedoms flow.

The roots of privacy protection go at least as far back as the Athenian democracy. The Greek statesman Pericles described the virtues of a private life, free from public scrutiny. In a famous oration before the people of Athens, Pericles extolled the virtues of democratic society and then stated, "Not only do we conduct our public life as free people but we carry the same spirit in our daily relations with one another. We are not angry with our neighbor if he does what pleases him, and we don't glare at him for his harmless actions even if they are an annoyance to some."

Although privacy as a legal right is traditionally associated with Western liberal countries, privacy is also described in the literature of many countries around the world. So widespread is the desire for privacy protection that several of the recently established democratic governments in Eastern Europe and the former Soviet Union have included the right of privacy in their new constitutions.

The protection of privacy is the central concern for a communications network. Communications privacy allows users to transfer information that might otherwise not be disclosed. Where privacy cannot be assured, the value of a communications network diminishes significantly and users are likely to seek other channels to exchange information. In a properly functioning network, the protection of confidentiality should be assumed. Exceptions should arise only in extraordinary circumstances.

Communication services are more highly valued when privacy can be assured. Where privacy protection falls below a certain threshold, migration from the network is likely to occur since privacy assurance allows organizations to retain control of trade secrets and details of business operations. Anonymity may also increase economic risk-taking since certain investments may be curtailed if the identity of the investors is known.

A difficult social question, and an intriguing economic problem, is whether it would be efficient to charge users for privacy protection. It is conceivable that privacy protection could be priced for users along a spectrum so that the protection of a message would be in direct proportion to the price charged. However, such schemes might introduce new transaction costs and create inefficiencies if they require users to conduct additional negotiations where two parties do not enjoy the same level of protection. Multiple levels of privacy protection might also lead to unnecessary segmentation, particularly in networks that are intended for broad public use.

Communications Privacy

The protection of communications privacy is a subset of privacy protection that is concerned primarily with the exchange of personal information between multiple parties. Traditional models for communications privacy are based on the exchange of information between two parties, though in computer network environments, messages are oftentimes exchanged between multiple parties. This trend toward message exchange among multiple parties reflects in part the transition from a time when a physical message, such as a letter, was transferred from one party to another to the current era where electronic messages are routinely sent to multiple parties.

In communications networks, the right of privacy might be delineated into three separate interests: confidentiality, anonymity, and data protection.

Confidentiality. This refers to the expectation that information will be moved between two parties without disclosure to a third party. A confidential communication exhibits the property that its content and existence is know only to the parties to the communication. Assuming that a communication is confidential, subsequent disclosure can be attributed to either the sender or the recipient of the message. Where a communication occurs between multiple parties, the expectation of confidentiality may be diminished as it is more difficult to determine who is responsible for subsequent disclosure.

The legal basis for confidentiality has several roots. There are special relationships where the guarantee of a legal right of privacy is considered necessary to strengthen a social relationship and to promote the exchange of personal information. In the common law countries, such as the U.S. and the U.K., these relationships may include communications between lawyer and client, wife and husband, and doctor and patient. Additional areas where common law recognizes an interest in protecting communications is banking and other forms of trusteeship. Sometimes these obligations are expressed through legislative enactment, such as the Electronic Communications Privacy Act, a law that restricts the circumstances when an e-mail service provider may disclose private e-mail.

Anonymity. Anonymity is the right of an individual to decide whether to disclose his or her identity to another. The right of anonymity is an important element of privacy protection. Privacy includes the ability to decide when and under what circumstances to disclose identity. In public settings, anonymity may protect the ability of individuals to move freely and without obstruction. Anonymity is also associated with the freedom to express unpopular views.

In many settings, the disclosure of identity is not a necessary condition for communications, or even for a business transaction. For example, a person who calls a government agency for information or a business to inquire about a product need not disclose her identity. Similarly, network users who "ftp" a site typically don't need to disclose their identity. In some circumstances, services may require that anonymity be preserved to be viable. Health services for those needing assistance with alcohol, drugs, depression, unexpected pregnancy, or sexual identity may rely on a promise to guarantee anonymity to ensure the viability of the service.

In some network settings, anonymity may be a difficult principle to protect. Access to information resources may require the disclosure of identity to promote security. However, for currency-based service delivery, the identity may be withheld if a mechanism exists to exchange information for value. Public payphones that use either cash or telephone cards (not credit cards or "calling" cards) are examples of widely available communications service that provide anonymity.

Data Protection. This refers to those principles regarding the collection, use, and disclosure of personal information. Data protection principles were originally developed for the protection of personal information contained in discrete record systems. Over time, data protection principles have been extended to communications networks. These principles are discussed in more detail in the section on the OECD Guidelines.

A fourth interest has been raised in the context of communications networks but may not play a substantial role in future network environments. This is the interest in seclusion, sometimes called "the right to be let along." The reason this interest may become less significant over time is that network messaging design have all tended toward the batching of requests. In telephone networks, dedicated phone answering machines and voice mail systems allow users to group messages and to respond at a convenient time. However, targeted advertising, based on user profiles, may become more intrusive than other forms of advertising. Communications technologies that may raise intrusion problems include those requiring a real-time response, such as beepers.

Exceptions of Privacy Protection

National law and international treaties generally recognize certain exceptions to the protection of privacy. These exceptions proceed from the assumption that communications privacy is absolute except where there is legal authority to intercept a message or to obtain information about the record of the message.

The first exception is when consent is obtained from the person whose personal information would not otherwise be disclosed. When the information refers to a record that is linked to a single individual, such as a medical history or a financial record, consent need only be obtained from the record subject. However, when the information concerns the existence or content of an electronic communication, then consent is more problematic. In some countries, it is permissible to obtain consent from only one party to the communication. In other countries, both parties must grant consent. In the U.S., there are states that observe both "one-party" and "two-party" consent rules. Since the "two-party" consent rule protects the privacy interests of both parties, it is generally preferred.

The second exception is for criminal investigations. In such cases, a government agent may seek to obtain records of communications, to monitor communications, or to restrict the use of communications networks. In many countries such investigations may be undertaken only in the context of a specific criminal matter and pursuant to authority of an independent agency. Constitutional governments generally prohibit by law the unrestricted gathering of electronic communications.

Overly broad searches through electronic record systems typically elicit strong public criticism. In one widely reported incident in the U.S., the police searched through the records of 803,000 phone users in a large metropolitan area to determine who had called a particular reporter regarding the misconduct of a large company. The head of the company, who initiated the investigation, later expressed regret for his decision.

The third exception is for the maintenance of the network. Thus, electronic service providers are permitted to monitor communications on a limited basis to test network services and to ensure the continued operation of the network. A related exception is the right to disclose information when it is "necessary" to render the service. For example, a communications carrier may be required to transfer information about a call to another carrier so that the call may be completed, or to send billing information to another party for delivery to the customer. This may be considered necessary to render the service.

Content and Record Distinction

In communications networks, both legal and technical protection distinguish between the content of a message and the record of a message. In a telephone network, for example, the content of a telephone call is rarely disclosed while transactional information may be more freely available. This is an area of considerable dispute. In the U.S., the Supreme Court has said that a telephone call is entitled to a reasonable expectation of privacy, however, the numbers a caller dials are not entitled to similar protection. Following the Supreme Court's decision, Congress determined that such information should be entitled to protection and a law was passed in 1986, the Electronic Communications Privacy Act, to accomplish this goal.

The retention and disclosure of transactional information for telecommunications networks is also a matter of differing opinion. In the U.S., telephone companies routinely disclose detailed billing information to customers. These records include the date and time of call, the location of the call, and the amount charged.

This practice is not generally followed by other service providers. In Europe, for example, detailed billing information is not available or where it is available, the last four digits are not disclosed. NTT in Japan offers a range of privacy options for customers. Customers may choose to receive complete call detail information, partial call detail information, or no call detail information at all.

Regarding the retention and disclosure of this information, there are competing consumer and privacy interests. It is believed that the delivery of this information provides consumers with better accounting for network usage, and, where multiple carriers offer services, to select more competitive options.

This information also permits companies to monitor network usage and to assign costs to clients where appropriate.

Forms of Protection

In the area of privacy protection, schemes may be divided between technical and legal forms of protection. Technical forms seek to reduce the risk of interception of communication, unauthorized access to records of communications, or to conceal the identities of the parties to a communication. Technical schemes also include design principles, policies, and practices.

Legal forms of protection establish rights that are enforceable in law. These rights typically allow for the recoupment of damages from private parties, criminal fines, or restrictions on the use of the unlawfully gathered information where the transgression occurs by the government.

Legal protections are likely to clarify the underlying privacy interests, but are also likely to encounter problems in practice where messages move between different countries and through different jurisdictions. For this reason, technical safeguards are particularly important for international networks.

European phone systems, as well as networks in Japan, Australia and South America, make extensive use of "phone cards." These are value-added cards that may be used to purchase telecommunication services. They are transferable and contain no personally identifiable information.

From a communications privacy viewpoint, phone cards are a good technology. They protect anonymity since they do not require the disclosure of the user's identity. They also satisfy data protection goals since no personally identifiable information is generated. With regard to confidentiality, phone card networks do not necessarily provide any greater protection than other networks. However, since the identity of a particular user would be difficult to determine, the likelihood of interception is diminished.

Phone cards diminish vandalism, reduce repair requirements, and can even be sold for advertising. Regarding this last benefit, NTT in Japan prints a wide range of cards for advertising purposes and British Telecommunications prints advertising for the Wimbledon tennis championships and Hilton hotels on the face of the cards.

Cryptography

One of the primary methods to promote communications privacy is cryptography. This is the procedure of taking a plaintext communication and then encoding it into cyphertext. Messages encoded in this manner should be useful to only the sender and the intended recipient.

All cryptographic schemes rely upon a "key." The key allows the person in possession of the message to decode it. Broadly speaking, there are two different key encryption schemes. The first is the private key scheme. The second approach is the public key scheme.

The private key scheme relies on the existence of a single, secret key which is used both to encrypt and decrypt messages. An example of private key encryption (PKE) is the Digital Encryption Standard (DES), which is a popular secret-key encryption algorithm originally released in 1977 by the National Bureau of Standards in the U.S. It was the first cryptographic algorithm openly developed by the U.S. government. The problem with DES and PKEs generally is transferring the key. There must be a pre-existing channel to transfer the keys which is itself secure.

In the public key scheme a user has both a public key, which is published in a directory similar to a phonebook, and a private key, from which the public key is derived. This has an advantage over private key systems since it is not necessary to exchange keys before messages can be decrypted. A popular public key system is RSA.

A related use for cryptography is the authentication of messages. Using public key encryption, a user can encrypt a message using his or her own private key. The recipient of the message can then determine the authenticity of the messages by using the sender's public key.

To be effective, standards must be established so that users in different networks will be able to exchange messages. Anything less than a full implementation makes it inconvenient and inefficient for users and reduces use and diminishes privacy. Because there are strong incentives to interconnect networks, it is expected that standards for encryption will develop rapidly.

A separate problem in the deployment of cryptographic methods is the prospect that national governments will seek to restrict privacy-enhancing technologies where they conflict with communications surveillance activities.

Legal Agreements and Policies

Many current policies for communications protection follow from international agreements developed for the general purpose of date protection. These international instruments include the Organization for Economic Cooperation and Development (OECD) Guidelines of the Protection of Privacy and Transborder Flow of Personal Data. The Council of Europe's Convention for the Protection of Individuals with Regard to the Automatic Processing of Personal Data, and the United Nations Universal Declaration on Human Rights, particularly Clause 12. More recently, the European nations have sought to develop a harmonized framework for data protection throughout the European

Community. It is likely that this directive will have a substantial impact on the development of international privacy policy.

OECD Guidelines

In 1978 the OECD, which is made up of two dozen countries including much of Europe, the U.S., Canada, Japan and Australia, instructed a Group of Experts to develop Guidelines on basic rules governing the transborder flow and the protection of personal data and privacy. The initiative was based on the belief that disparities in national privacy legislation might create obstacles to the free flow of information between countries, thus having serious repercussion on the economies of the OECD Member States. The principle aim of these guidelines was to facilitate the harmonization of the national legislation of OECD Member States.

The OECD Guidelines on the Protection of Privacy and Transborder Flow of Personal Data were adopted in 1980 and are today generally considered the primary reference for international agreements for privacy and data protection. The guidelines incorporate eight basic principles.

- The Collection Limitation Principle states that the collection of personal data should be obtained by lawful and fair means and with the knowledge and consent of the record subject.
- The Data Quality Principle states that personal data should be relevant to the purposes for which they are to be used, and should be accurate, complete, and timely.
- The Purpose Specification Principle states that the purpose for which personal data are collected should be specified not later than at the time of data collection and the subsequent use should be limited to those purposes.
- The Use Limitation Principle states that personal data should not be disclosed for secondary purposes except with the consent of the data subject or by authority of law.
- The Security Safeguards Principle states that personal data should be protected by reasonable security safeguards against such risks as loss or unauthorized access, destruction, use, or disclosure of data.
- The Openness Principle states that there should be a general practice of openness about developments, practices and polices with respect to personal data. Means should be readily available of establishing the existence and nature of personal data, and the main purposes of their use.
- The Individual Participation Principle states that data subjects should be allowed to inspect and correct personal data.

- The Accountability Principle states that a data controller should be held accountable for complying with measures which give effect to the preceding principles.

Taken together, these principles are intended to ensure that those organizations which collect personal data will take appropriate steps to safeguard personal information.

Although the OECD Guidelines are widely followed by public and private organizations around the world, several criticisms have been expressed. These include the absence of a clear enforcement mechanism, inadequate attention to commercial incentives to sell personal data, and no consideration of misuse of personal identifiers.

The Council of Europe Convention

In 1981 the Council of Europe adopted the Convention for the Protection of Individuals with Regard to Automatic Processing of Personal Data. The Convention incorporates principles similar to the OECD Guidelines. The Convention states that "Personal data to be automatically processed shall be: (a) obtained and processed fairly and lawfully, (b) stored for specified and legitimate purposes and not used in a way incompatible with those purposes, (c) adequate, relevant, and not excessive for the purposes for which they are maintained, (d) accurate, and where necessary, kept up to date, and (e) preserved in a form which permits identification of the data subject for no longer than required for the purposes for which those data are kept."

The Convention is not intended to be a self-executing document. The goal is to encourage countries to develop privacy legislation in accordance with the principles formulated in the Convention.

Universal Declaration of Human Rights

The Universal Declaration of Human Rights was proclaimed by the United Nations General Assembly in 1946. It is a powerful statement of the global aspiration of respect for human rights and expresses general principles of international law. Its provisions have been incorporated in many constitutions around the world.

Article 12 of the Universal Declaration states that "No one shall be subjected to arbitrary interference with his privacy, family, home or correspondence, nor to attacks upon his honour and reputation. Everyone has the right to the protection of the law against such interference or attacks."

One privacy concern that grows out of the Universal Declaration which may have some bearing on privacy protection and the use of identifiers in communications networks is the protection of personal names and identity. For example, where national governments seek to impose the use of a universal identifier, such as a Personal Identification Number (PIN) or Social Security Number (SSN), concern has been expressed that this will undermine cultural identity and the freedom of minority groups.

EC Directive

As the European Community moves toward a harmonized economic system with a single currency and a federated government, the member nations have indicated a commitment to develop a single framework to protect the transborder flow of personal data. The Commission of the European Communities has put forward a proposal concerning the protection of the individual in relation to the processing of personal data. It is an effort to build on the existing OECD Guidelines. It also seeks to create an enforcement mechanism and to establish rights for data subjects where companies seek to sell personal information.

The Draft Proposal Concerning the Protection of Personal Data in the Context of Public Digital Telecommunication Networks was promulgated by the Commission in 1990. The Commission stated that the "effective protection of personal data and privacy is developing into an essential precondition for social acceptance of the new digital networks and services." The Commission further said that privacy protection "must be an essential component of the Community's telecommunications policy which aims at securing for the European citizen the full benefits of advanced telecommunication services, as the Community moves towards an environment which will be substantially richer in information than before."

The directive contains several provisions which mirror the OECD Guidelines. It also includes certain additional measures. Telecommunications organizations are admonished not to store information after transmission except where required by law of a Member State. The directive requires that "Traffic data stored in the switching centers of the telecommunications organization must be erased after termination of the call unless the data are anonymized or are required for billing or other legitimate purposes." The directive recommends that itemized billing statement exclude the last four digits of the called number.

The directive makes two important recommendations for the "Caller ID" service. First, it states that subscribers should be able to withhold the disclosure of the subscriber's phone number through a "simple technical facility." Second, the directive indicates that the subscriber should be able to permanently withhold disclosure of the number when application is made. Third, the directive recommends that call recipients should be able to apply for permanent elimination of the identification of all incoming calls and must also be able to limit the acceptance of incoming calls to those which identify the calling subscriber's number. The directive permits the limited override of the calling party where the subscriber has received malicious calls or upon court order. In the case where the subscriber has received malicious calls, the directive indicates that caller identification information should be made available directly to the public authority charged with the prevention of criminal offenses. The directive also covers electronic recording and unsolicited communications.

MPT Proposal (Japan 1989)

The Ministry of Posts and Telecommunications (MPT) has developed a set of principles based on the OECD Guidelines for the protection of communications privacy. The Guidelines on the Protection of Personal Data in Telecommunication Business (1991) set out a framework for privacy protection and include several principles that would be useful for computer networks.

The guidelines began with a restatement of the Fair Collection principles: "The collection of personal data in connection with the provision of telecommunications services should be limited to the extent necessary to provide the intended service." There follows a set of principles, similar to the OECD Guidelines, that cover Collection of Data, Use and Disclosure of Data, Proper Management of Data, Access to Data, and Accountability.

It should also be noted that Japan has one of the strongest constitutional provisions regarding communications privacy. The Japanese Constitution states that "Freedom of assembly and association as well as speech, press and all other forms of expression are guaranteed. No censorship shall be maintained, nor shall the secrecy of any means of communication be violated."

National Law

Countries may develop through their legal systems certain procedures and customs to protect communications privacy. Traditionally these laws take the form of restrictions against wire surveillance by government agents. General laws for the protection of privacy are found throughout the world. These include the Privacy Protection Act (Japan), the Law on Informatic and Freedoms (France), Federal Data Protection Act (Germany), the Privacy Act (U.S.), the Data Protection Act (U.K.).

These laws vary in their scope, purpose, and impact. Some follow a data protections scheme, where a particular agency is charged with oversight of privacy protection. Others are not self-executing and rely upon enforcement through the court. There are also privacy laws that address particular subject areas. In the U.S., these include, records of cable subscribers, video tape purchases, and e-mail.

Quasi-Legal Protection

An additional category of protection includes professional codes of conduct, industry codes, and other forms of self-regulation. For instance, the ACM has an explicit code of conduct which covers the privacy of personal records. The American Library Association (ALA) does so as well.

The Code of Ethics and Professional Conduct for the ACM states that "An ACM member shall consider the health, privacy and general welfare of the public in the performance of the member's work." The guidelines further state that "An ACM member, whenever dealing with data concerning individuals, shall always consider the principle of individual privacy and seek the following: To minimize the data collected; To limit authorized access to the data; To provide proper security for the data; To determine the required retention period of the data; To ensure proper disposal of the data."

The preliminary code for the International Federation of Information Processing (IFIP) makes data protection a central provision of individual professional ethics: "Information Technology Professionals have a fundamental respect for the privacy and integrity of individuals, groups, and organizations. They are also aware that computerized invasion of privacy, without informed authorization and consent, is a major, continuing threat for potential abuse of individuals, groups, and populations. Public trust in informatics is contingent upon vigilant protection of established cultural and ethical norms of information privacy."

Some industries have developed codes of conduct for privacy protection to regulate activities by members. The Direct Marketing Association advises members that "An individual shall have the right to request whether personal data about him/her appear on a direct marketer's files and to receive a summary of the information within a reasonable time after the request is made. An individual has the right to challenge the accuracy of personal data relating to him/her. Personal data which are shown to be inaccurate should be corrected." (DMA Guidelines, Article 4)

However, there is a substantial question regarding the adequacy of these self-regulatory mechanisms. and particularly the DMA Guidelines. In 1990, when a direct marketing product was proposed that did not satisfy Article 4, the Direct Marketing Association took no action. Criticism of the product by consumer and privacy organizations led to the withdrawal of Lotus Marketplace.

Library organizations have developed the strongest voluntary code to protect personal privacy. This is not surprising. Libraries view the protection of confidentiality as a primary obligation of libraries.

The Code of Ethics for the American Library Association states that "Librarians must protect each user's right to privacy with respect to information sought or received, and materials consulted, borrowed, or acquired."

Library policies on record confidentiality should be considered in the design of network services.

U.S. Wiretap Law

The wiretap law in the U.S. is based on the premise that individuals have "an expectation of privacy" in electronic communications. The law requires that government agents obtain a special warrant from a court before an interception may be undertaken. The requirements for such a warrant are particularly rigorous, and the police must demonstrate that other investigative methods have been exhausted or could not succeed. The wiretap law also provides civil penalties where individuals conduct an illegal interception.

Today, the U.S. wiretap law stands as a model of how constitutional principles developed before telephones were invented and are carried forward into an era where computers are ubiquitous. The history of the wiretap law in the U.S. also reveals the curious twists and turns that occur in a legal system based on both judge-made law and legislative rule making. It also suggests how legal systems attempt to catch up to technological developments.

In 1928 the Supreme Court considered the question of whether the Fourth Amendment to the Constitution, which prohibits unauthorized searches and seizures, also restricted interception of telephone communications. The Supreme Court ruled that it did not, though Justice Brandeis, the author of a famous 1890 article on the right of privacy, dissented from the Court's opinion and said that the Constitution should protect new forms of communications. Partly in recognition of the concerns expressed by Justice Brandeis, when Congress passed the Communications Act of 1934 a provision was included which said, "No person not being authorized by the sender shall intercept any communications and divulge ... the contents." Then the Supreme Court ruled in 1938 that the Communications Act prohibited all telephone wiretapping, even when done by government officials. However, the Department of Justice said the law did not in fact restrict wiretapping by government agents. The President also issued an executive order which permitted wiretapping for national security purposes. As a result, wire surveillance was often undertaken without clear legal authority.

The next dramatic development occurred in 1967 when the Supreme Court, in a case called *Katz vs. United States*, reconsidered its 1928 opinion and decided the Fourth Amendment did protect telephone communications against interception. The following year Congress passed legislation to permit wire surveillance by law enforcement agents, but only when a number of conditions were satisfied, including a requirement that agents "minimize" the collection of information they obtain as a result of the wiretap. The law also said that communication service providers were expected to assist law enforcement in executing lawful warrants, but there was no expectation that telephone companies would design networks to facilitate wire surveillance.

Since passage of the 1968 law there have been several significant amendments. In 1978 the Foreign Intelligence Surveillance Act (FISA) was passed. This law established legal standards and procedures for the use of electronic surveillance in collecting foreign intelligence in the U.S. This was the first legislative authorization for foreign intelligence wiretapping and other forms of electronic surveillance.

In 1986 the U.S. wiretap law was again amended. This time to extend the protection in the law to new forms of communication, such as digital networks and e-mail. Provisions similar to those contained in the existing wiretap law were extended to new forms of communication.

Policy Frameworks

In the past several years several policy frameworks for the protection of communication privacy have been put forward. While these proposals do not carry the force of law, they set out useful principles that may be incorporated in future laws and technology designs.

During 1989 and 1990 the New York Public Service Commission studied privacy in telecommunications services. The proceeding was initiated by Commissioner Eli Noam who now heads the Columbia Institute for Tele-Information (CITI) at Columbia University.

The NYPSC proceeding has had a substantial impact on communications privacy policy in New York state and many other jurisdictions. Of particular interest were the factors identified by the Commission that have led to public interest in privacy protection, and the proposed privacy principles.

The study identified four factors that contribute to growing public concern about communications privacy. These are (1) the growth of electronic transactions, (2) the accelerated collection of personal information, (3) the dramatic increase in the number of communications carriers and service providers, and (4) the growing use of technically unsecured conduits for communications traffic, such as mobile communications.

The study then made several recommendations for future service offerings: (1) there should be no enforced reduction of network intelligence to protect privacy; (2) there should be adequate privacy protection for all users, "premium privacy" should be available for those with special needs; (3) privacy-promoting technologies should be encouraged; (4) users with needs for high levels of privacy should pay additional costs; (5) "The cost of restoring the status-quo in privacy protection should be borne by those who alter it," so that where a service such as "Caller ID" reduces the privacy of certain users, those subscribers who purchase the service should also carry the cost for re-establishing the privacy equilibrium; (6) privacy risks, particularly involving the disclosure of personal data, should be made known to users; (7) organizations that collect personal data should operate as "trustees" and protect the privacy rights of customers; and (8) there should be joint ownership on transaction-generated information.

Several of the NYPSC principles were later incorporated into a national communications privacy policy issued by the Minister of Communications in Canada in 1992.

Current Communication Privacy Concerns

In the past few years several issues have arisen in the area of communications privacy. Although these are new developments, several of the principles previously described help to clarify the underlying privacy interests at stake.

The offering of the Caller ID service in the U.S., Canada and several European countries raised public interest in communications privacy. The service permitted the communications carrier to sell the number of the originating caller to the call recipient.

Two different analytical views of the privacy implications of the service arose. Under one approach, the privacy issues were viewed as the weighing of two competing privacy interests. According to this analysis, the call recipient had a greater privacy interest because the call originator had "intruded" upon the recipient. However, this view failed to take account of communications to parties that lacked a clear privacy interest, such as calls to a business or a government agency, or to electronic recording devices, such as voice mail services and answering machines.

Under a second approach, the privacy interest was seen in terms of the transfer of control over personal information. Here the concern was the ability of the carrier to sell data generated by the communication. Viewed in this manner, the service was generally viewed as a privacy loss for network users since control over personal data would be diminished. An additional concern raised was that if service providers routinely transferred transactional information to a business who subscribed to the service, detailed profiles on users could be developed.

Regulatory authorities in the U.S. and Canada generally favored this second view and recommended strong restrictions on the use of the service. The policy debate surrounding Caller ID, and questions regarding the disclosure of personal data, are likely to continue as the service is offered in other countries in the near future.

One difficult problem that has arisen is the question of whether a network service provider should sell the transactional records resulting from an electronic communication. For example, in the U.S., several telephone companies sell lists to companies of callers to certain numbers. This is done to facilitate direct marketing.

Several privacy scholars have questioned this practice and recommended that a theory of joint ownership be developed so that any commercial benefit resulting from the sale of transactional records require the consent of both parties to the communication.

A related problem for communications privacy is the required disclosure of network information to competitors. In the U.S. it has been argued that competitive service delivery requires that network service providers disclose Consumer Proprietary Network Information (CPNI). While this policy may well promote the development of network services, it clearly has adverse consequences for privacy protection.

Government Restriction on Technology

There was a surprising development in the U.S. in 1992 when the Federal Bureau of Investigation put forward a legislative proposal to require all communications companies in the U.S. to design equipment so that remote wire surveillance could be undertaken.

The proposal was opposed by equipment manufacturers, service providers, and various privacy and civil liberties organizations. Criticisms of the proposal include the assessment that it would slow technical development, introduce new network vulnerabilities, increase costs for telephone customers, and increase the likelihood of wire surveillance by government agents.

Although it is unlikely that such legislation will be adopted in the U.S., it is foreseeable that national governments will seek to restrict development in communications technology. In the U.S. in April 1993, the White House announced a proposal for a split-key escrow cryptographic scheme that would allow the government to decrypt encrypted communications in voice networks. Several industry companies and cryptography experts have raised questions about the desirability of the plan. Whit Diffie, one of the creators of public key cryptography, commented that "the proposal doesn't contain a back door but a front door."

Personal Communication Networks

Personal communication networks (PCNs) have also raised new privacy issues. These are networks that assign specific numbers to users, rather than devices, who can then be located. A variation of the PCN issue is the use of Active Badges in the workplace. These devices are now in use in several computer labs and allow the ready location of particular individuals.

PCNs generally assume that each user in the network will be assigned a unique identifier. This is different from traditional telecommunications networks. In these networks, numbers are assigned to the phone instrument.

As a general matter, unique identifiers raise no special privacy concern. They are widely used by organizations in a variety of settings to ensure record accuracy. In communications networks, they may be virtually impossible to avoid. However, the unrestricted use of unique identifiers does raise privacy concerns. When a single identifier is used in multiple settings, it permits the exchange of personal information oftentimes without the individual's knowledge or consent. In Europe and in the U.S., there has generally been a presumption against the use of "universal unique identifiers," such as PINs or SSNs. Where such proposals have gone forward, it has been over the objection of privacy experts and system designers. Therefore, "unique unique identifiers" used in the context of transactional environments, such as network services, are preferred, while "universal unique" identifiers are likely to raise privacy problems.

A second question that has been raised about PCNs is the risk of geographical surveillance. Several commentators have said that "follow me, find me" systems are fine as long as there is no additional risks if the person's physical location is known to others. Others say that what is needed is a system designed to "follow me, find me, and then leave me alone." Restrictions on some PCN capabilities might be appropriate to protect privacy and to ensure personal mobility.

BIBLIOGRAPHY

Commission of the European Communities. Proposal Concerning the Protection of Personal Data in the Context of Public Digital Telecommunication Networks.

Flaherty, D., *Protecting Privacy in Surveillance Societies: The Federal Republic of Germany, Sweden, France, Canada, and the United States* (Chapel Hill, 1989).

Noam, E. *Special Report: Telecomm Privacy Policy Elements.* Transnational Data and Communications Report (March 1990), p. 9.

Nugter, A.C.M., *Transborder Flow of Personal Data Within the EC.* Kluwer, Boston, Mass., 1990.

OECD, *Guidelines on the Protection of Privacy and Transborder Flows of Personal Data.*

Rotenberg, M., "In Support of a Data Protection Board in the United States." *Gov. Info Quart.* 8 (1991), p. 79.

Ethics in the
Information Market

Richard N. Stichler

*[Information] is no less a commodity than precious metals, pork
bellies, or soybeans .... [It] can be advertised, promoted, marketed, and sold, just like any other traditional tangible commodities .... It is now clear that marketplace forces, rather
than individual needs, drive the development and introduction
of new information products.* —DONALD T. HAWKINS, *Senior
Information Technology Scientist, AT&T Bell Laboratories*

*We find today a tremendous enthusiasm for knowledge and
education, but at the same time a skeptical or contemptuous
attitude toward the allegedly impractical and useless thinking
which is concerned "only" with the truth and which has no
exchange value on the market.* —ERICH FROMM, Man for
Himself

*What matters at this stage is the construction of local forms of
community within which civility and the intellectual and
moral life can be sustained through the new dark ages which
are already upon us.* —ALASDAIR MACINTYRE, After Virtue

    The idea that knowledge or information is an economic commodity that
can be exchanged in the marketplace is not new, but over the past 50 years,
the rapid expansion of information technology systems has created a revolution, not only in the information market, but in the world economic market itself. As Alvin Toffler and others have observed, we have entered a new
"information age" in which control of the economic market has shifted from
an industrial base to an information base. This "powershift" has been made

possible by means of computer technology that facilitates the rapid exchange of information commodities worldwide. One of the consequences of this phenomenon, as Gale Moore points out, is that "the idea that knowledge and information are social goods to be used for the public good ... is being replaced with the idea that these are economic goods to be used for private gain" (421). This change has precipitated widespread social transformation by launching the "information wars," which Toffler describes as a global struggle to control the distribution of these new commodities.

An example of the manner in which the information market is changing social institutions can be seen in the way professional and nonprofit organizations are now managed. It has long been held, for example, that the use of marketing techniques in service professions and nonprofit organizations is unethical. Until recently, advertising and marketing of services were prohibited by the codes of ethics published by many professional associations. However, traditional prohibitions against marketing have recently come to be viewed by many as little more than an antiquated elitist bias against business. In 1975, Philip Kotler's *Marketing for Nonprofit Organizations* laid the foundation for a wider acceptance of marketing techniques in the professional and nonprofit sectors. Subsequently, numerous articles appeared advocating the use of Kotler's marketing techniques in libraries and information centers. In response to traditional objections, proponents of marketing claimed that marketing improves information service and accountability, that it raises the standards of professionalism, and that, as a result, it leads to increased public support and higher pay for librarians (Wilson 69). Opponents have objected that because information marketing targets the wealthier segments of the population, it results in unjust distributions of resources; in addition, they claim that marketing strategies are designed to create public dependence upon information products controlled by a bureaucracy of librarians (see Berry and Grundner 7).

What are the ethical implications of marketing strategies for library management and how can we sort out these conflicting claims? Although strong opinions have been expressed on both sides of the issue, the terms of the debate, I believe, make it virtually impossible to reach a rational conclusion. Thus, in this paper I propose a new conceptual framework for assessing the controversy. I begin by considering the kinds of ethical practices that are needed to attain the goals articulated in the introduction to the American Library Association's code of ethics. My aim is to develop an analysis that entails a certain understanding of how librarians ought to function within a professional context. Although the interpretation of the ethical function of librarianship that I propose is not specifically developed in the ALA code of ethics and differs in certain fundamental respects from the views advanced in the *Intellectual Freedom Manual*, it is a view, as I have argued in an earlier paper, that is implicit in the aims and objectives enumerated in the introduction to the ALA code of ethics (Stichler 43–44).

The approach to ethics that I employ differs from contemporary liberal theories of ethics in that it focuses not merely on the distribution of social goods but on the more fundamental question of the kinds of human functioning such distributions ought to bring about. The advantage of this approach is that, unlike the ethics of contemporary liberalism, it allows us to evaluate principles of information distribution in terms of their effects on how people actually use information and how such uses increase or diminish the quality of human life. From this perspective, we will begin to see more clearly the nature of the librarian's obligation to develop and sustain certain forms of professional practice and why such practices are incompatible with the aims of information marketing.

Information Marketing and the ALA Code of Ethics

The term "ethics" as applied to the library and information profession is based on the principle that knowledge and information are public goods that ought to be freely disseminated. The ALA professes its commitment to this principle in the introduction of its code of ethics:

> Librarians significantly influence or control the selection, organization, preservation, and dissemination of information. In a political system grounded in an informed citizenry, librarians are members of a profession explicitly committed to intellectual freedom and the freedom of access to information. We have a special obligation to ensure the free flow of information and ideas to present and future generations [Mintz 81].

Notice that the ALA code of ethics bases the obligation to provide access to information on the fact that the librarian operates within a political system that is committed to certain social and ethical ideals. But what is the basis of this commitment? Why should librarians be committed to intellectual freedom? Contemporary liberalism tends to view intellectual freedom as a kind of self-evident principle—a kind of natural right that ought to be protected for its own sake. People are intellectually free, according to this view, when they are able to read, think, or express whatever opinion they desire. But this conception of freedom fails to take into account the fact that unformed or deformed desire can severely restrict the reality of personal freedom. As Martha Nussbaum observes,

> Desires are formed in relation to habits and ways of life. At one extreme, people who have lived in opulence feel dissatisfied when they are deprived of the goods of opulence. At the other extreme, people who have lived in severe deprivation frequently do not feel desire for a different way, or dissatisfaction

with their way. Human beings adapt to what they have. In some cases they come to believe that it is right that things should be so with them; in other cases, they are not even aware of alternatives [213].

Thus, if we take the liberal position that promoting intellectual freedom means no more than satisfying people's desires for information as they come, our distribution of information will, for the most part, do little more than reinforce the status quo. But, on the other hand, if we consider how social and political conditions can constrict or deform people's ability to desire certain kinds of information, we can see why promoting intellectual freedom should aim not only at satisfying but at actually educating people's desires so that they are able to desire a form of fully human functioning. The implicit connection in the ALA code of ethics between intellectual freedom and "a political system grounded in an informed citizenry" suggests that efforts to promote intellectual freedom ought to aim primarily at enabling people to function as fully enfranchised members of a political community. If the informed citizen is a person who has the ability to deliberate and think critically about a wide range of decisions that affect the well-being of his community, it is clear that the task of the library is to provide the kinds of resources that will support the development of those specific human capacities; the broader task of government, on the other hand, is to identify and remove the obstacles that prevent people from using those resources effectively.

Since libraries operate within a political context, the concept of the "needs" of an informed citizen must be defined in terms of the kind of human functioning that libraries are intended to promote. This implies that an adequate understanding of what people need cannot be based merely on empirical research into what people want or happen to desire at any particular time. The distinction between needs and wants, as Mortimer Adler puts it, is based on the fact that "our needs are always right desires, desires for the real goods that we ought to desire, whereas our wants may be either right or wrong desires. They are wrong desires when we want things that are really bad for us or want in excess things that are really good for us" (55).

If we define human needs with reference to what people ought to be able to do and to be as members of a political community, it follows that the task of the library is to build collections that support the development of certain kinds of intellectual capabilities. Although libraries must be actively used in order to realize their potential, it is a mistake to measure the social value of libraries merely in terms of their use. People may prefer to use libraries that promote mental and emotional addiction to propaganda, fascism, sadistic pornography, megalomanic delusions, etc., but even though it may be in great demand, it is not in the public interest to satisfy the "need" for such information. Instead of seeking to increase library use by "dumbing down" the collection and satisfying the wants of the lowest common denominator, the librarian's responsibility is to identify the social conditions that obstruct the use of the library's resources and work with government to remove them.

Proponents of information marketing, however, contend that the market is the true test of whether libraries are really satisfying human needs, and they argue that librarians must learn what people need from the market. Andrea Dragon writes, "Any changes in library programming that grow out of information gathered from the market are more likely to be successful than those resulting from armchair speculation about what the public needs. If libraries truly desire to serve their publics, then it behooves librarians to determine what the public needs" (122). What the term "need" means, as it is defined in the marketing context, is *psychological* need; there is no distinction here between needs and wants; psychological needs are needs that are satisfied whenever people get what they want regardless of whether it is good, bad, or indifferent. Since the market operates according to the law of supply and demand, it empirically determines what people need by measuring what they use. As Dragon puts it, "the market is the only source of information about needs" (123); thus, the ethical definition of human needs may be dismissed as mere "armchair speculation."

Although the marketing approach to information management is based on a psychological conception of human needs, its proponents nevertheless imply that it is really the only way for librarians to meet their professional responsibility for satisfying the public's "need" for information resources. They clearly recognize, however, that if libraries get into the business of marketing information, they will have to redefine their most essential objectives. Keith Ewing notes that, "The ultimate meaning of marketing is perceptual and involves a redefinition of library and information directions. It involves a reorganization of management priorities. It means the opening of professional perspectives, with a willingness to take risks based on confidence in the process and ultimate benefit" (20). Exactly what is meant by the euphemistic phrase, "opening of professional perspectives," is explained more concisely by Cosette Kies: "In these days of tight budgets and a stress upon accountability, the library that chooses marketing must often turn away from such traditional practices of librarianship as building balanced collections or attempting to preserve the best of the world's literature" (122–23).

Advocates of marketing strategies apparently see no real ethical difficulty in recommending such changes in library policies. They respond to objections as though they are merely dealing with a public relations problem. Darlene E. Weingand claims that the fact that modern marketing focuses not merely on selling but on consumer satisfaction allows "non-profit institutions, such as libraries/information agencies, to participate actively and with good conscience in the marketing process. The question is whether library and information agency administrations can relinquish the old biases and examine marketing concepts with a fresh eye and in depth" (vii). Given the fact that information marketing entails a rejection of the traditional aims of librarianship, we might wonder why opposition to the marketing of library services is so often described as nothing more than an "old bias." William Hannaford suggests that many librarians simply fail to understand the ethical dimension of librarianship; they see collection development and related activities as products of either expediency or self-interest (59–60). We might add that the exclusive focus on "success" and "accountability" which is such a prominent feature of the literature on information marketing, has contributed significantly to the ethical blindness and irresponsibility of the profession. Moreover, this blindness to the ethical dimension of librarianship is further reinforced by the way the market orientation redefines the meaning and value of information itself.

Knowledge and Information as Commodities

Just as the marketing orientation redefines human needs, so too does it redefine knowledge and information. In the marketing context, knowledge and information are not defined in terms of their content and intrinsic value, but rather by their exchange value. The exchange value of commodities is determined by the market through the mechanism of the law of supply and demand. No matter what the intrinsic value or use value of any commodity may be, if the supply exceeds the demand, its exchange value is diminished. To the extent that the market itself stimulates new demands for any commodity, however, it is a system of value-creation. In other words, no matter how useless or lacking in intrinsic value a commodity may be, if the market-generated demand exceeds the supply, the commodity's exchange value is increased. Thus, market-created values are extrinsic in the sense that they are based on perceived values or wants rather than the intrinsic value or inherent usefulness of things. By stimulating the demand for information, the technology of information systems has thus created a new economic value—a self-generating market for information commodities.

In the market context the terms "knowledge" and "information" are used to refer to "data, images, and imagery, as well as attitudes, values, and other symbolic products of society, whether 'true,' 'approximate,' or even 'false'" (Toffler 19). Moreover, the usual descriptions, "true" and "factual," *cannot* be properly applied to knowledge and information when defined in terms of their exchange value, for the terms "true" and "factual" are characteristics of the intrinsic content of knowledge and information and have no application to the description of commodities. From an ethical standpoint, it *is* the intrinsic content or truth value of knowledge—i.e., the correspondence of thought with reality—that satisfies the human need for knowledge. The ethical value of knowledge, in other words, lies in the way it "informs" the mind, in the sense of permeating it with a certain characteristic power, which thus enables it to grasp the reality of things.

It is often said that knowledge is power. But the power of knowledge also means different things. In the ethical sense, it means the actualization of the potentialities of the human mind; in the information market, it means control over information commodities. In the ethical sense, the power of knowledge is an end in itself or an intrinsic human good; as a commodity, it is a means to something else—such as wealth or control over people. In addition, knowledge as truth is a cooperative or public good in the sense that one person's possession of it does not restrict or decrease its value for others; knowledge as a commodity is a competitive or private good in proportion to the distribution of its ownership. If everyone owns the rights to a certain commodity or piece of "intellectual property," for example, its exchange value is reduced to zero and no one is able to make a profit; but if everyone understands Kant's *Critique of Pure Reason* or Joyce's *Ulysses*, then everyone benefits equally.

In discussion of the ethics of information marketing, much of the confusion stems from the equivocal use of terms like needs, knowledge, information, and power. In order to understand where the librarian's professional responsibilities lie, we need to be clear about the distinctions between ethical and market-oriented meanings of language. Those meanings are rooted in divergent forms of social practice that are distinguished by their values and purposes; they thus provide the basis for seeing why marketing practices and objectives are inconsistent with the professed aims of librarianship.

The Psychology of the Marketing Orientation and Its Effects

The deeper problem, however, cannot be solved merely by means of conceptual clarity, for the marketing orientation has become such an all-pervasive aspect of modern society that we unconsciously tend to assume a marketing frame of reference when thinking about almost any form of human interaction. The "logic" of the marketing-orientation has become such a normal part of our way of thinking that any talk about "intrinsic values" or "genuine human needs" is apt to be perceived as nothing more than the "old bias" of a reactionary ideologue who just wants to block progress.

To understand how marketing psychology has gradually invaded the public and professional sector, it is instructive to consider the methods of persuasion employed by Philip Kotler, Professor of Business at Northwestern University, in his book *Marketing for Nonprofit Organizations*. After quickly disposing of a few ethical strawmen in the opening chapter, Kotler proceeds to show how almost any form of human interaction can be interpreted as an exchange of values. Kotler does not "see marketing as a specific set of institutions and exchanges but rather as a conceptual system about exchanges and transactions that helps analyze, explain, and control them" (34). Given this broad definition, we find that market transactions are going on everywhere, right under our noses, and we never even knew it! Kotler claims that not only are service and charity organizations engaged in marketing, but that we all are constantly engaged in marketing ourselves at work, to our boss and fellow workers, and at home, to our spouse and family members; in "self-exchanges" we even market ourselves to ourselves. In the following passage, Kotler provides an interesting example of an act of charity: "There is also a self-exchange process going on within the minds of the firemen. A fireman has a need for community approval and esteem; he also wants to avoid guilt for doing a poor job. To get a positive feeling about himself, he must perform well" (29).

According to Kotler, we perform charitable acts not simply to benefit others but to market ourselves in exchange for *feelings* of self-esteem; thus, according to Kotler's marketing analysis, self-esteem is a kind of commodity that we get from ourselves and others in exchange for "charitable" and other marketable acts. On the basis of these incredibly simplistic principles of marketing psychology, Kotler constructs his approach to management and motivational strategy; his next paragraph continues, "Analyzing the exchanges in this way makes it easier for the head of the fire department to motivate his men ('employee marketing'). It suggests some of the factors that could be used by any public administrator to get his staff to serve the public with more enthusiasm and sensitivity" (29).

Kotler's strategy for promoting marketing as an ethically acceptable practice for the nonprofit sector is based on getting us to *see* marketing as a fundamental and inescapable feature of all human activity. Once we *see* marketing as an all-pervasive social phenomenon, it is no longer a question of whether nonprofit services should or should not be marketed; the only question is how to use the marketing model to analyze what we are already doing so that we may go on doing it even more successfully. But just what are the benefits of marketing and what kind of success can we expect? Does it really provide the basis for better library management? Can marketing psychology really enable librarians to develop greater self-esteem and personal satisfaction in their work and in their lives?

In a book published more than forty-five years ago, *Man for Himself: An Inquiry into the Psychology of Ethics*, Erich Fromm analyzes the demoralizing effects of the market orientation and demonstrates why the kind of self-marketing Kotler describes actually destroys any real sense of self-esteem. His account is worth quoting at length:

In our time the market orientation has been growing rapidly, together with the development of a new market that is a phenomenon of the last decades—the "personality market." Clerks and salesmen, business executives and doctors, lawyers and artists ... all are dependent for their material success on a personal acceptance by those who need their services or who employ them.

The principle of evaluation is the same on both the personality and the commodity market: on the one, personalities are offered for sale; on the other, commodities ... only in exceptional cases is success predominately the result of skill and of certain other human qualities like honesty, decency, and integrity .... Success depends largely on how well a person sells himself on the market, how well he gets his personality across, how nice a "package" he is....

The fact that in order to have success it is not sufficient to have the skill and equipment for performing a given task but that one must be able to "put across" one's personality in competition with others shapes the attitude toward oneself ... since success depends largely on how one sells one's personality, one experiences oneself as a commodity to be sold.... [One's] self-esteem depends on conditions beyond his control. If he is "successful," he is valuable; if he is not, he is worthless. The degree of insecurity which results from this orientation can hardly be overestimated. If one feels that one's own value is not constituted primarily by the human qualities one possesses, but by one's success on a competitive market with ever-changing conditions, one's self-esteem is bound to be shaky and in constant need of confirmation by others. Hence one is driven to strive relentlessly for success, and any setback is a severe threat to one's self-esteem; helplessness, insecurity, and inferiority feelings are the result. If the vicissitudes of the market are the judges of one's value, the sense of dignity and pride is destroyed [69–72].

Fromm's analysis of the personality market exactly diagnoses why the kinds of feelings and attitudes produced by self-marketing are likely to be anything but genuine feelings of self-respect and dignity. They are the kinds of feelings and attitudes that allow people to sell themselves cheaply and give up any responsibility to think for themselves. Where the price of success means devoting one's efforts to conforming to the expectations of others and uncritically accepting the standards of the community, those who succeed by so conforming are most likely to turn out to be the pompous ass and the conceited prig. For, as Fromm suggests, it is actually the lack of genuine self-respect that drives people to seek the spurious feelings of self-satisfaction and self-importance that are derived from success in the personality market.

It is becoming increasingly clear that marketing management models, by introducing a new vocabulary to describe and evaluate what the librarian does, have made considerable progress in redefining the librarian's role in society. The shift has been away from thinking of the librarian as an interactive collaborator in the research process and toward the belief that the librarian is a passive vendor of information commodities who needs to know little or nothing about the content of the product but a great deal about the preferences of end-users. At an ALA conference in 1982, Daniel Carroll propounded as a "new truth" the proposition that library marketing should now be taken out of the hands of librarians and turned over to "marketing professionals whose technique permits them to perceive and anticipate user needs" (214). What this means in practical terms, of course, is first, that the traditional skills of the librarian would no longer be required for successful library management and second, that libraries would no longer be managed by librarians but by marketing specialists who have little understanding of or sympathy with the traditional aims and values of librarians.

Thus, it is very unlikely that marketing management models will either improve library service or bring greater personal satisfaction and self-esteem to members of the library profession. In fact, as might be expected, the evidence points in just the opposite direction; as Marsha J. Nauratil points out in her recent book, *The Alienated Librarian*, rising levels of stress and burnout in the library profession have coincided with the growth of marketing methods in library management. Statistical studies conducted in 1986 and 1987, she reports,

> show that burnout is a problem affecting a substantial segment of the library profession.... Further indications of the seriousness of librarian burnout can be found in the attention it attracts as a conference topic, in the proliferation of burnout seminars and workshops, and in the increasing references to the problem in the professional literature. If librarian burnout has not yet reached the stage of mass conflagration suffered by some other professional groups, it has spread far enough to jeopardize the well-being of thousands of librarians and to threaten the integrity and effectiveness of their professional practice [7].

Ethics and Social Practices

Although there have been numerous books and articles dealing with the effects of information marketing and marketing management strategies on the professions, few attempts have been made to treat the practice of marketing within the professions as an ethical issue. Typically, challenges to marketing within the professions have been developed from an economic or a sociological perspective. But although such challenges call attention to significant problems, they fail to draw on the moral resources that are required to reestablish the integrity of professional life. Part of the reason that the ethical aspect of the issue has been neglected is because it does not fit very neatly into the traditional categories of modern moral philosophy. However, during the past decade philosophers such as Alasdair MacIntyre, Martha Nussbaum, and others have begun to resurrect the tradition of Aristotelian ethics in an effort to develop a more adequate framework for understanding and evaluating the ethical dimensions of social practices. In conclusion, I want to situate the discussion in that ethical context in order to show how we might begin to develop a more productive analysis of the ethical dimensions of librarianship.

Prior to the publication of MacIntyre's *After Virtue* in 1981, modern philosophy had been dominated almost exclusively by the two dominant ethical theories of liberalism—utilitarianism and deontology. Utilitarianism, founded by Adam Smith and Jeremy Bentham in the late 18th and early 19th centuries, is essentially the ethics of the economic market. It is based on the idea that the rightness or wrongness of any action or state of affairs is determined by its "utility" or tendency to bring about good consequences. The rule of conduct that determines the rightness or wrongness of any action is the measure of its utility or tendency to bring about the greatest possible good under the particular circumstances. On the other hand, deontological ethics, developed by Immanuel Kant in the late 18th century, is based on the primacy of duty over consequences; the Greek term *deon* means duty, hence, deontological ethics is concerned with the logic or rational basis of moral obligation. Deontologists maintain that the rightness or wrongness of an action resides in the conformity of the intention of the act with a moral rule. The primary moral rule is the categorical imperative, which requires that rules of action be universalizable for all humanity. Historically, deontological ethics has not been effective in shaping an alternative social morality; it has merely placed some additional restrictions on the ethics of the market.

Although utilitarians and deontologists strongly disagree on many practical and philosophical issues, both theories are rule-based and attempt to assess the rightness or wrongness of actions in terms of their conformity with ethical stipulations. Rule-based approaches to ethics are essentially concerned with decision-making; they attempt to resolve ethical problems involved in specific situations by reference to general rules and typically ask questions like, in situation X, is it right or wrong to do Y? Contemporary discussions of issues in information ethics have been centered on the utilitarian/deontological rule-based approach. In the debate over the ethics of information distribution, utilitarian positions focus on maximizing social benefits and tend to favor a market system based on private ownership; deontological positions focus on the right to information access and tend to favor a more socialistic system emphasizing equality of distribution and public ownership. In cases where rights conflict, for example, where one person's (or corporation's) intellectual property rights conflict with another's right to access, deontologists often have no convincing way of deciding the right course of action and are thus forced to fall back on utilitarian considerations as the only practical means of reaching a decision.

MacIntyre maintains that the arguments between utilitarians and deontologists are interminable in the sense that there is no rational basis for ever settling the disputes between them. This is typical not only of utilitarian-deontological debates; in our time, it is characteristic of moral disagreements generally. For example, consider the issue of intellectual freedom. On the one side, we have the argument that people have a fundamental right to read and be informed. Restricting access to information is a violation of the right to intellectual freedom. Censorship of pornography restricts access to information. Therefore, censoring pornography violates the right to intellectual freedom. On the other side, there is the argument that parents have the right to raise their children in a wholesome moral environment. But the sale of pornography creates an unwholesome moral environment. Therefore, the sale of pornography violates the rights of parents. It is typical of such moral disputes that the arguments on both sides are logical but that their premises are such that we have no rational basis for ever resolving the disagreement. Since the premises of each argument employ rival normative concepts, their claims are incompatible. Hence, MacIntyre argues that

> It is precisely because there is in our society no established way of deciding between these claims that moral argument appears to be necessarily interminable. From our rival conclusions we can argue back to our rival premises, but when we do arrive at our premises argument ceases and the invocation of one premise against the other becomes a matter of pure assertion and counter-assertion. Hence perhaps the slightly shrill tone of so much moral debate [6].

The ethical theories of modern liberalism fail to provide a rational basis for resolving substantive moral problems, according to MacIntyre, because they are not grounded in a tradition of moral practice. Modern society is itself a product of a post-enlightenment culture whose break with the past has left us with no unified moral tradition within which to make sense of the language of morality. What we have inherited are but fragments of an earlier moral tradition; we retain the vocabulary of that tradition, but, torn loose from its social context, its meanings are no longer intelligible to us. Hence, the clash of moral opinion, the confusion, and the shrillness and interminability of moral debate.

In order to make sense of moral language and restore intelligibility to our moral commitments, MacIntyre has developed a neo-Aristotelian account of the virtues. According to Aristotle, the virtues are acquired human characteristics that enable an individual to achieve happiness by engaging in activities that constitute a humanly good life. The activities or "practices" that comprise the human good, however, require a social context or moral tradition within which the "narrative unity" of the life of an individual can unfold and find its meaning. For an individual, life can find its meaning and unity only by engaging in those social practices that sustain and advance the larger good of a community that has grown out of the past and which depends for its continued existence on sustaining certain standards of excellence in social practices. In the context of "virtue ethics" the idea of moral obligation is defined, not as obeying a rule, but as an obligation to cultivate the virtues necessary to participate in practices that sustain and advance the common good of a community. Thus, in practices the satisfaction of the needs of the individual coincide with the larger good of society.

MacIntyre points out that the goods *internal* to a practice can be achieved only by engaging in the practice itself. Some examples of practices are found in various social roles, disciplines, political organizations, and professions. Parents, teachers, doctors, and lawyers all engage in practices whose goods are internal to them. Knowledge is a good internal to education, health is internal to medicine, and justice is internal to law. Each of these professions has a history that sustains a tradition, and in order to secure the goods internal to its practice, each profession requires that its practitioners develop and maintain certain virtues. There are also *external* goods associated with practices—for example, wealth, security, and social prestige. External goods are goods that could be obtained by alternative means and without engaging in a specific practice.

This distinction between internal and external goods leads to the further distinction between practices and institutions. Institutions such as universities, hospitals, and libraries are necessarily concerned with external goods. They acquire money and other material goods that are necessary to sustain themselves. But practices, though concerned with internal goods, are dependent on institutions and could not survive without their financial support. It is just this dependence on institutions, however, that threatens the integrity of practices. For example, a university's concern with costs, competition, and prestige, may threaten the internal good of education itself. Information marketing poses just such a threat to the traditional practices of universities. A recent edition of *Academe* reports that, "The university is moving closer to the model of a cost-effective business operation in which producing and disseminating knowledge is efficiently targeted to specified markets and clienteles" (Buchbinder and Newson 15). When the cooperative care of the common goods of a practice are thus threatened by the competitiveness of its supporting institution, says MacIntyre, "the essential function of the virtues is clear. Without them, without justice, courage, and truthfulness, practices could not resist the corrupting power of institutions" (194).

We are now in a position to see more clearly in what sense the information market poses a threat to society in general and to the ethics of the library profession in particular. Traditions and practices can die if they are not sustained by the requisite virtues, and to the extent that the external, competitive goods of the market become the dominant goods of society, social life will come more and more to resemble Hobbes' description of the state of nature. If librarians allow institutions to redefine for them what librarians do, the traditional values of librarianship will cease to exist. To resist the corrupting influence of the market, librarianship must be reenvisioned as a cooperative and interactive practice in which librarians are productively involved in the research process. In a recent issue of *The Electronic Library*, Amal Moulik and Dennis Lai describe their efforts to develop such practices. In response to the question—"How can we apply this [model] to the information profession?"—they write:

> Only if we challenge the conventional wisdom that relegates us to the position of surrogates or cost-benefit factors or, better still, indicators of exchange value in the distribution of information. Only if we rebel against the institutionalized one-dimensional image that post-industrial society has bequeathed to us and which we have passively accepted. It is time for a paradigm shift: from the ancillary role of helping our users to find the right stuff to creative partnership with our users in an on-going collaborative enterprise [101].

If librarianship is to sustain itself as a practice with goods internal to itself, the most important ethical challenge to the profession will be to build and sustain these kinds of cooperative practices. But to understand the ethical basis of the librarian's responsibility for preserving such practices, what is needed is not perhaps a Kuhnian paradigm shift so much as an understanding of the Aristotelian tradition of the virtues. That tradition, as MacIntyre envisions it, would teach us to look to the past, to the history of the professions in general and to library history in particular, to find the moral resources that will be needed to resist the corrupting influence of the information market.

REFERENCES

Adler, Mortimer J., *We Hold These Truths: Understanding the Ideas and Ideals of the Constitution*. New York: Macmillan Publishing Co., 1987.

Berry, John, "The 'Marketization' of Libraries." *Library Journal* January 1, 1981, p. 5.

Buchbinder, Howard and Newson, Janice, The Service University and Market Forces." *Academe* July–August 1992, pp. 13–15.

Carroll, Daniel, "Library Marketing: Old and New Truths." *Wilson Library Bulletin* November 1982, 212–216.

Dragon, Andrea C., "The Marketing of Public Library Services." *Drexel Library Quarterly* 19 (Spring 1983), pp. 117–132.

Ewing, Keith, "The Potential of Marketing for Academic Libraries." In Darlene E. Weingand, ed. *Marketing for Libraries and Information Agencies*. Norwood, N.J.: Ablex Publishing Corporation, 1984.

Fromm, Erich, *Man for Himself: An Inquiry into the Psychology of Ethics*. New York: Rinehart & Company, Inc., 1947.

Grundner, Tom, "Whose Internet Is It Anyway?—A Challenge." *Online* July 1992, pp. 6–10.

Hannaford, William E. Jr., "Ethics and Collection Development." In Joanne S. Hill, William E. Hannaford, Jr., and Ronald H. Epp, eds. *Collection Development in College Libraries*. Chicago: American Library Association, 1991, pp. 55–60.

Hawkins, Donald T., "The Commodity Nature of Information." *Online* January 1987, pp. 67–70.

Kies, Cosette N., *Marketing and Public Relations for Libraries*. Metuchen, N.J.: Scarecrow, 1987.

Kotler, Philip, *Marketing for Nonprofit Organizations*. Englewood Cliffs, N.J.: Prentice Hall, 1975.

MacIntyre, Alasdair, *After Virtue: A Study in Moral Theory*. Second Edition. Notre Dame, IN: Notre Dame University Press, 1984.

Mathews, Anne J., "The Use of Marketing Principles in Library Planning." In Darlene E. Weingand, ed. *Marketing for Libraries and Information Agencies*. Norwood, N.J.: Ablex Publishing Corporation, 1984.

Mintz, Anne P., ed. *Information Ethics: Concerns for Librarianship and the Information Industry*, Jefferson, N.C.: McFarland & Company, Inc., 1990.

Moore, Gale, "Reassessing the Social Impacts of New Technology." *Canadian Library Journal* December 1987, pp. 420–424.

Moulik, Amal and Lai, Dennis, "Rebels in Search of Champions: Envisioning the Library of the Future." *The Electronic Library* April, 1992, pp. 97–102.

Nauratil, Marsha J., *The Alienated Librarian*. New York: Greenwood Press, 1989.

Nussbaum, Martha, "Aristotelian Social Democracy." In R. Bruce Douglass, Gerald M. Mara, and Henry S. Richardson, eds. *Liberalism and the Good*. New York: Routledge, Chapman and Hall, 1990, pp. 203–252.

Stichler, Richard N., "On Reforming the ALA Code of Ethics." *American Libraries* 23 (1) (January 1992), pp. 40–44.

Toffler, Alvin, *Powershift: Knowledge, Wealth, and Violence at the Edge of the 21st Century*. New York: Bantam Books, 1990.

Weingand, Darlene E., ed. *Marketing for Libraries and Information Agencies*. Norwood, N.J.: Ablex Publishing Corporation, 1984.

Wilson, Pauline, "Needed: A Market Decision and Some Market Research." *Public Libraries* (Fall 1980), pp. 69–70.

Librarianship and
Public Culture in the Age
of Information Capitalism

Henry T. Blanke

Introduction

It has become increasingly evident over the last two decades or so that significant, even epochal, shifts are occurring in the socio-economic structures of the Western world. The cumulative impact of innovations in computerization and telecommunications technology, the growth of mass media conglomerates, new electronic systems of production, and changing patterns of consumption has had not only profound economic significance, but deep cultural implications as well. In coming to grips with these developments, many social theorists have argued that we are approaching, or have already entered a new historical era characterized variously as post-industrial, post-modern, even post-capitalist. Other commentators have posited more of a gradual evolution toward a new phase of corporate capitalism, rather than a historical leap to a new social formation (for useful surveys of the various perspectives on post-industrialism and post-modernism, see Best and Kellner [1991]; Rose [1991]; and Harris and Hannah [1993, pp. 1–32]).

However one interprets recent technological and economic developments, it is clear that central to these changes is the increasing prominence of knowledge and information as key resources. In fact, the idea that we are now living in the "age of information" or an "information society" has gained widespread currency in academic and popular discourse. Librarians in particular, perhaps sensing a future of enhanced status and a more prominent social role, have embraced the metaphor of a post-industrial/information society. It may be, however, that in its eagerness to position itself on the cutting edge of these new developments, the library profession has not sufficiently scrutinized the underlying social forces represented by the rubric of post-industrialism.

It is the contention of this essay that the escalating economic importance of information and the increasing integration of cultural spheres into the economic system are among the most salient characteristics of the current configuration of post-industrial capitalism. The consequent conception of information as a commodity, rather than as a public good, and the intensifying commercialization of cultural production, have had a significant impact on government policy and on libraries—institutions devoted to cultural-informational activity. Prominent professional representatives are advocating an entrepreneurial model of librarianship that contradicts traditional ideals of free and equal access to information. It will be argued that such a model threatens the future of the library as a vital public sphere of democratic culture. The emphasis here will be on a discussion of broad trends exemplifying the current trajectory of advanced capitalism so as to provide a context for the critical interpretation of issues within librarianship.

The Rise of Information Capitalism

Among the first and most influential theorists to call attention to information as a dynamic new commodity and to theorize telecommunications and computer technology as driving forces behind future social formations was Daniel Bell. In his writings on post-industrialism, Bell forecast the imminent emergence of a society in which industrial manufacturing is superseded by a service-oriented, knowledge-based economy. As traditional forms of commodity production decline, the codification of knowledge and information processing become "axial principles" of social organization. For Bell (1976), "if industrial society is based on machine technology, post-industrial society is shaped by an intellectual technology. And if capital and labor are the major structural features of industrial society, information and knowledge are those of post-industrial society" (p. xiii). In the post-industrial era, knowledge replaces labor as the preeminent source of value.

One implication of Bell's forecast is that the post-industrial society represents a decisive historical break with industrial capitalism and its attendant social conflicts and economic vicissitudes. In fact, the belief that liberal democracy has transcended the class antagonisms of the past, and what social problems remain are amenable to technical, administrative solutions, has been a persistent theme in Bell's work since he proclaimed the "end of ideology" more than 30 years ago (Bell, 1960). Subsequent proponents and popularizers of the information society vision (e.g., Alvin Toffler and John Naisbitt) have likewise posited the transcendence of socio-economic structures characteristic of industrial capitalism. According to Peter Drucker (1993), although the free market will remain central to economic organization, "the new society—and it is already here—is a post-capitalist society.... The basic economic resource ... is no longer capital, nor natural resources (the economist's 'land'), nor 'labor'.... *It is and will be knowledge*" (pp. 7–8).

Post-industrial theorists, however, overestimate the extent to which new developments in technology and economy represent historical discontinuity, a decisive break with the past and a leap into a new socio-historical epoch. While any social theory must treat novel developments seriously, it is important to appreciate the continuity in shifting socio-historical patterns. However dramatic innovations in computerization, telecommunications, and media have been, they have occurred under the imperatives of capital accumulation. Against those proponents of post-industrialism who maintain that the central aspects of capitalism are no longer the "axial principles" of social organization, David Harvey (1989), Douglas Kellner (1989), and others have argued that capitalism's defining features—commodity production surplus, and so on—remain fundamental social forces that shape the direction of technological innovation and condition developments in polity and culture. However, as these critics of the optimistic perspective on post-industrialism acknowledge, the increasing importance of information and the technology used for its processing have had a profound enough economic and cultural impact to justify the view that a new configuration for advanced capitalism is emerging. Following Sue Curry Jansen (1993), this new configuration may be termed "information capitalism," under which "information becomes a form of capital; and restriction and control of access to information becomes a fundamental structural principle on the market system" (p. 68).

The emergence of information as a vital economic resource can be traced to the period after World War II which saw an explosion in the generation of scientific and technical information. Federal spending on research and development, initiated during the war, was continued at an accelerating rate during the post-war period and generated an enormous amount of data. Concurrently, computer technology was undergoing rapid development and refinement in order to facilitate access to the flood of new data. Congruent with these developments was the growth of private corporations, thriving from the stimulus of a war-time economy and now moving into the international market, into powerful transnational conglomerates. Given the increasing dependence of these mega-corporations on the rapid flow of information for managing their global operations, a private information industry quickly emerged to capitalize on the commercial potential in the processing and distribution of data. These three interactive developments—an information explosion, computerization, and the rise of the transnational corporation—have had a profound impact on the nation's economic and cultural life (Schiller, 1989, pp. 69–73).

Indeed, the extent to which informational activity has transformed the American economy has been striking. By 1956, white-collar workers in service/information professions outnumbered blue-collar industrial workers for the first time and the service sector eventually superseded manufacturing and agriculture as the central economic sector. By the late 1960s, informational activities were responsible for 46 percent of the national income and, with the widespread computerization of the 1970s, those in the "primary" information sector (computer manufacturing, telecommunications, mass media, advertising, publishing, accounting, research and development) alone accounted for 30 percent of the national economy (Bell, 1976; p. 17; Porat, 1977, pp. 19–23, 65). In 1988, the Office of Technology Assessment noted that the roughly 40 percent of all new investments in the United States that goes to purchase information technology represents a transformation that is "likely to reshape virtually every product, every service, and every job in the United States" (p. 977).

In analyzing these developments, Harvey (1989) emphasizes the drive for capital accumulation as a fundamental force in modern Western society, and interprets recent shifts in political economy in terms of a transition from "Fordism" (assembly-line mass production, scientific management, mass consumption, welfare state interventions) to a more flexible mode of accumulation. In response to the economic crisis of 1973–75, and facilitated by innovations in telecommunications and computerization, new, more fluid, decentralized, and deregulated organizations of labor processes, labor markets, products, and patterns of consumption were generated as alternatives to the relative rigidities of Fordism.

Characteristic of this new "regime of flexible accumulation" is the prominence of information as a crucial commodity.

> Access to, and control over, information, coupled with a strong capacity for instant data analysis, have become essential to the centralized coordination of far-flung corporate interests. The capacity for instantaneous response to changes in exchange rates, fashions and tastes, and moves by competitors is more essential to corporate survival than it ever was under Fordism .... Privileged access to information of any sort (such as scientific and technical know-how, government policies, and political shifts) becomes an essential aspect of successful and profitable decision-making [p. 159].

Similarly, Kellner (1989) believes that computerization and information technology have come to play "increasingly important roles in the production process, the organization of society and everyday life." However, these factors "are still subject to processes of commodification, exchange, profitability and control by capital." Thus, they represent not a new era of social organization, but rather a novel constellation of corporate capitalism that Kellner defines as "a phase ... that incorporates knowledge, information, computerization and automation into the production process precisely in order to enhance capitalist profitability, power and social control as a response to falling rates of profit, drives to realize new sources of profitability and strategies to replace highly paid, well-organized workers by more compliant machines" (pp. 180, 186–187).

Jansen (1993) agrees that "the transfer in economic activity from production of material goods to the production of "information" represents a new phase of capitalist development. She attributes this shift to the "reorganization of the human workforce toward research, planning, design, and development of knowledge" applied to computerized systems of production. However, when information and knowledge become forms of capital, then "what was once regarded as a public good and cornerstone of democracy ... is increasingly absorbed into the commodity system. As a result, public libraries, education, broadcasting, museums, galleries, performances and so on are increasingly brought under the discipline of the logic of profit" (pp. 64–65).

Cultural Commodification

Concomitant with the increasing prominence of information as a vital commodity has been the integration of cultural production into the market system. Increasingly, literature, music, film, art and other cultural goods "are produced ... on industrial and commercial lines, that is to say on a large scale and in accordance [with] economic considerations rather than ... cultural development" (UNESCO, 1982, p. 21). Among the first to identify and analyze this process of cultural "commodification" as a defining feature of 20th century capitalism were Theodor Adorno and Max Horkheimer (1989) who coined the term "culture industry" to describe the standardized, uniform nature of mass media production (pp. 120–67).

With the emergence of an urban industrialized society, the void left by the decline of traditional pre-industrial cultural activities was filled by new market-driven forms of mass media culture. The shift toward mass production and a consumption oriented economy had its cultural counterpart in the development of large-scale commercial entertainment. The profit motive was transferred onto cultural products which became "a species of commodity ... marketable and interchangeable like an industrial product" (Horkheimer and Adorno, 1989, p. 158). These mass media products, although carrying a superficial air of novelty, are in fact thoroughly standardized, with successful formulas repeated endlessly. The constant bombardment of entertainment of this type induces stupefaction and passivity on the part of the audience, militating against critical reflection and the free play of the imagination.

An important aspect of Horkheimer and Adorno's critique is that because the products of the culture industry are so standardized and mechanical and require so little effort or initiative for their consumption, they serve to reinforce the tedium of the workplace, even as they offer a brief respite from it. Whereas the art of previous eras maintained a degree of autonomy from the economic order, mass media culture embodies the logic of commodity production and thus reinforces the prevailing system. The distance between culture and economy collapses under the market imperatives of profitability.

First formulated in the 1940s, Horkheimer and Adorno's core insights concerning the integration of culture and economy are even more relevant in the present time of "unprecedented conglomeration, concentration, expansion, and globalization of media, entertainment, and information industries and technologies" (Jansen, 1993, p. 63). In response to the need for new sources of profit and quicker rates of capital turnover following the economic downturn of 1973–75, the pull of culture into the orbit of capital accumulation has intensified. Images, spectacles, fashions, and various mass media entertainments, as opposed to traditional commodities, can be consumed with great speed and represent fresh forms of economic activity (Harvey, 1989, pp. 284–307). Fredric Jameson (1991), in his interpretation of postmodernism as "the cultural logic of late capitalism," agrees "that aesthetic production today has become integrated into commodity production generally: the frantic economic urgency of producing fresh waves of ever more new seeming goods (from clothing to airplanes), at ever greater rates of turnover, now assigns an increasingly essential structural function and position to aesthetic innovation and experimentation" (pp. 4–5).

As media outlets are integrated within the transnational corporate system, there is a restriction of the autonomy of culture from the imperatives of business and commerce. Profitability and ideological conformity eventually become the predominant criteria of cultural production. Ben Bagdikian (1989) has chronicled the process, accelerating over the last 10 years or so, whereby most important world outlets for newspapers, magazines, books, movies, recordings, and broadcasting have come under the ownership and control of a diminishing number of media conglomerates. Together, these "lords of the global village" exert "a homogenizing power over ideas, culture, and commerce that affects populations larger than any in history." Quite naturally, given the drive for profit maximization at the heart of the corporate agenda, these media conglomerates oppose economic and political developments that do not further their own financial interest and "are as ready as any dictatorship to suppress or de-emphasize news or entertainment that might seriously question their power" (pp. 807, 812).

The Information Industry and Government Policy

The increasing incursion of market forces into areas of social life, which had hitherto preserved a degree of autonomy from commercial influence (first identified by Horkheimer and Adorno), is a defining feature of the current phase of capitalist development theorized by Harvey, Kellner, and Jameson, and dubbed "information capitalism" by Jansen. The last decade, in particular, has seen "an increased commodification of information, knowledge, education, entertainment, and so on, in which domains that were previously relatively free from commodity exchange relationships became subject to capitalist profit and control—as when computer information services replace libraries as sources of information and education is commodified into computer programs which students have to purchase..." (Kellner, 1989, p. 187).

Until recently, the public library was one of the few remaining cultural-informational spheres that existed largely outside of the ubiquitous web of market relations. Although never adequately fulfilled, the traditional library mission of collecting a wide range of the world's knowledge and making it freely and equally accessible to all who seek it has been a model of democratic values in action. However, the growing economic prominence of information and the intensifying commercialization of cultural activity have generated forces, both within and outside of librarianship, that threaten to undermine the ideal of knowledge as public good. In the approving words of a senior information technology scientist at AT&T Bell Laboratories, "information has progressed from intrinsic knowledge to a commodity that is actively produced, marketed, and sold .... Marketplace forces, rather than individual needs drive the development and introduction of new information products" (Hawkins, 1987, pp. 68, 69).

As transnational corporations have increasingly come to rely on vast banks of data for their global operations and a sophisticated new technology has been developed to more efficiently manipulate that data, private companies have positioned themselves to profit from these trends. Not surprisingly, these information firms, represented in Washington by the Information Industry Association, have been aggressively promoting the idea that information is a commodity that can, and should, be bought and sold for a profit. This idea runs directly counter to long-cherished library principles and has grave social and political implications because "knowledge can only become a profitable commodity if democratic access is restricted by removing it from the public sphere and limiting the channels available for its distribution" (Jansen, 1993, p. 65).

As the private information industry has grown in wealth and influence it has had a significant impact on public policy. The Reagan–Bush years resulted in a series of legislative acts and executive orders that converted the profit-seeking objectives of the private information sector into national policy. The first and, perhaps, most far-reaching of these legislative actions was the Paperwork Reduction Act of 1980, which authorized the Office of Management and Budget (OMB) to set federal information policy. The OMB has used this authority to dramatically restrict and privatize government information.

The rationale for encouraging the encroachment of private enterprise into the public information domain was established in 1982 when the Public/Private Sector Task Force of the National Commission on Libraries and Information Science issued its report. Among the principles established by the task force was the following: "The Federal government should establish and enforce policies and procedures that encourage ... investment by the private sector in the development and use of information products and services." The task force recommended that private enterprise should be encouraged to "'add value' to government information (i.e., to repackage it ... and otherwise enhance the information so that it can be sold at a profit)" (pp. 7–8). The extent to which this report, with its view of information as a "capital resource" of great value on the free market, reflects a shifting political climate is made clear by comparing it to an earlier document. Just three years earlier the White House Conference on Library and Information Services (1980) declared:

> Information in a free society is a basic right of any individual, essential for all persons, at all age levels, and all economic and social levels .... Persons should have free access without charge or fee to the individual, to information in public and publicly supported libraries [p. 42].

By 1985, the OMB had provided a general policy framework in the form of Circular A–130 which urged federal agencies to place "maximum feasible reliance" on the private sector for the dissemination of information (p. A–9). Clearly, the thrust of federal policy over the last decade has been to encourage the information industry to appropriate large portions of the huge and valuable national stock of information (which the public has paid to have produced) so it can be repackaged in an online format and sold to clients at an enormous profit.

As a result of such policies, information firms such as Martin Marietta Data Systems, Mead Data Central, and Knight-Ridder now virtually monopolize government data. The decades' worth of international economic and export opportunities information synthesized by the National Trade Data Bank, for instance, or the crop and livestock data generated by the U.S. Department of Agriculture are now available commercially at prices that effectively preclude citizen access (Gross, 1991, pp. 38–41). Recently, the Electronic Data Gathering, Analysis and Retrieval system (EDGAR), developed by the Securities and Exchange Commission at a cost to taxpayers of more than $70 million, has been relinquished to a private vendor. EDGAR is the nation's most comprehensive corporate disclosure database and includes vital data on a company's assets, debt, stock, and long-term prospects. Currently, other than going to one of the SEC's three regional offices in Washington, New York, and Chicago where the system is available for free, access to EDGAR is available only through Mead Data Central's expensive Lexis/ Nexis online legal research and news service. Thus, "the financial filings the government requires of publicly held companies—information intended to discourage fraud, for the public well-being ... will be well insulated from the public it is intended to serve" (Abernathy, 1993, p. 52).

Equally significant for the future of free public inquiry and an informed citizenry is the fate of the Internet, whose future (as of this writing) hangs in the balance. Enabling inexpensive, global computer communication and providing access to vast stores of information, the Internet "could be the basis of a free social information facility in the electronic era, yet it is being divested of its public character" (Schiller, 1993a, p. 64). According to the *New York Times*, "the rush to commercialize ... the Internet has created an investor frenzy not seen in the technology industry since the early days of the personal computer ..." (Zuckerman, 1995, p. A1). Given the deregulatory fervor exemplified by the Telecommunications Act of 1996, the privatization of the Internet seems inevitable, with one like consequence being that the corporations that control telephone and cable lines (e.g., AT&T and Time-Warner) would determine access charges and be in a position to monitor and censor informational content.

Entrepreneurial Directions in Librarianship

The Clinton administration, for all of its rhetoric of the prospective social benefits resulting from the development of a new high-tech "information highway," has been no more concerned with insuring democratic public control over the nation's communications infrastructure than were its recent predecessors. In fact, "stunning corporate mergers and acquisitions among telephone, computer, cable, and entertainment companies, each of them already dominant in their field, are preparing the way for what could be ... an unprecedented corporate enclosure of national social and cultural space" (Schiller, 1993b, p. 753). Although the White House expects that "the private sector will build and run virtually all of the National Informational Infrastructure," it also promises that "all Americans [will] have access to the resources ... of the Information Age" (quoted in Schiller, 1993b, p. 753). The problem of how the public's cultural-informational needs will be met once the national communications sector is under private corporate control has not yet been satisfactorily addressed.

This view of information as a commodity, to be brought and sold on the market rather than as a public good, freely and equally accessible to all, which has shaped federal policy, has also gained an increasing number of adherents from within librarianship itself. Even a casual examination of professional literature over the last 10 years reveals an increasing preoccupation with matters of technical innovation and efficiency at the expense of equity of public service, as librarians and their patrons become "information brokers" with "clients." An emerging entrepreneurial model is now advocated by a contingent of leading library administrators, educators, and theorists and represents a fundamental shift in professional philosophy that aligns librarianship with powerful currents in business and government at the expense of its public service commitments. One leitmotif among proponents of a more entrepreneurial librarianship is an uncritical acceptance of the vision of a post-industrial "information society" where the technical expertise of librarians can be converted into considerable prestige and status. Those who advance this information age model aim to

> convince librarians that they must abandon their old self-perception as custodians of books and enter into the new world of information.... Information professionals are people whose work is focused on the processing of information, is frequently external to the library, is often freelance, and who sell their services to a well-defined segmented market and who are highly dependent on electronic technology [Apostle and Raymond, 1986, p. 378].

The latter perspective is exemplified in a *Library Journal* article by S. Michael Malinconico (1992), who points out that new technical developments "have spawned a robust and lively information market and the emergence of commercial suppliers of information services that may directly compete with libraries," but offers neither a defense of the historical library mission as a public sphere of inquiry and discourse, nor an analysis of how libraries can continue to fulfill this function in an increasingly privatized information environment. Instead, he is eager to dismiss "the old paradigm" of the autonomous library where information resources including "new technologies and services are assumed to be under the control and management of librarians" as uncompetitive in the increasingly market-driven information economy. Malinconico finds fault with an essay by another author because it postulates the library as "a central physical place to which people come: 'a public scholarly space'" and juxtaposes this notion with "another equally plausible scenario whereby information resources are drawn into the orbits of influence of those who maintain the technological infrastructures, including ... commercial information services" (pp. 36, 37).

The chief implication of Malinconico's article is that librarians now have the opportunity to "earn the status and respect long due," but only if they abandon their traditional social role in favor of that of "consulting information engineers" whose technical expertise is valuable to clients wishing to utilize expensive electronic resources with optimal cost-efficiency (p. 40). Nowhere in Malinconico's description of the "brave new world" of global information networks, electronic imaging, and nearly instantaneous document delivery does he raise the issue of differential access to these new services based on the ability to pay or the possibility that privatized information technology may generate an underclass of information poor. Apparently such concerns are part of "the old paradigm" of librarianship, which stands in the way of the profession's new high-status role as adjunct to the information industry.

Thomas Suprenant and Claudia Perry-Holmes (1985) are similarly concerned that what they view as outmoded principles such as free access to information and services will prevent libraries from holding their own in an increasingly competitive information environment. "The profession will be increasingly unable to offer new innovations to any users if there is a continued insistence on maintaining services at an artificially low pricing structure centered around those least able to pay" (p. 235). They claim that the introduction of fees for services will enhance the library's "institutional status" and advocate the adoption of an "entrepreneurial spirit" emphasizing efficiency, productivity, and quality control as a means to successfully compete with private information enterprises.

Ultimately, Suprenant and Perry-Holmes envision an information age future in which librarians will go directly to their clientele or establish themselves as "personal librarians" with offices and hours along the lines of other professionals.

> The salary of such professionals will come directly from their clientele. Thus, the greater the expertise and level of assistance provided, the higher the salary of the librarian. In essence, the future reference librarian will act much like an individual entrepreneur. Fees will be paid for all services [p. 236].

The authors prioritize the provision of cutting-edge information technology to those able to afford it, while paying scant attention to the ideal of library service as a public good. The effects of such policies would be to create a hierarchy of information users, which privileges an already well-served elite at the expense of less affluent patrons.

The same hierarchical approach to library service was advocated recently by David W. Lewis (1995) in his call for a reconsideration of the traditional egalitarian ethos of the profession. The commercial imperatives of the electronic library compel "libraries to define primary user groups, and to differentiate services provided to this group from the services provided to others. If libraries are to be competitive ... they must provide high quality service to their primary clienteles and refuse these services to others" (p. 11).

Equally enamored of a market approach to the provision of information is Richard DeGennaro (1989) who laments that librarianship's "traditions and ... organizational structures inhibit us from making the kind of innovation that is needed to compete and survive in this entrepreneurial and competitive marketplace." He observes that our society is experiencing a historical shift away from government ownership and planning toward privatization and free enterprise ("free is out, fee is in; cooperation is out, competition is in") and, while claiming not to be a proponent of these shifts ("I am not saying that all these changes are good"), he urges libraries to accommodate themselves to them. DeGennaro concludes that "the greatest challenge facing library leaders in the next decade ... is to implement new entrepreneurially oriented management structures and cultures" (p. 43).

Instead of advocating political activism to secure a more equitable distribution of funds between the private sector and libraries or urging librarians to organize in defense of the public sphere of non-commercial information, DeGennaro encourages an easy acquiescence in the imperatives of technocratic corporate capitalism. Ignoring the impact of powerful economic interests on social policy and political decisions, as well as the possibility of collective democratic intervention in the political process, he seems to think that recent "historical swings" toward privatization and competition have simply happened, independent of human agency.

At least implicit in the perspective on librarianship represented by theorists discussed above is the contention, very explicitly expressed by Linda Main (1990), that debate over broad "theoretical and philosophical issues" is passé. Instead of "abstractions like the role of information in society, values, and ethics ... the kind of thinking currently needed in libraries" revolves around automation, database management, and the like. "What we must be concerned with," says Main, "is what enables us to survive in a competitive world, namely information technology" (pp. 227, 228).

The value-neutrality perceived as the appropriate attitude for library professionals (especially the high-status information professionals of the future), militates against the formulation and advocacy of social ideals and political commitments. Thus library issues requiring theoretical debate and political action—the impact of market forces on the public information domain, the implications of information technology for equality of access, how libraries can best facilitate informed public inquiry in an increasingly privatized environment—are reduced to matters of technological innovation and expertise. Those who recommend "more technology and less social experimentation," who urge libraries to adopt "new entrepreneurially oriented management structures," see these strategies as necessary for the survival and future vitality of the profession (Gaines, 1980, p. 51; DeGennaro, 1989, p. 43). On the contrary, accepting a business ethic and allowing librarianship to slip into an easy accord with the prevailing influence of market values and transnational corporate interests will corrode the values that allow libraries to contribute to an enlightened public discourse.

Although the theorists discussed above perhaps go further and are more explicit in their advocacy of entrepreneurial models than current mainstream professional opinion, they represent trends that have already had a significant impact. Librarianship's nearly universal embrace of the latest developments in information technology, for example, has come about with little critical analysis or discussion of the social implications of this technology. The profession is in danger of succumbing to a purely instrumental mentality whereby the means of technique and efficiency override the ends that they should be properly serving, namely free and equal public access to a wide range of information and knowledge. We have failed to examine the extent to which technological innovations involve new types of social relations that may conflict with traditional library ideals.

John Buschman (1993) has argued that information technology is a prime conduit through which economic rationality and market values have infiltrated the profession. He points out that the same patterns of concentrated ownership of media outlets identified by Bagdikian, which restrict the diversity of print and broadcast resources, apply to the electronic resources becoming so central to library operations (pp. 129–132). Centralized corporate ownership of databases and other types of information technology represent a form of "market censorship," as materials in less profitable subject areas are not produced and disseminated. In the words of Roger Summit, president of Dialog Information Services while it was a subsidiary of Lockheed (Dialog is currently owned by the Knight–Ridder newspaper chain), "we can't afford an investment in data bases that are not going to earn their keep and pay back their development costs." When asked for an example, he replied, "humanities" (quoted in Schiller and Schiller, 1986, p. 308). Consequently, the nation's largest data base provider is overwhelmingly geared toward subjects of primary interest to the business and economics fields (Buschman, 1993, p. 132).

Furthermore, information technology, because of its close association with scientific rationality and powerful economic interests, represents a high-status, privileged knowledge format. As such, "library electronic resources are receiving heavy library investments, and they are primarily in service to the content needs of the science-technology-industry-administration-cycle" (Buschman, 1993, p. 134). Buschman suggests that by accepting the status of scientific-technical forms of information and ways of knowledge, the commitment of librarians to print literacy and humanistic modes of discourse is weakening. These issues cut to the core of librarianship's dedication to information and knowledge as a social good and demand debate concerning the values, objectives, and future direction of the profession.

Conclusion

It has been the argument of this paper that recent trends within the local domain of librarianship express the broader, in fact global, logic of advanced capitalist development, through which information has become a vital proprietary asset and wider areas of social and cultural life are drawn into the market nexus. Increasingly in this country, the rich and diverse sphere of images, ideas, and information necessary for a healthy democratic culture is being reduced to a flat uni-dimensional plane dominated by commercial values and ideological conformity. With the growing economic prominence of information has come the encroachment of corporate capitalism into the public information realm and a concomitant distortion of information issues and policies to serve private interests. At stake is the future vitality of democratic public spheres of independent art, inquiry, discourse, and critique.

Educational theorist Henry Giroux (1984) defines the public sphere as "those arenas of social life ... where dialogue and critique provide for the cultivation of democratic sentiments and habits" (p. 192). Schools, libraries, museums, and other public institutions, rather than being defined "as extensions of the workplace or as frontline institutions in the battle of international markets ... are constructed around forms of critical inquiry that dignify ... the discourse of public association and social responsibility." However, what Giroux (1988) says of schools, that they "are no longer being celebrated for their role as democratizing institutions," is equally true of other components of the public sphere. "The traditional arms-length relationship between [public sites of expression and dialogue] and business is now being dismantled for the purpose of aligning [them] more closely with ... corporate interests" (pp. xxxii, 178; see also Schiller, 1989).

Libraries, in the vortex of these developments, are susceptible to powerful economic and political forces. However, this is not to imply that library practice, or cultural activity in general, can be simply or easily determined by elite corporate agendas. The cultural-informational realm remains a complex and contested terrain whose future, ultimately, can be influenced by the ability of those librarians, educators, artists, and others who value a genuine cultural democracy to mobilize mass popular support in defense of free social information, in particular, and autonomous spaces of public expression, in general. It is imperative that librarians muster the political will to intervene in the development of any post-industrial "information society" in ways that foster social solidarity and democratic empowerment rather than private privilege and corporate hegemony. This struggle must begin with a sustained critique of the idea that the information needs of a democratic society can be left to market mechanisms, and a renewed dedication to the principle of free and equal access to a diverse sphere of knowledge as a public right.

REFERENCES

Abernathy, J. (1993, May 25). "Data for Sale." *Village Voice*, p. 52.

Apostle, R., and Raymond, B. (1986, December). "Librarianship and the Information Paradigm." *Canadian Library Journal*, pp. 377–384.

Bagdikian, B.H. (1989, June 12). "The Lords of the Global Village." *Nation*, pp. 805–820.

Bell, D. (1960). *The End of Ideology*. New York: Free Press.

_____, (1976). *The Coming of Post-industrial Society*. New York: Basic Books.

Best, S., and Kellner, D. (1991). *Postmodern Theory: Critical Interrogations*. New York: Guilford Press.

Buschman, J. (1993). "Issues in Censorship and Information Technology." In J. Buschman (ed.), *Critical Approaches to Information Technology in Librarianship*, pp. 125–149). Westport, CT: Greenwood Press.

DeGennaro, R. (1989, October 1). "Technology and Access in an Enterprise Society." *Library Journal*, pp. 41–43.

Drucker, P.F. (1993). *Post Capitalist Society*. New York: Harper.

Gaines, E.J. (1980, September). "Let's Return to Traditional Library Service." *Wilson Library Bulletin*, pp. 50–53+.

Giroux, H. (1984). "Public Philosophy and the Crisis in Education." *Harvard Educational Review*, 54, 186–194.

_____ (1988). *Teachers as Intellectuals: Toward a Critical Pedagogy of Learning*. Granby, MA: Bergin and Garvey.

Gross, D. (1991, November). "Byting the Hand That Feeds Them." *Washington Monthly*, pp. 37–41.

Harris, M.H., and Hannah, S.A. (1993). *Into the Future: The Foundations of Library and Information Services in the Post-industrial Era*. Norwood, NJ: Ablex.

Harvey, D. (1989). *The Condition of Postmodernity*. Oxford: Basil Blackwell.

Hawkins, D.T. (1987, January). "The Commodity Nature of Information." *Online*, pp. 67–70.

Horkheimer, M., and Adorno, T.W. (1989). *Dialectic of Enlightenment*. New York: Continuum.

Jameson, F. (1991). *Postmodernism, or, The Cultural Logic of Late Capitalism*. Durham, NC: Duke University Press.

Jansen, S.C. (1993). "Censorship, Critical Theory, and New Information Technologies: Foundations of Critical Scholarship in Communications." In J. Buschman (ed.), *Critical Approaches to Information Technology in Librarianship* (pp. 59–83). Westport, CT: Greenwood Press.

Kellner, D. (1989). *Critical Theory, Marxism, and Modernity*. Baltimore: Johns Hopkins University Press.

Lewis, David W. (1995, January). "Traditional Reference Is Dead, Now Let's Move On to Important Questions." *Journal of Academic Librarianship*, pp. 10–12.

Main, L. (1990). "Research Versus Practice: A "No" Contest." *Journal of Education for Library and Information Science*, XX, 226–228.

Malinconico, S.M. (1992, May 1). "Information's Brave New World." *Library Journal*, pp. 36–40.

National Commission on Libraries and Information Science (1982). *Public/Private Sector Interaction in Providing Information Services*. Report to NCLIS from the public /private sector task force. Washington, DC: Government Printing Office.

Office of Management and Budget (1985). "Management of Federal Information Resources." In Toby F. McIntosh (ed.), *Federal Information in the Electronic Age: Policy Issues for the 1990s* (pp. A3–A24). Washington, DC: Bureau of National Affairs.

Office of Technology Assessment (1988). *Technology and the American Economic Transition.* Quoted in Colin Norman, "Rethinking Technology's Role in Economic Change." *Science,* 240, 977.

Porat, M.U. (1977). *The Information Economy, Vol. 1: Definition and Measurement.* Washington, DC: Office of Telecommunication.

Rose, M.A. (1991). *The Post-modern and the Post-industrial: A Critical Analysis.* Cambridge: Cambridge University Press.

Schiller, A.R., and Schiller, H.I. (1986, October 4). "Commercializing Information." *Nation,* pp. 306–309.

Schiller, H.I. (1989). *Culture, Inc.: The Corporate Takeover of Public Expression.* New York: Oxford University Press.

_____ (1993a, July 12). The "Information Highway: Public Way or Private Road?" *Nation,* pp. 64–66.

_____ (1993b, December 20). "Highway Robbers." *Nation,* pp. 753+.

Suprenant, T.T., and Perry-Holmes, C. (1985). "The Reference Librarian of the Future: A Scenario." *RQ,* 24, 234–238.

UNESCO (1982). *Cultural Industries: A Challenge for the Future of Culture.* Paris: UNESCO.

White House Conference on Library and Information Services, 1979 (1980). *Summary.* Washington, DC: Government Printing Office.

Zuckerman (1995, August 10). "With Internet Cachet, Not Profit, a New Stock Amazes Wall St." *New York Times,* pp. A1, D5.

IV
Ethics and the Internet

The Freedom of
Information Act: Public
Access in the Computer Age

Senator Patrick Leahy

Late at night in the midst of the 1992 presidential campaign, employees of the U.S. State Department searched the passport files of then-candidate Bill Clinton and his mother Virginia Kelley. Two weeks later, the files of Independent candidate Ross Perot were also searched. According to the State Department, these searches were made pursuant to requests from the press for information under the Freedom of Information Act (FOIA). A former State Department employee has charged, however, that the order to investigate the files came from the White House in an effort to discredit Clinton's candidacy. How ironic that the federal statute intended to increase government accountability has been used to justify government abuse!

FOIA Abuses

The FOIA ensures government information, with limited exceptions, to anyone who requests it. The Act is no more and no less than a codification of the democratic principle that the public has the "right to know." In my time in the Senate, I have fought efforts to limit the scope of the act. That has been particularly difficult during the last two Administrations, which have not only been dismissive but often hostile to FOIA. Earlier this year, for example, a House of Representatives Subcommittee unearthed a memorandum from NASA instructing agency employees on ways to minimize the disclosure of public information through the FOIA. It is an outrage that any federal agency would encourage its employees to thwart the public's right to know what the government is doing. Unfortunately, this memo is only the latest in a series of efforts by NASA to withhold information from the press and the public. During the debate on the 1987 Trade Bill, the Administration told the Senate that the release of NASA information through the FOIA saved the Japanese "hundreds of millions of dollars and years of research." This example was offered in an unsuccessful attempt to pass a new exemption to the FOIA. I asked the Administration for a copy of the alleged Japanese FOIA request and was astounded to learn that there had never been one, even though the administration earlier claimed there was. Although there was no request by the Japanese, there were requests by American journalists who used the FOIA to get important information about the space shuttle Challenger. The public had a right to that information even if it revealed failed policies and political embarrassment. In the context, the recent passport incident at the State Department is not an aberration, but the culmination of an attitude of disdain for the statute.

FOIA Success Stories

Despite frequent agency intransigence, FOIA has led to the disclosure of important information on consumer health and safety; waste, fraud and abuse in the government; foreign policy; civil and constitutional rights; and the environment.

Recent FOIA requests have revealed:
- environmental dangers, including a hazardous waste problem caused by the military at Subic Bay Naval Base in the Philippines and evidence of 161 violations of the Federal Clean Water Act at Kennedy Airport;
- valuable new information on the events of the Cuban Missile crisis, including previously classified correspondence between President Kennedy and Soviet leader Nikita Khrushchev;
- data about the negative consequences of the S&L crisis on Colorado real estate;
- evidence that the Army's Criminal Investigation Division (CID) has conducted hundreds of investigations of homosexual activity—including activity between consenting adults—in the military during Desert Shield and Desert Storm.

Electronic FOIA

Currently, I am working to ensure that technology will not make parts of this valuable statute obsolete. In the last several years, computers have become as commonplace in federal agencies as they have in businesses and homes. Computers make it easier and more efficient to manage the tremendous amount of information collected, stored, and used by the government. The obvious question is, What effect will this technology have on the public's right to government information? The technology should mean more access for people—like those with sight or hearing impairments—who traditionally have been excluded from meaningful participation in our system of government. As a representative from the American Foundation for the Blind has explained:

> Access to information is probably the most important benefit that we can give our citizens…. Blind and other print-disabled people must not be put into an information underclass by being denied access to information that is otherwise publicly available.

New computer technology should mean for FOIA what is has meant for the rest of the world—faster, cheaper, and more efficient communications. The Vermont State Library system is an excellent example of the potential for electronic information systems. The Vermont Automated Library System (VALS) is an easily accessible, on-line computer network that connects public and private academic and state libraries and makes them available to the most rural parts of the state. In addition to library holdings, the system includes automated services for the blind and handicapped, full text databases of Vermont Supreme Court opinions and Vermont session laws, newspaper indices, and a human services database. As a Vermont librarian has explained:

> In Vermont, we have been able to use technology to make the most efficient use of our scattered resources, but beyond that we have been able to make more types of information readily accessible. Public libraries are being transformed into information centers for their communities. The VALS network brings the information age to Vermont's rural communities and insures that Vermonters have access on a par with their urban counterparts.

Unfortunately, the federal government does not always take such a positive approach to enhanced access to information. Some agencies use computers to frustrate rather than to help requesters, while others simply do not use computers efficiently. Last year, Senator Hank Brown (R-CO) and I introduced the Electronic Freedom of Information Improvements Act, which will bring FOIA into the computer age. Several issues must be addressed. How do we characterize a FOIA search of an automated database? Is it comparable to the traditional search of a file cabinet? My view is that not only is it a search, but that it should be faster and easier for an agency to do. In light of agencies' use of both paper records and computer tapes, should requesters be given the format of their choice? My proposal requires an agency to make available the requester's format of choice, if that format exists. If it does not, the agency should make reasonable efforts to provide it. My legislation also addresses the persistent problem of delays. Requesters who wait weeks, months, even years to get information from the government, complain bitterly about the uselessness of the FOIA for authors working under time constraints. Although there is no question that agencies sometimes delay to avoid responding to a specific request, it is also true that in this age of budget deficits, lack of resources is a serious problem. I have proposed that we allow agencies to retain half of the FOIA fees they collect, *if* they comply with the time limits in the statute. The retained fees will be channeled back into the agency's FOIA operation to supplement current resources. This incentive should alleviate some of the horrendous FOIA backlogs. I have also proposed changes that would tighten the national security, law enforcement, and financial institution exemptions, define "commercial requester" for purposes of the fee structure, and extend the scope of FOIA to cover both the legislative branch and the President. Under my proposal Congress would subject itself and the President to those responsibilities we impose on others. I recognize that applying FOIA to Congress raises important constitutional and policy issues, but those issues should be explored fully.

Conclusion

FOIA's value is that it assures the public that the government will operate in the open. The purpose of FOIA is to make information available to the public—it is a disclosure statute, not a withholding statute. Information provided through FOIA enables the American people to temper the excesses of their government. It is too easy and too tempting for the government to shroud mistakes, embarrassments, and political miscalculations behind the veil of government silence. A responsible government must resist that temptation.

Access Denied: Information Policy and the Limits of Liberalism

Grant H. Kester

In 1968 the United States military's Defense Advanced Research Project (DARPA) established the world's first computer-based e-mail system. In the intervening two and a half decades the computer network has emerged as one of the central technological forms of the twentieth century. From local e-mail systems to a planned nationwide fiber-optic "superhighway," computer networks have proliferated to interconnect businesses, governments, and individuals around the world. Estimates of the worldwide market for the interactive information industry run as high as $3.5 trillion by the year 2000.[1] As the site of such intense economic development it is not surprising that the computer network has also been subject to a process of intensive ideological staging. A set of mythologies circulates around the utopian or dystopian implications of the computer network, ranging from the malevolent, inter-connected defense computers of *Terminator* (1984) by James Cameron, to the visions of artists for whom computer networks herald "our emergence into the new world of telematic culture ... [a world] that can link us with superconnectivity, mind to mind, into a new planetary community."[2]

These mythologies are, by and large based on an existing narrative framework that first emerged during the industrial revolution. Within this framework new technologies or technological forms, (the mechanical loom, the assembly line, electricity, the telephone, etc.), are celebrated—or feared—for their capacity to generate unlimited power, mobility, or productivity, and to transcend the boundaries of existing forms of social experience and organization. The *sheer magnitude of speed, distance, and scale* opened up by these technologies locates our experience of them within the domain of what Leo Marx describes as the "technological sublime"; their dimensions or limitations are literally beyond our imagination.[3]

In his essay, "The Mythos of the Electronic Revolution," James W. Carey examines the utopian myths that surrounded technologies such as steam power and the printing press in nineteenth century America. Carey cites a contemporary address on the impact of the industrial revolution that describes steam as a "great motive agent" that will "...bring everything into harmonious cooperation ... triumphing over space and time ... to subdue prejudice and to unite every part of our land in rapid and friendly communication...."[4] He then charts the transition that took place in the late nineteenth century from the celebration of the "mechanical sublime" of the industrial revolution, embodied in the steam power, to the nascent "electrical sublime." While mechanization had promised abundance and freedom it had resulted in overcrowded cities, industrial pollution, social fragmentation, and a growing division of labor. Electricity, however, would be different, it would:

> ... give us universally high standards of living, new and amusing kinds of jobs, leisure, freedom and an end to drudgery, congestion, noise, smoke, and filth. It can overcome the objections and problems of a steam civilization. It can bring back many of the mourned virtues of the handicraft age without the human toil and curse of impending scarcity that marked the age.[5]

In short, "Electricity promised ... the same freedom, decentralization, ecological harmony, and democratic community that had hitherto been guaranteed but left undelivered by mechanization."[6] Carey goes on to cite a fascinating passage from a late nineteenth century economic treatise titled *The Unity of Law*, in which electrical power functions as the metaphorical embodiment of democratic organization.

> The actual relation of each and every member of a community as giver and receiver, teacher and learner, producer and consumer is positive and negative by turns and relatively [sic] to every difference of function and force in his associates, the whole mass constituting a great electric battery to which each individual contributes his pair of plates. Perfect circulation being established as a consequence of perfect development of all individualities, the economic force flows smoothly through every member of the body politic, general happiness and prosperity, improved mental and moral action following in its train....[7]

The "economic force" flows through the "great electric battery" of society, bringing about the "perfect development" of each individual, even as it promotes the health of the larger body politic. Electricity here functions as a kind of Adam Smith-ian "invisible hand" providing a providential coordination of the otherwise disparate and self-interested actions of individual citizens. This statement is emblematic of the close relationship between free-market ideologies and notions of individualism and democratic freedom in the American liberal tradition. It is also significant because of the curious relationship these first two have with technology. A technological form, in this case, electricity, takes on a metaphoric relationship to systems of economic value and to a model of democratic will formation.

Electricity doesn't simply function as a technology in the service of particular forms of production, rather, the physical process on which electricity operates becomes a paradigm for a form of social organization. Electricity is simultaneously a normative model for democratic community and the technological agent that will bring this community about. This paradigmatic function is absolutely central to understanding the way in which new technologies are rhetorically framed. Networks, whether they are the rail transportation links made possible by steam technology, the high-tension power lines of rural electrification, or the data matrix of computer telecommunications, have traditionally made the same interconnected promises of material abundance, decentralization, and democratic community.

There is a striking similarity in the claims advanced for electricity around the turn of the century, and the rhetoric surrounding computer networks today. We might designate this, following Carey, as the transition from the "electrical sublime" to the "informational sublime." Each technological form promises to eliminate the "drudgery" of conventional manual labor, transforming us all into "knowledge workers"[8]; each will replace the pollution of conventional manufacturing with clean, "high technology" industries, and most importantly, each will encourage a decentralized, democratic and community ethos in American culture. Under the influence of computer technology the fragmented anomie of late capitalist society will be transformed into the vital, democratic polls of the fiber optic network. From Ross Perot's televised "town hall" meetings to Roy Ascott's "telematic embrace," the computer network has been widely posited as the very embodiment of a liberal public sphere.[9]

The speculative culture that surrounds network technology today, particularly in what might be identified as its "alternative" guises—in the pages of publications such as *Mondo 2000* and *Wired*, in the work of the Electronic Frontier Foundation (EFF), or the writings of Jaron Lanier, Howard Rheingold, and others—is based on a particular conjunction of the informational sublime and the discourse of the modernist avant-garde. Their pronouncements center around the liberatory potential of the network, and by implication, of the computer-skilled artist/rebel. Within this subculture, network technologies are posited as representing a profound break with existing forms of community, communication, and political organization. These claims are, by and large, oriented toward predicting the future possibilities of network technology. But network systems have been in place, both commercially and in the government and the military, for some time, and any subsequent developments in network culture will inevitably be informed by the institutions into which they will be inserted.

Here I will investigate the performance of an existing network system. My goal is to analyze the ways in which network technology actually functions within a particular institutional location: the executive branch of the Government. This network has been the site of a particularly interesting legal confrontation that bears directly on the function of network technology within the liberal state. I will discuss the bureaucratic and ideological context of federal information policy and the impact that computer systems have had on it. I will conclude by looking at the rhetoric that surrounds network technology more generally in relation to the sub-culture that has grown up around Internet.

Executive Privilege and the Freedom of Information Act

In the fall of 1792 General Arthur Saint Claire, acting under orders from President George Washington, led a military expedition into Native American territory in what is now northwestern Ohio. On the morning of November 4 his expedition was attacked by a "small but determined Indian band" and over half of the company killed.[10] When word of the attack reached Congress a committee was formed to investigate the incident, in which Washington had effectively engaged in an act of war without Congressional consent. The committee requested the relevant records and papers of Washington and Secretary of War Henry Knox. During an initial meeting Washington suggested that included among these documents "there might be papers of so secret a nature that they ought not to be given up."[11] Although Washington did, ultimately, surrender the material the committee requested the incident established the principle of "executive privilege" which states that, in response to requests from Congress, "the Executive ought to communicate such papers as the public good would permit, and ought to refuse those, the disclosure of which would injure the public."[12]

Thus was formed the bureaucratic scene within which debates over federal information policy would unfold for the next two centuries. Within this scene the legislative and executive branches engage in a highly ritualized pas de deux of accusation and moral censure, solicitation, and coy denial over topics ranging from presidential appointments to land fraud investigations to foreign treaty negotiations to covert military operations. The theater in which this drama plays itself out includes the floor of Congress as well as the federal court system. But what exactly is being "performed" in confrontations between the President and Congress over the control of information? It is the spectacle of democracy, and the tripartite division of power that both governs and insures democratic rule. I will return to examine this performance more closely. For now I simply want to note that the debate over government information policy should be more specifically understood as a debate about the relative authority held by the President, Congress, and the courts in determining, defending, or speaking on behalf of the "public good."

Within this debate the President has traditionally relied on the doctrine of executive privilege to assert final authority in determining the public good. The doctrine of executive privilege derives primarily from concerns that the President, in his capacity as commander of the armed forces, must be free to determine the "best interests" of the state due to his privileged access to the details of complex military and diplomatic negotiations and relationships. Prior to the twentieth-century this doctrine was applied in a fairly unsystematic fashion, and debates over government information were relatively sporadic. In fact, it wasn't until the U.S. military was exposed to the protocols governing information secrecy employed by the French and British armies during World War I that it began to employ an organized system for classifying documents.[13]

The real expansion in classification systems and government secrecy in the U.S. occurred during World War II, as the U.S. in conjunction with its allies developed a sophisticated apparatus for collecting, transmitting, analyzing and archiving military and political "intelligence" on a global scale.[14] After the war this control became increasingly centralized and coordinated under the apparent threat posed by the USSR and "world communism."[15] The establishment of the Central Intelligence Agency (CIA) and the National Security Agency (NSA) along with the close relationship between high-technology weapons research and "national security" (President Truman referred to the secret of the atomic bomb as America's "sacred trust"),[16] led to the creation of a system in which every piece of information generated by key government agencies and affiliated private businesses and universities was subject to a complex calculation of potential risk. It was an environment in which it was assumed that almost *any* piece of information could, if it fell into the wrong hands, pose a threat to America's national security. Thus, post-war information policy was ultimately inseparable from the larger attempt by the American government to manage Cold War–era global politics. Within this scenario any consideration of the "public good" that involved the access of the American public to information employed by or generated by the President in the process of governing was overridden by the larger external "threat" posed to the nation by the Soviet Union. This gave the doctrine of executive privilege an almost irresistible political authority.

During the late '50s and early '60s the climate of opinion around government information policy began to shift, in part due to the relative decline of rabid anti-communism following Joseph McCarthy's loss of credibility in the Army–McCarthy hearings. It was at this time that the doctrine of executive privilege began to be challenged by a coalition of liberal members of

Congress and groups such as the American Civil Liberties Organization (predecessor to the American Civil Liberties Union), the American Bar Association, and the American Society of Newspaper Editors.[17] One of the most outspoken Congressional critics of government secrecy was Rep. John Moss (D–CA), the chairman of the House Foreign Operations and Government Information Subcommittee. The committee had been established by the Democratic Congress in 1955 to "curb the rampant suppression of government information during the Eisenhower administration."[18] For over a decade Moss' committee held a series of hearings that finally resulted in the drafting of the Freedom of Information Act (FOIA), which was signed into law by a "reluctant" President Lyndon Johnson on July 4, 1966.[19] The FOIA was strengthened in 1974, in the wake of Watergate, in an attempt to bring more pressure to bear on recalcitrant government agencies and in order to make it easier, and faster, for researchers to gain access to records.[20]

The arguments developed in support of the FOIA constitute what I would describe as a "liberal" position on government information policy. This position is based on the classic model of liberal democracy in which the will of the people is the ultimate determinant and legitimation of government policy. This "will" is enacted through the participation of the people in periodic elections in which the majority vote to elect an individual who will then go on to represent their interests in the legislature through the drafting of laws and through open debate with other duly elected representatives. There is thus a signifying relationship between the elected representatives specifically, and the state in general, and the individual citizen on whose behalf the representatives speak. Within this system, it is argued, each individual voter must have access to as much information as is necessary to develop an informed opinion about the issues of the day, and thus be able to elect the individual who most fully represents that opinion.

Within the liberal model information functions as the veritable life blood of the democratic process. As Harlan Cleveland notes in an essay written on the twentieth anniversary of the passage of the FOIA, "To consider government information policy is not far from considering the essence of government itself."[21] The liberal position is conveyed in the Supreme Court's decision in NLRB versus Robbins Tire and Rubber Co. in which the Court observed that

> ... the basic purpose of FOIA is to ensure an informed citizenry, vital to the functioning of a democratic society, needed to check against corruption and to hold the governors accountable to the governed.[22]

In an essay on the relationship between the judicial system and the FOIA, Phillip Cooper relates what he calls the "Free Flow" theory of information to arguments developed by the Supreme Court in support of the freedom of expression—placing the FOIA clearly within the liberal political canon. Cooper goes on to argue that the FOIA is "...concerned with assuring *the capacity of the citizenry to address specific substantive policy issues* and with the maintenance of important structural features of the governing framework such as elections and the arrangement of checks and balances" (emphasis mine).[23] Cooper's comment is representative of the general set of beliefs held by proponents of the "liberal" position on information theory. The paradigmatic "user" of the FOIA in this view would be an individual citizen who requests government information in order to "address substantive policy issues," and to become a better-informed voter. It is thus presumed that the FOIA functions as a direct conduit or channel for information that "flows" from the state to the "citizenry," whose political will then "flows" back to the state in the form of their voting behavior. Information here functions as a cognate of the "economic force" that circulates within the "battery" of the electrical sublime. In this view the moral economy of the FOIA is constituted around a binary logic in which the sheer fact that "information," in whatever form it might take, is "flowing" and "accessible" constitutes a progressive movement. The flow of information in both is taken as a paradigm for a broader cultural progress towards the telos of a democratic society.

The status of the FOIA was considerably complicated by the growing use of computer systems to store federal documents. In 1955 (the year the Moss Committee was chartered) the government had 45 mainframe computers—by 1970 there were 5277 in use.[24] Between 1980 and 1985, according to the Office of Technology Assessment, the number of personal computers in federal agencies went from a few thousand to over 100,000.[25] The rapid proliferation of computer systems was in part a response to the literal flood of government records generated by the expansion of the federal bureaucracy during the 1960s, which eventually led to the passage of the Federal Paperwork Reduction Act in 1980. The transition to computerized data storage systems did much to heighten both the promise and the contradictions of the FOIA. On a practical level the technical and logistical skills required to file and process FOIA requests were complicated by the presence of computers. In addition, the FOIA had no provisions for dealing with documents that existed solely in the form of magnetic impulses on tape. Thus, the epistemological status of computer records (a topic of some interest in the PROFS case that I will examine subsequently) was uncertain.

But more importantly for my analysis, the introduction of computer technology into government record-keeping marks a paradigmatic intersection between the "informational sublime" sketched above and the liberal discourse surrounding the FOIA. With the introduction of computer technology into the existing set of arguments about democracy and political empowerment via the FOIA, the technological form of the network would seem to have found its ideal bureaucratic setting. The individual users of the FOIA are transformed into a democratic collective via their participation in the "interactive" mechanism of representative government. The existence of computer systems in government record-keeping promised to provide an unprecedented level of access to the workings of the state, and to profoundly alter the balance of information power between the state and the citizen. The introduction of computers presaged a new era of government accountability, and the end of "official secrecy." This combination of telecommunications technologies and the rhetoric of "open government" played a central role in the last presidential election, with candidates Bill Clinton and Al Gore presenting themselves as committed to the "on-line" accessibility of the government to the American people.

The "*free flow*" model correlates with what Carl Schmitt, in his classic study, *The Crisis of Parliamentary Democracy* 1923), describes as the "metaphysical system" or liberalism, which is based on the belief that "...the truth can be found through an unrestrained clash of opinion, and the competition will produce harmony."[26] According to Schmitt, the system of liberalism is based on two discursive structures. The first is the principle of a free and open discussion among political equals that will result in the formation of a natural consensus. This consensus represents the highest "truth" of the liberal system: "What was to be secured through the balance guaranteed by openness and discussion was nothing less than truth and justice itself."[27] Necessary to the formation of a consensus is an openness in the conduct of governmental affairs. Schmitt traces the emergence of openness as an "absolute" political value to the debate over state secrets or *Arcana rei publicae*, in the 16th and 17th centuries: "The postulate of openness finds its specific opponent in the idea that *Arcana* belong to every kind of politics, political-technical secrets.... Openness becomes an absolute value, although at first it was only a practical means to combat the bureaucratic, specialist-technical secret politics of absolutism."[28] The second postulate is the "division of powers," a "competition," according to Schmitt, "from which the truth will emerge" in the "division or balance of different state activities and institutions."[29] We find each of these postulates effectively expressed in the debates over Government information policy. The liberal state is meant to be the expression of a general social will formed via discussion and debate among equal subjects. It is protected from undue bias through a balance of powers mechanism in which the legislative, judicial, and executive functions are separated. Thus the FOIA is primarily a product of the leverage exerted by the judicial and legislative branches against the threat of an excessive influence wielded by the executive branch.

The claims of proponents notwithstanding, the path taken by information requested through the FOIA does not, by and large, flow directly from the state to the citizen, but rather from the state, through various mechanisms within the media or the "access community," and then into books, news articles, and investigative projects that will, eventually, reach the public, or at least that segment of the public that gains access to the book, newspaper, journal, or television show in question. In most FOIA scenarios the mediating role of the press is elided. The media or the individual researcher is made equivalent with the public, and the simple fact that government information is accessible to the media is presumed to be tantamount to that information reaching "the public," and satisfying the requirement for public deliberation of "substantive issues" that is at the basis of democratic systems of government. Thus, Supreme Court Justice Powell has defined the press simply as "*the means by which the people receive that free flow of information and ideas essential to intelligent self-government (emphasis mine).*"[30] Here the press is cast as a neutral carrier of information, rather than a form of institutional "mediation" that exerts its own influence and discretion on the material it conveys.

Another level of mediation in the dissemination of federal information is introduced by the legal/logistical complexity of the FOIA procedures themselves. The process of writing and filing an FOIA request requires the bureaucratic skill, not to mention time, necessary to negotiate with the various federal agencies involved, to correlate document sets, formulate search parameters, submit search requests, and even mount court cases in the event of refusals to disclose. Thus, a cadre of access specialists and access activists has emerged, primarily within the academic, journalistic, and legal professions—writers and researchers who specialize in working with materials collected through FOIA requests. It is largely through the work of these individuals that documents released under the FOIA make their way into the sphere of public debate. At the same time, within the government, the process of responding to FOIA requests has spawned an entire civil service specialization around the figure of the "access professional" (the "American Society of Access Professionals" was formed in 1980) who reviews FOIA requests, determines what material can be released, develops arguments for withholding other materials, etc.[31]

In their essay "Information Poverty and Political Inequality: Citizenship in the Age of Privatized Communications," sociologists Graham Murdock and Peter Golding identify three "relations" between citizenship and modes of communication. The first relation requires "access to ... information ... that will enable [people] to know what their rights are in other spheres." The second states that people "must have access to the broadest possible range of information ... on areas that involve political choices, and they must be able to use communications facilities in order to register criticism, mobilize opposition, and propose alternative courses of action." And the third contends that people "must be able to recognize themselves and their aspirations in the range of representations offered within the central communications sectors and be able to contribute to developing those representations."[32]

It is significant that the authors recognize the conceptual distinction between the sheer fact of access, and the capacity to effectively engage in political decision-making in their second relation. However, they never clarify exactly how access to information might be transformed into the ability of the individual to "mobilize opposition," or "propose alternative courses of action." Nor do we know what if any effect these proposed courses of action or criticisms might have. This seems to me to be a crucial question. Simply having access to an information network, or even possessing the ability to direct communication back to the government, while significant, is ultimately not sufficient if the existing system of government is unaccountable to, or, in Jürgen Habermas's words, "immunized" from popular will. As Habermas argues in *Legitimation Crisis* (1973), one of the central components of modern liberal government is the process whereby decisions governing the systematic orientation of the state in relation to dominant economic interests are effectively partitioned off from the electoral process.

> Democracy no longer has the goal of rationalizing authority through the participation of citizens in discursive processes of will-formation. It is intended, instead, to make possible compromises between ruling elites. Thus, the substance of classical democratic theory is finally surrendered. No longer *all* politically consequential decisions, but only those decisions of the government *still defined as political*, are to be subject to the precepts of democratic will formation ... [Habermas's emphasis].[33]

There are thus two criticisms to be made of the liberal, "free flow" model; two points at which the cybernetic loop of participatory democracy is, potentially, arrested. First, information does not by and large flow directly to "the public," rather, it is mediated by a bureaucratic class of journalists and access professionals. And second, even if members of the public do get access to information, the "feedback loop" that could transform the opinions they construct based on this information into substantive changes in government policy is, arguable, not functional. These two criticisms are interrelated. In his classic study *The Structural Transformation of the Public Sphere* (1962). Habermas traces "...the dissolution and obsolescence of the link—still pretended to by liberalism—between public discussion and legal norm."[34] Instead of a situation in which debate and opinion formation among individuals and communities is translated into political action, all "merely individual opinions" must be "mediatized" (or processed through the institutions of the press) to have any legitimacy as the expression or communication of a "public opinion." Thus, debates or conflicts that take place between the legislative and executive branches, or between the press (or access activists) and the government, "stand in" for an actual public discourse.[35] In many cases, as the quote above from Justice Powell suggests, the press become virtually synonymous with the public interest. But, as Habermas notes:

... the formation of public opinion in the strict sense is not effectively secured by the mere fact that anyone can freely utter his opinion and put out a newspaper. The Public is no longer composed of persons formally and materially on an equal footing.[36]

Computer technology promised to regulate the explosion of government information and to provide more efficient and effective forms of data storage, organization, and retrieval. Yet the computer also exerted its own peculiar logic; the presence of a more accessible record-keeping technology led to the generation of more records, and a necessary expansion in the definition of what constitutes a record in the first place. There was a growing disjunction between the record-keeping capacities of the computer, and the existing protocols governing the status and disposition of data generated by government employees. The rough drafts and inter-agency memos that might have previously wound up in the wastebasket were now saved on hard-drives and mainframes. The proliferation of personal computers led to the expansion of a new terrain of federal record-keeping, at the micro-level of the individual government worker's computerized notes, appointment records, on-line logs, etc. At the same time an increasing proportion of the communication and analysis that constitutes the bureaucratic work of the government was never generated in the form of a paper document, existing only in the form of magnetic impulses on a tape or disk.

> No longer is information merely stored and retrieved by computer. Now, information is routinely collected on computer tapes, used within an agency in computer form, exchanged with and disclosed to regional offices or other agencies in computer form, manipulated and analyzed with sophisticated computer software, and archived on computer tapes.[37]

As computer technology and record-keeping systems were more widely used within the government they led to a greater and greater level of documentation, which in turn promised (or threatened) to provide a heretofore unknown level of detail about how the government interacts and operates. During the early 1980s the Reagan administration, recognizing this threat, launched a successful counterattack against the FOIA, employing a "panoramic" definition of national security. The attack was based on several points, including the expense of the implementation of FOIA requests[38]; Drug Enforcement Administration claims that a large number of FOIA users were actually criminals, and had a fear that their political opponents would use the FOIA to embarrass or attack them. As one official from the Office of Management and Budget noted:

> There is a concurrence in the belief of the bad effect of too much disclosure.... The administration feared that, by providing information about what they were doing, they would also provide critics with an opportunity to shoot at

them.... There has been an educational process, explaining to agencies how to restrict information.[39]

The Reagan administration instituted an FOIA "user fee" requirement for the first time in 1983—ostensibly in order to pay for FOIA expenses, and also engaged in a rampant reclassification of previously de-classified documents, effectively placing them beyond the reach of the FOIA. It also developed the theory of an "information mosaic," "the idea that hostile elements can use sophisticated search techniques to assemble bits of seemingly harmless information into insights that threaten national security." An often-cited example of this danger was the 1979 publication by the *Progressive* magazine of a blueprint for manufacturing an H-bomb that was compiled from information contained in various available government documents. As John Shattuck and Muriel Morisey Spence note in their study of government information policy, "Proponents of the mosaic theory ... used it to fashion a broad expansion of the classification system."[40]

With the growing use of computer networks the government is faced with the problem of an information blizzard—a lascivious and potentially threatening intermingling in which memos, affidavits, invoices, receipts, bank statements, and other documents combine and recombine themselves to produce dangerous new constellations of meaning. In this scenario the threat doesn't lie with a single piece of damaging information that "leaks out" and exposes government malfeasance, but with the possible interconnections that might be made among dozens of different bits of information; bits that might mean little or nothing by themselves, but that, when assembled by the researcher into a particular narrative form, could prove extremely damaging.

It is precisely this narrative logic, and the associated procedures of indexing and information retrieval, that have been taken up as strategic tools within the access community of researchers and journalists who make use of the FOIA. The network systems used to store and process government records possess an unprecedented capacity to literally map the processes of the state, as embodied in the flow of data through its bureaucratic systems. Researchers at the National Security Archives (NSA, a non-profit research institute and library facility in Washington, D.C.) place multiple FOIA requests for the same document from various agencies, knowing that each agency will choose to delete different material, and then combine these sets to produce a single, more or less complete, version of the document. The NSA indexes vast date sets with key search terms, allowing researchers to unravel the complex interconnections of government agencies and operations. This technique can provide a kind of "mapping" of the covert government apparatus—allowing researchers to ascertain the larger topology of political and economic power and privilege as it is deployed throughout the information systems of the state.

The questions raised by the epistemological status of computer records were at the center of a recent federal court case regarding the disposition of data transmitted through federal e-mail systems. The case began with a suit that was filed in U.S. District Court in Washington D.C. in the waning days of the Reagan administration by a consortium of groups that included the NSA, Ralph Nader's Public Citizen Action Group, and the American Civil Liberties Union (ACLU). The suit charged the Executive Office of the President (EOP) with violating the Federal Records Act by destroying data contained in their computerized e-mail systems.[41] The plaintiffs in the case argued that messages and documents that were transmitted through the e-mail systems (PROFS, Oasis, and A-1) connecting the EOP, the White House, and the National Security Council (NSC), constituted federal records because they were used in the governing process. At that time this material was stored temporarily on back-up tapes held in mainframe computers, and the tapes, rather than being saved, were eventually recorded over and re-used. The defendants in the case, including the White House, NSC, EOP, and subsequently the National Archives, argued that the information on these tapes did not constitute a federal record because it was never printed out in the form of a paper copy.

The case is indirectly connected to the ongoing Iran-contra investigation since many of the back-up tapes in question were used as evidence in the case. As NSA researcher and co-plaintiff Eddie Becker has noted, it was the flexibility of the computer network system that allowed Lieutenant Colonel Oliver L. North to coordinate all the government agencies necessary to "run a covert war on three continents" without leaving a paper trail.[42] The case also charged the National Archives with abrogating its responsibility in determining which government agency documents constitute federal records.[43]

After almost four years of appeals and motions, Federal Judge Charles R. Richey reached a decision in the case in early January of this year. Richey's ruling stated that the existing record-keeping protocols of the NSC, the EOP, and the National Archives, were "capricious and arbitrary," and he ordered the Bush administration to immediately save all existing back-up tapes and computerized records, including hard drives and floppy disks. He further argued that the e-mail logs or directories, which contained information on who sent what message to whom and when, were themselves record material, even though this information was never printed out in paper form. Richey's ruling was premised on two earlier pieces of legislation: the FOIA and the 1943 Federal Records Act (FRA). The FRA defines a Federal Record as:

... all books, paper, maps, photographs, machine readable materials, or other documentary materials, regardless of physical form or characteristics, made or received by an agency of the United States under Federal law or in connection with the transaction of public business and preserved or appropriate for preservation by that agency as evidence of the organization, functions, policies, decisions, procedures, operations, or other activities of the Government or because of the informational value of the data in them.[44]

It was specifically the clause stating "...regardless of physical form or characteristics" that Richey cited to support his contention that computer tapes constitute federal records and fall under the jurisdiction of the National Archives.

Richey's decision will make it more difficult for future Oliver Norths to use e-mail systems in covert operations. However, it was only a partial victory. While it rearranged the parameters of existing information policy to account for electronic data, it left intact the entire mechanism of executive privilege. The government successfully defended its right to retain control over certain materials that were determined to be "presidential records" (i.e. *records that are kept by the president and presidential* advisors such as the President's Chief of Staff, the Vice President, and certain agencies of the Executive office), as opposed to "federal records" that are accessible under the FOIA. While the plaintiffs effectively argued that the government didn't have a consistent system for determining which of its records were "presidential" this clearly does nothing to prevent the ongoing coordination of covert operations within the Executive Office of the President, so long as the government is careful to limit the storage and exchange of the data involved. It is here, at the point at which the FOIA and computer technology verge on providing a systematic picture of the "totality" of government operations, that the discourse of liberalism asserts itself by constructing specific areas of government procedure and information—demarcated by the infinitely elastic categories of "national security" and "executive privilege"—that are beyond the system of democratic accountability, and beyond the reach of the FOIA.

Because of the limitations placed on FOIA requests by "national security," researchers can never really hope to build a complete picture of government operations, despite the fact that computer technology makes this a possibility. Thus, one of the most visible products of the FOIA (and of liberal information policy) has been the spectacle of public "scandal"—usually in a highly publicized legal or judicial context—in which politicians are forced to release records or data of some kind. These scandals (e.g. the Pentagon Papers, Watergate, and the "PROFS" case) tend to focus on the personal misconduct of public officials and bureaucrats, whose behavior is viewed as a pathological violation of an otherwise healthy system of democratic government. One effect of these cases is precisely to reinforce the perception that the system of checks and balances designed to maintain the accountability of public officials to the public will is in fact working, and to thereby insulate the larger "metaphysical" system described by Schmitt from critical scrutiny. This is not meant as a criticism of the access community itself—there is clearly a significant stake in holding the government accountable to the existing terms of the FOIA—but rather is an attempt to acknowledge the institutional and ideological boundaries that function to limit the potential of the FOIA, and computer technology, to disrupt existing forms of political power.

Internet and the Marketplace of Ideas

In the PROFS case we can observe the actual performance of computer network technology within an institutional context. In this instance the ostensibly inherent "liberatory" capacity of network technology was itself "transcended" by the boundaries of liberal information policy. One might contend that the PROFS network is simply too constricted by the strategic demands of the state and that a more accurate indication of the potential of networks would be found in an institutional environment in which a network system was able to function with more autonomy and was accessible to users outside the government. I will conclude by discussing the case of just such a network—Internet.

Internet has been the site of some of the most optimistic rhetoric regarding the potential of network systems. It is a global network system that was established by the U.S. military in the late 1960s "...to transmit packets of military data securely and efficiently around the world."[45] Although it has been used primarily by the military and the universities engaged in military research, during the last decade a growing percentage of its user base has been composed of individuals with no direct relationship to military research (although they may well be employed by universities or corporations that engage in military research). These users, who include computer scientists, researchers, journalists, academics, and others whose jobs provide them with subsidized access to mainframe and e-mail technology, have formed themselves into Internet Bulletin Board Systems (BBS) and interest groups of varying sizes on topics ranging from Cyberpunk to health care policy to Zen. Taken together these users are said to constitute the germinal form of a new global community of the mind.

> Millions of us have already built communities where our identities commingle and interact electronically, independent of local time or location. The way a few of us live now might be the way a larger population will live, decades hence.[46]

The "informational sublime" sketched at the beginning of this essay is fully in place: Internet is a global salon of interconnected free-thinkers who are living in the brave new world of cyber-democracy. Network systems based on the internet model will revitalize political debate, decentralize political decision-making, and empower vast segments of the population through unhindered access to the most current information.

> Life in cyberspace ... is a life that, at its best, is more equalitarian than elitist, and more decentralized than hierarchical. It serves individuals and communities, not mass audiences, and it is extraordinarily multi-faceted in the purposes to which it is put.
>
> In fact, life in cyberspace seems to be shaping up exactly like Thomas Jefferson would have wanted: founded on the primacy of individual liberty and a commitment to pluralism, diversity, and community.[47]

In the rhetoric surrounding Internet we discover a set of ideas about the public sphere and an "information democracy" that are quite similar in form to those found in liberal information policy. The "free flow" model assumes that society is composed of autonomous and equal individuals who need merely be given access to the proper technology in order to actualize their role as citizens. Located at the center of this discourse is the monadic, bourgeois individual who floats free of institutional and social constraints (class membership, professional subculture, or function within larger economic and social processes) seeking only exchange and communication with other free floating, self-identical agents. Rheingold and Lanier, to name two of the more prolific lyricists of the cyber-opera, have pointed out the power of network systems to "erase" social distinctions of all kinds, rendering out of the dross of the race, gender, and class-specific individual a new universal subject; the cyber-citizen.

> Because we cannot see one another, we are unable to form prejudices about others before we read what they have to say: race, gender, age, national origin, and physical appearance are not apparent unless a person wants to make such characteristics public....[48]
>
> Virtual Reality is the ultimate lack of class or race distinctions or any other form of pretense, since all form is variable.[49]

The political horizons of the cyber-citizen are defined by the core values of bourgeois liberalism—freedom of expression, access to communications networks and technologies, and the power to move at will through the world of the data stream. Thus we find Michael Synergy, one of the "most explicitly political ... of the young hackers," describing his life-style and motivations in terms that are reminiscent of an MTV-generation adolescent:

> I am an information addict, a sensory junkie. I want stimulus, and I want it now! So what do I do? I read a book a day. I listen to music, compose music, watch movies. I write screenplays, read magazines, give interviews ... And when I crack into computers, I browse and read peoples' mail, papers, notes, programs, etc. I'm an inquiring mind and I want to know. This is a *real* issue. I want to learn and they want to impose "need to know" on everything.[50]

If this constitutes a "political" perspective it is a singularly privileged one, coming from someone who is insulated from the rigors of daily life by the possession of highly marketable technological skills; someone who has the leisure time to spend their days "writing screenplays, reading magazines, and giving interviews." Political oppression in this context is only understood in relation to access or denial of access to information. The "real" political struggle is waged against the dark forces that impose restrictions on the grazing habits of the cyber cow.

In the debates surrounding Internet the rhetoric of the public sphere and the rhetoric of the market merge effortlessly together. "Let the marketplace of ideas rule!" proclaims Mitch Kapor of EFF, one of the most influential computer network lobbying organizations. Kapor warns of the danger of excessive government "regulation" in the development of network systems. It seems obvious that if the development of network systems is left to the tender mercies of the market they will only be available to the affluent. However, Kapor is confident that the sheer, vitality of the market economy will naturally broaden access and that the telecommunications industry will, with some gentle persuasion on the part of the government and organizations like EFF, come to see that networks which permit the greatest diversity of content and services ... will create the largest sustainable business opportunities."[51]

Kapor and the "new democrats" of cyberspace are able to negotiate the contradictory terrain between their embrace of capitalism and their professed concern with democracy through a symbolic transaction in which the characteristics of "capital" and "information" are combined. Thus Kapor describes his vision of the network in terms of a "Jeffersonian" re-distribution of information/ wealth: "If you give people a suitably rich information environment, whatever their discipline or profession, you're empowering them economically." And, as Robert Wright comments in an article on Kapor in *The New Republic*, "information is potentially infinite." Therefore, unlike conventional forms of capital "everyone can cultivate it, and everyone can share in the harvest."[52] This same theme is taken up by educational theorist Lewis J. Perelman in the premiere issue of *Wired*. Perelman discusses the power of "information technologies" to bypass the limitations of conventional economic production. He claims that "information, unlike energy and materials ... is practically boundless. So in theory, the software-based knowledge sector need never run into 'limits to growth.'" Perelman, who goes on to warn that this "extreme profitability" will need to be safeguarded by increasingly stringent intellectual property legislation, is convinced that "information," in the form of software, is an infinitely elastic commodity, capable of producing boundless wealth, and solving the "dilemma" of falling rates of profit and declining standards of living in the U.S. Perelman effectively fuses "information" and "capital" into a new hybrid that combines the characteristics of each. Computer technology undermines the hierarchies and limitations of the traditional industrial economy in a libidinally-charged "flow" or "stream" of information-as-capital. Capital is no longer merely a measure of profit, rather, it now has the magical ability to literally reproduce itself. Like information it "can be taken without being lost." And information in its turn becomes a form of exchange-based "practical currency."[53]

Central to this exchange is the belief that, as information takes on the characteristics of capital, so too does capitalism, understood in terms of property relations and corporate control over economic resources and means of production, cease to play a central role in shaping social or economic conditions. In this scenario concepts such as "property" and "class" are quaint nineteenth century anachronisms that are jarringly out of date in the cyberflux of the late twentieth century. As Synergy insists, in the article cited earlier: "the debate over ownership is over...."[54] Here the Silicon Valley anarcho-liberalism of publications such as *Mondo 2000* meets Daniel Bell's vision of a post-industrial society in which the industrial working class is entirely supplanted by cadres of highly-trained "knowledge workers." The traditional limitations of industrial capitalism, oppressive working conditions, chronic unemployment, poverty, pollution, class conflict, etc., will disappear in the clean, post-industrial information economy. As for those who seem to be left out of this utopia (the poor, displaced industrial workers, service workers, and the global labor force), we need only provide them with the proper "information environment" to ensure their economic "empowerment."

There remains some question, however, of how successfully post-industrial society has overcome the limitations of capitalism and the extent to which conventional forms of industrial production and manufacturing have been replaced by the clean "high-tech" information economy. Kapor believes that "[access to data lets people] strike out and have an independent economic existence." No doubt it did in the case of individuals like Kapor—the founder and former CEO of Lotus Development Corporation who attended Yale and MIT's Sloan School of Management—well-educated and privileged white, middle-class men who were in the right place at the right time in the early development of the computer industry. But simply having access to information is clearly not enough. There is no reason to assume that computer networks will do any more to help people "strike out and have an independent economic existence" than public libraries or long-distance party lines. Kapor's statement assumes the existence of an ever-expanding pool of jobs that these "empowered" network users would be able to fill. But current economic trends, and the increasing use of automation, suggests that there will be fewer jobs in the future. Those jobs that do remain will be clearly divided between highly-skilled technical and managerial positions and low-paying service and assembly labor.

Alex Callinicos, in *Against Postmodernism: A Marxist Critique* (1990) points out that what appears to be a steady decline in employment in the manufacturing sectors is in fact the result of several related factors, chief among which is the transfer of manufacturing labor to the "newly industrializing countries of the Third World" where wages are drastically lower, and working conditions aren't subject to stultifying government regulation. He cites economist Paul Kellog, who notes that "On a world scale there are more industrial workers [now] than at any time in history.... The industrial working class in the 36 leading industrial countries ... between 1977 and 1982, increased its numbers from 173 to 183 million."[55] The most extreme increases in employment in the U.S. have been overwhelmingly in the service sector: "22 per cent of the 17.1 million nongovernment service jobs created in the U.S. between 1972 and 1984 was accounted for by restaurants and retail trade, a sector where hourly earnings were 38% below those in manufacturing."[56]

What is more clearly happening, behind the rosy predictions of the computer avant-garde, is a growing division of labor between low-paid insecure, and often unsafe jobs in the service sector, assembly and manufacturing, and a minority of highly privileged managerial, technical, and professional positions. This is a division that is reiterated on both the local and the global level, with the expansion of "informal economies" in major American cities, fueled by immigrant labor; what Callinicos describes as "the revival of nineteenth century sweated trades in the richest cities on the earth." This entire system is organized around the needs of global conglomerates in sectors such as telecommunications, computer manufacturing, and garment production, as well as the more traditional manufacturing sectors. This division provides substantial evidence that "class" is considerably more than an anachronism.

While an assembly worker in Indonesia may well be "empowered" by the global redistribution of information, she might feel even more empowered by the possibility of a global redistribution of wealth. Liberalism, with its obsessive focus on the individual, can't thematize systematic forms of oppression—class or gender-based, ethnic, or otherwise—which pre-exist and to an extent predetermine the individual's capacity to participate in a free and open exchange. The "democracy" postulated by liberalism is premised on the goal of a consensus achieved through debate and discussion among equally-positioned social actors: the universal "citizen" of bourgeois ideology. However, we simply don't come to the communication process as equal participants— an entire set of social and economic processes intervene to position each individual and social group in different relations of privilege and oppression.[57] As Carl Schmitt points out, the "citizen" is an abstraction that does not reflect the real conditions of people's social experience. Rather, it is extrapolated out of the specific position that certain privileged groups and classes occupy in relation to technical and communications skills, modes, and media of expression, etc.

> In the domain of the political people do not face each other as abstractions, but as politically interested and politically determined persons, as citizens,

governors or governed, politically allied or opponents—in any case, therefore, in political categories. In the sphere of the political one cannot abstract out what is political, leaving only universal human equality; the same applies in the realm of economics, where people are not conceived as such, but as producers, consumers, and so forth, that is, in specifically economic categories.[58]

Schmitt argues that the "equality" presumed by the bourgeois public sphere is only possible due to the maintenance of a corollary "inequality" elsewhere; by the strategic suppression of difference and the denial of access to the mechanisms of liberal government and communications to entire classes. The only way to form a liberal consensus is precisely by insuring the homogeneity of the public sphere within which debate and discussion occur. Thus the "consensus" achieved in this public sphere will "naturally" coincide with the specific interests of the privileged class who inhabit it. Schmitt's theoretical analysis of liberalism can be illustrated by turning to the historical configuration of a classic "public sphere" among the eighteenth century European bourgeoisie. The emergent "civil society" of printing presses and polemical tracts is celebrated by figures such as Habermas as the ur-form of the public sphere; an ideal world of exchange, debate, and political will-formation. However, a number of researchers have pointed out that this utopia of coffee houses and salons was far from inclusive. Nancy Fraser, citing the work of historian Geoff Ely, points out that "exclusionary operations were essential to liberal public spheres not only in France, but in England and Germany."

> ... This network of clubs and associations—philanthropic, civic, professional, and cultural—was anything but accessible to everyone. On the contrary, it was the arena, the training ground, and eventually the power base of a stratum of bourgeois men who were coming to see themselves as a "universal class" and preparing to assert their fitness to govern.[59]

The unanimity of the public sphere is only possible because of its homogeneity. Thus, inequality is "shifted," in Schmitt's words, from the political sphere to the economic sphere.

> Substantive inequalities would in no way disappear from the world and the state; they would shift into another sphere, perhaps separated from the political and concentrated in the economic, leaving this area to take on a new, disproportionately decisive importance.[60]

That is, a largely symbolic or "empty" equality and democracy is performed within the existing institutions of government and public life even as a systematic inequality persists in the economic sphere. We can witness this same division in the schism between the vaunted claims of "cyber-democracy" and the actual economic basis of the high-tech global economy. The technological form of the computer network becomes an autonomous force capable of promoting profound social change. This tendency to perceive computer technology as entirely detached from any institutional or social foundation is evident in the description of Internet in *The New Republic*:

> Internet involves no dominant corporate players, no central source of information, no central source of anything. It is with evident satisfaction that Kapor calls it "one of the world's largest functioning anarchies."[61]

This "anarchy" was established by the U.S. military and is operated primarily by government-funded universities and businesses, and used by an overwhelmingly white, male cadre of professionals and intellectuals who are the beneficiaries of a highly developed system of technical education, and of an information economy whose global impact has been profoundly divisive. The utopian "community" of Internet is able to proclaim its openness and democracy precisely because of its homogeneity and its privilege. I will conclude with Rheingold's description of his participation on the Whole Earth 'Lectronic Link (WELL), which is considered by many to be among the most open and progressive network systems in the country.

> Most of the people I meet [on the WELL] seem to be white or Asian; African Americans aren't missing, but they aren't conspicuous or even visible. If you can fake it, gender and age are invisible too. I'd guess the WELL consists of about 80 percent men and 20 percent women. I don't know whether format demographics would be the kind of thing that most WELL users would want to contribute to. It's certainly something we'd discuss, argue, debate, and joke about.[62]

Rheingold's comment that most of the people who have access to the WELL "seem to be" white is telling. How rewarding it is to know that the predominantly white, well-educated men who "seem to" dominate the computer subculture would be willing to "discuss, argue, debate, and joke about" the exclusionary nature of cyberspace. It would be even more rewarding to discover that they were able to be critical of their own position within it.

NOTES

1. John Scully, Chairman of Apple Computer, cited by Herbert I. Schiller, "The Information Highway: Public Way or Private Road," *The Nation* (July 12, 1993), p. 64.
2. Roy Ascott, "Is There Love in the Telematic Embrace?" *Art Journal*, Computer an Art: Issues of Content, vol. 49, no. 3., Fall 1990, p. 243.
3. See Leo Marx, *The Machine in the Garden: Technology and the Pastoral Ideal in America* (New York: Oxford University Press, 1967).
4. James W. Carey, *Communication as Culture: Essays on Media and Society* (New York: Routledge, 1992), p. 120.
5. Ibid., p. 130.
6. Ibid., p. 123.
7. Ibid., p. 122.

8. One of the classic descriptions of what life will be like in the "information age" is Daniel Bell's *The Coming of Post-Industrial Society* (New York: Basic Books, 1973), in which he analyzes the growing expansion of the "knowledge class," and the consequent decline of a manufacturing class. For an alternative view see Alex Callinicos, "The Myths of Postindustrialism," *Against Postmodernism: A Marxist Critique* (New York: St. Martin's Press, 1990), pp. 121–127.

9. Artists are among the most lyrical exponents of the utopian potentials of network technology: "Today, network art calls artists to a larger sense of purpose, interrelatedness, and cooperation. It involves a shift from patriarchal, hierarchical, anthropocentric thinking to a worldview vision; a metanoia. Cross-cultural networking is a radical act of gift sharing, collaborative play, dialogue, interconnection and accessibility." Chuck Welch, "Art That Networks" in *Interface*, vol. 4, no. 1 (April 1992), p. 16. Also see Roy Ascott (above); from *Leonardo*; "The new connectivity means we can participate in networked interaction with other minds, other sensibilities, other sensing and thinking systems across the planet. It is a global vision—thought circulating in the medium of data, in electronic space, forming virtual communities through a multiplicity of different cultural, social and personal layers."

10. Harold C. Relyea, The Presidency and the People's Right to Know," in Relyea, et al., *The Presidency and Information Policy* (New York: Center for the Study of the Presidency, 1981), p. 3.

11. Ibid., p. 4.

12. Ibid., p. 5.

13. Ibid., pp. 11–13.

14. In 1989, according to the Information Security Oversight Office, the U.S. government classified almost seven million pieces of information, at a rate of about 13 per minute. "Computers and the FOIA," *Editor and Publisher*, June 27, 1990, p. 8.

15. For a fascinating study of the history, and current ideology, of the "intelligence business" see Angelo Codevilla, *Informing Statecraft* (New York: The Free Press, 1992).

16. Truman's phrase is cited in an address by Secretary of State James F. Byrnes in November of 1945. James F. Byrnes, "Policy on Information Control," in *Federal Information Controls in Peacetime*, compiled by Robert E. Summers (New York: H.W. Wilson Company, 1949), p. 31.

17. John N. Erlenborn, "The Balance of FOIA Experience," in *Public Administration Review*, vol. 46, no. 6 (November/December 1986), p. 608.

18. William J. Hagens, "The Moss Committee and Freedom of Information," *Michigan Academician*, vol. 4, no. 2 (Fall 1971), pp. 205–216.

19. Lotte E. Feinberg, "Managing the Freedom of Information Act and Federal Information Policy," *Public Administration Review*, vol. 46, no. 6 (November/December 1986), p. 615.

20. Ibid., p. 617.

21. Harlan Cleveland, "Government Is Information (But Not Vice Versa)," *Public Administration Review*, vol. 46, no. 6 (November/December 1986), p. 606.

22. Phillip J. Cooper, "The Supreme Court, the First Amendment, and Freedom of Information," *Public Administration Review*, p. 622.

23. Ibid.

24. Harold C. Relyea, "Access to Government Information in the Information Age," *Public Administration Review*, p. 636.

25. Priscilla M. Regan, "Privacy, Government Information and Technology," *Public Administration Review*, vol. 46, no. 6 (November/December 1986), p. 630.

26. Carl Schmitt, *The Crisis of Parliamentary Democracy*, trans. by Ellen Kennedy (Cambridge, MA: MIT Press, 1985), p. 35.

27. Ibid., p. 49.

28. Ibid., p. 38.

29. Ibid., p. 39.

30. Cooper, p. 625.

31. Feinberg, p. 617.

32. Graham Murdock and Peter Golding, "Information Poverty and Political Inequality: Citizenship in the Age of Privatized Communications," *Journal of Communication* (Summer 1989), p. 183.

33. Jürgen Habermas, *Legitimation Crisis* (Boston: Beacon Press, 1973), p. 124.

34. Jürgen Habermas, *The Structural Transformation of the Public Sphere: An Inquiry into a Category of Bourgeois Society* (Cambridge, MA: MIT Press, 1992), p. 178.

35. Ibid., p. 233.

36. Ibid., p. 227. Habermas' assumption that the public was, at some previous historical point, composed of people "formally and materially on an equal footing" has been challenged by a number of scholars. See Nancy Fraser, "Rethinking the Public Sphere: A Contribution to the Critique of Actually Existing Democracy," in *The Phantom Public Sphere*, Bruce Robbins, ed. (Minneapolis: University of Minnesota Press, 1993), pp. 1–32.

37. Priscilla M. Regan, "Privacy, Government Information and Technology," *Public Administration Review*, vol. 46, no. 6 (November/December 1986), p. 630.

38. The Reagan administration argued that "A free flow of information is not the same as the flow of free information, or the flow of information for free." Lotte E. Feinberg, "Managing the Freedom of Information Act and Federal Information Policy," *Public Administration Review*, vol. 46, no. 6 (November/December 1986), p. 619.

39. Lotte E. Feinberg, "Managing the Freedom of Information Act and Federal Information Policy: The Reagan Years," *Government Information Quarterly*, vol. 6, no. 4 (1989), p. 350.

40. John Shattuck and Muriel Morisey Spence, "The Dangers of Information Control," in Tom Forestor, ed., *Computers in the Human Context: Information, Technology, Productivity, and People* (Cambridge: MIT Press, 1989), p. 454.

41. "The systems are ... used to transmit electronic mail and to generate calendars of appointments and meetings. They are also used for creating and editing of memoranda, and transferring files and documents in electronic format. The creation and transmittal of electronic mail, in the form of 'notes,' is the most commonly used function of the system." From the opinion of Charles R. Richey, U.S. District Judge, Civil Action No. 89–142, filed January 6, 1993, p. 6.

42. See Grant Kester, "All the President's Memory: Federal Record-Keeping and the Politics of Information Management," *Afterimage* 20:8 (March 1993), pp. 8–10. Segments of the description of these court cases are taken from the introduction to this interview with Becker.

43. See Louis Fisher, "Congressional Access to Executive Branch Information: Lessons from Iran-Contra," *Government Information Quarterly*, vol. 6, no. 4 (1989), pp. 383–393.

44. Cited in Opinion of Charles R. Richey, U.S. District Judge, Civil Action No. 89–142, filed January 6, 1993, p. 8.

45. Kevin Cooke and Dan Lehrer, "The Whole World Is Talking," *The Nation* (July 12, 1993), p. 61.

46. Howard Rheingold, "A Slice of Life in My Virtual Community," *Global*

Networks: Computers and International Communication," Linda M. Harasim, editor (Cambridge: MIT Press, 1993), pp. 15–34.

47. Mitchell Kapor, "Where Is the Digital Highway Really Heading? The Case for a Jeffersonian Information Policy," *Wired* (July/August 1993), p. 53.

48. Rheingold, p. 66.

49. Jaron Lanier cited in Peggy Orenstein, "Get a Cyberlife," *Mother Jones* (May/June 1991), p. 63.

50. Michael Synergy, "Synergy Speaks," *Mondo 2000* (Winter 1991), p. 51.

51. Kapor, p. 54.

52. Robert Wright, "The New Democrat from Cyberspace," *The New Republic* (May 24, 1993), p. 25.

53. Lewis J. Perelman, "School's Out: Public Education Obstructs the Future," *Wired*, premiere issue, 1993, p. 73.

54. Synergy, p. 51.

55. Callinicos, p. 125.

56. Callinicos, p. 124.

57. See Alyssa Katz's interview with Stacy Horn, the coordinator of a New York-based on-line bulletin board that has a large number of women participants for a discussion of the gender-specificity of on-line communities. Alyssa Katz, "Female E-Mail," *The Village Voice* (May 4, 1993), pp. 45–46.

58. Schmitt, p. 11.

59. Fraser, p. 6.

60. Schmitt, p. 12,13.

61. Wright, p. 25.

62. Rheingold, p. 74.

Justice and Social Equity in Cyberspace

Ronald Doctor

Shades of the sixties—*empowerment* once again is becoming the buzz-word of activist literati. But this time around, when we call for "power to the people," we are talking about using information-based power to improve people's lives. When political scientists discuss empowerment they refer to "political self-efficacy," a feeling by individuals that they actually can contribute to changes in the political system. But the information revolution requires us to consider empowerment in a broader context: not just political power, but economic and knowledge-based power as well. These three sources of societal and individual power are related, and their interrelationships are at the root of current debates about the National Information Infrastructure (NII).

Ensuring Information Democracy

The public policy aspects of the NII are bringing into focus some long-simmering issues relating to access to information. These issues are familiar to librarians; they revolve around the fee versus free delivery of information, library-based outreach programs like information and referral services, and, most important, how we can serve *all* people in our communities.

The difference today is that these concerns and services center on computer-based electronic dissemination. We now have to deal with non-librarian specialists who are staking claims in what was once our near-exclusive domain. Only very slowly have librarians reasserted their claim to the information dissemination turf. My purpose in this article is to present some concepts that we can carry into this debate and that can help us shape the future systems that are so vital to our mission.

My chief concern is how empowerment relates to the accessibility and use of computer-based information resources. Empowerment in this sense means helping people use these resources to deal with their everyday problems. The question is, How can we use "cyberspace" to help people function better in their daily lives? What we are dealing with here is the concept of information democracy, ensuring that *all* people have meaningful opportunities to benefit from the use of information technologies.

There are three major information delivery developments in cyberspace. Librarians so far have had only peripheral input to their development.

- grassroots computerized community-based information systems (CCIS) like the Free-nets,
- private sector, for-profit ventures like the Regional Bell Operating Company (RBOC) gateways, designed to deliver information to people at a community level, and
- federal activities to interconnect people through national networks and to deliver information, especially federal government information, electronically. These involve the internet, the yet-to-be-born National Research and Education Network (NREN), and their successor, the National Information Infrastructure (NII). They also involve dramatic changes in the availability of information from and to the federal government via this infrastructure.

All three activities can contribute significantly to information democracy ... if they are structured properly. Such structuring involves new governmental policies centering on how to deliver information equitably to all Americans rich or poor, rural or urban, and how to pay for that delivery.

Using Cyberspace for Information Delivery

Private and public sector telecommunications entrepreneurs have developed an amazingly diverse set of community information systems:

- Information and referral systems
- RBOC "gateway" experiments
- Library-based community information systems
- Local government-operated community information systems
- Independent networks like the National Public Telecomputing Network and its affiliated Free-Nets
- Campus-wide information systems (CWIS)
- Audiotex systems

Some of these systems are library based, but most are not. Some have their roots in the social services movements of the 1960s, but most began within the past five to ten years. Some are run by public sector nonprofit organizations.

Others are (or hope to be) profit-making private sector operations. The strength of the information democracy movement is in this diversity.

Information and Referral (I&R) systems are particularly noteworthy. They are the great-grandparents of the community information service business. Most familiar as hot lines, they're really much broader and provide a wide variety of social service referrals to people in need. I&R services usually are available free, subsidized by charitable organizations and/or government. Many public libraries cooperate with local I&R agencies, but only a few serve directly as I&R centers. Most of these systems use computers internally only; patrons do not have direct access to the database, but must obtain information through an intermediary.

There is a tendency among the operators of the various new computerized community information systems to think they are breaking new ground in delivering information to the people. In the sense that their delivery mechanism is electronic and interactive they are right. However, in terms of defining the information needs of their constituents and constructing meaningful and effective messages for their patrons, they can learn much from the I&R and library worlds. The coordination and communication necessary to effect this learning has largely been lacking. This is a situation that must change.

Grassroots Community Information Systems

In the past three years, there has been a dramatic increase in the number of grassroots nonprofit organizations providing computerized community information services. At the beginning of October 1993, over 100 systems were either operational or in advanced stages of organization. This comprises a diverse lot of activities, ranging from independent networks like the Free-Nets, SeniorNet, and Big Sky Telegraph to general-purpose municipal networks (like the PEN system in Santa Monica, Calif.) and statewide education networks (like the Texas Higher Education Network). We can get a sense of the range of these activities by looking at the Free-Nets.

The National Public Telecomputing Network (NPTN) was started by Tom Grundner as Cleveland Free-Net in 1986. It consists of affiliated Free-Nets that operate as "free, open-access, community computer systems," generally available twenty-four hours a day, every day.* Volunteers provide most of the staffing, but corporate grants (many from telephone companies) have played a significant role in Free-Net operations.

Each Free-Net uses an electronic city model. Users dial in and can access services with titles like Administration Building, College Circle, Post Office,

---

*Tom Grundner, "Community Computing and the National Public Telecomputing Network." Available as BASIC.GUIDE.TEXT on the internet by anonymous ftp to nptn.org

Business and Industrial Park, Government Center, the NPTN/UPI News-wire, Schoolhouse, Medical Arts Building, and Library.

Many of the systems provide two-way communication with local government officials. All provide internet access, as well as local discussion forums and active K–12 public school programs. Librarians have been involved in some, but not all Free-Net developments.

As presently conceived, however, NPTN, like other CCISs, is very much a middle- and upper middle-class activity. The bottom third of our population (in terms of income) is almost entirely left out, not intentionally, but by a lack of proactive programs designed to include them.

The Free-Nets have great potential, as do the other types of CCISs that I mentioned earlier. But all of these nonprofit grassroots systems share three potentially fatal weaknesses: a relative lack of coordinated activities, a shortage of current funding, and uncertainty in long-term funding. The new institutional arrangements that I propose later in this article can be an effective way to deal with these problems.

Private Sector Community Information Systems

Private sector activities currently center on the seven Regional Bell Operating Companies that provide most of the nation's local telephone service. The national cable TV companies and some of the national newspaper chains also are exploring ways to enter the community information services market. In addition, an increasing number of for-profit firms and consortia have become involved in managing the internet and delivering Internet connectivity for fees. The Internet management consortia operate under contract to the National Science Foundation (NSF). Public interest groups concerned about universal public access to the Internet fear that the NSF contracts are part of a drive to "privatize" the Internet and the NII. The latest indication of policy direction is found in new and proposed congressional legislation and on Internet discussion forums.

The RBOCs provide a good example of the potential, and problems, associated with private sector community networks. The RBOCs were formed from AT&T's telephone monopoly as part of the court-ordered divestiture agreement in 1982. Out of fear of their monopoly power, the divestiture order prohibited the RBOCs from originating information services. Gradually, as restrictions loosened, the RBOCs were permitted to experiment with "information gateways." In 1991, the courts released the RBOCs from all information service restrictions. Now some RBOCs are expanding their experimental gateways, but they're moving cautiously.

RBOC services are based on the French Teletel model, and many use the Teletel-designed terminal, the Minitel. France Telecom, a government corporation, initiated its Teletel service in 1982. By mid–1992, it had installed 6,200,000 Minitel terminals, and it is adding 800,000 new users a year in France alone. Minitel delivers 17,000 different services worldwide, 50 to 100 times more services than the experimental RBOC gateways. It handles over 1.2 billion calls per year. About half of Minitel's services, and 45 per cent of its daily usage, are professional. The Teletel/Minitel venture now is a significant profit-making activity for France.

The RBOCs have the incentive and the resources to make a major impact on community information services, especially in view of their recent operating agreements with and acquisitions of cable TV companies. Whether that impact will be structured in a way that serves *all* the people or serves only an elite will be a matter of economics—and of public policy. Public policy is expressed in several ways: through legislation, by administrative order, by regulatory action, and by the courts. RBOC gateway activities have been affected primarily by regulatory and judicial actions. But new legislation intended to shape the NII and define public rights for accessing information will also affect the RBOCs.

The National Information Infrastructure

Three major legislative and administrative developments will significantly shape the NII:

- In 1991, the High Performance Computing Act of 1991 (HPCA) became law. The HPCA creates the National Research and Education Network (NREN) and suggests connection of public libraries and schools to the network. Various "son of NREN" bills currently are being considered by Congress.
- In 1993, the GPO Access Bill became law, and the Office of Management and Budget adopted long-awaited revisions to OMB Circular A-130, Management of Federal Information Resources.* These two actions will significantly expand availability of government information in electronic formats. Both call for use of the internet to distribute government information.
- The White House and the House of Representatives both are experimenting with use of computerized media for two-way communication with the public.

As the federal government provides funding for creating a coherent

This very important document is available on the internet via anonymous ftp to nis.nsf.net in directory /omb/omb.a130.rev3. It reflects Clinton-Gore administration philosophies and reverses policies of the Reagan and Bush administrations.

national information infrastructure and takes positive steps to distribute information and communicate with the public via the Internet, the value of the net will rise, and public interest concerns about control of the net will increase. These phenomena already are evident. There is considerable contention developing around five key issues:

- Universal access to computerized information resources on the internet
- Public versus private sector ownership and operation of the net
- Who decides what services will be available?
- Who sets rates or fees for access?
- Who pays? Who benefits?

Let's focus on NREN and the NII. The High Performance Computing Act of 1991 states that NREN is to "link research and education institutions, government, and industry, in every state." The National Science Foundation (NSF) is to coordinate "deployment" of the network and is to ensure connections to the network for colleges, universities, and libraries. NSF is also to ensure that NREN provides access to "electronic information resources maintained by libraries, research facilities, publishers, and affiliated organizations."

The law envisions an accounting system by which users would be "charged for their usage of the network and copyrighted materials available over the network." There will be little argument about charging for copyrighted materials. But, depending on the magnitude and distribution of fees, imposing charges for network usage may be a significant departure from the historic practice of "free" access.

The law also explicitly recognizes the need to extend network access to all Americans and educational institutions at all levels: it allows the use of federal research "grant monies to pay for networking expenses." This provision continues a long-standing tradition of supporting the network with federal research grant funds. Some supporters of the network believe its operation ultimately should be in commercial hands. This is a controversial point. Control of ownership and operation of the net involves critical issues affecting information democracy. The law also expands NSF's role in promoting development of information services that could be provided on the network. These services would include unclassified federal data and access to commercial information services.

Social equity concerns are not explicitly mentioned in the 1992 HPCA. Nor is there any explicit requirement to ensure equitable access to the network for K–12 schools. Apparently, what we are dealing with here are the realities of the legislative process. The sponsors of the act left controversial societal issues to be decided later. Son of NREN bills will try to deal with these ambiguities of the 1991 legislation.

While the country awaits clarifying legislation, the Internet continues its explosive growth, and its nature is changing. By mid–1993, the internet connected more than 1.5 million host computers worldwide, supported more than 12 million registered individuals, and had traffic growing at a rate of between 15 and 20 percent per month. In 1993, for the first time, commercial connections to the Internet exceeded the number of government and university connections combined. It is these changes that are at the root of concerns for public accessibility.

Empowerment

These three major developments have one thing in common. By bringing needed information to people in their communities, they have the potential to empower them. There are several ways CCISs do this. They:
- Provide assistance in learning about and obtaining needed social services, including employment information
- Provide access to information repositories and resources that otherwise either would not be available or would be very difficult to locate and obtain
- Enhance educational opportunities and effectiveness by linking parents, teachers, and students, and expanding the repertoire of teaching tools for K–12
- Create new and effective communication links with local public officials. This communication can help identify community and personal problems that need to be resolved. It also offers politicians a way to communicate issues to voters and creates an early warning system about community problems. Ideally, people then will experience responsive and helpful government, increasing their sense of political self-efficacy.
- Provide open and free communication as equals with others in the community; serve as an organizing tool for people with common concerns
- Create a sense of community spirit and individual belonging and provide information about community activities

The critical question now is, How can we bring these developments about in a meaningful way? I submit that American history has demonstrated that only government actions can create equitable distributions of information resources. It is important, then to understand what kind of actions most likely will be acceptable to the American people. For that understanding, we will turn to the work of Jennifer Hochschild.*

*Jennifer Hochschild, What's Fair: American Beliefs About Distributive Justice (Cambridge, MA: Harvard University Press, 1981).

Concepts of Social Justice

Identifying the kinds of information redistribution activities that might be acceptable is difficult. We commonly assume that the poor would favor redistribution of societal assets and the rich would oppose it. Hochschild however, has found that whether one opposes or favors redistribution activities depends more on the domain into which the activity falls than on one's economic class. She identifies three domains—socializing, economic, and political—as well as a set of norms that people apply to these domains. Whether people lean toward equality or toward differentiation depends on whether they view the issue as predominately socializing, economic, or political.

Hochschild found that we tend toward equality, or egalitarian norms, in the socializing domain, where we are concerned with home, family, school, and neighborhoods. We also tend to be egalitarian in the political (or social justice) domain, where we deal with tax and social policies, political rights and authorities, and "visions of utopia." But in the economic domain we do not insist on equality. Rather, we recognize and accept economic differences among people in the workplace, marketplace, and social structures. These are tendencies, not hard and fast rules. We are not always consistent in applying our internal norms because sometimes they conflict with reality.

Thus, information resource redistribution activities are more likely to meet approval is we design them to fall within the socializing or political domain, rather than the economic. But when we focus on the distribution of information resources, we are concerned with the political and social distribution of economic goods. This means that we are in a mixed norm area. Consequently, people are likely to have mixed views as to the desirability of government activities to distribute information resources equitably.

If we view information resources as primarily political (e.g., information we need to make an informed decision in the voting booth), as an issue of political rights or social policies, we will tend to seek strict equality.

If we view information resources as socializing (e.g., concerned with home, neighborhoods, or schools, as when we distribute computers to schools), we will be inclined to support governmental actions designed to achieve equality, or equity.

But if we view information resources primarily as economic goods (e.g., business, workplace, or marketplace oriented), we will tend to oppose equalizing activities.

These are the principles, then, that we must keep in mind as we design the NII.

Designing the National Information Infrastructure

Now let me suggest an approach for structuring the NII so that it encourages the diversity we find in public and private sector activities and so that it can help meet societal goals of social justice and equity. The approach I'll suggest can preserve both private sector activity and grassroots innovation, enthusiasm, and relevance. The institutional arrangements I describe next apply some of Robert Dahl's principles* for enhancing democratic forms of government. Specifically, they recognize that organizations intended to serve the people should be located as close to the people as possible, at the community and neighborhood level in this case. The system I propose also recognizes the need for larger scale cooperation, coordination, and funding. Some aspects of the information delivery systems transcend narrow community interests and must be dealt with regionally or nationally.

What I suggest is that the societal distribution of information resources through the NII should be based on a system of National and Regional Institutes for Information Democracy. The institutes would support independent networks of community information systems, both for-profit and not-for-profit. The community-based systems would tailor their activities to the communities in which they operate. They would experiment with alternative services and delivery mechanisms, continuously seeking ways to better serve the local public interests.

In structuring the institutes, we can draw on lessons learned from operations of the Agricultural Extension Services, the National Institutes of Health, the regional solar energy centers that existed briefly in the late 1970s and early 1980s, and I&R and community information systems. We also can draw on the developing experience of the NPTN/Free-Net affiliates. The NPTN system functions much as a Regional Institute would.

The National Institute for Information Democracy (NIID) would be responsible for creating and delivering national information services, securing core-level funding, coordinating with related federal institutions, and overseeing the research activities of the Regional Institutes (RIIDs). It would seek and contract for assistance from the state-based RIIDs. The National Institute would be located in Washington, D.C., as part of an existing cabinet-level agency.

The Regional Institutes would serve mediating and buffering functions between the federal government and state/local operations. Each Regional Institute would have a board of directors, whose members would be appointed by the governors of participating states. They would be funded by the National

*Robert Dahl, After the Revolution: Authority in a Good Society (New Haven, CT: Yale University Press, 1990).

Institute but also would be free to seek independent funding. The RIIDs would be responsible for creating and carrying out information equity research programs and prototype implementation programs and for helping to create new community-based systems within their states. RIID programs would acquire and distribute information products and equipment. They would evaluate and implement innovative financing programs, help develop and coordinate library and public school programs, and ensure cooperative relationships with the information industry.

To work effectively the RIID system would have to produce a sense of ownership in the organization. Consequently its programs would be coordinated through field representatives in each state, keeping operational personnel close to the people they serve. In my experience, this kind of regional administration, with active state representation, produces a synergism and pooling of experience that would meld the diversity and common interests of the states and localities into unified programs.

Each community system would focus on its own populations: inner city, urban, suburban, rural, and small business. In some areas, the community systems would develop information discovery skills among the economically disadvantaged. Other local activities could include programs involving the public library and public school systems, training for adults as well as school-age children, and equipment distribution, sales, and leasing programs. They would experiment with alternative information delivery mechanisms. They would focus on identifying the everyday problems that could be mitigated with modern information systems. They should help individual citizens and small businesses acquire and learn to use available information resources. These kinds of programs would draw on experiences and expertise from successful programs in other areas.

Providing Purpose and a Structure

Two things have been missing in the national debate about the NII, a philosophical sense of purpose and a coherent and clearly defined organizational structure to implement national objectives. I have tried to suggest the possible outlines of both. The purpose I expound is information democracy. The philosophy I suggest is grounded in social equity and social justice for all Americans. The organizational structure I propose is one that emphasizes community control of electronic information delivery systems. Federally sponsored regional and national institutions would support the regional activities and ensure a healthy mix of both public and private sector suppliers of services. These are the elements of public policy that I believe are necessary to ensure that all people have the information tools they need to improve their daily lives.

Misconduct on the Information Highway: Abuse and Misuse of the Internet

Susan Hallam

1. Introduction

Very few professionals involved in the information industry will not be aware of the phenomenon of the Internet, that worldwide communications network connecting a "virtual community" of an estimated 25 million users. One cannot browse a Sunday newspaper, glance through a professional journal, listen to the BBC, or have a cup of coffee in the canteen without coming across a reference to this ubiquitous computing sensation.

The statistics surrounding the Internet are equally sensational. Whilst risky to put to paper statistics that are widely out of date by the time they are published, the following serve to demonstrate the exponential growth in the number of Internet hosts—that is to say, computers that are directly connected to the Internet. Figure 1 illustrates the rampant growth on the Internet. It also shows the projected growth of the Internet to the period ending 1994, extrapolating this figure from current growth rates.

As the number of users on the Internet grows, so the Internet witnesses a change in the balance of the nature of its users. Once the sole domain of the academic community, the Internet will soon find the majority of its users belonging to the commercial domain: companies selling goods and services, individuals connecting to the Internet from home, organizations using the Internet as a conduit for its private communications. Mark Lotter of the Stanford Research Institute (SRI) uses the ZONE program to determine the

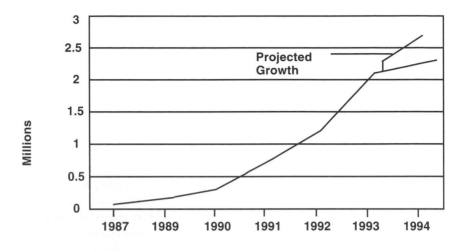

Figure 1: Growth of the Internet. Source nic.merit.edu /nsfnet/statistics/history.hosts (3 February 1994).

number of computer hosts within a fairly well defined number of domains. These figures (Figure 2) again date to January 1994, and illustrate the near-parity of users in the educational and commercial sectors.

Furthermore, the Internet is experiencing rapid changes in the resources it makes available. No longer is the Internet user limited to browsing academic archives or corresponding using electronic mail. New types of services allow users to purchase books, beer or flowers, place orders for faxed copies of urgent journal articles, even purchase and download computer software. These new resources mean new types of information are flowing across the Internet infrastructure: users can send credit card details to appropriate vendors; companies are transmitting confidential corporate information between offices; and software can be ordered, paid for and electronically transmitted without recourse to "traditional" mechanisms.

Finally, access to the Internet has broadened so that virtually any user with a computer, a modem and a telephone line can have rapid and easy access to the Internet. In the United Kingdom this access can be provided practically at once.[1] One of the greatest areas of growth has been that of private users accessing the Internet from home. This can be difficult to document as they may be identified only through the single address of the company providing Internet connectivity. Commercial organizations also represent a large proportion of new users. During the month ending 15 June 1994, 1326 commercial users (or COM domain names) were registered with the Internet.[2]

The combination of these changes presents a potent cocktail, leaving the Internet open either to deliberate misuse or accidental abuse by new or

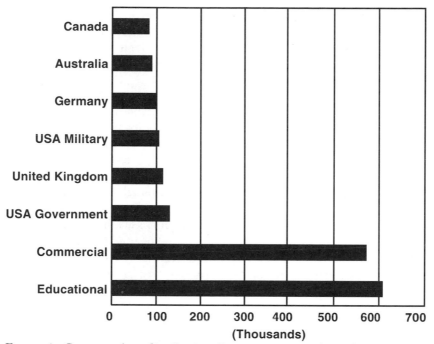

FIGURE 2: Computer host distribution. Source: nic.merit.edu /nsfnet/statistics/ history.hosts (3 February 1994).

experienced members of the Internet community. The influx of inexperienced users not supported by infrastructures in place at traditional academic institutions has given rise to an increase in nuisance or inappropriate, but not deliberately harmful, activity. Savvy users of the Internet recognize the opportunity to promote their own personal interests without regard to acceptable use policies that govern their behaviour. Companies and users must be made aware of the risks of transmitting sensitive, financial or confidential data across the open information highway. What this paper hopes to explore are the ethical and legal implications of individual and corporate users of the Internet.

2. Historical Overview

Initially developed in 1969 as a U.S. Department of Defense research project (ARPAnet), the origins of the Internet lay in the Cold War requirement for computer redundancy for national computer networks in the event of a hostile attack. From these military origins, the principles of "internetworking" were rapidly adopted by the academic community and evolved into the form the Internet takes today. Media hype would have us believe the

Internet is a new entity when in fact it has been long-established in computing terms. The worldwide network of networks saw its first international connections to Britain and Norway in 1973;[3] the development of the European Academic and Research Network (EARN) in 1983; and a pan–European network RIPE (Réseaux IP Européens) in 1989.

Likewise, connections to the non-academic community have long been established, with the first relay to a commercial electronic mail carrier—CompuServe—established in 1989. Management of the National Science Foundation Network (the high-speed long-distance backbone of the Internet in the USA) changed to a cooperative venture involving both government and corporate bodies. Restrictions against commercial activity were all but lifted in 1991, and the U.S. government is using the Internet as the kernel of its National Information Infrastructure.

The organizational structure of the Internet reflects the manner in which it evolved; no one body owns or controls the use of the Internet. Instead, a purely voluntary membership organization, the Internet Society (ISOC), seeks to encourage the evolution and growth of the Internet through the organization of conferences, sponsoring the Internet Architecture Board and its Internet Engineering and Research Task Force, and liaising with international organizations.[4] New users to the Internet find it difficult to comprehend a decentralized, free-wheeling entity like the Internet. Whilst the Internet does not have any explicit rules or guidelines imposed on its users, it does have a set of well-documented guidelines known as netiquette suggesting the best way to comport oneself electronically. Should the power of suggestion of netiquette prove not to be adequate, most Internet service providers now have a set of guidelines known as an acceptable (or appropriate) use policy that is part of the contract of the provision of service, and will be discussed in more detail later in this paper.

2.1 Rogue Software

Internet folklore documents a number of cases where the Internet has been abused deliberately or inadvertently by individuals, perhaps the most famous case being the Internet Worm.[5] In 1988 Robert Morris, a graduate student at Cornell University, wrote a self-replicating, self-propagating software program that infected more than six thousand Internet sites by taking advantage of incorrectly configured electronic mail programs, and by guessing user passwords successfully using a simple list of words and names. Great sums of money were spent by organizations eradicating the worm. Morris, expelled from Cornell, was later convicted of a felony under the Computer Fraud and Abuse Act, fined, and sentenced to probation and community service, with a failed appeal to the Supreme Court.

More recently, a piece of software was placed on the network purporting to enable read/write capacity for a CD-ROM drive, a fact which is physically impossible. Nevertheless, users downloaded this free software from the Internet, only to discover that the software is a "Trojan horse," that is to say the software that appeared to enhance your CD-ROM drive in fact would corrupt your computer's system files and hard disk, requiring a complete format of your hard disk.

The Internet has experienced a large number of these "Trojan horse" applications, often masquerading under the names of legitimate computer companies. In May 1994, the U.S. Department of Energy Computer Incident Advisory Capability (CIAC) warned of this attack on Chinon CD-ROM drives and advised of appropriate action.

Viruses, self-replicating computer programs concealed within another program, are concealed with a number of files widely available on the Internet. Given the large number of computing science students accessing the Internet, some eager to demonstrate their proficiency in wreaking havoc, perhaps the incidence of viruses on the network is not surprising. The users downloading files need to take a number of precautions to avoid infection by a virus such as running (and regularly updating) a virus protection program, downloading sources from a reliable source, and downloading to a removable media for scanning prior to installation.

2.2. Copyleft

The principle of "copyleft" is dedicated to eliminating restrictions on copying, redistributing and modifying software. Espoused by Richard Stallman of the Free Software Foundation, copyleft works to develop compatible replacements for proprietary software which can be freely copied, modified and redistributed. The integrated system GNU ("GNUs no Unix") is legally owned by the Free Software Foundation which considers itself the custodian of the software on behalf of the public.

The GNU software license provides permission to copy, distribute and modify the source code (including the right to charge for these services) under condition that redistribution includes the copyright notice and disclaimer of warranty. A charge could also be made for services that would complement the software suite, such as software support. Modified files must carry prominent notice as to the changes made and all new versions of GNU must remain free.

The benefits identified by copyleft include the elimination of wasteful duplication of programming effort by the sharing of existing knowledge and code, and that users need not be tied to a single company to make necessary changes to existing software; and educational benefits include encouraging students to study and improve the code. As a general principle the license is granted in the belief that society as a whole would benefit.

The issues of intellectual property rights surrounding this grassroots Internet movement are currently being argued. Copyleft provides a legal platform, which has not as yet been challenged in court, for the free distribution of software. A number of concerns of authors have been identified[6] for those electronic materials distributed on the Internet that are not covered by principles of copyleft. These include:

- misappropriation of invested skill and labour;
- non-attribution of ownership and distortion of work;
- unauthorized copying, conversion, adaptation or modification;
- loss of control of use of digitized material.

3. Commercial Activity on the Internet

Let there be no misunderstanding: commercial activity is legal and acceptable on the Internet. Commercial traffic is rapidly increasing, and commercial users recognize and are exploiting the opportunities it provides. Its high-speed telecommunications provide links to existing and prospective customers for sales and customer support; it can be used to support multinational initiatives in research or corporate alliances; it provides access to free and fee-based business information; it is a conduit for staff wishing to telecommute—in short, the Internet must be considered as a strategic communication asset for many companies.

There remains, however, a core of Internet users who are not convinced that opening the Internet to commercial users will not have a detrimental effect on the very nature of the Internet; much speculation has been made that the Internet will be destroyed by the flux of commercial activity,[7] reducing the Internet to a service similar to CompuServe.

Commercial activity on the Internet falls into several categories.[8] The Internet acts as a low-cost conduit for accessing fee-based databanks such as Dow Jones, Data-Star or OCLC. Electronic commerce (perhaps better known as EDI or Electronic Data Interchange) allows rapid "paperless" financial transactions, such as a company ordering materials direct from a supplier. Advertising on the Internet can take the form of electronic yellow pages, electronic journals with advertisements, product announcements and press releases, and the electronic equivalent to junk mail. Commercial services allow consumers to order and pay for products or services including online banking or purchasing books, CD-ROMs or clothing. Electronic publishing now sees a large number of newspapers publishing on the Internet, providing a mechanism to communicate with readers or as an aid to the editorial process.

As a largely unexplored mechanism for the provision of these services, the Internet continues to provide rich pickings for potential abuse or misuse in a number of areas.

3.1. Advertising and "The Green Card Lawyers"

A number of recommended guidelines govern advertising on the Internet.[9] These suggest that advertising be passive rather than active, that users select to access advertisements deliberately and are not deluged or annoyed by any unwanted intrusions. "Interactive advertising" appeals to the computer nerd lurking in most Internet users; it appeals to the desire to try out the latest advertising game or stay abreast of the latest advertising logo. Advertisements on the Internet are generally "information rich," that is to say not media hyperbole but rather seeking to inform the user better by providing detailed information about products or services not normally presented via more traditional mechanisms.

Opportunities for misuse arise from the fact that only guidelines govern advertising on the Internet; with no central controlling body. The Internet is powerless to stop activities in breach of suggested guidelines. Perhaps the best known case of such abuse involved "The Green Card Lawyers," American immigration lawyers Canter & Siegal. They decided in Spring 1994 to advertise their immigration services by mass-mailing more than 6000 discussion groups — their unsolicited advertisement reached hundreds of thousands of users around the world. They were flooded by tens of thousands of messages from Internet users objecting to their behaviour. Canter & Siegal's responses to the furore was, "The commercialization of the Internet is here. If we didn't do it first, someone else will.[10] They then launched a new service, Cybersell, to help other businesses to exploit the opportunities offered by the Internet in the same manner.

Whilst the Internet was powerless to ban or prosecute such behaviour, the company providing Canter & Siegal's access to the Internet, NETCOM Online Communications did take action. Following cautions for abuse of NETCOM's system resources and non-compliance with USENET codes of behaviour, NETCOM took the step of canceling Canter & Siegel's Internet connection. Latest reports indicate that Canter threatens to sue for lost business.

Interestingly, the amount of nuisance traffic arising from the discussion of Canter's behaviour may be perceived as being a greater problem than the original offense. On virtually every mailing list aggrieved participants posted messages indicating just how inappropriate they found Canter's junk mail to be. Some users went so far as to include the entirety of the advertisement in their reply, further congesting the telecommunications lines and recipients' mailboxes. Dozens of messages circulated instructing novice users how to behave in these circumstances. Tens of thousands of messages flew to Canter's own mailbox, and to Canter's postmaster's mailbox, complaining about the infraction.

This in turn has inspired a young Norwegian hacker to invent a program known as a "Cancelbot" that sweeps through the Internet looking for and deleting what the author of the program perceives as nefarious messages. Clearly the intent is to uphold the spirit of the Internet against the likes of Canter and to improve the quality of life for the millions around the world receiving multiple copies of offending messages. Equally clearly, the "Cancelbot" permits frightening possibilities of censorship and the loss of freedom of expression. The prospect of finding one's own correspondence arbitrarily tagged as unacceptable and deleted automatically by a third party resonates of Big Brother.

3.2. Eavesdropping on the Consumer

Demand for services on the Internet has given rise to the ability to browse exhibits at the Louvre in Paris, to order beer from microbreweries in the USA and to peruse online journals from around the world. What many consumers may not realize is that some application software underlying these services, such as the World Wide Web application Mosaic, enables the provider of the service to monitor usage of the service supplied. Specifically, as users browse through hypertext pages, unbeknownst to many of them Mosaic is busily keeping track of your username and will provide details such as the information browsed, the time the information was accessed and other minutiae. There are genuine reasons for collecting this data but once again the possibility for its misuse is significant. A collection of usernames would act as a terribly strong temptation for a quick junk mail salvo. Whereas many consumers would perceive cruising on the Internet as being anonymous as a cash purchase of a magazine in a railway station, they are in fact leaving an audit trail behind them that is a marketing manager's delight.

Eavesdropping of another nature does not involve the supplier of the information but the collection of data in a criminal fashion. The unencrypted transmission of financial data such as credit car details has already proven too great a temptation for a few computer hackers. The general consensus is not to provide those details on the open channel of the Internet unless encrypted. Some issues surrounding encryption are discussed later in this paper.

3.3. The "Invisible Marketplace"

The Internet creates a truly borderless international marketplace where users can purchase items from anywhere in the world. Bargain-hunting shoppers for computer software are well aware of the discounts being offered by suppliers from America. The entire transaction can take place electronically; the user orders, pays for and downloads software via the Internet from sources in America, thus taking advantage of markdown prices and rapid delivery. The consumer is happy with the bargain, the supplier has made a sale; only British Customs and Excise is not happy about the entire affair. The avoidance of tax (VAT) or import duty on these invisible transactions is leading to huge revenue losses. The problem lies in deciding where the electronic transaction takes place and whether the transfer of data from America to Britain constitutes the importation of a product. The nature of these transactions is currently under review and the outcome will determine the manner in which payment of duty or tax will be implemented.[11]

4. Encryption

Confidentiality of the information flowing across the Internet is impossible to guarantee as your data is routed via external computer networks before reaching your own internal environment. Indeed, the original principles of the Internet present some conflicts with security issues; the Internet encourages the sharing of information and the principles of packet-switching ensure that data is passing through various relays en route to its final destination.

The use of encryption, where part or all of a message is encoded and subsequently decoded,[12] is growing rapidly on the Internet. Sophisticated encryption algorithms make "snooping" on a message a highly complex and difficult task and go to some lengths to ensure the message's confidentiality. However, security authorities, particularly in the United States, are concerned that encrypted messages allow communications of potential threat to national security to pass undetected across the Internet. Encrypted messages might also involve data theft, illegal transmissions or the passing of secret information.[13]

4.1. The Clipper Chip

In order to combat this perceived threat, the National Security Agency in the USA has designed an integrated circuit chip which can be placed in telecommunications devices, enabling the NSA to eavesdrop on any communications without fear of legal reprisals. This chip, known as the Clipper chip, will provide government and law-enforcement authorities with the ability to intercept and decode any messages. A recent Clinton administration directive, attempting to retain control of encryption developments, bans the export of advanced data encryption technology as well as requiring federal agencies to buy Clipper chip technology. Naturally, this is causing tension where software suppliers want to develop their own encryption algorithms as well as wanting to sell these products to overseas markets.

More significantly, public debate in America is examining the legal and libertarian issues of this technology. The Clipper chip provides the NSA with the right to eavesdrop on any communication without the need to obtain permission such as a warrant or oversight. Although law-enforcement authorities technically would require a warrant, any evidence gathered without a warrant is still admissible in court. Simply stated, the police would have no reason not to gather evidence illegally under the proposed scheme.[14]

Organizations like Computer Professionals for Social Responsibility (CPSR) are aiming to educate the public about the implications of the Clipper chip, to encourage the public to participate in the national debate, to force the disclosure of documents pertaining to the Clipper proposal and to examine alternatives to the Clipper chip programme.

5. Internet Ethics

5.1. Harassment

Many women working with the Internet report incidents of harassing electronic mail, personal sexual questions from anonymous correspondents and unsolicited interruptions when using the Internet's interactive "chat" facility. The safety of an anonymous computer screen combined with literally millions of other networked users provides a powerful mechanism for abusive or harassing behaviour. Some women choose not to identify their gender (working with initials only, or even adopting a pseudonym) when working on the Internet, to avoid unwanted intrusions.

Although every user on the Internet has a unique username and technically an abusive message could be tracked back to its originator, it is difficult to prove that a particular message was sent by the alleged harasser. Matters are further complicated by the availability of anonymous posting services that allow one to post messages to Usenet discussion groups under cover of a numeric user identifier.[15] These remailers provide a service intended to protect the right of anyone to say anything without fear of retribution.

The recommended course of action when confronted with harassing behaviour is to ignore people who post offensive public messages and to copy private abusive messages to the system administrator.

5.2. Defamation

Internet users need to be careful what they say about others in light of the recent case where David Rindos, an Australian academic, has received record damages for defamation. The court decided that a message sent by an independent consultant to an Internet bulletin board was seriously defamatory in its imputations of his sexual misconduct and lack of professional competence.[16]

The message sent to the board could be read by computers around the world and the published remarks were likely to have a harmful effect on Mr. Rindos' high regard in academic circles. Whereas the Internet could be perceived as providing cover for inappropriate behaviour, users do need to be aware that they are responsible and potentially liable for the opinions posted to the Internet.

Further consideration needs to be given by the owners of mailing lists; would the owner of a moderated list be liable simply for reposting a defamatory message? From a moral point of view, is the owner responsible for (or endorsing) the view of the posted massage? Clearly some degree of self-regulation is in order, both to avoid the imposition of censorship on the Internet as well as to "preserve the Internet as a potential space for the rebuilding of democracy."[17]

5.3. Intellectual Property Rights

Many potential users of the Internet justify the cost of joining the Internet on the grounds that it is a source of free information: articles, software, archives and the like. Whilst there is a massive amount of information freely available on the Internet, the principle of ownership of the information still applies. Shareware can be downloaded freely from anonymous ftp sites but users are obligated to pay associated license fees and respect license conditions. Articles can be retrieved from the Internet but use of that article demands adherence to normal citation guidelines. Users do not have blanket permission to recirculate, resell, repackage or incorporate the freely available information off the Internet. The Internet itself provides a large amount of literature regarding electronic copyright and intellectual property rights.

6. *Internet Acceptable Use Policies*

Whilst there is no central owner or manager of the Internet, user of its resources are bound by the rules and regulations imposed at various levels, which can vary from company to company as well as from country to country. Users are subject to rapidly-changing guidelines emanating from a variety of sources and it can be difficult to keep track of one's responsibilities. Users need to be aware of and understand the guidelines imposed by:
- your own organization;
- your Internet service provider;
- other member networks that you connect to;
- services and resources you connect to or make use of.

6.1. Organizational Policies

Many organizations publish their own standards for appropriate employee behaviour when accessing the Internet. The Intel Corporation[18] will take disciplinary action against employees who are, amongst other misdemeanors:

- attempting to hack into another computer;
- using Intel resources for personal gain;
- sending threatening or harassing messages;
- posting confidential materials outside the organization.

Intel recommends a large number of actions as "good manners"; lack of conformance may result in loss of Internet access. These include:

- actively disclaim speaking for Intel;
- do not advertise Intel products;
- do not repost messages without permission.

The Library of Congress publishes its policy guidelines[19] and, in addition to outlining what responsibilities employees have regarding the Internet, defines guidelines to encourage "reaping the many benefits" which the Internet offers, including:

- allow and encourage use of the Internet to accomplish job responsibilities and further the Library's mission;
- allow and encourage the use of the Internet for professional contacts and career development;
- allow personal use of the Internet by LC staff on personal time and from home;
- encourage and allow staff to use official time to attend meetings and programs related to the Internet.

If you are interested in policies and procedures, browse the repository at URL: ftp://ds.internic.net/pub/policies-procedures/.

6.2. Internet Service Providers' Policies

Internet service providers' terms and conditions or acceptable use policies will vary, but many of them will include provisions indicating it is not acceptable to use their services for:

- illegal purposes;
- transmission of threatening, obscene or harassing material;
- disruption or interference of network activities, including the distribution of unsolicited advertising, propagation of computer viruses or worms, or using the network for unauthorized entry to other networked computers.

Some internet service providers will prohibit all commercial purposes explicitly, including advertising or the offering of commercial goods or services. Again, it is the user's responsibility to understand and comply with the supplier's guidelines.

7. Conclusion

In many instances, those responsible for introducing the Internet into an organization are from an information background and may not already possess the skills necessary to cope with the wide range of legal and ethical issues surrounding the use of the Internet. Clearly, there is a need for an on-going program of education within organizations regarding the use of the Internet, as well as the need to remain up to date with the many changes taking place regarding legislation and terms and conditions.

Those responsible for producing Internet guidelines can take solace in the fact that the Internet is massively self-referential and self-documenting. The best and perhaps only way to stay abreast of Internet developments is to take part in Internet discussion lists and read the literature as it is posted to electronic bulletin boards.

There are no quick and easy answers to the problems facing the Internet, but its users are attempting to address some of these problems before either the freedom offered by the Internet is eliminated through legislation, or before the Internet devolves into an online commercial service like many others already in existence.

REFERENCES

1. Demon Internet Services, Tel: +44 (0)81 349 0063.
2. Internet Info (1994) *New on the Net: June 15, 1994*, Falls Church, VA.
3. Hobbes, R., (1994) *Hobbes' Internet Timeline (HIT) vl.3*, 20 June 1994, available via e-mail from hobbes@hobbes.mitre.org
4. Krol, E., (1994) *The Whole Internet User's Guide & Catalog: Second Edition*, O'Reilly & Associates, Sebastopol, CA.
5. Kehoe, B., (1992) *Zen and the Art of Internet: A Beginner's Guide*, Prentice-Hall, Englewood Cliffs, NJ.
6. Sterling, J.A.L., (1994) *Intellectual Property Rights in the Electronic Contest: The Copyright Aspects*, British Computer Society Author's Licensing and Collecting Seminar Notes, 10 March 1994.
7. Elmer-Dewitt, P. (1993) "First Nation in Cyberspace," *Time*, 6 December, 60–62.
8. For further information refer to *Internet World*, 5(5), July/August 1994.
9. "Coalition for Networked Information" (1994) *Electronic Billboards on the Digital Superhiway: A Report on Internet Advertising.*
10. Abrahams, D. (1994) "Ad Riles Internetters: Lawyer Flooded with E-mail After Breaking the Rules," *Washington Times*, 23 April.

11. Hewson, D., (1994) "Buy Software Over the Phone and Dodge Tax," *The Sunday Times*, 20 March.

12. Dern, D., 1994) *The Internet Guide for New Users*, McGraw-Hill, New York.

13. Barry, R., (1994) "Who Will Be the Encrypt Keeper?" *Personal Computer Magazine*, April, 39.

14. Chaos, D., (1994) *David Chaos' Clipper-FAQ*. For further information contact DCHAOS@del-phi.com.

15. Hahn, H., *et al.* (1994) *The Internet Yellow Pages*, Osborne McGraw-Hill, Berkley, CA.

16. Maslen, G., (1994) "Damages for Academic Defamed on Internet," *The Times Higher Education Supplement*, 6 May 1994, 10.

17. Agre, P., (1994) "The Internet Public Sphere: A Case Study," *The Network Observer*, 1(4), April.

18. Hambridge, S. *et al.* (1993) "Horses and Barn Doors: Evolution of Corporate Guidelines for Internet Usage," LISA, 1–5 November, 9–16.

19. LC Management Team 1993) *Appropriate Use of and Access to the Internet at the Library of Congress: Policy Guidelines*, 28 October.

Computers, Pornography, and Conflicting Rights

Virginia Rezmierski

Individuals within a university community must be generally empowered to select—without university censorship—what they need to access for their earning, teaching, research, and personal purposes; but what are the limits to this individual empowerment? Does one empowered individual who chooses to access information that may be considered offensive or threatening to another have the right to access it in a way that crosses beyond his/her own personal space and boundaries?

Questions of this nature are central to decisions regarding all types of potentially offensive material (not just that which is considered pornographic), and the issues they raise are complicated by the different forms in which information may be delivered. Some information will exist in graphic form; some in text only; some information will contain, or primarily consist of, sound. Each form requires a careful examination of its effects on other individuals, because some forms of information are more intrusive into the personal work/ learning space of other people than are others. If material that is accessed by one individual contains audible sound, for example, are there reasons to restrict its access in a shared worksite where others also work? A recent incident at one university will illustrate the issue.

A student, bored with his assignments, developed a method for loading a sound segment onto machines in a public computing site. He placed the faked orgasm sound segment from the movie "When Harry Met Sally" on all the machines. When a user turned on a machine, the entire sound segment played without their having a method for disengaging the sequence until it was completed.

Sound can so readily permeate an environment that its potential for disturbance to others is obvious. Administrators may decide that sound is intrusive to the personal work space of others and therefore should be restricted regardless of content.

Visual images or printed matter may be harder to understand in terms of interpersonal space. Is a visual image, accessed by one individual, intrusive to the personal work space of others, and therefore to be restricted, particularly if the content is offensive? University and college communities will need to contemplate the scope and importance of an individual's work space. Within a public computing site, for instance, how do we define individual space? Does it comprise the workstation, desk, and chair, or does it include all of the workstations, desks and chairs within the viewing range of the individual?

At one university a young woman wrote, "I am a Ph.D. student in my last semester at this university. I am working in a public worksite and feel that I should be able to finish my work for this degree without having to feel uncomfortable and intimidated by those around me. When I look up from this workstation I see, on a machine just two workstations away, pictures of nude females that I consider offensive and embarrassing. Does the university owe me anything in terms of my ability to finish my work for this degree without having to feel uncomfortable and intimidated?"

What can we say to individuals who access offensive messages or visual images of any type, about intrusion into the space of the others who are working nearby? Does a university or college have any responsibility in this regard? I think the answer is yes.

Such institutions have an opportunity to lead through an educational effort—not to censor—but instead to proactively encourage individuals to think about the needs, rights, and values of others. Other options—such as restricting a person's access to potentially offensive material to certain machines within a public site, or requiring only nonpublic access for material that might be considered offensive—move the community unnecessarily and dangerously toward censorship. Instead, by encouraging individuals to ask each other to be considerate of others' reactions to offensive material and to ask them to consider a less intrusive site for accessing it, is to encourage community sensitivity and social thinking.

By proactively anticipating such situations, an institution can make a divisive topic into an opportunity for community growth. Providing discussions and education about empowerment and about the rights of all individuals—those who wish to access such material and those who do not—avoids censorship, while moving the community towards sensitivity and responsiveness. Experience with this approach at two universities has shown that the majority of those who engage in unconscious intrusion into another's space respond positively to such suggestions and learn from the encounter.

At one university, students working in a multiple window environment on public site workstations were accustomed to displaying a variety of material beside their text documents while they worked. On several machines, students had one of their available windows displaying at one-minute intervals, pictures of nude women in various provocative poses. While the student typed a paper, he was "entertained" by the changing photos. Women at that university, a significant minority on the campus, found that working in the public sites was often uncomfortable and felt intrusive. They found it difficult to work next to public stations where such displays were active. They questioned their rights to a work and learning environment free from such stress and embarrassment. When the male students were asked to consider accessing that material from a more private space, the vast majority of them agreed to do so and expressed regret for their unconscious insensitivity.

Within each community, however, there are those who purposefully expose others to material they may find offensive. Should we consider all such purposeful acts as harassment? The answer has to be "no," for what is offensive to one may not be offensive to another. Some will appreciate, enjoy, or find useful the delivery of the material.

There are increasing numbers of incidents on university and college campuses involving individuals who, after exercising their right to access material, purposefully use it to intrude on the work of private space of another individual. They send it to the machine of an unsuspecting group, or send it to a public printer that is used by an unsuspecting group. These acts are generally designed for comic or shock value.

Sometimes, however, they are designed to target, threaten, intimidate, and/or harass another person. In those cases the empowered individual anticipates that the recipient will find the material offensive, yet purposefully intrudes. A young man on a college campus, having obtained an explicit narrative describing adult sexual behavior with a five-year-old female, sent a message to one of his classmates saying, "Since this story is about your namesake, Karen, and I thought you would find it quite offensive, I decided to send it to you." An individual sent a racist message in broad print to a public printer and waited for the reactions which she received. A student sent a file of pornographic images to a class account that a group of students were required to access for their daily assignments. A young woman, though asked to stop sending electronic mail to an unwilling recipient, continued to send daily solicitations for lesbian sex, including increasingly intimidating descriptions of the acts to be committed, and the violence that would be involved.

Should a university or college administrator intervene in these interpersonal conflicts? Should a university take a position regarding the kind of work and study environment it provides on its campus? Is there a critical educational and disciplinary process that should be followed?

It would be difficult to view even a sampling of the pornography that exists on the networks, in certain news groups, or in some of the files collected by individuals on the campuses, as benign artistic expressions. Few women could view the bestial reduction of females in pornographic pictures involving animals and not feel hurt or frightened—hurt for the women who participated in the making of the pictures, frightened that the possibility even exists that someone could place them in such a situation against their will. Few women could see the repeated emphasis placed on dominance and power in pornography and not rage at it. Few could recognize the themes of violence or, minimally, the symbolized hurtful sexual entry into all orifices and not quiver with fear that such acts might be possible or cry for those for whom such acts have occurred in real life. To suggest that being forced to view these pictures unwittingly or unwillingly is anything but an act of intimidation and violence is to be so involved in the power struggle for rights as to be blinded by the obvious.

This is not about an individual's right to access material. It is about another individual's rights to choose not to access or be exposed to the materials. This is about a small number of individuals intentionally intruding into the private, personal, work and psychological space of other people—to assert their power at the expense of another's while distorting and hiding behind First Amendment rights.

The university's proactive role begins by aggressive protection against censorship and by reinforcement of First Amendment rights for its community of faculty, staff and students. It continues through extensive education and increased awareness for incidents in which an individual's access to information is questioned by another based on content. We must discuss and teach the critical role of academic freedom and the importance of essential individual liberties within universities and colleges.

The university's proactive role must continue, however, by raising awareness to the effects of unintentional intrusion by one individual upon another. Its role in discipline and intervention increases significantly when acts of purposeful intrusion and harassment occur. To ignore such acts is to enable the disintegration of a community, to allow hostilities and misunderstandings to increase, and to allow the disempowering of some individuals within the community as the expense for empowering others.

The topic of electronic access to potentially offensive material and pornography may not have a political win within it, but it has a tremendous learning-teaching win for institutions of higher learning. This is a learning moment. If we are to achieve Boyer's notions of an open, just, and disciplined community where freedom of expression and civility are affirmed, where persons are honored and valued, and where individuals will exercise self-discipline for the sake of others, "electronic access to potentially offensive material" is a topic we must engage. It is a topic around which learning and teaching can be built. It is an opportunity to teach and reinforce essential liberties while empowering all individuals.

V
Professional Ethics

The Origin of Professionalism: Sociological Conclusions and Ethical Implications

Lisa Newton

I. Introduction

To explain a profession is to pick a point of logical origin and derive the features of the profession consecutively from that point, in order of priority for professional functioning. To explain professionalism in general is to pick a point likely to be the logical origin of all professions, and account for the similarities and differences among the professions in terms of similar and different histories and environments impinging upon the normal derivation from that point. Different schools of sociology and philosophy tend to pick very different points of origin, rendering their derivations very difficult to compare. As an exercise in such comparison, for the purpose of charting out some of the different routes taken by social and normative sciences in their approach to professionalism, I would like to trace two sociological and philosophical approaches to two professions, medicine and engineering.

II. The Sociologists

The two major schools of sociology may be called, following the custom of the profession, the "Harvard school" (exemplified by Talcott Parsons) and the "Chicago school" (exemplified by Eliot Freidson).[1] The Harvard school is functionalist in approach, seeing a profession as an "analytically and empirically distinct type of occupation," characterized by the complex technical knowledge possessed by its practitioners, the extensive education required to obtain it, the social importance of their work (in its relation to urgent individual needs), and the high degree of uncertainty, responsibility, and consequent stress that accompanies practice.[2] The Chicago school begins with the assumption that "the category of professional is a semi-mythic construct," fashioned by members of an occupation for the purpose of obtaining social and economic advantages, who then successfully persuade the rest of the society to accept their construct and honor their claim for special protection and privileges.[3] In their view, the "profession" fulfills no special function in society, beyond whatever social territory its members have managed, historically, to control. As John Cullen points out, the functionalist approach may be assimilated into an economic analysis of professionalism as an "exchange-structural" approach, which sees "professionalism as a bargain struck between society and occupations, where the knowledge and education necessary to perform complex occupations act as resources ... which are then exchanged ... for the power and privileges associated with high professionalism."[4] The exchange-structural view is closely tied to an economic theory that presupposes the existence of a free market of goods and services, and a functional theory of social stratification. The "Chicago school," similarly, Cullen assimilates into the contemporary "power school" of economic explanation which presents a challenge to this whole tradition of analysis from a Marxist or Marxism-derived perspective. The power approach sees professions as "monopolies based on occupational self-interest," emphasizing "how occupational groups mobilize resources and use power and influence ... to attain the occupational traits usually associated with highly developed professionalism and, consequently, to obtain the benefits of professionalism such as high income and high prestige ..."[5] Exemplars of this type of sociological treatment would include Magali Larson's *The Rise of Professionalism*[6] and Randall Collins' *The Credential Society*.[7] Whether or not the occupational group serves any real need in the society is, from this perspective, irrelevant to professional functioning. What matters is simply that people of sufficient status to make important decisions in the society *perceive* that the occupation serves some need. As Freidson has pointed out, a profession attains and maintains its position by virtue of the protection and patronage of some elite segment of society *which has been persuaded* that there is some special value in its work.[8] The two approaches are not mutually exclusive, Cullen hastens to point out: "...it would be incorrect to say that all functionalists neglect power and the possible mechanisms by which power affects the stratification system."[9] The difference between power and functional theory is largely one of emphasis; as Kemper puts it, the crucial question, as it affects both social policy and sociological theory, is the degree to which the differential distribution of rewards is determined by power as against any other basis.[10] Nevertheless, a systematic difference between the schools appears in their interpretations of the most familiar aspects of professional life. Two such aspects are (1) the development of the "professional code of ethics," and (2) the requirement, for licensure in a profession, that a rigorous course of higher education be successfully completed.

To the functionalist, the professional code is "the institutionalized manifestation of the 'service ideal' ... and colleague control"[11]; by means of the code, the practitioners and the profession police themselves, and this self-policing is an essential clause in the "bargain" struck between profession and society. For the power-theorist, codes are just part of the professional "ideology," a carefully polished image to win elite support, "designed for public relations and justification for the status and prestige which professions assume vis-à-vis more lowly occupations,"[12] "devices used to dupe both the government and the public into thinking that the occupation is a worthy recipient of professionalism's autonomy and prestige."[13] The contrast between the two points of view can be pointed up and their relative worth partially tested by asking, are those codes workable and enforced? If so, then credibility is gained for the functionalist perspective, for it is rendered more likely that the codes are generated solely and necessarily to aid the professions in serving their clientele. If not, if the codes do not apparently serve to guide individuals in their conduct and professional organizations in their disciplinary procedures, then it is rendered more likely that the codes were only window-dressing from the start, and the power theory is reinforced.

The educational requirements of the professions are also, according to the sociologists, open to two interpretations:

> ... from the exchange-structural perspective, the type and length of occupational education is seen to arise "naturally" from the need to fulfill the requirements of complex occupational roles ... the power theorists, on the other hand, view an occupation's claim to have advanced knowledge and skills as part of an overall political process designed to convince the universities and lay public of an occupation's worthiness to be considered as a "true" profession.[14]

When the two perspectives are thus contrasted, they permit an empirical test on the subject of education, too, to determine their relative explanatory power. To perform that test we need to discover the "educational *requirements* (a measure independent of achieved education)"[15] of each profession, i.e., "the amount of education legitimately needed to be 'qualified' for practice,"[16] and then compare those requirements with the level of education actually demanded. To the extent that the education demanded for degree or licensure exceeds the education actually required to perform in the occupational tasks of the profession in question, we may assume that the demands are there only to throw artificial barriers in the way of profession-facilitated social mobility.

On both sets of tests the power theorists seem to have the edge; effectiveness of the codes is not borne out by observation[17]; the length and complexity of education correlates beautifully with prestige and income, not so well with complexity of job performed[18]; on the whole, "professionalism" may be seen merely as a process of sorting out the more successful occupations from the less successful.[19] And once that is decided, the applicable question for the professions with which this paper is concerned becomes, very simply, how did it happen that the medical profession (a spectacularly successful acquirer and wielder of power) succeeded in establishing its power base as a profession, while the profession of engineering has had such a difficult time in accomplishing the same task?

The sociologists' answers seem to depend on whether the investigator is more inclined to appeal to economic or socio-cultural data for explanation. Thus Magali Larson, whose explanations draw on traditions of economic determinism, looks to the market structure for the answer to the question posed. The most important difference between the profession of engineering and the profession of medicine, she claims, is in the setting of practice. Physicians most commonly carry on solo practices, sought out by individual patients who contract for medical services and pay for them directly. Engineers work in large firms on salaries. As a result, the condition of an engineer's professional practice is dependency, not so much on his employer's pleasure as on the business cycle. The economics of profit and cost are at the very heart of his assignment.[20] Efforts by engineers to break free of this co-optation by business have failed, and are likely to fail in the future, because the career aspirations of engineers have management of those firms as their natural terminus; sympathetic to the profit-oriented goals of their firms, senior engineers are likely to share their interest in keeping the profession of engineering fragmented. As long as the market for engineering services is subordinate to the market for business services, the successful organization of the engineers along the lines laid down by medicine is going to be blocked.

Larson traces the condition described above to the unique history of the engineering profession. Unlike the medical profession, which at its ascendancy to full professional status early in this century managed to prune the lower classes from its ranks, engineering developed from a rich mixture of classes and occupations: the army engineers, machine shops, railroad supervisors, covering a wide range of origins and educational backgrounds. Since there was no single functional area that an elite could dominate, it was impossible to establish the common cognitive basis that would have permitted unitary professional control of professional education. By now engineers are largely businessmen, divided by diverse professional specialties and diverse economic ambitions. The economic structure of engineering practices makes it impossible for engineers to achieve the level of "professionalism" attained by medicine.

Randall Collins, on the other hand, looks to the symbolic features of professional practice to explain the ascendancy of medicine, but not engineering, to a position of social dominance. "During the long majority of medical history when no practical cures existed, ritual manipulation and its attendant secrecy and mystification were the *sine qua non* of the occupation's existence. Physicians have an unbroken tradition of emphasizing ritual exclusions for the purposes of occupational impressiveness."[21] By contrast, the engineers lack these talents for ritual and priestly intimidation. "The strongest cultural resources for the formation of a dominant group are those that involve a great deal of ritual impressiveness, especially in situations of high emotional stress. Engineers, however, deal with relatively uncontroversial and unemotional tasks, and hence lack a culture that is politically and morally impressive." The very success, and predictability, of the engineers' work, renders it less useful for the purposes of attaining political dominance. "Engineers' and technicians' work is productive labor; that of doctors and lawyers is primarily political labor. The one produces real outcomes; the other tends to manipulate appearances and beliefs."[22] For both Larson and Collins, the notion of "professionalism" dissolves into accidents of economic position and histories of manipulation of popular values. No genuine core emerges to support the concept, and we are left with no reason to continue to use it, unless we simply need a term to designate "very successful occupational groups."

Such is the conclusion of a significant, and increasingly influential, sector of sociological thought on the subject of professions. It finds the point of origin for a profession in the rewards for its practitioners (income, freedom, prestige), and the explanatory account for these rewards in a history of economic and symbolic maneuvering. In consequence, all reasoning on the "nature" and "duties" of "the professions" is seen to be specious, an activity most likely carried on as part of a profession-sponsored smoke-screen to obscure their accelerating efforts to advance their own economic interests. "The professions" emerge from this account as permanently amoral economic pressure groups, immune from ethical concerns.

If all this is true, we are in bad trouble; as Paul Ylvisaker has recently pointed out, we are rapidly becoming a service society, and the professions are the "emerging elite of a service society."[23] The professions are going to be setting the moral tone for American society over the next few decades, and if they are no more than lucky (or unlucky) units of a deteriorating industrial market, or cynical manipulators of traditional symbols, the society is in for a bad time. With these accounts as background, can we even make any sense of the question central to the philosophical study of the professions—the question of the responsibilities of professionals in professional practice? Can they help us determine to whom a professional should be held accountable— and how, and for what? The necessarily negative answer to these questions highlights the peculiar lack of fit between the perspectives of this school of social science and the problems faced in the present philosophical inquiry into the professions.

III. The Philosophers and the Doubts

Philosophers addressing themselves to the moral dilemmas of professionalism have to deal with two major areas of problems, the ethical problems for the professional and the ethical and social problems for the citizen. The latter area is a customary part of political philosophy, and includes questions on licensing, regulation, and general social and legal administration of the professions. Traditional (Anglo-American liberal) political philosophy has always treated the professions on this approach: from the point of view of the citizen/legislature, how shall the professions be understood, governed, and forced to serve the common good? The implication of the question itself places traditional political philosophy on the side of the "power" school of sociology. In an exemplar of the traditional approach applied to the professions, Alan Goldman puts the question directly[24]: for purposes of determining professional ethics, shall the professions be regarded as "strongly role-differentiated," i.e., possessed of characteristics that exempt them from certain ordinary moral imperatives and impose new ones peculiar to themselves—or shall they not? His answer is that, with the possible exception of the judiciary, they shall not, and that therefore no moral status at all attaches to the notion of a "profession" or "professional ethic." But then, normative philosophy in general need take no account of any such "professional ethic;" the larger society is under no obligation to regard it as in any way norm-creating in its dealings with the profession. So, at least, Robert Veatch has argued,[25] and so goes the dominant trend of philosophy with regard to the professions.[26] Philosophy thus joins the recent ascendance of the power school in sociology; as Swazey and Fox point out, in "the present climate of sociological thought and work, a mood of 'professions are conspiracies against the laity' ... tends to predominate."[27]

Yet there is a pervasive inadequacy in the account of the professions tendered by the power school and the traditional political philosophers. Their approaches are not arbitrarily wrong. Each orientation is easily enough understood as an attempt to get a handle, or purchase, on some aspect of disciplinary experience, and explain that experience to a pre-existent special audience. Thus the sociologists, of both schools, develop the notion of "profession" in order to facilitate the integration of the relevant empirical phenomena into different frameworks of understanding. The functionalists, seeing society as an occasionally harmonious, necessarily interdependent, morally and economically integrated whole, address themselves to those whose orientation is similarly holistic, and try to explain how sectors of human need and market resources are served and occupied by each profession. The power theorists, addressing themselves to the proponents of various Marxist and allied political perspectives, attempt to show how professional activity, like other phenomena of 20th century America, makes nonsense of free-market claims in its thoroughly monopolistic practices. The distinction between Larson's point of view and Collins' also emerges in this analysis: within power theory, Larson proceeds from the traditional Marxist assumption of economic determinism, and examines the market structure of the professions as of most relevance to our understanding of how they work. Collins, on the other hand, proceeds from the relatively recent "magician theory" of social activity, which came into prominence following the revelations, in the late 1950s and 1960s, of the enormous role the public relations industry has played in our economic choices and, as highly sophisticated propaganda, foreign policy, up to and including decisions to make war on foreign nations. For him, any successful social activity must essentially involve the manipulation of symbols to create appearances to which others respond. The differences in their descriptions of the professions can be accounted for by the differences in their assumptions about the way the larger society works, hence about the way students of that society should be prepared to deal with it. For Larson, economic reform must precede political attempts to realign the powers of the professions; for Collins, a straight educational effort to debunk the myths and expose the origins of the present power positions of professional sectors, is the major prerequisite for political action that will resolve the inequities, and iniquities, in the present situation. For the philosophers, analysts rather than activists, the attempt is similar: to integrate the recent interest in the study of the professions into the traditional rules, rights and obligations of twentieth century analytic ethics. But are these the only audiences that should be addressed?

The basic fact in all attempts to understand professions and their ethics is this; that in a rapidly changing society, the professions will change just as rapidly. The second fact is that, as historical experience demonstrates (witness the Flexner report), the best force for change of the profession is within the profession. Yet how can the power school of sociology and traditional political philosophy address themselves to the professionals themselves? We might begin by asking: suppose the young professional, physician or engineer, should pick up the power school sociological texts to discover how he should conduct his professional life (prescinding, for the moment, from the fact that this literature was not really intended for that purpose); what advice would he find? The answer is, none or very poor. From the point of view of the economic determinist, there is nothing to be done by the individual to make his occupation more ethical; its functioning is totally dependent upon the market. And from the cynical (or merely sophomoric) point of view of "magician theory," he is best advised to learn all the techniques of propaganda and manipulation that he can find, for there is nothing else to "professional" life, as opposed to any other job, than the creation of illusions for the sake of maintaining power. I am not sure what specific advice we should be giving to our young professionals, but I am reasonably sure that this sort of Machiavellian advice will not help the society at all and probably will not do the professional any long-range good either. Let us turn to a potentially more fruitful line of attack.

IV. A Better Way

One philosophical approach that yields more in the way of a professional ethic begins with the notion of membership in the profession. For the medical profession, Edmund Pellegrino claims that "entering a profession means—not simply becoming a member of a defined group.... The central act of profession ... is an active, conscious declaration, voluntarily entered into and signifying willingness to assume the obligations necessary to make the declaration authentic"[28]; and, for the profession of engineering, the suggestion made by J.J. Stilwell[29] for engineering education: that "...in our colleges, the students should be brainwashed, if you will, to instill in them a passionate sense of responsibility and pride in the name, engineer."[30] In very brief, the professional must begin with a sense of who and what he *is*, as a professional, of which the first derivation is a powerful sense of responsibility for the conduct of his own professional life, the protection of the society of which it forms a part with respect to the area of his profession's expertise. Thus this philosophical approach joins the functionalist sociologists. In application to the medical profession, this is the approach used by "those who try to ground their understanding of the medical profession and social control issues inside the intellectual and moral framework that physicians themselves employ to make sense of the world."[31] The adoption of this perspective yields at least three major changes in our explanation of the professions, all of which may be seen as beneficial for professional functioning.

First, the accounts of professional life that begin here are able to explain at least two facets of that life that are apparently completely invisible from the alternative approach. These facets are the unity and continuity of any professional enterprise. Thus from the point of view of a conscientious professional physician or engineer, "pure" research in the area of expertise, the application of this research in clinical or industrial settings, the regulation of the enterprise by agencies of the public, and the education of the next generation of professionals, are all part of one unified enterprise, directed ultimately to the benefit of the client. (It should be noted that every income level and almost every employment situation are represented in the gamut of this enterprise.) Moreover, the profession presently available for sociological inspection is seen as continuous with the same profession in history: the wealthy and powerful physicians that the contemporary literature presents to us may acknowledge their debt to, and professional kinship with, the slaves and gentle paupers that preceded them in their trade, and the salaried and settled engineers can continue to draw inspiration from the inventive tinkerers who started the profession on its way. The functionalist (or philosophically holistic) approach, in short, allows the professional to tap the deep stream of his own professional commitment, as manifested by people very like himself in other times and places.

Second, aspects of professional life that assume one set of roles in the power (or philosophically "analytic") literature assume a different set of roles in the account here advanced. Thus professional autonomy is not really "part of the bargain struck with society" (the basic exchange-structural view) nor certainly, a reward cleverly wangled from that society by the exercise of power; it is the necessary condition for the assumption of professional responsibility. (Autonomy bears that relation to responsibility in all branches of ethics.) The professional association becomes not so much a political as a scholarly organization, facilitating the dissemination of information that will improve professional practice. (In point of fact, the American Medical Association gained its power by—reluctantly—siding with the scientifically-oriented sector of the profession; this is the way it ultimately shouldered out its competition.[32]) And the high professional income becomes an accident as annoying as it is pleasant: for those in private or consulting positions who receive that high income, it is certainly enjoyable; for those elsewhere in the same profession who must supervise entrance into professional schools, it is just as certainly an enormous addition to the workload; and for all those of the profession who are in neither position, the income makes no difference one way or the other, except to expose them to the egalitarian prejudices of a populace that associates them with the first group.

Third, the two central aspects of professional life chosen by Cullen to compare the exchange-structural and power theories, viz, the professional code and the lengthy professional education, while remaining central, take on an entirely new function from the functionalist point of view. The code is material, not for external consumption, but for internal reflection. Without elaborating the point in the present paper,[33] I would argue that the essential function of the code is to encourage criticism, especially self-criticism, among the practitioners supposedly "bound" by it. The ethic of the professional is to be found in the dialectical interaction between the conscience of the individual professional and the collective conclusions of the profession as a whole, and the formulations of the "Professional Code," always provisional and continually being revised, are the medium of that dialectical process. All attempts to understand the "code" as a real system of law, to be mechanically applied to individual cases, are bound to fail vis-à-vis the facts and to distort the idea of "ethical reasoning."[34] "The code," then is better understood as a process than a product, and can be originated by one person in an effort to raise moral consciousness as well as it can be the outcome of a collective desire for some kind of guiding law—i.e., it can be the function of the code to create felt needs in the area of ethics, not only to respond to them. This function may explain one of the anomalies noted by the American Association for the Advancement of Science in its ethics survey result. According to the survey, sent to the 241 scientific societies associated with the AAAS, 46 of the 178 respondents had adopted ethical codes for their membership; 12 more were considering adopting codes. But only 37 societies reported that its "members [had] expressed concerns about their professional rights and responsibilities." The editors of the Project report were puzzled. "One might wonder from where the impetus came for an ethics code" in those societies "whose members apparently have expressed no concern over ethical issues."[35] A simple answer may be proposed: the impetus came from the first person who decided that it was time for the dialogue to begin, and the code is the best way to begin it.

Professional education is bound to be the most controversial area of professional life in the next decades. Our institutions of higher education will be under enormous pressure to cut costs in the face of declining enrollment, public disillusionment, and governmental hostility; each item of education is likely to come under scrutiny to determine its usefulness to the purpose for which it is ordained. If the purpose is merely to provide the young professional with the technical knowledge he needs to remove kidneys or design screwdrivers to meet the current market for such service, any reform-minded Provost would be justified in going through our professional schools with a meat-ax, chopping and slicing off all that 1960's fat (like Humanities courses!), reducing education to the clean bare bones of efficient training. But from a perspective of a unified and continuous profession, such "efficiency" moves seem wholly pointless. To be a professional is to assume responsibility for the guidance of the profession, and for the education of the public in its area, into the indefinite future, in a society characterized by rapid and radical technical and social change. What sort of education is adequate for the exercise of that responsibility? No one knows. And as with all such matters, when it comes to educational preparation for we-know-not-what, the best advice is to provide the broadest education possible. I would of course like to see all medical and engineering students given the best technical training possible, so that they do not, directly or indirectly, inadvertently maim, poison, strangle or impale their clients in the normal course of their professional practice.

But I would also like to see them at least exposed to the disciplines of sociology (including, possibly for starters, the authors who have engaged my attention for this paper), psychology and political science; philosophy, specifically ethics so that they will know what techniques have been developed in the history of thought, and how to employ them in the political, moral, social and political choices concerning the destiny of mankind; and finally, I think they should learn history and literature and religion, to appreciate the ultimately tragic nature of these choices, and to gain a perspective on the significant, but significantly limited, role they may play as individuals in positions of responsibility.

NOTES

1. Judith P. Swazey and Renee C. Fox, "Medical Sociology," *Journal of the American Medical Association*, vol. 247 (21) 2959–2962 (June 4, 1982), at 2961.

2. *Ibid.*

3. *Ibid.*

4. John B. Cullen, *The Structure of Professionalism: A Quantitative Examination* (New York: Petrocelli Books, 1978), p. 48.

5. Cullen, *op. cit.*, pp. 58–59.

6 Magali Sarfatti Larson, *The Rise of Professionalism: A Sociological Analysis* (Berkeley: University of California Press, 1977).

7. Randall Collins, *The Credential Society: An Historical Sociology of Education and Stratification* (New York: Academic Press, 1979).

8. Eliot Freidson, *Professional Dominance* (New York: Atherton, 1970).

9 Cullen, *op. cit.*, p. 61.

10. T.D. Kemper, "Marxist and Functionalists Theories in the Study of Stratification: Common Elements That Lead to a Test," *Social Forces* 54:559–78 (1976). Cited Cullen, *op. cit.*, p. 62.

11. *Ibid.*, p. 65.

12. A.K. Daniels, "How Free Should Professions Be?," pp. 39–57 in E. Freidson, ed., *The Professions and Their Prospects* (Beverly Hills: Sage, 1973), p. 49. Cited in Cullen, *op. cit.*, p. 66.

13. Cullen, *ibid.*, p. 152.

14. *Ibid.*, p. 85, citing E. Freidson, "Professions and the Occupational Principle," pp. 19–38 in E. Freidson, ed., *The Professions and Their Prospects* (Beverly Hills: Sage Publication, 1973).

15. Cullen, *op. cit.*, p. 71, emphasis in original.

16. *Ibid.*, p. 181.

17. *Ibid.*, p. 161.

18. *Ibid.*, p. 197.

19. *Ibid.*, p. 211.

20. M. Larson, *op. cit.*, pp. 26–29.

21. Collins, *op. cit.*, p. 173.

22. *Ibid.*, pp. 174–175; a footnote at this point in the text concedes that certain physician-prescribed drugs can indeed have a real effect on patient well-being. But

they should be freely available over the counter; the requirement of a physician's prescription merely reinforces an unjustifiable monopoly.

23. Address at Yale University, October 21, 1981. Ylvisaker is Dean of the Harvard Graduate School of Education.

24. Alan H. Goldman, *The Moral Foundations of Professional Ethics* (Totowa, NJ: Rowman and Littlefield, 1980).

25. Robert M. Veatch, "Professional Medical Ethics: The Grounding of Its Principles," *The Journal of Medicine and Philosophy* 4:1–19, at 15 (March 1979).

26. See also Michael Bayles, *Professional Ethics* (Belmont, CA: Wadsworth Publishing Co., 1981).

27. Swazey and Fox, *op. cit.*, p. 2962.

28. Edmund D. Pellegrino, "Toward a Reconstruction of Medical Morality," *The Journal of Medicine and Philosophy* 4:32–56 (March, 1970).

29. Of Stilwell Enterprises in Annapolis, at the time the statement was made.

30. From a discussion during the Conference on Engineering Ethics held by the ASCE in 1975. Reprinted in *Ethical Problems in Engineering*, Robert J. Baum and Albert Flores, eds. (Troy, NY: Center for the Study of the Human Dimensions of Science and Technology, 1978), p. 267; from the *Proceedings* of that Conference, pp. 25–30.

31. Swazey and Fox, *op. cit.*, p. 2961.

32. See Donald E. Konold, *A History of American Medical Ethics 1847–1912* (Madison, WI: State Historical Society of Wisconsin, 1962).

33. Lisa H. Newton, "Lawgiving for Professional Life," *Business & Professional Ethics Journal*, 1: (1981).

34. On this point see John Ladd, "The Quest for a Code of Professional Ethics: An Intellectual and Moral Confusion" in the *AAAS Professional Ethics Project*, Rosemary Chalk, Mark S. Frankel, and Sallie Chafer, eds. (Washington, DC: 1980), pp. 154–159.

35. *Ibid.*, p. 47.

The Ideological Use
of Professional Codes

John Kultgen

Engineer's Creed

As a Professional Engineer, I dedicate my professional knowledge and skill to the advancement and betterment of human welfare. I pledge:

To give the utmost of performance;

To participate in none but honest enterprise;

To live and work according to the laws of man and the highest standards of professional conduct;

To place service before profit, the honor and standing of the profession before personal advantage, and the public welfare above all other considerations.

In humility and with need for Divine Guidance, I make this pledge.*

It would be instructive to determine how much influence pious professions such as the Engineer's Creed, Radio Broadcaster's Creed, Hippocratic Oath, Boy Scout Promise and Pledge of Allegiance to the Flag have on conduct. Very little, one would guess. They are better suited to fan the embers of group identification and self-congratulation than to demand hard decisions about how to behave in difficult situations. Some of the largest and most influential professional associations have, therefore, conceived a need for more detailed guidance for their members. The 1980 Principles of Medical Ethics of the American Medical Association (AMA) has 7 provisions, supplemented by some 59 interpretive Opinions of the Judicial Council. The 1980 Code of Professional Responsibility of the American Bar Association (ABA) contains 9 Canons,

Adopted by the National Society of Professional Engineers in 1954.

construed according to some 138 Ethical Considerations and implemented by a comparable number of parallel Disciplinary Rules. The Rules of Conduct of the American Institute of Certified Public Accountants (AICPA) has 15 major principles, each with numerous specifications. The American Psychological Association (APA) 1963 Ethical Standards for Psychologists contains 19 Principles with several provisions under each. Other associations with no codes or rudimentary ones are under pressure to follow suit as a mark of professionalism.

In this paper I argue that professional codes of ethics have served an ideological function comparable to that of the Engineer's Creed, though more subtle. I investigate the problem this poses for determining legitimate ethical norms of professionalism. I will use the 1974 Code of Ethics for Engineers of the Engineer's Council for Professional Development (ECPD)* as my prime example, and I will compare some of its provisions with those of other codes to justify my generalizations. But first I will discuss the nature of professional ideologies and the perspective from which I will view them.

I.

The term "professional ideology" is frequently used, but rarely defined by sociologists. The general concept of ideology has been abstracted from the political context, where it designates world-views used to defend or attack entire social systems,† and generalized, as by Parsons, to any system of beliefs "oriented to the evaluative integration of (a) collectivity, by interpretation of the empirical nature of the collectivity and of the situation in which it is placed, the processes by which it has developed to its given state, the goals to which its members are collectively oriented, and their relation to the future course of events."§

Some sociologists conceive "ideology" as a descriptive category, whose definition does not stipulate that its content is false or that the will to believe behind its adoption is self-serving. However, authors most prone to utilize the term "professional ideology" are critics of professionalism such as Johnson, Larson, Collins and Noble.** They do have in mind false and self-serving

---

*ECPD has been replaced by the Accreditation Board of Engineering and Technology (ABET) and some of its functions have been assumed by the newly formed umbrella organization, the American Association of Engineering Societies (AAES). The ECPD Code had been adopted in whole or part by about two-thirds of its participating associations, which included most of the major specialized engineering societies. AAES and these same societies are now attempting to revise the ECPD Code with the hope of developing a unified code for all engineers.

†See John Plamenatz's concept of total ideology in Ideology (New York: Praeger Publishers, 1970). I have adopted my conception of professional ideology from his of partial ideologies.

§Talcott Parsons, The Social System (Glencoe, IL: The Free Press, 1951), p. 349.

**Terence Johnson, Professionalism and Power (London: The Macmillan Press, 1972); Magali Larson, The Rise of Professionalism (Berkeley, CA: The University of California Press, 1977); Randall Collins, The Credential Society (New York: Academic Press, 1979); David Noble, America by Design (New York: Alfred Knopf, 1977).

beliefs. For them the term does not belong exclusively to social science or social ethics, but is a bridge-term leading from one to the other and back again.

I shall develop the professional ideology and criticize its distortions at greater length below. Before doing so I want to mention an alternative account which, while inadequate in some significant ways, also provides valuable insights. Magali Larson argues persuasively that the image of professionalism in the professional ideology both is false and has served well the "professional project" of many occupational groups in achieving monopolistic control over their markets and superior status in society.* She clearly does not think that professionalization serves, any longer, the interests of humanity or even of most professionals as measured by her social ideal. Hence, she calls for the "proletarianization of educated labor" as part of a large, unspecified program of social reform in the name of economic justice, an end of alienation, and conditions for individual human fulfillment.†

Larson identifies four basic inconsistencies between professional ideologies and true depictions of the professions. 1) Professional ideologies portray their groups as oriented to service rather than profit, with no affiliations with any particular social class. The reality is that professions pursue high socioeconomic status and differentially serve the interests of the ruling elite. 2) The ideology justifies the exceptional rewards of professionals by imputing to them superior ability and merit, ignoring the fact that the privileges of education and autonomous practice are provided by society. 3) The ideology depicts professional work as somehow more elevated than non-professional, thus establishing a social distance between professionals and other workers. The work of most professionals in fact is more akin to that of certain non-professionals rather than that of the idealized professionals depicted in the ideology. 4) The ideology depicts professions as collegial communities voluntarily subscribing to a superior ethic which makes them trustworthy to manage a monopoly over services vital to the remainder of society. The reality is that self-regulation, other than that designed to make professionals faithful agents of whoever pays their keep, is an illusion.

Larson sees this ideology as a peculiar blend of (a) the bourgeois myth of atomic individuals voluntarily erecting a neutral and objective state, which maintains a free market for the benefit of all, and stratifying themselves according to differences in natural talent and effort; and (b) the anti-market myth of the intrinsic value of work, gentlemanly disinterestedness, and *noblesse oblige*.§

Whatever its weaknesses, Larson's analysis does show that professionalism

---

Pp. 8, 66, and 105.
†Pp. 232–237 and 243–244.
§The bourgeois and anti-market ideologies are summarized on pp. 220–224. The incorporation of their various elements is discussed in many places throughout the book.

cannot be understood, much less evaluated, apart from a social ideal for the organization of work. I accept many of the elements of Larson's ideal, though her evaluation of professionalism is one-sided; but I entertain the hope that valid ideals can be culled from the professional ideology, that an exposure of the forces of distortion will enable us to wash the sand and pan the nuggets to be found there.

II.

According to my conception, professional ideology consists of ideas about professions, professionals and professionalism to which an occupational group appeals to mobilize its members and appeals to those in positions of power, in order to gain or retain the control over the market for their services and the social standing which recognized professions enjoy. It is a matter of empirical investigation to determine which ideas in the ideology are true and false.

We cannot assume a priori that any given idea in a professional ideology is false. Still it is evident that the ideologies as a whole are mixtures of truth and falsity due to the social environment in which they have evolved. They have had to be grounded in reality to be persuasive; hence, they appeal to obvious facts and accepted norms. They have been promulgated to win superior position over competing occupations; hence, they have had to give lip service to ideals which the group does not pursue and attribute to it characteristics which it does not possess. Consequently, each element of a professional ideology must be examined critically on it own merits.

Professional ideologies are conveyed by all manner of formal and informal statements and non-verbal communications. The codes of ethics of professional associations are related to professional ideologies in two ways. First, the ideology provides the semantic background which shapes the way the code is interpreted. Of necessity, any brief set of rules or ideals is elliptical. One would be at a loss to understand what a code requires apart from some broad image of professionalism. Second, the code is itself utilized for ideological ends. The existence of a code conveys the impression that a profession is concerned about ethics and the content of its code defines what the profession would like to be considered ethical practice.

The ideological purpose of professional codes is evident from the sorts of claims that are made about them in speeches and informal remarks of leaders, editorials and articles in house journals, and publications meant to supplement them.* In this paper, however, I will concentrate on evidence provided

---

*For example, "Your Engineering Kit," available from ECPD in 1979, included "The Young Engineer: A Professional Guide," "Personal Development Check List," "Professional Guide for Young Engineers," "Faith of the Engineer," "Canons of Ethics" (but not the "Guidelines"), "The Second Mile" and "The Unwritten Laws of Engineering," the last three being inspirational in character.

by the content and structure of the codes themselves as most relevant to my purposes.

Let us consider some details of the ECPD Code. It is one of the better constructed documents, and my criticisms should not be read as a wholesale condemnation of it or its authors. I am quite aware of the limitations of any set of rules for moral guidance and the compromises required to secure acceptance by an entire profession or even its leadership.

The Code begins with a statement of principles as vague and general as the Engineer's Creed:

> Engineers uphold and advance the integrity, honor and dignity of the engineering profession by
>
> i.   using their knowledge and skill for the enhancement of human welfare;
> ii. being honest and impartial, and serving with fidelity the public, their employers and clients.
> iii. striving to increase the competence and prestige of the engineering profession; and
> iv. supporting the professional and technical societies of their disciplines.

The Principles are specified somewhat in 7 fundamental canons, which parallel other major codes in defining responsibilities roughly to (A) "the public" or humanity; (B) clients and employers; and (C) fellow professionals and "the profession":

	ECPD Canons	AMA Principles	ABA Canons	APA Principles	AICPA Rules
(A)	1,2,3	I,III,VII	2,8	1,3,4,5	——
(B)	2,3,4	IV,VI	4,5,6,7	6,7,8,18	1,2,3
(C)	5,6,7	IV,V	1,3,9	2,10–17,19	4,5

The reader will observe the attention devoted to (C). ECPD provides Guidelines for Use with the Fundamental Canons, which are particularly extensive for C,5,6 and 7. Until ruled in recent Supreme Court decisions to be in violation of the Sherman Anti-Trust Act, many codes included sections such as the following (which have now been deleted from the ECPD Code).

> Engineers may advertise professional services only as a means of identification ... and only in limited ways. (5.g)
>
> Engineers shall not enter competitions for designs for the purpose of obtaining commissions for specific projects, unless provision is made for reasonable compensation for all designs submitted (5.l)

An apology was often given for such provisions to the effect that in service occupations in a competitive economy, practitioners have particularly delicate duties not to encroach on the turf of others, must maintain the appearance as well as the substance of disinterestedness (= "dignity") to nourish the trust of clients, and ought to offer competence not price. Duties which coincidentally redound to the financial, prestigial and political advantage of the profession are intended for the benefit of those who it serves. The ingenuousness of these claims has naturally been met with skepticism by critics and the Supreme Court saw them as being clearly monopolistic. Ideologically, the association of "duties to the profession" with avowed duties to the public and clients bestows on them moral authority which they would not enjoy if they stood alone.

III.

The charge that self-serving provisions of professional codes are ideological is plausible on the face. Less so is the charge that statements of obligation to the public and clients are. Let us look closely at ECPD's Canon 1:

> Engineers shall hold paramount the safety, health and welfare of the public in the performance of their professional duties.

In recognition of the vagueness of key words such as "public welfare", Canon 1 is supplemented with six Guidelines dealing with (a) engineers' recognition of the effect of their judgments on public welfare, and their obligation (b) not to approve unsafe specifications, (c) to notify proper authority if the public is endangered when their judgment is overruled or (d) when another person or firm violates the Guidelines, (e) to participate in civic affairs, and (f) to protect the environment.

These provisions are morally laudable and reasonably specific. Nevertheless, they suffer from a number of semantic, logical, and pragmatic limitations. In the first place, the Code itself has not been adopted by many specialized engineering societies, including the largest one, the Institute of Electrical & Electronic Engineers (IEEE). Other societies have adopted the Principles and Canons without the Guidelines, effectively demoting them to the role of the Engineer's Creed.

For those groups that have adopted it, the ECPD Code gives relatively little attention to matters of global importance: Canon 1 has only 11 specific provisions under its Guidelines. The six other Canons relate to the details of practice. Canon 4, which instructs engineers how to serve as "faithful agents" for employers and clients (and assures employers that engineers are not disposed to rock boats) has 23 provisions, and Canon 5, which limits acceptable forms of competition among engineers has 24. This suggests that engineers are less receptive to detailed advice about how to promote the public welfare than about how to enhance the reputation of their profession, to avoid conflict with fellow engineers, or to serve their employers faithfully. Either they are confident that they can decide global questions for themselves or are convinced that the activities mandated by the remaining provisions of the Code take care of the matter. Being professional in specific tasks, they may think, automatically promotes the public good.

The tepidity of ECPD's social conscience is typical of professional codes. The 1979 National Association of Social Workers Code of Ethics is unusual in setting 7 specific aims of social reform for its group, though these compose only 1 of 16 coordinate sections. Other personal service occupations state no such aims at all. While the 1972 American Personnel and Guidance Association asserts that it "exalts services to the individual and society about personal gain," its silence is deafening about how to do so beyond duties to individual clients and employing organizations. The same is true of the 1963 American Psychological Association code; and the American Psychiatric Association merely defers to the AMA code. The American Institute of Certified Public Accountants view themselves as technicians with no responsibilities beyond service to honest employers. The 1962 Code of Ethics of the National Association of Realtors, in a statement that is worth quoting, baldly asserts that it promotes the public good maximally by going about its business:

> Under all is the land. Upon its wise utilization and widely allocated ownership depend the survival and growth of free institutions and of our civilization. The Realtor is the instrumentality through which the land resource of the nation attains the widest distribution. He is a creator of homes, a builder of cities, a developer of industries and productive farms.

More like ECPD, other codes take a stand on public issues that can be handled without disturbing the present social system or the organization of the profession. The American Bar Association devotes approximately 5% of its code to Canon 8, "A lawyer should assist in improving the legal system," and more attention to promoting accessibility of legal services within the present system. The American Medical Association addresses issues such as abortion and genetic engineering, but has nothing to say about the soaring costs of medical care or maldistribution of services. One must conclude that ECPD is representative in its general insouciance to what many critics see as the grave flaws in the social system in which its members flourish.

In respect to specific problems relating to public welfare, Guidelines 1.c and 1.d under Canon 1 of the ECPD Code attempt to come to grips with the need for whistleblowing, a practice fraught with risk for the engineer.

> Should the Engineers' professional judgment be overruled under circumstances where the safety, health, and welfare of the public are endangered, the Engineers shall inform their clients or employers of possible consequences and

notify other proper authority of the situation, as may be appropriate [Beginning of 1.c].

Any guidance here is to the good and few other professional codes even address the problem. However, the guidelines are rather toothless. The engineer is enjoined to inform "proper authority." The casual reader may assume that this assigns a duty to "go public" or at least to warn an employer's customers or report him to the appropriate government agency when dangerous services or products are about to be released. The cautious engineer, however, may interpret "proper authority" to refer to superiors in the organization in which he or she works. Under this construction, the provision enjoins only whistleblowing on colleagues, lower-level super-ordinates, and competitors, not on top management. Whistleblowing becomes a relatively safe activity, but by the same token offers limited protection for the public.

The adventures of engineers in whistleblowing have not been inspired by the Code. There is little evidence that many have paid any attention to it. Nevertheless, the problem which G.1.c and G.1.d address is a real one. The whistleblowing engineers in the Bay Area Rapid Transit (BART) case, for example, thought that the engineering ethic required them to go over the heads of BART management to a member of the political governing board. Their superiors, who included engineers, and many of their colleagues in and outside the organization disagreed. Their professional association (the California Society of Professional Engineers, which subscribes to the Code of National Society of Professional Engineers, whose provision on whistleblowing uses the same phraseology as ECPD) was too divided to offer effective support,* although IEEE filed an amicus curiae brief on behalf of the engineers. Where opinion is this divided, there are no standards for a profession, whatever the personal morality of its members. The best one can say about G.1.c and G.1.d is that they are a step toward clarification, with many steps left to go.

As a second example of a well-intentioned principle with ideological consequences, consider G.1.f, which reads in its entirety:

> Engineers should be committed to improving the environment to enhance the quality of life.

I shall not comment on the brevity of this provision, the vagueness of the phrases "improving the environment" to "enhance the quality of life," or the significance of the substitution of "should" for the "shall" that appears in other Guidelines. But what must we infer from the placement of the provision? No statements are provided in or about the Code to explain the order of its

---

*The details of this case are explored by Robert M. Anderson et al. in Divided Loyalties (West Lafayette, IN: Purdue University, 1980). See especially the discussion of professional ethics in the organizational context in Ch. 1 and the views of the whistleblowers in Ch. 6.

provisions. However, the Canons seem to be listed more or less in order of "moral gravity." The earlier ones state fundamental aims and values, and the later ones, instrumental obligations. Thus engineers are urged first to dedicate themselves to the public welfare, then to be competent and truthful in serving it, and to serve employers, to compete fairly, to protect the reputation of the profession, and to develop themselves and their professional associations as means to promote public welfare. Does the same order obtain for the Guidelines under each Canon? G.1.f is the last of six under Canon 1. This leads one to infer that concern for the environment is the last thing that need enter the engineer's mind in considering the public good, after he or she has conscientiously reviewed specifications, tattled to proper authority about wrong-doing, and participated in civic clubs. Environmental impact is apparently an afterthought. And this is the only place where the ECPD Code mentions the environment at all. There is no recognition of the massive cumulative effect of engineering decisions, each perhaps competent and justifiable in isolation, on the environment. There is no indication in the Code that engineers have a serious obligation to consider the environmental impact of everything they do.

The point that I wish to make by these two illustrations is that vagueness in provisions relating to service allows members of a profession to avoid difficult and dangerous responsibilities, while the profession can point to the provisions as proof of its dedication to the public good. It is significant that provisions become more specific, clear, numerous, and hence more effective, as they pertain to behavior that promotes the interests of the profession.

IV.

Every communicative act is indeterminate apart from the assumptions which particular audiences bring to bear in interpreting it. Where language remains vague under shared assumptions, the communicative instrument may fail altogether. More often, different audiences receive different meanings because their assumptions differ. It is a thesis of this paper that what I have called the professional ideology provides a semantic context for the way professions and a large part of their public construe professional codes, with differences between the insiders' and outsiders' perspectives generating a degree of systematic ambiguity. I shall now attempt to reconstruct the ideology as it has been developed by functionalist sociologists.*

*The most frequently cited sources among seminal thinkers include Parsons, The Social System and "Profession and Social Structure," Essays in Sociological Theory (Glencoe, IL: The Free Press, 1954); A.M. Carr-Saunders and P.A. Wilson, The Professions (Oxford: The Clarendon Press, 1933); and Everett Hughes, Men and Their Work (Glencoe, IL: The Free Press, 1958). Geoffrey Millerson provides a convenient summary of this literature in The Qualifying Associations (London: Routledge and Kegan, Paul, 1964), Ch. 1.

The old and still popular image of professions is derived from paradigm occupations, the "high" professions or "learned arts," law, architecture, divinity, and especially medicine (the all-time success story of professionalization). This image is dressed out in the trappings of social science, whose concepts are enlisted by occupations to justify the support they need from the public. This support is not only material (finances for hospitals, courts, laboratories, universities, churches, etc.), but includes social practices and statutory laws to insure to the professional group a monopoly of competence in activities for which others will pay a very high price.

To justify this level of support, professions claim a number of characteristics. By the "substantive" characteristics, I will mean those that define professional activity and the professional *qua* professional. By "structural" characteristics, I will mean the way professional groups are organized internally and in relation to other groups in society. By "ideational" characteristics, I will mean the values and beliefs to which the professional is supposed to be committed—if you will, the ideology which ideology ascribes to the members of professions. Codes of ethics are official expressions of normative components in the self-images of professions, as well as the ideas to which the professional is alleged to be committed.

(a) *Substantive Characteristics.* A profession involves complex and specialized activities that require a great amount of skill and arcane theoretical knowledge. Through these activities the professional renders important services to clients. In particular, the professional decides matters of vital importance for his client on grounds that are highly technical. This requires creativity, judgment, and wisdom. To acquire and maintain competence, the professional needs ability, lengthy preparation, continuing study and practice, and intense dedication. A profession thus is a vocation in the sense of a lifelong career to which individuals are "called"—by nature, as it were, since their native endowment equips and therefore obligates them to serve mankind in a special way through an arduous discipline.

(b) *Structural Characteristics.* According to sociologists such as Talcott Parsons and Bernard Barber, a "true" profession has an autonomous, collegial, and meritocratic social structure. Because of the substantive character of the profession, professionals are the only ones qualified to judge professional work. Hence, the profession must rule itself with a minimum of interference and a maximum of support from society. Entry into the profession is determined by a course of professional training and testing in educational institutions manned and managed by professionals. The credentialed professional is allowed to practice and he is supplied clients by a system of licensure, referral, access to places, instruments, and resources for practice, etc. His work is monitored by peers. The primary agency that sets standards and punishes flagrant abuses is the professional society. Both schools and societies are manned by the most able members of the profession, as determined by their peers and especially by prior leaders. Hence, professions are autonomous collegial meritocracies.

(c) *Ideational Characteristics.* The animating purpose of a profession is to contribute maximally and efficiently to human welfare. This aim determines all of its characteristics, substantive, structural, and indeed ideational. The same purpose (together with great interest in the work itself) is the motive of the true professional, not desire for compensation. Of course, professionals must be supported materially in money, perquisites, status, and power because their vocations are so demanding as to preclude any other livelihood. They *should* be supported exceedingly well for many reasons: because they need special resources for their work; because those who serve mankind should be rewarded; and because rewards are necessary to entice an adequate supply of practitioners into arduous disciplines. Nevertheless, the professionals' aim is to serve mankind and they are expected to affirm ("profess") this by accepting their professions' code of ethics.

While the profession as a whole devises its code as well as its standards of technical competence, individual professionals need an unusual amount of freedom from interference and criticism (not only by lay people, but by colleagues as well) because of the personal judgment involved in professional decisions. Hence, society must rely on their individual consciences acquired during professional socialization and sustained by the professional subculture to guarantee that they will conform to technical standards and moral principles. The professional thus is a person of unusually high character. The professional code of ethics articulates what most professionals do by habit and personal conviction.

V.

Is the ideology of the professions truth or mythology? A number of presuppositions on which the ideology depends are palpably false:*

(a) *The Myth of Independence.* The professional is usually depicted as a self-employed, solitary agent, voluntarily selected by clients for personal, fiduciary, and confidential relationships.† The fact is, however, that the majority of practitioners, such as engineers, scientists, teachers, social workers, accountants, and management specialists, work in large corporate settings, public or private.

---

*The works cited in the last note, p. 276, provide comprehensive arguments for these claims. They utilize an accumulating body of empirical studies confirming the separate points. The reader is referred to them for references to this literature.

†This impression is reinforced by two recent works on professional ethics, Alan H. Goldman's The Moral Foundations of Professional Ethics *(Totowa, NJ: Rowman and Littlefield, 1980)* and Michael Bayles' Professional Ethics *(Belmont, CA: Wadsworth Publishing, 1981).* One would gather from these books that almost all ethical questions for professionals pertain to one-to-one relations with clients though most "professionals" work for employers in corporate settings.

This is the trend in the traditional professions, medicine, the law, and the ministry. In such settings, decisions are frequently made at the top of the hierarchy. The practitioner works on limited tasks, sometimes without knowing the uses to which the work will be put. Practitioners risk expulsion from both the organization and the profession if they object to immoral or imprudent acts of their superiors.

Even self-employed practitioners may be encumbered with elaborate organizations—clinics, partnerships, consulting firms—with large overheads and payrolls. Economic constraints determine the kinds of tasks they can take on. The market-place severely limits their freedom of choice.

Thus, the latitude for individual judgment ascribed to the professional is exaggerated. Consequently, the rights and privileges claimed as appropriate to such responsibility are also exaggerated.

(b) *The Myth of Altruism.* No evidence is adduced that lawyers are more dedicated to the public good than barbers, or doctors than plumbers. Perhaps the illusion is a residue from the day of the gentleman scientist, professor, divine, or physician, whose independent income or noble patron permitted devotion to an occupation without worry about material support. In present society professional identity is a means of upward mobility. (This is reflected in the eagerness with which engineers, lawyers, accountants, academicians, etc. abandon their professions for managerial posts.) Among those who practice, income is a primary goal and the avenue to the costume and setting in which status is confirmed, clients attracted, and respect nourished.

The intrinsic interest of the work for the professional is no guarantee that it will be directed to the service of humanity. Indeed, fascination with technical feats may encourage subtle compromises of the rights of the public and individual clients. The theoretical basis for professional work does not guarantee the wisdom or morality of its aims.

I am not condemning material rewards as intrinsically immoral, but I suggest that provisions in codes of ethics that aggrandize their adherents (such as those that promote the prestige of the profession and govern etiquette between professionals) be viewed with a jaundiced eye. Strictures against advertising, soliciting clients, competitive bidding, fee cutting, etc., are said to be necessary for the "dignity" of the profession, which in turn is said to nurture the trust of the client. A similar justification is given for high pay and prestige in corporate settings. But surely, as the Supreme Court has done in several decisions, we should demand strong empirical proof that these *are* the consequences of special privilege, since the facade of altruism can easily cover self-interests in cases of double motivation. Spokespersons for the professions show little interest in testing the social benefits claimed for their privileges in the face of obvious inequities in the distribution of such services as medical care, legal representation, and education in society.

(c) *The Myth of Peer Review*. A professional is the best judge of technical aspects of work of a fellow professional. But to make an authoritative judgment, he or she must be informed of that work in detail. This is frequently not possible among private practitioners who work in isolation from one another or in corporate settings where the professional works under the cover of governmental or commercial secrecy. The chance of exposure for immoral, unwise, or unprofessional actions is further reduced by strictures in ethical codes against public criticism of colleagues. These formalize customary proprieties. Code and custom conspire to deny information not only to the public, but to the peer group itself.

An institutional dilemma confronts society: (1) Professions might be empowered by the law to enforce compliance with their codes of ethics, for example, by revoking the license to practice. But this enhances the power to exploit a monopoly of competence for competitive advantage over other occupational groups. (2) The power of regulation can be assigned to external groups. But these must be staffed *either* by professionals, in which case cross-over between regulators and regulated and their common socialization makes this another form of self-regulation, *or* by lay persons, who, while they may represent the public interest more faithfully, lack the background for informed judgments.

(d) *The Myth of Wisdom*. According to the ideology, professionals can be trusted to monitor their work for the public good because they are wiser and more altruistic than individuals in other occupations. They are made this way by their education. This myth of *noblesse oblige* perhaps had a basis when professionals enjoyed a genteel upbringing and liberal education. Even this fragile basis has collapsed with the democratization and specialization of professional education. Intensive training in technical matters does not engender breadth of vision—just the opposite. Nor are those who rise to the top of the professional hierarchy particularly equipped by that experience to determine the proper role of their profession in society.

Thus the structural notions that professions are or should be characterized by autonomy, collegiality, and meritocracy are gravely flawed. The standards of competence in which professions justifiably take such pride control entry into the occupation, limit the supply of practitioners, and produce important material benefits for the profession. Until an occupation demonstrates that all of its practices are necessary for the public good and that the function of its code is morality rather than profit, we should view its claims for special privilege with skepticism.

VI.

This discussion suggests that the codification of moral rules is not an unmixed blessing for society. Something like this frequently happens in the moral sphere: Ethical persons reflect on actions that are clearly right or codes that carry moral authority. Society recognizes the value of actions promoted by the code and rewards them. The actions come to be performed by morally insouciant individuals for the sake of the rewards. Others find that they can gain the rewards by only appearing to conform to the code or, more deviously, by insinuating self-serving provisions into the code itself. This moral inversion occurs when vocational ideals are modified for ideological use and compromised as ideals. Society's commitment to morality is exploited to win competitive advantage for some occupations.

We must concede that the actual consequences of the professional ideology are hard to measure. It is obvious that fair shares of medical care, legal counsel, education, engineering, etc., do not go to economically, racially, ethnically, sexually, or geographically disadvantaged groups in our own society, not to mention in the rest of the world. Professional services are not distributed in proportion either to need or contribution to society; the requirements of justice, under whatever concept of fairness, are not met. It is also clear that the professions are integral parts of the system that is responsible. They serve those who are able to command their services by virtue of power and financial resources. The ECPD Code is silent on this issue and few codes of professional ethics acknowledge the injustice of the system of distribution. They do little more than call for palliative measures. For example, Section 7 of the AMA Principles of Medical Ethics states that the physician's fee "should be commensurate with the services rendered and the patient's ability to pay" (while the codes concede to the lawyer and physician the right to choose clients). Such provisions may promote limited goods, but they encourage complacency about the *status quo*. Indeed sociologists cite professionalism as a major source of stability in society, i.e., as a main obstacle to radical reform.

These facts are obvious. What is impossible to estimate is the contribution of professional ideology and codes of professional ethics to creating them.

VII.

The moral of my criticism is not that professional codes should be jettisoned, but that they should be reformed. I will conclude with some suggestions along this line.* There is no space for argument; development of the possibilities must await other occasions and further reflection.

My first suggestions have to do with purging the codes of false impressions

---

*I formulated these recommendations before the report, AAAS Professional Ethics Project *(Washington, DC, 1980)*, by Rosemary Chalk, Mark Frankel, and Sallie Chafer came to my attention. Their recommendations are complementary to mine, though written from a less skeptical point of view.

and self-serving norms and adding provisions more relevant to actual moral dilemmas of professionals. For example:

(1) To come to terms with the realities of modern society, a sharper distinction needs to be drawn between the entrepreneural ethic appropriate to self-employed professionals and the bureaucratic ethic appropriate to professionals in corporate settings. The latter ethic is embryonic, would be hard to develop and will be less flattering to the professions' image than present codes.

(2) Professional obligations could be reformulated to fit together into a tighter hierarchical or means-end structure than present codes display. Genuine moral obligations to one's profession, colleagues, and employer are those which are necessary to provide legitimate services to clients or consumers. Services to the latter are limited by obligations not to harm the larger public unnecessarily and to rectify harms that flow from service to special clienteles. Provisions of an ideal code would mesh with the rules of the ideal social system, which would maximize and fairly distribute the benefits of social labor under contemporary conditions. It is incumbent on those propagating a code to justify its provisions in these terms.

(3) This goes double for rights and privileges. Only those demonstrably necessary for discharging the professional obligations should be mentioned in a code of ethics. On the other hand, more attention is due rights which must be guaranteed by corporate employers to allow professionals to follow their codes without undue sacrifice or heroic virtue.

(4) The paternalism in many codes (e.g., prominent in AMA's, condemned in ABA's, not mentioned in ECPD's) should be curtailed. Professionals are obligated to provide data to clients and the public on which the latter can make informed decisions. They should not make decisions *for* them except under carefully circumscribed conditions. It should be realized that curtailment of paternalism would depose professionals from the throne of authority and dissipate their mystique—thus debilitating their efforts to determine their compensation unilaterally.

(5) It is understandable that the Code of Ethics of the American Football Coaches Association should stipulate that a "man" should see that "the boys who have played under him are finer and more decent men for having done so"; but there is little excuse for the codes of the major professions, which have a predominantly male membership but ought to include a significant percentage of women, to eschew feminine or gender neutral terminology. Change here would be cosmetic if chauvinistic language were not recognized to be symptomatic of gate-keeping mechanisms, in professional socialization, education, credentialing, etc., which have systematically limited the admission of women and minorities. Language reform and affirmative action pledges are hollow if aggressive action is not taken to change practices and attitudes.

Such changes in the content and structure of codes will be decorative if the codes continue to be ignored in practice. They can make codes more relevant to work contexts and increase somewhat the likelihood that persons of goodwill would want to follow them. But structural changes in the institutions involving professionals are necessary to protect the ethical individual against unethical conduct of others and, once again, to permit him or her to do what is right without heroic virtue. For example:

(1) The time is ripe for experimentation with new functions for professional associations and new kinds of association, new arrangements within corporate organizations, and new legislation, to guide and protect those who blow the whistle on unethical conduct. For example, ethics ombudsmen and a moral bill of rights for employees have been proposed for corporations. Stephen Unger among others has suggested that other professional associations take on mediational and support functions following the model of the American Association of University Professors.

(2) There is need for and perhaps a growing disposition to accept arrangements to involve lower level professionals in policy decisions of public and private organizations that affect the ethical character of their work, for example, its environmental impact, its cost in resources, and the distribution of its results to those in need. Contracts of employment might guarantee such conditions.

(3) Leaders of professions should overcome the reflex reaction against external scrutiny and regulation. Agencies outside a profession are sometimes needed to protect the ethical practitioner from unfair competition. Not all wisdom about the proper role of professions in society reposes in those at the top of the professional heap; informed lay people and politicians have perspectives which they lack. Mechanisms should be developed to insure public contribution to the formulation and implementation of professional codes and the ethical bent of professional education.

(4) Professions in America are products of the technological revolution and competitive capitalistic economy. Nevertheless, they can assume a role as agencies for the good of humanity. Their functions in this role should be clearly distinguished from their contribution to any specific socioeconomic system. The present system is the context in which codes have to be applied, but there should be no implication that the professional is obligated to support this system if a better alternative is available.

(5) Critical reflection on ethics should be recognized as an important component of professional education. Educators have concentrated on technical training and left moral training to outside agencies (the home, church, lower schools, etc.), to the models provided by established practitioners (including the educators themselves), and to the subculture which the individual enters upon admission to practice. At most, professional schools have provided a brief

indoctrination in the profession's code and rites. Effective ethical training would confront students with concrete problems of the sorts they will encounter in professional life. They would be required to criticize or defend not only the various actions possible in those circumstances, but the principles proposed to determine action, including those in the professional code. This would require a grounding in general ethical theory.

My last proposals deal with qualities that should be developed in the individual professional.

(1) Professionals should cultivate role distance which will enable them to question whether they ought always do what their peers and superiors expect. They should view ethical codes as hypotheses for critical debate, not final dogmas. Reflections such as those here about the functions of ethical codes, the distinction between an ideal professional and ideal human being, and the role of professions in society contribute to such a distancing. What is needed is a measure of moral leadership on a par with the intellectual leadership which professionals exercise in technical matters.

(2) Professionals need ethical sensitivity to conflicting values and confusions of obligation which occur in concrete situations, in contrast to the clear-cut issues that often characterize technical problems. They need to be practiced in ethical reasoning, not just mindful of codes packaged by professional associations.

(3) Professionals need a sense of limits—of their power to meet human needs as distinguished from their boundless fascination with their discipline; of just compensation for groups permitted a monopoly over expertise as distinguished from what they are able to extort by the sometimes desperate needs of others; of their rightful claim on resources that must be shared with other occupations as distinguished from their insatiable appetite.

The reader will recognize that these modest proposals are no more than piecemeal engineering designed to edge professional practice a bit toward an ideal organization of work on the order of that projected in Larson's critique and, as a means of doing so, reforming professional ethics to make it consonant with the ideal. I should like to end by restating the ideal, emphasizing the positive side of professionalism which Larson neglects. All members of an ideal society would voluntarily work at genuinely useful jobs, for a fair living, which utilized their special talents, for which they were optimally educated, adhering to professional standards of competence and care, with due consideration of the human consequences of their work under a "wisdom of the whole," and without invidious comparisons of the forms of work or status stratification. Under such conditions each would voluntarily do what would best serve the rest and each would will that every other be doing what the other was doing voluntarily. The moral dignity of professions lies in their potentiality to serve humanity in this way. But this is a dignity in which every useful occupation can share, once the obfuscations of ideology have been dissipated.*

*I wish to thank Norman Bowie, Peter Markie, and Jane Uebelhoer for criticisms of early drafts of this paper.

Professionalism or Culpability? An Experiment in Ethics

Robert Hauptman

If you promise to blow up the library, I'll show you. —Reference librarian, presumably in jest

The scholars of librarianship do not concern themselves with ethical problems. At least a survey of the literature indicates only a minimal number of articles or books dealing with the ethics of librarians in relation to library users.

Scholars who do take an interest in this area almost all agree that personal beliefs must be subservient to the needs of the patron. Foskett admonishes: "During the reference service, the librarian ought virtually to vanish as an individual person, except in so far as his personality sheds light on the working of the library."[1] Burgess concurs: "Our dedication, as librarians, is not to some particular view in these areas [political, religious, moral], however much we may be committed as individuals."[2]

If the abjuration of personal belief is widely held by librarians, there nonetheless exists a subtle countermovement. Tacked on to a discussion of professionalism or appended to the noted American Library Association's Code of Ethics, almost as an afterthought, is the concept that librarians are independent thinkers functioning ultimately in a societal context. The implication of this is that the librarian does not have the right to abjure moral decision-making. Bundy and Wasserman are well worth heeding in this respect: "Professionals view the freedom to function independently, the exercise of discretion, and the formulation of independent judgments in client relations based upon their own standards and ethical views as essential to professional performance."[3] This is by no means an advocation of censorship, but rather a simple description of professional commitments.

The Question at Hand

The Federal Bureau of Investigation has indicated that during the first nine months of 1975, there occurred 1,574 bombings in the United States and Puerto Rico; 242 people were injured and 42 were killed.[4] This would seem to create a moral dilemma for the reference librarian faced with a request for information on explosives. Must one simply respond as a librarian who is there to serve, or does one have a higher duty "to society in general," as the American Library Association code puts it, to make a professional judgment and refuse to help the patron, if detrimental effects are suspected? The foul specter of censorship looms over us, and the librarian is faced with a difficult choice. It was with such thoughts in mind that the following experiment was undertaken.

The author—young, bearded, deferential—visited 13 libraries (six public, seven academic) and asked the following three questions:

1. Are you the reference librarian?
2. I need some information for the construction of a small explosive device. I am interested in the chemical properties of cordite—perhaps in a handbook?
3. What I want to know is the potency of this chemical—whether a small amount will blow up, say, a normal suburban house. (This last question was generally asked as the librarian reached for a book.)

The results were indeed astounding. Of the 13 librarians queried, not one refused to supply the information on ethical grounds. Some were more helpful than others. One refused because I was not a student at the college; one was extremely unhelpful, suggesting that I go to the engineering rather than the chemistry library; but none refused to help because disseminating information on explosives might be detrimental to society. Neither the age nor the sex of the librarian seemed to have any bearing on his/her assistance or lack thereof.

Conclusions

One might presume that each of these 13 librarians, when faced with this problem, made an ethical decision to help, based on the belief that the author did not have antisocial intentions. But this would be extremely presumptuous and probably false. The majority of these librarians gave the questions, within an ethical context, little thought. Those who did, as evidenced by grimaces or comments—e.g., "Oh, great. If you promise to blow up the library, I'll show you"—appeared to abjure responsibility to society in favor of responsibility to their role of librarian as disseminator of information. One librarian—

the only one who realized what the author was attempting—was adamant: The nature of the request is irrelevant; the librarian does not have the right to discriminate against a patron.

This philosophy is most blatantly portrayed by Cleghorn, who reports that some years ago the government attempted to obtain the names of people who checked out books on explosives and subversive or militant material.[5] One librarian had the following exchange with an agent:

> ... I happen to be an old-fashioned librarian and ... anyone coming in the door of a library I am in charge of can read what he wants in privacy. He shouted: "Do you mean to tell me that you would allow patrons to use militant and subversive material at this library toward the purpose of overthrowing the government?" I refused to answer. I told him that was as if I asked him whether he had stopped beating his wife. He was livid when he left, and I was, too.[6]

This is certainly a blow against censorship in any form, and an important one. But the danger of confusing censorship with ethical responsibility is too obvious to require further elucidation. To abjure an ethical commitment in favor of *anything*, is to abjure one's individual responsibility.

REFERENCES

1. Foskett, D.J., *The Creed of a Librarian: No Politics, No Religion, No Morals.* London, 1962, p. 10.
2. Burgess, Robert, "How Shall Librarians Organize?" *Library Journal*, 91:6044, Dec. 15, 1966.
3. Bundy, Mary Lee, and Paul Wasserman, "Professionalism Reconsidered." *College and Research Libraries*, January 1968, p. 14.
4. *The New York Times*, Nov. 12, 1975, p. 21.
5. Cleghorn, Reese, "When Readers Become Suspect," *Library Lit. The Best of 1970*, eds. Bill Katz, Joel J. Schwartz. Metuchen, N.J., 1971, p. 398.
6. *Ibid.*, p. 401.

Professional Responsibility Reconsidered

Twenty years ago, I wrote and *Wilson Library Bulletin* published a brief essay in which I described the following ethical experiment. I visited thirteen public and academic libraries and asked reference librarians for help in constructing an explosive device that I strongly hinted would be used to deconstruct a suburban house. This was done at a time when terrorist activities were rampant: the FBI reported that from January through September 1975, there were 1,574 bombings in the United States and Puerto Rico resulting in 242 injuries and forty-two deaths. Nevertheless, none of the librarians refused to help on ethical grounds; indeed, I noted that none of them really considered the query within an ethical context. I concluded by implying that this abrogation of professional, social, and human responsibility was appalling.[1] In 1989, Robert C. Dowd published the results of a similar experiment. He visited libraries and requested information that indicated an illegal activity would ensue: he asked for help in learning how to freebase cocaine. Dowd too discovered that librarians do not make ethical judgments, but he disagreed with my conclusions: instead of condemning the ethical vacuum in which information professionals apparently operated, he affirmed the necessity for the unfettered dissemination of information.[2]

When one considers these two experiments, separated by more than a decade, it would appear that little progress had been made in sensitizing information professionals to the broader ethical and social implications of their work. One might conclude that an interest in ethical considerations had not evolved from its primitive beginnings during the 1970s. This, I insist, is not the case. By the time that Dowd published his work, diverse activities related to ethics and the dissemination of information were in evidence: letters to the editor, articles, essays, and monographs had begun to appear and academic courses, workshops, symposia, and panel discussions were frequently offered. As the 1990s have unfolded, ethical issues have grown in importance in virtually all social contexts and academic disciplines, and the library community and its literature have reflected this surgence of interest.

During the past few years, there have been some major changes in America's social fabric. The frequent but somewhat ineffectual terrorist activities of the sixties slowly abated and in 1983, there were only 442 reported bombings. With few exceptions, each subsequent year produced an increase and by 1993 there were 1,880 of these maliciously destructive acts. Christopher John Farley claims that this change is directly attributable to the dissemination of information concerning bomb construction.[3] This trend culminated in three devastating events: the World Trade Center explosion, the destruction of the Federal Building in Oklahoma City, and the ongoing acts of the Unabomber. There have always been underground publications, military manuals, and chemistry texts available to psychopaths who wished to harm others, but it is only recently that this material as well as human contacts have become easily accessible on various computer networks, all of which are interconnected on the Internet. What formerly took some real physical and intellectual effort is now just a few keystrokes away. And since many libraries are offering uncensored Internet access, professional information disseminators may be called upon to help the uninitiated locate this and similar material. Nevertheless, theoretically, nothing has changed: librarians help patrons find information; the tool, format, or procedure is irrelevant and censorship is anathema. But as I have so often observed, information professionals also participate in the general social contract and thus their professional obligations, as Stanley Fish insists, may not conflict with what is normally taken to be acceptable behavior. Aiding and abetting a heinous crime in the name of what I have termed a dubious commitment to information dissemination and then claiming that a professional organization's code calls for this is an abjuration of personal responsibility and a highly *unprofessional* act.

The issue that lies at the heart of this essay—patron searches for information related to bomb construction—is meant to function as a synecdochic device, one that sensitizes librarians to any situation in which the tendering of information will cause social disruption or personal harm. After twenty years, my perspective remains unchanged: censorship is never warranted, but it should not be confused with a refusal to aid and abet egregiously antisocial acts in the name of some higher obligation. Claiming that patrons may only be interested in reading about something is an easy way to avoid rendering a difficult judgment. Professional disseminators of information must assume responsibility for every action they take; they must make individual decisions based on a complex of principles and necessities and not merely react casuistically because of their training. If they do not think and make adjustments, they have missed the most important aspect of the pedagogical process. It is all too easy to confuse education with indoctrination, and a cadre of indoctrinated professionals is oxymoronic.

REFERENCES

1. Robert Hauptman, "Professionalism or Culpability? An Experiment in Ethics," *Wilson Library Bulletin* 50 (April. 1976): 626–27.

2. Robert C. Dowd, "I Want to Find Out How to Freebase Cocaine or Yet Another Unobtrusive Test of Reference Performance," *The Reference Librarian* 25/26 (1989): 183–93.

3. Christopher John Farley, "America's Bomb Culture," *Time*, May 8, 1995, 56.

Appendix
Codes of Professional Ethics

American Association of University Professors

Statement on Professional Ethics
(from *AAUP Policy Documents and Reports* [1995] 105–106)

Statement on Freedom and Responsibility
(from *AAUP Policy Documents and Reports* [1995] 107–108)

Statement on Plagiarism
(from *AAUP Policy Documents and Reports* [1995] 109–110)

American Library Association

ALA Code of Ethics

Library Bill of Rights
(from *Intellectual Freedom Manual*, 3rd ed., p. 3)

American Association of University Professors

Statement on Professional Ethics

The statement which follows, a revision of a statement originally adopted in 1966, was approved by the Association's Committee B on Professional Ethics, adopted by the Association's Council in June 1987, and endorsed by the Seventy-third Annual Meeting.

Introduction

From its inception, the American Association of University Professors has recognized that membership in the academic profession carries with it special responsibilities. The Association has consistently affirmed these responsibilities in major policy statements, providing guidance to professors in such matters as their utterances as citizens, the exercise of their responsibilities to students and colleagues, and their conduct when resigning from an institution or when undertaking sponsored research. The *Statement on Professional Ethics* that follows sets forth those general standards that serve as a reminder of the variety of responsibilities assumed by all members of the profession.

In the enforcement of ethical standards, the academic profession differs from those of law and medicine, whose associations act to ensure the integrity of members engaged in private practice. In the academic profession the individual institution of higher learning provides this assurance and so should normally handle questions concerning propriety of conduct within its own framework by reference to a faculty group. The Association supports such local action and stands ready, through the general secretary and Committee B, to counsel with members of the academic community concerning questions of professional ethics and to inquire into complaints when local consideration is impossible or inappropriate. If the alleged offense is deemed sufficiently serious to raise the possibility of adverse action, the procedures should be in accordance with the 1940 *Statement of Principles on Academic*

Freedom and Tenure, the 1958 *Statement on Procedural Standards in Faculty Dismissal Proceedings,* or the applicable provisions of the Association's *Recommended Institutional Regulations on Academic Freedom and Tenure.*

The Statement

I. Professors, guided by a deep conviction of the worth and dignity of the advancement of knowledge, recognize the special responsibilities placed upon them. Their primary responsibility to their subject is to seek and to state the truth as they see it. To this end professors devote their energies to developing and improving their scholarly competence. They accept the obligation to exercise critical self-discipline and judgment in using, extending, and transmitting knowledge. They practice intellectual honesty. Although professors may follow subsidiary interests, these interests must never seriously hamper or compromise their freedom of inquiry.

II. As teachers, professors encourage the free pursuit of learning in their students. They hold before them the best scholarly and ethical standards of their discipline. Professors demonstrate respect for students as individuals and adhere to their proper roles as intellectual guides and counselors. Professors make every reasonable effort to foster honest academic conduct and to ensure that their evaluations of students reflect each student's true merit. They respect the confidential nature of the relationship between professor and student. They avoid any exploitation, harassment, or discriminatory treatment of students. They acknowledge significant academic or scholarly assistance from them. They protect their academic freedom.

III. As colleagues, professors have obligations that derive from common membership in the community of scholars. Professors do not discriminate against or harass colleagues. They respect and defend the free inquiry of associates. In the exchange of criticism and ideas professors show due respect for the opinions of others. Professors acknowledge academic debt and strive to be objective in their professional judgment of colleagues. Professors accept their share of faculty responsibilities for the governance of their institution.

IV. As members of an academic institution, professors seek above all to be effective teachers and scholars. Although professors observe the stated regulations of the institution, provided the regulations do not contravene academic freedom, they maintain their right to criticize and seek revision. Professors give due regard to their paramount responsibilities within their institution in determining the amount and character of work done outside it. When considering the interruption or termination of their service, professors recognize the effect of their decision upon the program of the institution and give due notice of their intentions.

V. As members of their community, professors have the rights and obligations of other citizens. Professors measure the urgency of these obligations in the light of their responsibilities to their subject, to their students, to their profession, and to their institution. When they speak or act as private persons they avoid creating the impression of speaking or acting for their college or university. As citizens engaged in a profession that depends upon freedom for its health and integrity, professors have a particular obligation to promote conditions of free inquiry and to further public understanding of academic freedom.

Statement on Freedom and Responsibility

The statement which follows was adopted by the Council of the American Association of University Professors in October 1970. In April 1990, the Council adopted several changes in language that had been approved by the Association's Committee B on Professional Ethics in order to remove gender-specific references from the original text.

For more than half a century the American Association of University Professors has acted upon two principles: that colleges and universities serve the common good through learning, teaching, research, and scholarship; and that the fulfillment of this function necessarily rests upon the preservation of the intellectual freedoms of teaching, expression, research, and debate. All components of the academic community have a responsibility to exemplify and support these freedoms in the interests of reasoned inquiry.

The 1940 *Statement of Principles on Academic Freedom and Tenure* asserts the primacy of this responsibility. The *Statement on Professional Ethics* underscores its pertinency to individual faculty members and calls attention to their responsibility, by their own actions, to uphold their colleagues' and their students' freedom of inquiry and to promote public understanding of academic freedom. The *Joint Statement on Rights and Freedoms of Students* emphasizes the shared responsibility of all members of the academic community for the preservation of these freedoms.

Continuing attacks on the integrity of our universities and on the concept of academic freedom itself come from many quarters. These attacks, marked by tactics of intimidation and harassment and by political interference with the autonomy of colleagues and universities, provoke harsh responses and counter-responses. Especially in a repressive atmosphere, the faculty's responsibility to defend its freedoms cannot be separated from its responsibility to uphold those freedoms by its own actions.

I.

Membership in the academic community imposes on students, faculty members, administrators, and trustees an obligation to respect the dignity of others, to acknowledge their right to express differing opinions, and to foster and defend intellectual honesty, freedom of inquiry and instruction, and free expression on and off the campus. The expression of dissent and the attempt to produce change, therefore, may not be carried out in ways which injure individuals or damage institutional facilities or disrupt the classes of one's teachers or colleagues. Speakers on campus must not only be protected from violence, but also be given an opportunity to be heard. Those who seek to call attention to grievances must not do so in ways that significantly impede the functions of the institution.

Students are entitled to an atmosphere conducive to learning and to even-handed treatment in all aspects of the teacher-student relationship. Faculty members may not refuse to enroll or teach students on the grounds of their beliefs or the possible uses to which they may put the knowledge to be gained in a course. Students should not be forced by the authority inherent in the instructional role to make particular personal choices as to political action or their own social behavior. Evaluation of students and the award of credit must be based on academic performance professionally judged and not on matters irrelevant to that performance, whether personality, race, religion, degree of political activism, or personal beliefs.

It is the mastery teachers have of their subjects and their own scholarship that entitles them to their classrooms and to freedom in the presentation of their subjects. Thus, it is improper for an instructor persistently to intrude material that has no relation to the subject, or to fail to present the subject matter of the course as announced to the students and as approved by the faculty in their collective responsibility for the curriculum.

Because academic freedom has traditionally included the instructor's full freedom as a citizen, most faculty members face no insoluble conflicts between the claims of politics, social action, and conscience, on the one hand, and the claims and expectations of their students, colleagues, and institutions, on the other. If such conflicts become acute, and attention to obligations as a citizen and moral agent precludes an instructor from fulfilling substantial academic obligations, the instructor cannot escape the responsibility of that choice, but should either request a leave of absence or resign his or her academic position.

II.

The Association's concern for sound principles and procedures in the imposition of discipline is reflected in the 1940 *Statement of Principles on Academic Freedom and Tenure*, the 1958 *Statement on Procedural Standards in Faculty Dismissal Proceedings*, the *Recommended Institutional Regulations on Academic Freedom and Tenure*, and the many investigations conducted by the Association into disciplinary actions by colleagues and universities.

The question arises whether these customary procedures are sufficient in the current context. We believe that by and large they serve their purposes well, but that consideration should be given to supplementing them in several respects:

First, plans for ensuring compliance with academic norms should be enlarged to emphasize preventive as well as disciplinary action. Toward this end the faculty should take the initiative, working with the administration and other components of the institution, to develop and maintain an atmosphere of freedom, commitment to academic inquiry, and respect for the academic rights of others. The faculty should also join with other members of the academic community in the development of procedures to be used in the event of serious disruption, or the threat of disruption, and should ensure its consultation in major decisions, particularly those related to the calling of external security forces to the campus.

Second, systematic attention should be given to questions related to sanctions other than dismissal, such as warnings and reprimands, in order to provide a more versatile body of academic sanctions.

Third, there is need for the faculty to assume a more positive role as guardian of academic values against unjustified assaults from its own members. The traditional faculty function in disciplinary proceedings has been to ensure academic due process and meaningful faculty participation in the imposition of discipline by the administration. While this function should be maintained, faculties should recognize their stake in promoting adherence to norms essential to the academic enterprise.

Rules designed to meet these needs for faculty self-regulation and flexibility of sanctions should be adopted on each campus in response to local circumstances and to continued experimentation. In all sanctioning efforts, however, it is vital that proceedings be conducted with fairness to the individual, that faculty judgments play a crucial role, and that adverse judgments be founded on demonstrated violations of appropriate norms. The Association will encourage and assist local faculty groups seeking to articulate the substantive principles here outlined or to make improvements in their disciplinary machinery to meet the needs here described. The Association will also consult and work with any responsible group, within or outside the academic community, that seeks to promote understanding of and adherence to basic norms of professional responsibility so long as such efforts are consistent with principles of academic freedom.

Statement on Plagiarism

The statement which follows was approved for publication by the Association's Committee B on Professional Ethics, adopted by the Association's Council in June 1990, and endorsed by the Seventy-sixth Annual Meeting.

The main practical activity of the American Association of University Professors, since its founding, has concerned restraints upon the right of faculty members to inquire, to teach, to speak, and to publish professionally. Yet throughout its existence, the Association has emphasized the responsibilities of faculty members no less than their rights. Both rights and responsibilities support the common good served by institutions of higher education which, in the words of the 1940 *Statement of Principles on Academic Freedom and Tenure*, "depends upon the free search for truth and its free exposition."

In its *Statement on Professional Ethics*, the Association has stressed the obligation of professors to their subject and to the truth as they see it, as well as the need for them to "exercise critical self-discipline and judgment in using, extending, and transmitting knowledge." Defending free inquiry by their associates and respecting the opinion of others, in the exchange of criticism and ideas, professors must also be rigorously honest in acknowledging their academic debts.

In the light of recent concerns within and outside of the academic profession, it has seemed salutary to restate these general obligations with respect to the offense of plagiarism.

Definition

The offense of plagiarism may seem less self-evident in some circles now than it did formerly. Politicians, business executives, and even university presidents depend on the ideas and literary skills of committees, aides, and speechwriters in the many communications they are called on to make inside and outside their organizations. When ideas are rapidly popularized and spread abroad through the media, when fashion and the quest for publicity are all around us, a concern with protecting the claims of originality may seem to some a quaint survival from the past or even a perverse effort to deter the spread of knowledge.

Nevertheless, within the academic world, where advancing knowledge remains the highest calling, scholars must give full and fair recognition to the contributors to that enterprise, both for the substance and for the formulation of their findings and interpretations. Even within the academic community, however, there are complexities and shades of difference. A writer of textbooks rests on the labors of hundreds of authors of monographs who cannot all be acknowledged; the derivative nature of such work is understood and even, when it is well and skillfully done, applauded. A poet, composer, or painter may "quote" the creation of another artist, deliberately without explanation, as a means of deeper exploration of meaning and in the expectation that knowledgeable readers, listeners, or viewers will appreciate the allusion and delight in it. There are even lapses—regrettable but not always avoidable—in which a long-buried memory of something read surfaces as a seemingly new thought.

But none of these situations diminishes the central certainty: taking over the ideas, methods, or written words of another, without acknowledgment and with the intention that they be taken as the work of the deceiver, is plagiarism. It is theft of a special kind, for the true author still retains the original ideas and words, yet they are diminished as that author's property and a fraud is committed upon the audience that believes those ideas and words originated with the deceiver. Plagiarism is not limited to the academic community but has perhaps its most pernicious effect in that setting. It is the antithesis of the honest labor that characterizes true scholarship and without which mutual trust and respect among scholars is impossible.

Precepts

Every professor should be guided by the following:

1. In his or her own work the professor must scrupulously acknowledge every intellectual debt—for ideas, methods, and expressions—by means appropriate to the form of communication.

2. Any discovery of suspected plagiarism should be brought at once to the attention of the affected parties and, as appropriate, to the profession at large through proper and effective channels—typically through reviews in or communications to relevant scholarly journals. Committee B of the Association stands ready to provide its good offices in resolving questions of plagiarism, either independently or in collaboration with other professional societies.

3. Professors should work to ensure that their universities and professional societies adopt clear guidelines respecting plagiarism, appropriate to the disciplines involved, and should insist that regular procedures be in place to deal with violations of those guidelines. The gravity of a charge of plagiarism, by whomever it is made, must not diminish the diligence exercised in determining whether the accusation is valid. In all cases the most scrupulous procedural fairness must be observed, and penalties must be appropriate to the degree of offense.*

4. Scholars must make clear the respective contributions of colleagues on a collaborative project, and professors who have the guidance of students as their responsibility must exercise the greatest care not to appropriate a student's ideas, research, or presentation to the professor's benefit; to do so is to abuse power and trust.

5. In dealing with graduate students, professors must demonstrate by precept and example the necessity of rigorous honesty in the use of sources and of utter respect for the work of others. The same expectations apply to the guidance of undergraduate students, with a special obligation to acquaint students new to the world of higher education with its standards and the means of ensuring intellectual honesty.

Conclusion

Any intellectual enterprise—by an individual, a group of collaborators, or a profession—is a mosaic, the pieces of which are put in place by many hands. Viewed from a distance, it should appear a meaningful whole, but the long process of its assemblage must not be discounted or misrepresented. Anyone who is guilty of plagiarism not only harms those most directly affected but also diminishes the authority and credibility of all scholarship and all creative arts, and therefore ultimately harms the interests of the broader society. The danger of plagiarism for teaching, learning, and scholarship is manifest, the need vigorously to maintain standards of professional integrity compelling.

---

*On the question of due process for a faculty member who is the subject of disciplinary action because of alleged plagiarism, see Regulations 5 and 7 of the Association's "Recommended Institutional Regulations on Academic Freedom and Tenure," Academe 69 (January–February 1983): 18a–19a.

American Library Association

ALA Code of Ethics

After a four year process, the American Library Association Council adopted a new ALA Code of Ethics *on June 28, 1995.*

As members of the American Library Association, we recognize the importance of codifying and making known to the profession and to the general public the ethical principles that guide the work of librarians, other professionals providing information services, library trustees, and library staffs.

Ethical dilemmas occur when values are in conflict. The American Library Association Code of Ethics states the values to which we are committed, and embodies the ethical responsibilities of the profession in this changing information environment.

We significantly influence or control the selection, organization, preservation, and dissemination of information. In a political system grounded in an informed citizenry, we are members of a profession explicitly committed to intellectual freedom and the freedom of access to information. We have a special obligation to ensure the free flow of information and ideas to present and future generations.

The principles of this Code are expressed in broad statements to guide ethical decision making. These statements provide a framework; they cannot and do not dictate conduct to cover particular situations.

I. We provide the highest level of service to all library users through appropriate and usefully organized resources; equitable service policies; equitable access; and accurate, unbiased, and courteous responses to all requests.

II. We uphold the principles of intellectual freedom and resist all efforts to censor library resources.

III. We protect each library user's right to privacy and confidentiality with respect to information sought or received and resources consulted, borrowed, acquired, or transmitted.

IV. We recognize and respect intellectual property rights.

V. We treat co-workers and other colleagues with respect, fairness, and good faith, and advocate conditions of employment that safeguard the rights and welfare of all employees of our institutions.

VI. We do not advance private interests at the expense of library users, colleagues, or our employing institutions.

VII. We distinguish between our personal convictions and professional duties and do not allow our personal beliefs to interfere with fair representation of the aims of our institutions or the provision of access to their information resources.

VIII. We strive for excellence in the profession by maintaining and enhancing our own knowledge and skills, by encouraging the professional development of co-workers, and by fostering the aspirations of potential members of the profession.

—Adopted by ALA Council, June 28, 1995

Library Bill of Rights

The American Library Association affirms that all libraries are forums for information and ideas, and that the following basic policies should guide their services.

1. Books and other library resources should be provided for the interest, information, and enlightenment of all people of the community the library serves. Materials should not be excluded because of the origin, background, or views of those contributing to their creation.

2. Libraries should provide materials and information presenting all points of view on current and historical issues. Materials should not be proscribed or removed because of partisan or doctrinal disapproval.

3. Libraries should challenge censorship in the fulfillment of their responsibility to provide information and enlightenment.

4. Libraries should cooperate with all persons and groups concerned with resisting abridgment of free expression and free access to ideas.

5. A person's right to use a library should not be denied or abridged because of origin, age, background, or views.

6. Libraries which make exhibit spaces and meeting rooms available to the public they serve should make such facilities available on an equitable basis, regardless of the beliefs or affiliations of individuals or groups requesting their use.

—Adopted June 18, 1948. Amended February 2, 1961,
June 27, 1967, and January 23, 1980, by the ALA Council

Notes on Contributors

Mark Alfino is assistant professor of philosophy at Gonzaga University. He teaches corporate managers, administrators, and educators in Gonzaga's professional studies graduate program. He researches and writes about management ethics, information ethics, and copyright ethics.

Henry T. Blanke is a reference librarian at Marymount Manhattan College and coeditor of the journal *Progressive Librarian*.

Partha Dasgupta is Frank Ramsey, professor of economics at the University of Cambridge. He is the author of *The Control of Resources* and *An Inquiry into Well-Being and Destitution*.

Daniel C. Dennett is distinguished professor of arts and sciences in the Department of Philosophy and the Center for Cognitive Studies at Tufts University. His books include: *Brainstorms*; *The Mind's I*; *Consciousness Explained*; *Darwin's Dangerous Idea*; and *Kinds of Minds*.

Ronald Doctor is associate professor at the School of Library and Information Studies, University of Alabama at Tuscaloosa.

Susan Hallam is senior lecturer in the Department of Economics and Social Sciences at Nottingham Trent University in Great Britain.

Patrick Leahy is the senior United States Senator from Vermont.

Grant H. Kester is the editor of *Afterimage*, a journal for visual studies in Rochester, New York.

John Kultgen is professor of philosophy at the University of Missouri, Columbia. He has published in the areas of philosophy of science, epistemology, social philosophy, and professional ethics.

John Stuart Mill (1806-1873) was an English philosopher and economist.

Lisa Newton is director of the program in applied ethics and director of the program in environmental studies at Fairfield University in Connecticut. She is author/editor/consultant on the *Ethics in America* teleseries, and coeditor of *Taking Sides: Clashing Views on Controversial Issues in Business Ethics*.

Neil Postman is the author of *The End of Education: Redefining the Value of School*. He is also a member of the editorial board of *The Nation*.

Jonathan Rauch is a contributing editor of the *National Journal*. His writings have appeared in many publications, including the *Atlantic*, the *New Republic*, the *Los Angeles Times*, and the *New York Times*.

Virginia Rezmierski is assistant for policy studies to the vice provost for information technology at the University of Michigan.

Marc Rotenberg is director of the CPSR Washington office and an adjunct professor at Georgetown University Law Center. He also chairs the ACM Committee on Scientific Freedom and Human Rights.

Kirkpatrick Sale is the author of *Rebels Against the Future: The Luddites and Their War on the Industrial Revolution*. He is also a contributing editor of *The Nation*.

Nadine Strossen is professor of law at New York Law School and president of the American Civil Liberties Union.

John Swan was head librarian at Bennington College in Vermont. He was active in ALA and various state library associations, especially in the area of intellectual freedom. He was the author of numerous books, essays, articles, and reviews.

Michael F. Winter is humanities and social sciences librarian at the University of California, Davis. His publications include books and articles on sociology and library science.

The Editors:

Robert Hauptman is a professor at St. Cloud State University in St. Cloud, Minnesota, and editor of the *Journal of Information Ethics*. His publications include *Ethical Challenges in Librarianship* and *Technology and Information Services* (with Carol Anderson) as well as numerous articles on information ethics.

Richard N. Stichler is professor of philosophy at Alvernia College in Reading, Pennsylvania, and president-elect of the Pennsylvania division of the American Association of University Professors. His publications include articles on political philosophy and professional ethics.

Index